The HAMBROS 1779–1979

IN DEO

Bo Bramsen & Kathleen Wain

MICHAEL JOSEPH
LONDON

First published in Great Britain
by Michael Joseph
44 Bedford Square, London WC1B 3EF, 1979

© by Bo Bramsen and Kathleen Wain

ISBN 0 7181 1852 9

Film set in 11/13 point Baskerville
Printed and bound in Great Britain
by W & J Mackay Limited, Chatham

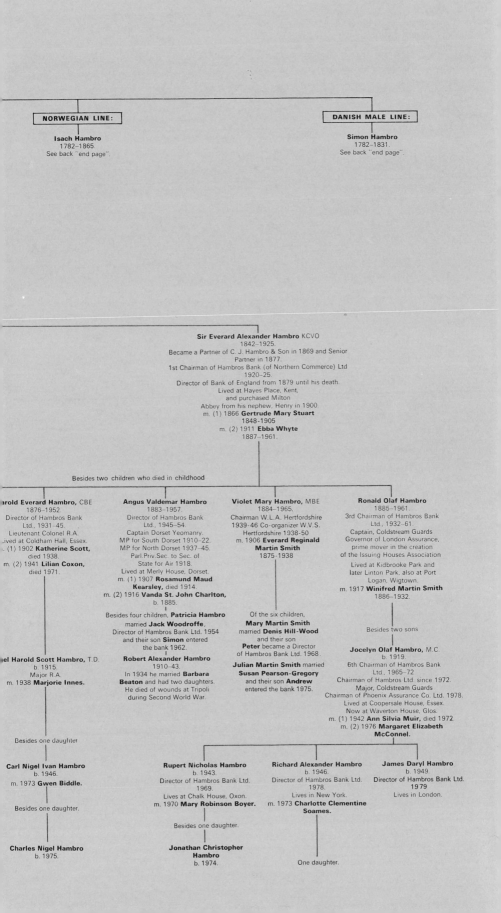

NORWEGIAN LINE:

Isach Hambro
1782–1865.
See back "end page".

DANISH MALE LINE:

Simon Hambro
1782–1831.
See back "end page".

Sir Everard Alexander Hambro KCVO
1842–1925.
Became a Partner of C. J. Hambro & Son in 1869 and Senior
Partner in 1877.
1st Chairman of Hambros Bank (of Northern Commerce) Ltd
1920–25.
Director of Bank of England from 1879 until his death.
Lived at Hayes Place, Kent,
and purchased Milton
Abbey from his nephew, Henry in 1900.
m. (1) 1866 **Gertrude Mary Stuart**
1848–1905
m. (2) 1911 **Ebba Whyte**
1887–1961.

Besides two children who died in childhood

...arold Everard Hambro, CBE
1876–1952.
Director of Hambros Bank
Ltd., 1931–45.
Lieutenant Colonel R.A.
...ived at Coldham Hall, Essex.
.. (1) 1902 **Katherine Scott,**
died 1938.
m. (2) 1941 **Lilian Coxon,**
died 1971.

Angus Valdemar Hambro
1883–1957.
Director of Hambros Bank
Ltd., 1945–54.
Captain Dorset Yeomanry.
MP for South Dorset 1910–22.
MP for North Dorset 1937–45.
Parl.Priv.Sec. to Sec. of
State for Air 1918.
Lived at Merly House, Dorset.
m. (1) 1907 **Rosamund Maud
Kearsley,** died 1914.
m. (2) 1916 **Vanda St. John Charlton,**
b. 1885.

Besides four children, **Patricia Hambro**
married **Jack Woodroffe,**
Director of Hambros Bank Ltd. 1954
and their son **Simon** entered
the bank 1962.

Robert Alexander Hambro
1910–43.
In 1934 he married **Barbara
Beaton** and had two daughters.
He died of wounds at Tripoli
during Second World War.

Violet Mary Hambro, MBE
1884–1965.
Chairman W.L.A. Hertfordshire
1939-46 Co-organizer W.V.S.
Hertfordshire 1938-50
m. 1906 **Everard Reginald
Martin Smith**
1875–1938

Of the six children,
Mary Martin Smith
married **Denis Hill-Wood**
and their son
Peter became a Director
of Hambros Bank Ltd. 1968.
Julian Martin Smith married
Susan Pearson-Gregory
and their son **Andrew**
entered the bank 1975.

Ronald Olaf Hambro
1885–1961.
3rd Chairman of Hambros Bank
Ltd., 1932–61.
Captain, Coldstream Guards
Governor of London Assurance,
prime mover in the creation
of the Issuing Houses Association
Lived at Kidbrooke Park and
later Linton Park, also at Port
Logan, Wigtown.
m. 1917 **Winifred Martin Smith**
1886–1932.

Besides two sons

Jocelyn Olaf Hambro, M.C.
b. 1919.
6th Chairman of Hambros Bank
Ltd., 1965–72.
Chairman of Hambros Ltd. since 1972.
Major, Coldstream Guards
Chairman of Phoenix Assurance Co. Ltd. 1978.
Lived at Coopersale House, Essex.
Now at Waverton House, Glos.
m. (1) 1942 **Ann Silvia Muir,** died 1972.
m. (2) 1976 **Margaret Elizabeth
McConnel.**

...el Harold Scott Hambro, T.D.
b. 1915.
Major R.A.
m. 1938 **Marjorie Innes.**

Besides one daughter

Carl Nigel Ivan Hambro
b. 1946.
m. 1973 **Gwen Biddle.**

Besides one daughter.

Charles Nigel Hambro
b. 1975.

Rupert Nicholas Hambro
b. 1943.
Director of Hambros Bank Ltd.
1969.
Lives at Chalk House, Oxon.
m. 1970 **Mary Robinson Boyer.**

Besides one daughter.

**Jonathan Christopher
Hambro**
b. 1974.

Richard Alexander Hambro
b. 1946.
Director of Hambros Bank Ltd.
1978.
Lives in New York.
m. 1973 **Charlotte Clementine
Soames.**

One daughter.

James Daryl Hambro
b. 1949.
Director of Hambros Bank Ltd.
1979
Lives in London.

Contents

		page
List of Illustrations		2
Acknowledgements		9
Introduction		11
1	Thobe and Calmer	15
2	The Surprising Zipora	34
3	Simon, the Fleet Painter	43
4	The Practical Isach	57
5	The President of the Storting	80
6	Theodora's Grandchildren	120
7	The Imperturbable Joseph	142
8	The Government Adviser	166
9	Joseph's Later Years	178
10	The Development of the Business	201
11	Carl Joachim, the Baron	237
12	My Friend Cavour	262
13	The Baron's Two Elder Sons	284
14	Everard, the Youngest Son	298
15	Changes at Milton Abbey	337
16	Military Warfare	350
17	Economic Warfare	361
18	A Break with the Past	370
19	The Depression	385
20	The Bank in World War II	397
21	The Post-War Era	416
22	The Bank Today	438
Bibliography		443
Index		445

List of Illustrations

		page
1	Calmer Hambro's Licence to Trade	13
2	Evening on Nicolaifleet	16
3	View of Hamburg	17
4	Map of Hamburg, 1804	18–19
5	The Gate to Copenhagen	21
6	Calmer Hambro	22
7	Thobe Hambro	23
8	The Tombstone of Nachman Levi	24
9	The Fire of Copenhagen, 1795	26–7
10	The Milliner's Shop	28
11	Jewish Tradesmen	29
12	Round Tower and Trinity Church, Copenhagen	31
13	Calmer Hambro's First Entry in the Guild Register	32
14	The Tombstone of Calmer Hambro	33
15	Zipora Hambro	35
16	The Church at Fredensborg Castle	36
17	Carl Wilhelm Wulf-Borup	37
18	Niels Borup	38
19	Julius Theodor and Marie Borup	40
20	Johan Borup	41
21	Carl Simon Hambro	44
22	Jeanette Hambro	45
23	The Destruction of the Danish Fleet	46–7
24	The Naval Yards of Holmen	48
25	A Danish Fire Officer	49
26	View of Copenhagen	50–1
27	Caroline Frederikke Hambro	53
28	Ørholm Paper Mill	54
29	Henrik Leonhard Danchell	55
30	Carl Ancker	56
31	Tyskebryggen in Bergen	58
32	Street Scene in Bergen	58
33	Entrance to Bergen Harbour	60
34	Joseph Hambro's Press Announcement	61

page

35 The Norwegian National Assembly   62–3
36 Isach Hambro   64
37 Marie Hambro   65
38 Map of Bergen *c.* 1800   66
39 Carl and Angelique Hambro   68
40 Carl Hambro's Home and Shop in Bergen   69
41 Carl Hambro's Cotton Mill   70
42 Edvard I. Hambro   72
43 Edvard I. Hambro   73
44 Edvard Isach, Nicoline, Elise and Carl Joachim Hambro   75
45 The Hambro School at Stavhusgaten   77
46 Nico Hambro   78
47 Elise and Carl Joachim Hambro as Students   81
48 Carl Joachim and Gudrun Hambro   83
49 Carl Joachim Hambro's Five Children   85
50 Carl Joachim Hambro *c.* 1928   87
51 Caricatures of Carl Joachim Hambro   89
52 Quisling, Hagelin and Hitler   93
53 King Haakon VII of Norway   95
54 Meeting of the Storting in Hamar   99
55 The Elverum Authority   101
56 President Hambro and Otto Ruge   103
57 King Haakon, 10 April 1940   105
58 Norwegian Fishing Boats   106
59 The Storting, 1942   107
60 Crown Prince Olav and Carl Joachim Hambro   109
61 Carl Joachim's Return to Oslo   111
62 Vidkun Quisling   112
63 Drawing of Carl Joachim Hambro, 1947   113
64 Gyda Christensen   114
65 The UN General Assembly in New York   115
66 Portrait of Carl Joachim Hambro, 1951   117
67 Edvard Isak, Cato, Carl and Johan Hambro   119
68 Johan Randulff Bull   120
69 Theodora Hambro   121
70 Lithograph of Oslo's Main Street, Karl Johan   122
71 Painting of Oslo's Main Street, Karl Johan   123
72 Edvard Isach Hambro Bull aged Five   124
73 Kristiania University   125
74 Caricatures of Bjørnson, Ibsen and Grieg   126
75 Edvard Isach Hambro Bull, *c.* 1900   127

3

page

76 Ida Marie Bull and her Four Children — 128
77 Edvard Bull — 130
78 The First Norwegian Labour Government, 1928 — 133
79 Edvard Bull, Junior — 134
80 Caricature of Edvard and Francis Hambro Bull — 135
81 Francis Bull, 1948 — 137
82 Francis Bull in Grini Prison — 139
83 Young Intellectuals in Kristiania, 1887 — 140
84 Edward and Stine Hambro — 141
85 Joseph Hambro in Copenhagen — 143
86 The British Assault on Copenhagen, 1801 — 144–5
87 Erichsen's House in Copenhagen — 146
88 Erich Erichsen c. 1800 — 147
89 The Picturesque City of Hamburg — 149
90 The Alter Rabe Inn, Hamburg — 149
91 The Hamburg Bourse — 150
92 Martin Joseph Haller — 151
93 Ruben Henriques Junior — 152
94 The Henriques Broking Premises, Copenhagen — 153
95 The Second British Attack on Copenhagen — 155
96 Mendel Levin Nathanson — 156
97 David Amsel Meyer — 157
98 Georg Gerson — 158
99 Joseph's Home in Copenhagen — 159
100 Kongens Nytorv, Copenhagen with the Premises of
C. J. Hambro & Son — 160–1
101 Count Ernst Schimmelmann — 162
102 Johan Sigismund von Møsting — 163
103 Carl Joachim Hambro's Childhood Home — 165
104 The Copenhagen Bourse — 167
105 Uprising outside The Raphael Brothers' Shop — 168
106 The Second Day of the Jewish Persecution — 169
107 The Fourth Day of the Jewish Persecution — 171
108 The Main Entrance to the Copenhagen Bourse — 173
109 King Frederik VI of Denmark — 175
110 The King's Weekly Audience — 176
111 The Town of Kristiania, 1830 — 180–1
112 Nicolai von Holten — 183
113 Conrad Hinrich Donner — 184
114 Martin Johan Jenisch — 186
115 Jenisch's House in Hamburg — 187

		page
116	Georg Gerson's Compositions	189
117	Andreas Hansen	191
118	Nathan Rothschild, Thomas Wilson and Adolf Goldschmidt	193
119	Bertel Thorvaldsen	195
120	The New Synagogue in Copenhagen	197
121	Carl Joachim Hambro as a Student	199
122	The Port of Copenhagen	203
123	Bodenhoffs Plads, later Hambros Plads	204–5
124	Map of Copenhagen, 1840	206–7
125	The Road to Christianshavn	209
126	Hambros Factory at Hambros Plads	210
127	Entrance to Christianshavn	210
128	The Hambro Bakery	211
129	Arrival by Boat at Hambros Plads	211
130	Øregaard in 1840	212
131	The Present Øregaard	213
132	Caroline Gostenhofer	215
133	Count A. W. Moltke	217
134	Miniature of Carl Joachim Hambro	219
135	View of Gamla Stan, Stockholm	220–1
136	King Carl Johan XIV of Sweden	223
137	The Tombstone of Marianne Hambro	224
138	Carl Joachim's Winter Home in Copenhagen	225
139	View of Old Broad Street, London	227
140	Charles and Percival Hambro as Children	229
141	Jenny Lind	230
142	Hans Christian Andersen	231
143	Johan Hambro	233
144	Edvard Hambro	234
145	Marble Bust of Joseph Hambro	235
146	Site of Joseph Hambro's House in Copenhagen	236
147	Emile le Maire and Wilhelm Smidt	239
148	The Danish War, 1848–51	240–1
149	Frederik Treschow	242
150	King Frederik VII of Denmark	243
151	Count Wilhelm Sponneck	244
152	Carl Joachim Hambro	245
153	Carl Joachim's Commoner's Coat-of-Arms	247
154	The Danish Design	248
155	The Royal College of Arms Design	249

page

156 The Modern Symbol — 250
157 View of Milborne Valley — 251
158 View of Milton Abbey and Hall — 252–3
159 Aerial View of Milton Abbey and Hall — 254
160 The Abbey Church at Milton Abbey — 255
161 Baptismal Font at Milton Abbey — 257
162 Joseph Hambro's House on Putney Heath — 258
163 Carl Joachim Hambro — 259
164 Eliza Turner — 261
165 Camillo Cavour — 263
166 Caricature of Cavour from Fischietto — 265
167 King Victor Emanuel II of Sardinia — 267
168 Caricature of Cavour from Fischietto — 268
169 Two Caricatures of Cavour from Fischietto — 269
170 Napoleon III's Army in Northern Italy — 271
171 Meeting of the Austrian Emperor and Napoleon III — 271
172 The Piedmontese Army at Martino — 273
173 The Battle of Calatafimi — 273
174 The Danish Church, Wellclose Square, London — 274–5
175 Prince Vilhelm, later George I — 277
176 Carl Joachim Hambro — 278
177 The Hambro Public Baths, Copenhagen — 280
178 The Second Public Baths, Copenhagen — 281
179 Effigy of Carl Joachim Hambro — 282
180 Charles, Percival and Everard Hambro — 285
181 Charles Hambro — 286
182 'The Great Court of Trinity College, Cambridge' — 289
183 West Lawn front of Milton Abbey and Hall — 290–1
184 Colonel Charles Hambro — 292
185 'The Cut. Triumph of Woman over Man' — 293
186 The Outdoor Servants at Milton Abbey — 294
187 The Indoor Servants at Milton Abbey — 294
188 Percival and Grace Hambro — 297
189 Everard Hambro at Cambridge — 299
190 Everard and Mary Hambro — 300
191 Angus, Violet and Olaf Hambro as children — 301
192 Junius Spencer Morgan — 302
193 John Pierpont Morgan — 303
194 The Bank of England — 305
195 The Royal Exchange — 305
196 Map of London — 306–7

page

197 E. C. Baring — 308
198 Lord Rothschild, Lord Revelstoke and Everard Hambro — 311
199 The Baron Alphonse de Rothschild — 313
200 C. F. Tietgen — 316
201 'Sunset over Genoa Harbour' — 317
202 'A Scene on Change, Pillars of the City' — 318
203 Everard Hambro — 321
204 Villa Espoir, Biarritz — 322
205 Gannochy Lodge, Scotland — 325
206 Sketching beside the North Esk — 325
207 The Hambros at Gannochy, 1898 — 327
208 Eric Hambro shooting on the Milton Abbey Estate — 329
209 'A Dirty Crossing' — 333
210 Court of Directors of the Bank of England, 1903 — 334–5
211 'Dividend Day at the Bank of England' — 336
212 Harry Hambro — 338
213 Milton Abbas Schoolchildren — 339
214 The Village of Milton Abbas — 340–1
215 Everard Hambro and Martin Ridley Smith — 343
216 Violet Hambro — 345
217 The Royal Shooting Party at Milton Abbey — 346–7
218 The Beaters at the Royal Shoot — 348
219 The Gamekeepers and Loaders at the Royal Shoot — 349
220 Lt. Norman Joachim Hambro — 351
221 Major-General Sir Percy Hambro — 352
222 Lady Hambro and her three children — 353
223 Harold Hambro in Africa — 355
224 Wedding Photograph of Angus and Vanda Hambro — 356
225 Harold Hambro at Swaythling — 357
226 Angus and Olaf Hambro playing golf at Biarritz — 358
227 Bertram Hambro — 359
228 Val Hambro — 360
229 Knut Wallenberg — 362
230 Sir Everard, Sybil and Eric Hambro — 364
231 Eric Hambro — 366
232 Sybil Hambro — 367
233 British Bank of Northern Commerce — 371
234 Hambros Bank, 41 Bishopsgate — 373
235 Christmas at Milton Abbey, 1919 — 374–5
236 Gerard d'Abo — 376
237 Charles Hambro fishing in Iceland — 378

page

238 Shooting at Gannochy, 1921   379
239 Queen Mary and Captain Olaf Hambro   381
240 Winifred Hambro   382
241 Pamela Hambro   383
242 'Cricket on College Field'   384
243 J. Pierpont Morgan, Junior   386
244 The Court of Directors of the Bank of England 1932   388
245 Olaf Hambro   390
246 Kidbrooke Park   393
247 Harold Hambro   394
248 Nigel Hambro as a boy   395
249 The Hyde, Bedfordshire   398
250 The Hyde in Wartime   399
251 Evy Bingham Hambro and family   403
252 Wedding Photograph of Jocelyn and Silvia Hambro   404
253 Alec Hambro   406
254 Jack Hambro   408
255 Charles and Dorothy Hambro   409
256 Sir Charles Hambro   413
257 The Three Chairmen   417
258 Jocelyn Hambro and family   418
259 Coopersale House, Essex   419
260 Wedding Photograph of Andrew and Jean Elphinstone   422
261 Charlie Hambro at Eton   423
262 Sir Charles Hambro, Chairman of the Anglo-Danish
     Society   425
263 Jack Hambro, fifth Chairman of Hambros Bank   427
264 Jocelyn Hambro at Newmarket   434
265 Acceptance Figures and Balance Sheet Totals,
     1879–1978   437
266 Jocelyn Hambro, sixth Chairman of Hambros Bank   439
267 Charlie Hambro, seventh Chairman of Hambros Bank   440
268 Rupert, Richard and James Hambro   441

Acknowledgements

We are deeply indebted to each of the following for all their assistance in the completion of this book. In the Danish chapters we received help from:

Mr S. Ingemann Jensen for the investigation of older Danish documents concerning Joseph Hambro; Mr Julius Margolinsky for information about Calmer and Thobe Hambro as members of Danish Jewish society; Mr Johannes P. Jensen for Hambro correspondence with Bertil Thorvaldsen and Elizabeth Jerichaū-Baūmann; Mr Sv. Tito Achen for information about the Hambro coat-of-arms; the Reverend Paul Fabricius for information about the former Danish Church in London; Mrs Edith Moltke-Leth, Mr Steffen Borūp and Mr Jens Mortensen for information concerning the Danish descendants of Zipora and Simon Hambro and Mr Henrik Henriques for details of the Hambro-Henriqūes relations. We are grateful for pictures from the Royal Library in Copenhagen; the Frederiksborg Historical Museum in Hillerød, Copenhagen town museum, the Staatsarchiv, Hamburg, the Stockholm Town Museum and the Royal Collections at Stockholm Castle; and the Danish newspapers *Berlingske Tidende* and *Politiken*. We are especially indebted to Mr Sv. Voigt-Andersen, who designed the geneaological tables.

In the Norwegian chapters we are pleased to acknowledge the help of: Mr Hans Bāll for early pictures of the Norwegian Hambros; Mr Per Monsen, the Norwegian Telegrambureau, the University Library in Oslo, the Town Museūm in Oslo, the Bergens Art Gallery, the Bergens Historical Museum, the publishing houses of Norsk Gyldendal and J. W. Cappelen, and the newspaper *Aftenposten* for nearly all the later illustrations in the Norwegian chapters.

For the translation of both the Danish and Norwegian chapters we are indebted to Mr and Mrs F. C. J. Crowley.

In the English chapters individual thanks go to Professor Sayers, Sir Michael Perrin, Mr Harry Sporborg, Lord Ramsay and Colonel Philip Fielden for their important contributions to special sections of the book and to Mr C. Sheers of Lewis Photos and Mr M. Gostelow as our photographers. We are especially grateful for the valuable assistance given by the officers of Hambros Bank, in particular Mr R. G. Sheffield, and also to the staff of the Guildhall Library including Miss D. Parker who has painstakingly catalogued the bank's archives. Furthermore, we are indebted to many banks both in London and abroad for their willingness to provide colourful illustrations and to give access to their manuscript material. Special mention should be made of the assistance given by Mr E. M. Kelly and his staff at the Bank of England in the Historical Research Section.

Above all we are extremely grateful to each member of the Hambro family living either in Norway or England who has made available their photographic and personal archive material. Without their help the Hambro history would be a mere skeleton.

A book of this size has demanded a great deal of research and there are numerous people throughout Denmark, Norway and Great Britain who have given up their valuable time to help us. We regret insufficient space prevents us mentioning them all by name but we most sincerely thank them.

Bo Bramsen and Kathleen Wain
Copenhagen and London

Introduction

Two hundred years ago the 29-year-old Hamburg merchant Calmer Joachim Levy secured an entry permit and was granted a Jewish tradesman's licence in Copenhagen, dated 14 April 1779. On the same day the family name of Hambro came into being. Following the Danish custom, young Calmer wanted to adopt the name of his native town, but the Copenhagen Corporation made spelling errors in his licence, and from their garbled versions of Hembroe and Hambroe Calmer himself chose to spell his new name 'Hambro'.

The first part of this book describes the modest family that Calmer quickly founded following his arrival in Copenhagen at Christmas 1778. He was already engaged by written agreement to marry Thobe Levi. He had never seen her, but in the good Jewish manner he accepted her as his wife under a contract between his father and his future father-in-law. They were married shortly after his arrival, and lived an industrious, frugal and devout life together in Copenhagen until his death in 1806. Within three years of the marriage Thobe had produced four very dissimilar children, the last two of whom were twins.

The one daughter, Zipora, contracted two Jewish marriages and then arranged to be baptized before marrying Niels Borup, a Christian lawyer, in Copenhagen in 1813. She founded a family associated with the church and higher education, and of an ultra-patriotic Danish stamp.

Of Calmer and Thobe's three sons, Carl Simon, the elder of the twins, was the only one to spend his entire life in Copenhagen, where he became a respected master craftsman. His story is so typical of the period of Jewish emancipation in Denmark that it deserves to be told. The female line of his descendants – he had four daughters but no sons – produced two pioneers of industry and the arts, who are still remembered and highly regarded in Denmark.

Calmer's other twin son, Isach, went to Norway in 1810 to trade as a merchant. He married a Norwegian woman, and his family and descendants became established in Bergen and Oslo. This branch of the family is now generally thought to be native Norwegian, for the name Hambro has a decidedly Norwegian sound. The second generation rejected Isach's trading activities and became academics, a tradition that is still continuing. The Leader of the Norwegian Parliament during World War II, Carl Joachim Hambro, was the most remarkable of them.

The eldest and most gifted of Calmer's sons, Joseph, followed in his father's business and became banker to King Frederik VI of Denmark. His only son Carl Joachim married an Englishwoman, and in 1839, with the help of Joseph, C. J. Hambro & Son was founded in London. After his father's death Carl Joachim displayed the distinctive, if impulsive, talent in which old Joseph had never placed much trust. The family and bank continued through six generations of Hambros, and some of Carl Joachim's descendants became prominent in England as major landowners, politicians and officers in the armed forces. Joseph's story is told last of the four children, owing to his close connection with the English branch of the family.

When Carl Simon's third unmarried daughter Caroline died in 1892 the Hambro family name died out in Denmark, but the memory of Joseph and Carl Joachim's achievements in and for Denmark lives on. Both father and son have streets named after them in Copenhagen. Today Joseph Hambro's portrait hangs in the Copenhagen Stock Exchange, and there is a bust of him in the collection of sculptures of famous Danes at the Frederiksborg Nation History Museum.

A point of interest, characterizing the period, is the book's description of how, after the death of their devout father in 1806, three of the four Hambro children were prepared to abandon their Jewish faith at moments of crisis. Zipora's motives in allowing herself to be baptized in 1808 were personal; but Isach's in 1810 were purely practical. The baptism of Carl Simon and his entire family in 1819 arose entirely from fear since the adoption of the Christian faith was the best security for the family's future. Only the proud Joseph demonstrated his personal independence throughout his life by formally adhering to his father's faith, although he allowed his only child, Carl Joachim, to become baptized in 1821.

Surprisingly little has been written about the Hambros and no biographer has looked at the extensive family as a whole, and it is this

---

Calmer Hambro's licence to trade as a 'merchant of the Jewish nation', issued in Copenhagen on 14 April 1779. Calmer had wanted to be named Hamburg, but Copenhagen Town Hall misunderstood him, and in this licence he was called Hembroe; the name Joachim was also spelt incorrectly. Before the end of the year he had chosen for himself the name of Calmer Joachim Hambro, which sounded very Danish. Copenhagen Municipal Archives.

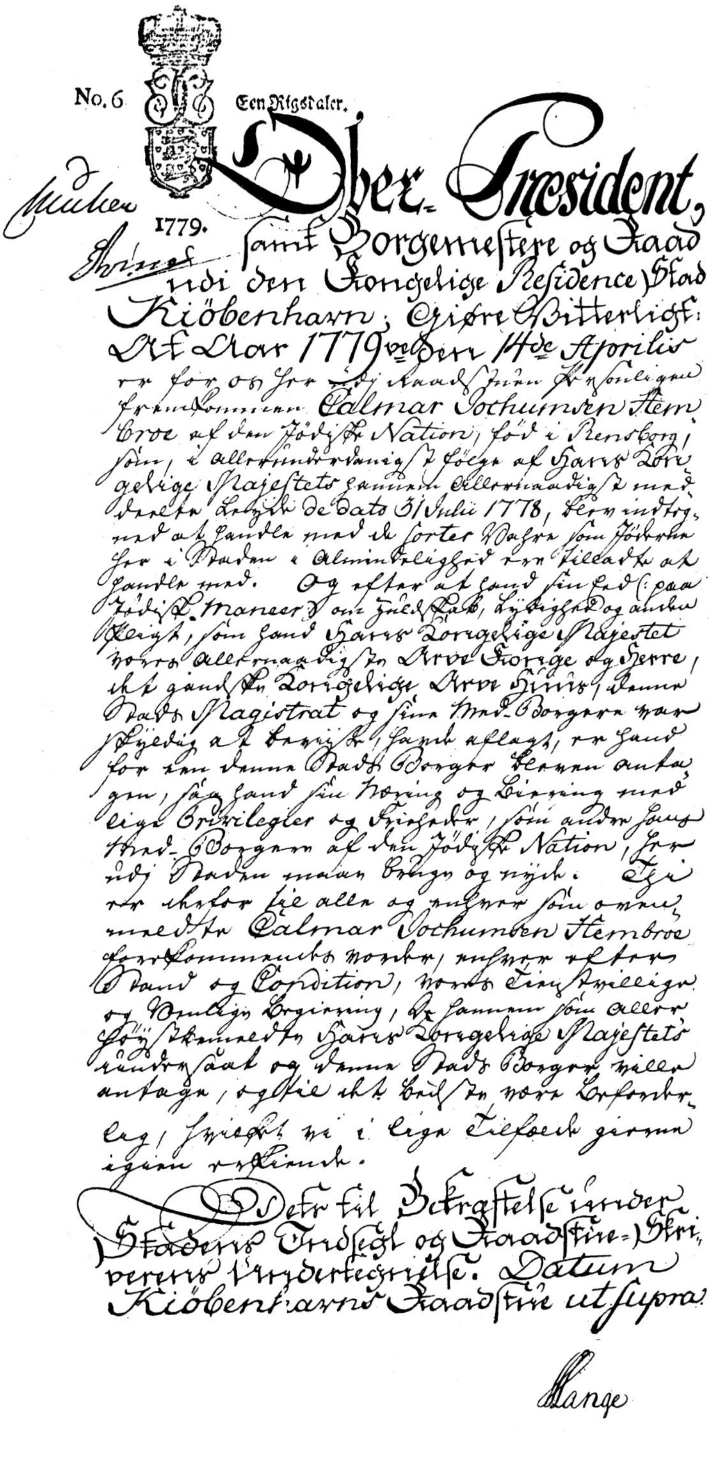

No. 6 Een Rigsdaler.

1779.

Ober-Præsident, samt Borgemestere og Raad udi den Kongelige Residence Stad Kiöbenhavn, Giöre Witterligt: Af Aar 1779 ved den 14de Aprilis er for os her udi Raadstuen personlig fremkommen Calmar Jochumsen Hambroe af den Jödiske Nation, föd i Rensborg, som i allerunderdanigst Fölge af Hans Kongelige Majestets hannem allernaadigst meddeelte Bevilling de dato 31 Julii 1778, [illegible] med at handle med de Sorter Vahre som Jöderne her i Staden i Almindelighed ere tilladte at handle med. Og efter at hand sin Eed (: paa Jödisk Maneer :) om Huldskab, Lydighed og anden Pligt, som hand Hans Kongelige Majestet vores allernaadigste Arve Konge og Herre, [illegible] Kongelige Arve Huus, denne Stads Magistrat og sine Med-Borgere var skyldig at beviise, havde aflagt, er hand for en denne Stads Borger hermed antagen, saa hand sin Næring og Biering med lige Privilegier og Friheder, som andre sine Med-Borgere af den Jödiske Nation, her udi Staden maae bruge og nyde. Thi er [illegible] alle og enhver som ommeldte Calmar Jochumsen Hambroe [illegible] efter Stand og Condition, vores Tienstwillige og Venlige Begiering, at hannem som allerforskrevne Hans Kongelige Majestets Undersaat og denne Stads Borger ville antage, og sig ikke [illegible] vores Erfordring, hvilket vi i lige Tilfælde gierne igien erkiende.

Des til Bekræftelse under Stadens Indsegl og Raadstue-Skriverens Underskrivelse. Datum Kiöbenhavns Raadstue ut supra.

Lange

Our main concern throughout this book has been to tell the story of the older generations and their pioneering achievements. Calmer and Thobe now have some eight hundred descendants, and only the family's most prominent representatives in the three countries can be dealt with here . Even so, it has been necessary to exclude nearly all of the female lines who, by marrying, had to renounce the name of Hambro.

What will probably strike the reader most is the family's incredible adaptability under new and often wholly strange conditions, and its versatility which, combined with the sudden exploitation of latent ability, has produced over the two centuries that concern us some outstanding public figures in a wide variety of fields.

Finally, we wish to express our special thanks to Hambros Bank for making available such a comprehensive and colourful range of illustrations. The book contains not only old pictures of the best-known members of the family and their closest associates, but also illustrations of contemporary society in the various countries over two hundred years.

Bo Bramsen and Kathleen Wain
Copenhagen and London

1 Thobe and Calmer

In 1778, Nachman Joachim Levy, a devout Jewish merchant and draper of Hamburg, had good reason to feel satisfied. Although he was now fifty-three his third wife had just given birth to yet another son, whom they had named Jokev. This was his eleventh child; he already had seven sons and three daughters. Such a large family was not an undue worry to him. They were all healthy and intelligent, and he was sure that he would be able to launch all his sons into a trade and find suitable husbands for his daughters.

Since leaving his native town of Rendsburg in the Danish duchy of Holstein about twenty years earlier he had succeeded in building up a large and well established business. He had already been able to give his older children a very much better education than was normal for Jewish families in north Germany. They not only spoke faultless German but could also read and write the language, while less educated Jews spoke only Yiddish. Nachman's eldest son Isaak was at thirty-two already well established in the butter trade in Amsterdam, and his third son, twenty-eight-year-old Jekev, had recently been sent to London to open a branch of his father's business. This was the normal pattern for all good Jewish families – from the Rothschilds downwards – at the end of the eighteenth century. The second and fourth sons, Calman, aged twenty-nine, and fifteen-year-old Mathias, were his two favourites and he wanted to keep them in Hamburg to take over the business. He had great expectations of Calman, who had already shown a talent for the cloth trade, the most important area of his father's activities.

But in spring 1778, Nachman received an unexpected letter from Denmark which forced him to revise his plans for the family. A distant relative in Copenhagen, the trader Isach Joseph Levi, wrote that he was now sixty-eight and so frail that he expected to die very soon. His great desire was to see his only daughter Thobe, now twenty-two, happily married. The old man knew that Nachman had many sons, and he begged him to allow one of them to try his luck in Copenhagen and marry Thobe. Copenhagen, he wrote, was of course well known to be second only to Amsterdam in its fair treatment of the Jews. Old Levi added that almost all trades were prospering there as never before, and

15

Evening on Nicolaifleet, Hamburg's great canal, seen from the Customs House. The old warehouses were located here, and German and foreign ships could sail straight in at high tide to load and unload. In the background is St Katharina church. French lithograph, c. 1820. Royal Library, Copenhagen.

he hoped soon to be able to leave his own modest enterprise to Thobe's husband.

The letter ended with some purely financial, but of course significant, information. If one of Nachman's sons came to marry Thobe, her father could procure the safe conduct that the Copenhagen Corporation always required of immigrating Jews. This document would prove that on arrival in Denmark the petitioner would possess £100, and that he was already betrothed to a girl in Copenhagen. Of the £100 Thobe's father would be able to find £70.

Nachman realized at once that Isach Levi's offer was fair and sincere, but unfortunately his only son of a suitable age was his favourite, the promising and able Calman. A family conference was held, and Calman himself agreed to the proposal provided that his father also agreed. This was the proper reaction for any young Jew then, although Calman had never seen Thobe nor previously known of her existence. Moreover, he had never visited Copenhagen, though he knew that many able young Hamburg and Altona Jews had already gone to Copenhagen for the same reasons. Nachman Levy accepted on behalf of his son, and added another £70 so that the young couple could enter into marriage with a capital of £140, which was equal to at least two years' earnings for a modest young merchant.

Thobe's father took immediate action as soon as he received this welcome letter, and on 15 June he approached the Copenhagen Corporation for permission for his future son-in-law to settle 'as a merchant of the Jewish nation'. The Corporation asked the Jewish Council of Elders in Copenhagen for their views. They immediately replied that they knew Isach Joseph Levi to be a 'worthy citizen', and that Thobe's betrothed from Hamburg might also be considered a 'proper person'. On 17 July Thobe's father was summoned to the Town Hall to produce the marriage contract and to prove the existence of the £140. All that now remained was to seek the King's approval of the safe conduct, which was in fact no more than a formality since the unfortunate King Christian VII had been mentally ill for several years. On 31 July, Thobe's father was able to send the Danish safe conduct to Hamburg. All four gates to Copenhagen then stood open to Calman; he might enter the town and meet the bride he had never seen.

The origin of the family name of Hambro, which has become so well known all over Europe, must be mentioned at this stage. Its origin is in itself a somewhat surprising tale.

Even in the early 1770s only a few Copenhagen Jews used a true family name. Only first names were used, which made registration by the authorities difficult when censuses were introduced. It therefore became necessary during the 1770s for immigrating Jews to adopt a family name, and in Denmark they usually adopted the name of their

The approach to Hamburg from the North Sea through the estuary of the Elbe, near the entrance to the city's port. Behind the ramparts can be seen St Michaelis church and the inner harbour. Coloured etching by Friedrich Rosenberg, 1803. Staatsarchiv, Hamburg.

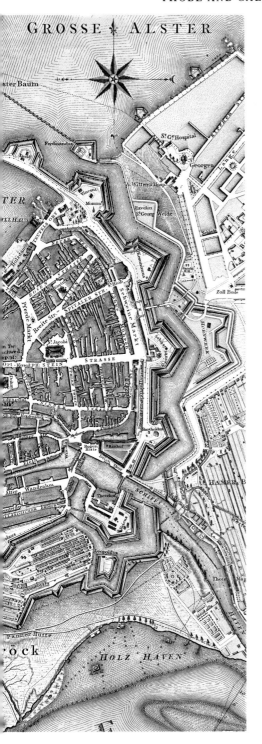

Hamburg in 1804. Until 1815 the city was squeezed between its fortifications and ramparts north of the Elbe. The river linked the city with the interior of Germany, and also with the North Sea which gave it excellent communications with London and the rest of the world. A system of canals between the river and the Alster lake formed the city's internal transport routes, along which numerous warehouses and factories were situated. The Hamburg stock exchange stood on its own wide canal in the centre of the city's oldest quarter, near St Nicolai church. In about 1800, Hamburg had a larger population than Copenhagen (125,000 as against 100,000), and also a substantially stronger commercial position. However, the city's trade suffered during Napoleon's occupation of 1806–14, and after the great fire of 1842 it completely changed its character. Royal Library, Copenhagen.

native town. The majority of immigrants came from Germany, and even today Jewish families in Copenhagen bear family names such as Dessau, Trier and Warburg. Some even allowed themselves a flippant 'von' in front of the name – for example, von Essen, von Halle or von Minden – which suggested to the uninitiated a completely false concept of German nobility.

There were of course several old Jewish families in Denmark who merely turned one of their first names into a family name, calling themselves, for example, Cohn, Gerson, Levin, Levy, Marcus, Nathan, Philip, Raphael or Salomon.

In 1778, against this background, Calman's father-in-law Isach Levi, old and almost illiterate, not unexpectedly proposed to the Corporation that his future son-in-law should be named Hamburg or (in Danish) Hamborg. But they either misunderstood him or a clerk made an error, since in Calman's safe conduct and later in his licence to trade his old first names and his new surname were thoroughly distorted. Calman became Calmar, Joachim became Jochumsen and Hamborg became first Hembroe and then Hambroe. But no one wanted to delay the matter, and no objection was raised. Before long Calman himself chose to sign as Calmer Joachim Hambro, or merely C. J. Hambro. His first name Calman, which became Calmar and then Calmer, was eventually rendered completely Danish when his grandson was named Carl Joachim, a name that later, in England, became Charles Joseph.

But the name-mangling at the Town Hall was by no means a disadvantage. The new name sounded wholly Danish, since 'bro' means 'bridge' in Danish, and family names such as Solbro and Wibro already existed. Later, in Norway, where Danish was spoken until relatively recently, the name also sounded entirely Norwegian, and it has always been easy to pronounce in English.

In September 1778, Calmer left his home in Hamburg and set out for Copenhagen. He never saw his father again; the old man died five years later. Calmer travelled by stagecoach through Holstein and his father's native town of Rendsburg to Fredericia. From there he went by coaster across the narrow sound to Funen, and then on by coach across Funen to the Great Belt. After the usual few days' wait here for transport and favourable wind conditions came the last seventy miles across Zeeland to the Danish capital. Calmer arrived at last at Vesterport and before evening he was seated with his bride-to-be and her happy and relieved parents. Calmer was a good-looking, polite young man, and his behaviour at grace before the meal showed that he came from a Jewish home with the same lifestyle and domestic customs as those prevailing in Thobe's home. For the first time he realized that the Jewish ability to

In 1778, when Calmer Hambro arrived in Denmark, Copenhagen, the old seat of the Danish kings, was the largest town in Scandinavia, although it had only 90,000 inhabitants. The picture shows Vesterpont, through which Calmer entered the town. Anonymous painting from about 1800. Copenhagen City Museum.

adapt to strange conditions arose largely from the fact that, wherever they travelled in the world, they could expect their fellow believers to be people with an identical attitude towards life as themselves.

It had been agreed in the marriage contract that for the first two years Calmer and Thobe would live with her parents – then the custom in Jewish families, and, indeed, part of the bride's dowry. This helped the family to become well acquainted, and of course it eased the newly-weds' finances.

Shortly before Christmas 1778 Thobe and Calmer were married beneath the Jewish bridal canopy in the Copenhagen synagogue in Læderstræde. Old Joseph Levi was happy and proud that he had arranged his daughter's wedding so well, then he quietly took to his bed and died a few weeks later. Thobe's mother, Elkele, died four years later. The young couple were thus left with no relations at all in Copenhagen and sometimes felt a little lonely, but they soon had a family of their own. In 1779 Thobe gave birth to a daughter, Zipora. In 1780 Joseph arrived, and in 1782 the family was completed with the twins, Isach and Simon. Joseph was named after his maternal grand-

Miniature of Calmer Levi Hambro the clothier (1747–1806), the first to bear the name of Hambro. The picture must have been painted in about 1800 when he was in his early fifties. By then he had worked up a substantial clientèle among Copenhagen's upper classes, who appreciated not only his fine goods but also his honesty. He never became wealthy; later generations thought of him as a poor man, but this is because his affluent son, Joseph, took pleasure in emphasizing the modest circumstances surrounding his youth. Owned by the Norwegian family.

father and Isach after his devout great-grandfather, who had been leader of the synagogue at Rendsburg.

By 1779 Calmer had acquired the promised licence to trade, entitling him, 'as a member of the Jewish nation', to trade in 'goods in which Jews are normally permitted to trade'. This was intentionally a vague form of words, displaying on the one hand the Government's sympathy towards Jewish merchants, but signifying on the other that Jewish tradesmen must always expect guild members such as the drapers, hosiers and glovemakers to seek any opportunity to make life difficult for them, and that if the Jews dared to venture into the fancy goods trade the town's clockmakers and goldsmiths would likewise give them no peace. Since permission to run a business 'in open shop' – that is, a proper shop – was reserved to guild members, Jewish traders normally had to resort to street trading or to peddling second-hand clothes and certain fancy goods not expressly referred to in the ancient guild rules.

In this sensitive atmosphere Calmer chose the cloth trade in which he had been trained, ordering his goods from his father – and later from his brother Mathias – in Hamburg. This enabled him not only to provide himself with quality goods but also to get the credit necessary to carry a wide range. He ran the business from his home, and industriously and systematically built up a first-rate clientele. Probably neither he nor his sons ever had to offer their goods for sale in the street, but

Miniature of Thobe Hambro (1756–1820), who was the daughter of a Jewish tradesman. Her father, Isach Joseph Levi, had come to Copenhagen in 1751, but the family had lived in Denmark for several generations. Thobe's mother, Elkele Goldzieher, was also a Jewish tradesman's daughter. Elkele's father had a grocer's shop at Christianshavn. In her last fourteen years of widowhood, and after the baptism of three of her four children, she called herself Dorothea. She is buried in the Jewish cemetery at Copenhagen. Owned by the Norwegian family.

they were often to be seen with their large selection in boxes on their way to clients in the better quarters of the town. This was the form of trading that the oldest son, Joseph, liked to talk about in his old age. The favourite wares were silks, wool and linen, and later calico and cashmere, supplemented by fancy goods such as silk stockings, silk scarves, shawls, lace and neckwear. No Copenhagen Jew was able to gain admittance to the drapers' guild until 1798, although his business might be larger and better than those of many of the lesser guild members.

But Calmer and Thobe quietly accepted this, particularly after they moved in 1786 to a larger house in Admiralgade where there was room for the four children and the growing stock of goods. In his old age Joseph liked to make much of his childhood poverty, but in fact his background was merely somewhat modest compared with his own subsequent wealth. In 1783 Calmer inherited £150 from his father in Hamburg, and his contributions to the synagogue set him in the middle class of the Jewish community. Within the home, in Calmer's time, the entire family led the quiet, rather withdrawn life of devout, orthodox Jews, the life that Calmer and Thobe had known in their own homes. The three daily prayers were scrupulously conducted. Calmer's own morning prayers lasted half an hour. Grace was the normal procedure before all meals, and the food was always ritually prepared. On Friday evening at sunset, when the Sabbath began, Thobe lit the two candles and the whole family sang the Sabbath hymn. On Saturday they all went to the synagogue in Læderstræde, spending the morning listening to Hebrew prayers and choral music. In the intervals they met their friends and acquaintances, since the synagogue was the focal point of the community.

The community's Council of Elders arranged all matters of civil law among its members: marriage, divorce, funerals, probate, namings and social assistance, all based on Jewish law which in many fields differed greatly from Danish law. Until 1805, education was the biggest problem. The children of poor Jews in fact received no education, and normally spoke only Yiddish, the mixed German-Hebrew language. This of course made them alien in Danish eyes.

At first only German was spoken in Calmer and Thobe's home, but while the children were growing up the whole family learnt to speak, read and write Danish. Joseph's letters written in the 1820s to various Danish authorities and ministers of finance are all in his own hand, and the language is excellent. The writing is neat, stylish and easy to read. Later in life his letters in English became just as correct as his German ones had been in his youth. In Norway, too, his brother Isach's descendants were later astonished by the elegant letters he wrote in his old age

Calmer's father, Nachman Levi, died in Hamburg on 4 April 1783 aged sixty-three. The Hebrew inscription on his tombstone in the Jewish cemetery at Altona reads: 'Here rests an honest man who was zealous and active, and acquired great merit. He was one of the faithful who came to the synagogue morning and evening; one who served the Lord and read the holy scriptures. He undertook everything with honesty. The venerable and highly respected Mr Nachmann, son of Mr Isach from Rendsburg. Blessed be his memory. He died and was buried on Friday the 9th of Nisam in the year 5543 after the Creation. May his soul be preserved in life's preservatory.'

to relations and friends. There is no doubt that Calmer took great pains to educate his children in languages. It was of course taken for granted that they were all very well versed in Hebrew.

In 1795 the everyday life of the Hambro family suffered a serious blow that was shared with hundreds of other Copenhagen homes. Within three days a quarter of the capital was burnt in a great fire, and as Admiralgade was at the centre of the blaze the Hambro home was reduced to ashes on the first day. Calmer managed to save his stock, and in his quiet way reflected that it was perhaps just as well that Jews were not yet allowed to own property in Denmark.

Much worse, the synagogue in Læderstræde also fell victim to the flames on the second day of the fire. It was not rebuilt for another forty years. This was indeed a tragedy. The ever-growing community of 1500 or 2000 devout souls was now without a synagogue, since the Council of Elders could not agree on anything at all during the great conflicts and birth of emancipation in Jewish society that marked the early years of the century. Three of the Hambro children – like so many other young Copenhagen Jews – allowed themselves to be baptized, and Joseph after deep reflection also agreed to have his only son baptized. The lack of a synagogue as a focus of spiritual guidance was undoubtedly one of the causes. Of course, baptism also improved the social position of able Jews in Danish society, particularly after the end of the eighteenth century. As a result, even the most loyal and orthodox Jews felt themselves to be on shaky ground; their whole ideology was based on self-sufficiency and conscious isolation.

Until 1833, when the new Krystalgade synagogue was consecrated, Copenhagen Jews had to be content with small makeshift places of worship in private homes, and were often led by ill-informed and primitive refugee rabbis. Such services could neither inspire nor captivate intelligent young Jews, who were now enjoying greater access to all that Danish society had to offer, including the Danish National Church. No doubt it was this that attracted Zipora Hambro, the first of her family, in 1808. But while Calmer lived none of his children gave a thought to rebelling against the faith of their fathers.

In 1788 the guilds suffered the humiliation of being ordered to accept as apprentices Jews who otherwise met the general requirements, which meant that within ten years the town would see its first Jewish apprentice masters. Calmer's youngest son, Simon, was the only son who showed no aptitude for commerce, so he was apprenticed to a house-painter in 1796. Zipora married a Jew in 1799. Two years earlier, Calmer had arranged for seventeen-year-old Joseph to go to Hamburg

25

for three years' training. He lodged there with his father's brother, his Uncle Mathias, and worked diligently for the Fürst Haller & Co., a German trading company. When Joseph returned home in 1800, Isach went to Hamburg in his turn. Joseph now became his father's partner, and the firm was re-named C. J. Hambro & Son, the name used by the present bank in London until 1920. Joseph respected his father's pioneering efforts so highly that he always looked on Calmer as the true founder of the Hambro undertaking. From 1800 until Calmer's death in 1806 Joseph assisted his father in the business, and they appear never to have had a cross word.

Until the very last years of his life Calmer had been able to carry on his business without falling foul of the drapers' guild, although around 1800 the guild master, Bernhard Thortsen, submitted to the Copen-

In 1795 the Hambro family witnessed the great fire of Copenhagen, which in three days reduced the central districts to ashes. The unfavourable strong winds caused the spire of Nicolai church in the centre of the picture to catch fire on the first day. A few hours later the tower collapsed on to the densely populated quarter around the church, and the fire then quickly raged westwards along the canal. The Hambro family lived at the foot of the church, and shared the fate of 1,200 other Copenhagen families. Coloured engraving by G. F. Lahde, 1795. Royal Library, Copenhagen.

hagen police repeated complaints about the guild's difficulties in the face of Jewish competition. In 1800 the guild master sent the following letter – in vain – to Copenhagen's chief of police:

A horde of Jewish boys and girls whose number is increasing daily have posted themselves at Amagertorv where they offer for sale all kinds of silk and florentine ribbons, woven lace and various kinds of cloth goods. This, under its rules, is the trading monopoly of the Drapers' Guild. On behalf of the Guild, therefore, I respectfully request that these vagabonds be moved away, if possible today as tomorrow is market day, that they be apprehended, that their goods be taken from them and that they be punished according to the law.

These Jewish children were in fact offering for sale goods more or less the same as those in which Calmer had traded for twenty-three years, and he finally saw that the time had come to apply for membership of

27

the guild. He had looked on in some surprise when in 1798 Crown Prince Frederik, the future King Frederik VI, ordered the guild – in his insane father's name – to accept two well-known drapers, the brothers Moses and Aaron Philip. Equally surprisingly, this was repeated in 1800 for Moses Meyer and Isaak Cohn. More comprehensible was the admittance in 1801 of Moses Ruben Henriques, who had the advantages of a privileged Portuguese origin.

In 1803, therefore, Calmer, strongly encouraged by Joseph, at last applied for admission to the guild, only to receive the coolest of rejections. This he accepted with resignation. To him it was no more than a matter of morality, self-respect and a wish to avoid trouble. His business was doing well, and in any event he was growing old. In fact he no longer needed the permission to trade from an 'open shop' that had formerly been so desirable.

But Calmer could not keep out of trouble with the guild. It must be appreciated that the guild master's position at this time was far from easy. His far too numerous guild brothers gave him no rest in their efforts to force him to take action against growing competition from the

Shops with large display windows first began to appear in Copenhagen at the end of the eighteenth century. The leaders in this field were the members of the drapers' guild, who liked to tempt their customers with a large selection of goods. Until 1814 Jewish tradesmen were not allowed to keep 'open shop' except by royal licence. Drawing by Peder Klæstrup. Royal Library, Copenhagen.

Tradesmen organized in guilds had a monopoly of shopkeeping. Until 1814, therefore, Jewish tradesmen in Copenhagen were to a large extent forced into street-trading. Coloured engraving of Jewish street traders by G. F. Lahde, 1815.

ever-increasing body of Jewish traders in Copenhagen. For example, on 17 January 1805 his guild brothers pushed him into making yet another attack by letter to the chief of police:

The Jew, Mr Calmer Hambro, who lives at Mr Blankensteiner's Store Købmagergade No. 101, 1st floor, sells to all and sundry, on both large and small scale, cloth, cashmere and numerous other goods in which the drapers have a trading monopoly under Sec. 2 of their Guild Regulations. If he denies this, it can be proved by many persons. On behalf of the Guild, therefore, I respectfully request that the said Hambro be called before the Copenhagen Police Court and, insofar as no Royal licence gives him permission to conduct this kind of trade, that he then be punished under Sec. 2 of the Guild Regulations.

When this letter was shown by the chief of police to Calmer, now aged fifty-eight, his main reaction was of deep offence. Young Joseph on the other hand was so thoroughly outraged on his father's behalf that in his will, forty-five years later, he was careful to exclude all guild members from the benefits of his great charitable foundations. But he also reacted without delay. There is no doubt that it was Joseph – later so outstanding a stylist – who wrote the letter sent by Calmer to Crown Prince Frederik personally. This letter was dated 2 February 1805, two weeks after the master's abusive letter to the chief of police, who was still waiting for a reply. The magnificently worded letter touched politely but firmly upon all the considerations that might influence a future absolute ruler, whose constant wish was to be seen as the father of his country's children, always anxious to come to the aid of subjects suffering injustice. Formally and very correctly, the Crown Prince was made aware that Calmer, a citizen of Copenhagen for twenty-six years, had always supported himself and his family by a trade that was legal in every respect. Nevertheless, in his old age he had been subjected to humiliation by the drapers' guild who wished to deny him his rights to this trade, in spite of the fact that his activities had been known all these years, since he had often supplied guild members with the higher class of goods they could not come by themselves. He went on to say that he had never kept 'open shop', nor had he any need to do so. All his distinguished clientele travelled daily to visit him, and were served on the first floor at Købmagergade where he lived. He considered the guild to have acted basely and contemptibly in seeking to ruin a respectable citizen, and he hoped he would live to see the day when there would no longer be guilds in His Majesty's capital. He said that as a member of the Jewish community in Copenhagen he had the same claim to protection as other subjects of the Crown, and he therefore begged to be allowed to continue to carry on his business as he had all these years.

Then followed the main point of the letter, a request that the Crown Prince should exercise his royal prerogative to compel the guild to admit Calmer without more ado. Calmer added here that the guild had rejected him two years earlier, and he confirmed that he was willing to enter on the customary terms for other, more substantial, members – undertaking to buy £400 worth of goods each year from the guild's Danish textile factory.

The most impressive aspect of the letter was that during the fourteen days available to him Joseph had collected the signatures of nine of his father's most distinguished customers, who all recommended that Calmer should be given the royal privileges. Among them were Møsting, the minister of finance; A. G. von Lowzov, Marshal to the Crown Prince; Counsellor Peder Giersing, Minister Ove Malling's son-in-law; and the immensely rich merchant Frederik Gustmeyer.

Calmer's letter had the desired effect. On 5 April 1805 the Crown Prince ordered Thortsen, now wild with rage and deeply offended on

During the last years of his life, Calmer lived on the first floor in Købmagergade, which ran from Nørreport to the town centre. In the middle of the long street stood Christian IV's seventeenth-century observatory, the Round Tower and Trinity Church, which are still to be seen. Joseph Hambro arranged for his fourteen-year-old son Carl Joachim to be baptized and confirmed in this church on the same day in 1821. Coloured engraving by H. G. F. Holm, 1830. Copenhagen City Museum.

behalf of his guild, to enter Calmer's name in the register of members, the guild's sixth Jewish member to be admitted by special royal decree.

Calmer and his family were happy and relieved that circumstances for Jews in Copenhagen now permitted a denunciation addressed to the police to be turned around into membership dictated by no less a person than the Crown Prince. It is not surprising that the Hambro family's devotion to the future Frederik VI reached its zenith in 1805.

But Calmer's pleasure at his guild membership did not last long. He died on 18 January 1806, only nine months after his admission. His life ended in fact at a well chosen time – 1806 was the momentous year in which Denmark's entire economic outlook underwent a catastrophic change. Calmer was spared the British bombardment of Copenhagen in 1807 and the state bankruptcy in 1813, which ruined so many of his colleagues. A devout and generous Jew throughout his life, he was buried in the presence of a large body of fellow believers in the Møllegade Jewish cemetery, where his tombstone with its beautiful Hebrew inscription is still to be seen.

Calmer Hambro did not succeed in entering the drapers' guild until eight months before his death, and then only because Frederik VI ordered the guild to admit him. After twenty-seven years in Copenhagen he received his first regular trading licence on 24 April 1805. Here is his entry in the guild register, with a note that acceptance was by royal command. Drapers' Guild Register, Copenhagen Town Hall.

Under Calmer's will, Joseph as the oldest son received the lion's share, since it was his duty to carry on the business and to become head of the family. The two twins each inherited £750. Joseph had to make these payments on taking over the business, as well as giving a sum of money to his sister, Zipora. Calmer also left a trust fund of £250, drafted in great detail in Hebrew by the Council of Elders, which was to be used to provide fuel for poor Jews. During the recent severe winters there had been a fuel shortage in Copenhagen, and this generous gesture was much welcomed within the Jewish community.

Thobe, who survived Calmer by twelve years, was entitled as a widow of a guild member to continue the business, employing the necessary expert assistance, which of course Joseph and Isach were able to provide. Soon after Calmer's death she tried to arrange for Joseph, who had been a partner in the firm since 1800, to be admitted to the guild in his father's place. The guild had no hesitation in using this unique opportunity for revenge, and flatly refused the application. It even had the effrontery to assert that there was no evidence that Joseph had had the training he claimed, or that he had completed his apprenticeship test. On this occasion Joseph did not react, although he realized once again and with increasing bitterness that the Danish guild system should be abolished without delay. The system was dissolved in 1857, but by that time Joseph had been dead for nine years. However he could safely trade in 'open shop' on the strength of Thobe's privileges, which he began to do in 1806. At this time the firm of C. J. Hambro & Son moved into larger and better premises at the more fashionable end of Købmagergade.

During 1806–7 Joseph and Isach ran the business jointly, but in 1807 they agreed that Isach should go to Norway – preferably Bergen – to start a trading enterprise which could co-operate with Joseph in Copenhagen and Uncle Mathias in Hamburg.

Thobe withdrew from day-to-day work in the shop in 1808. She was now fifty-two, and from that date lived quietly in a little apartment in Store Kongensgade. It was mainly Zipora who kept contact with her there until Thobe's death in 1820. Thobe had remained true to her Jewish faith until the end, but she was not entirely unmoved by the baptism of her three children and by Joseph's preparations to have his only son baptized. In her later days she had unofficially changed her name to Dorothea and was entered in the Copenhagen Directory as D. Hambro, draper's widow. But in the end, on her tombstone in the Jewish cemetery, she was named Thobe Hambro. The Jewish community had no patience with outrageous modern whims.

Calmer Hambro died at home, aged fifty-nine, on 18 January 1806. He was buried in the Copenhagen Jewish cemetery. His tombstone still stands, and the Hebrew inscription reads: 'A weak and humble voice is heard in the world. The splendid clothes are now exchanged for the ribbons of sorrow. Today, from on high, a beloved man was called, a man respected and honoured, and of high repute. Alas! Nachmann's son, you have departed from us and your house, and from your sweet children whom you loved. But now you are happy, for your spirit has ascended to its dwelling, and among the glorious creatures it will now live in undisturbed peace. The influential, highly respected and generous Mr Calmer, son of Nachmann from Rendsburg, died on Friday the 27th of Teweth and was buried on Sunday the 1st of Schewat in the year 5566. May his soul be preserved in life's preservatory.' Photographed in 1920, when the text was still legible.

33

2 The Surprising Zipora

Zipora, born in 1779, was the first child of Calmer and Thobe Hambro, and their only daughter. Looking today at her somewhat stiff portrait painted in 1841 when she was sixty-two, it is hard to imagine that as a girl she was very beautiful and so temperamental that she was an endless cause of disturbance in her family's placid home. It is said that when young she had raven-black hair and a delicate, attractively pale complexion. She was the only one of the children with what might be called typical Jewish looks. Even as a young man Joseph had the look of a Danish aristocrat, and from childhood the twins could be taken for two healthy, red-cheeked, Danish peasant boys.

The beautiful Zipora was married in 1799, when she was almost twenty, to a 26-year-old Jewish hosier, Lazarus Raphael. The marriage gave Calmer and Thobe every reason for satisfaction, for young Lazarus was not only the son of a prosperous Copenhagen draper, Raphael Jacob, but also, even more significantly, the grandchild of Jacob Raphael, once highly respected in Jewish circles. This grandfather, who had died in 1786, had been a member of the Council of Elders and one of those who in 1778 had vouched for Calmer on his arrival in Denmark. What is more, in 1766 the bridegroom's grandfather had given the community its synagogue in Læderstræde, the synagogue which the entire Jewish community had so sadly missed since its destruction in the great fire of Copenhagen four years before Zipora's marriage. But although the lack of a synagogue meant that Zipora's wedding could not be celebrated in the same festive surroundings as her parents' wedding twenty-one years earlier, she had none the less married into one of the wealthiest and most highly respected families in Copenhagen's small and close-knit Jewish community. Moreover, she had secured a husband who, by virtue of his upbringing, was as orthodox as her own father.

Zipora and Lazarus settled in Brolæggerstræde in the centre of the town, where the father-in-law and Lazarus' brother Joseph also carried on their joint business, in many ways similar to Calmer's but concentrating more on luxury fancy goods. In this field the name Raphael was already well established by the turn of the century, but in the following decade the name 'Raphael Brothers' came to mean Copenhagen's most

Zipora (Hanne Sophie) Hambro (1779–1852), Calmer and Thobe Hambro's eldest child and only daughter, at the age of sixty-two. In her youth she was the most restless member of the family, and she married three times. Her road to Christianity was complex, but had effective results. Painting by A. H. Hunæus, 1841. Owned by the Danish family.

exclusive and fashionable shop in the town's most elegant shopping street, Østergade.

A little further along Brolæggerstræde lived another, more modest, family of Jewish drapers. Here the widow Caroline Wulf, with her two sons, twenty-eight-year-old Wulf Marcus and the younger Joseph, continued the business founded by their father.

We know very little of Zipora's marriage to Lazarus, the young and ambitious hosier, apart from the fact that two children soon arrived, Lazarus junior and a daughter, Thea. One thing is certain: in 1806, a few months after the death of Zipora's devout father, Lazarus and Zipora were divorced! At that time divorce in Jewish circles was very rare and cause for embarrassment. The matter was arranged by the Jewish Council of Elders, but the documents have not survived, so it is impossible to say why the marriage failed.

It is in any event certain that almost immediately after the divorce Zipora married the elder of her neighbour's sons, Wulf Marcus Wulf, and in the same year bore him a son. Without wishing unjustly to tarnish Zipora's honour, it must be assumed that it was she who was the cause of the divorce, which cannot have added to her reputation within Copenhagen's strictly moral Jewish circles. Lazarus Raphael never married again. He died in 1833 aged sixty-one, the senior partner of Raphael Brothers. His large tombstone towers in isolation in the Møllegade cemetery.

A little church linking two buildings is part of the great Fredensborg Castle complex in North Zeeland, still the Danish royal family's favourite summer palace. It was here, twenty miles north of Copenhagen, that Zipora came in 1808 to be baptized with as little attention as possible. Contemporary drawing. Royal Library, Copenhagen.

Little is known about Zipora's marriage to Wulf. Apart from her first son, Carl, born in 1806, she produced in 1808 another son, Gustav. In the same year, when Wulf became very ill, she was expecting his third child. His illness, which rapidly worsened, would certainly have saddened her, but probably also caused her moments of panic. Her sadness arose from her undoubted fondness for him; otherwise she would scarcely have given her daughter, born shortly after his death in 1809, the strange and ugly name of Wulfine. But one must also have been deeply distressed by the thought that, at only thirty years of age, she might be alone with five dependent children, knowing that she was generally disliked by the Jewish community which until then had formed her very narrow world. This was the desperate situation in which she found herself when Wulf died, at the early age of thirty-nine.

But Zipora was a realist throughout her life, and in this threatening situation she made a surprising arrangement. Wulf must have known about it before his death, and probably advised her to carry it through. On 30 April 1808, with the utmost secrecy, she had been baptized. Her conscience had come to terms with the fact that when she became a widow she would have to escape from her Jewish world, a world that would never forgive her for the divorce. And as a future breadwinner in the drapery trade for which she had been trained she had to safeguard herself against the malice shown by the guild towards her father, who had only his Jewish trade licence. As a Christian, she would be able to acquire ordinary citizenship immediately. As a mother responsible for five children, she felt that she must disregard all other considerations. She would scarcely have dared to discuss her plans with any of her three brothers, but she no doubt turned to her mother, Thobe, for advice.

As early as March 1808 the Danish Chancellery had given her permission to be baptized, and later she agreed to the ceremony itself with the court chaplain of Fredensborg Palace Chapel, twenty miles north of Copenhagen. On Sunday 30 April 1808 she was baptized in the beautiful little church by the rural dean, Frederik Carl Gutfeld. At her baptism, and according to the custom of the time, she changed her first names from Hannah Zipora to Hanne Sophie, which were the two Danish names closest to the Jewish. She had taken an unusual step, since before the persecution of the Jews in 1819 baptism of Danish Jews was still quite rare. In any case, it was unique for a married Jewish woman to become baptized without her husband and children being baptized simultaneously. She chose a remote church because she wished to attract as little attention as possible. She at least owed Wulf that consideration! And so Zipora became the first Hambro to desert the Jewish faith.

In the year after Wulf's death and Wulfine's birth she was able to settle without great difficulty in Købmagergade, where she opened a little milliner's shop specializing in stockings and ladies' shoes. She ran the shop with the usual Hambro energy and perseverance for ten years,

Carl Wilhelm Wulf-Borup (1806–59), Zipora's eldest son by her marriage to Wulf Marcus Wulf. Following the Persecution of the Jews, he was adopted with his two siblings, Gustav and the unmarried Wulfine (1810–88), by Attorney Borup, and at this time baptized. Carl Wilhelm matriculated in 1824 and emigrated to the USA in 1827, with support from Joseph Hambro. Here he married a Canadian, Elizabeth Beaulieu (1815–83), and had a splendid career as a businessman in St Paul. They had nine children, all of whom became American citizens and soon lost contact with Denmark. One of the daughters married Emmet, the American envoy at The Hague, who had been the senior partner in Theodore Roosevelt's firm of attorneys before Roosevelt became President of the USA in 1901.

Niels Borup (1787–1860), Zipora's third husband, was a son of the chairmaker Lars Borup, and became a lawyer. Photograph of a miniature of about 1820, now lost.

and in 1813 she married for a third time. The thirty-four-year-old 'Madam Hanne Sophie Wulf, Milliner', with five children, found a Christian husband. Zipora's irresistibility can be judged by the fact that her third and last husband was a law student eight years younger than his bride, a bride already blessed with five children, and that, the marriage having been celebrated on 12 November 1813, Zipora was able to gladden her twenty-six-year-old husband by presenting him with twins only six weeks after the wedding!

Her new husband was a senior official, Niels Borup, the intelligent son of a chair-maker. Since the age of sixteen he had been employed by the Prefect's Office, first at Roskilde and later at Copenhagen, but he had begun to study for law examinations in 1811. He met Zipora in Copenhagen at about this time – perhaps as a customer in her newly opened shop in Købmagergade. They must have felt the mutual attraction of opposites – he was from an environment quite unknown to her, and to him she was something strange, beautiful and mysterious. The picture above shows him as a handsome young official in about 1813, when he began to study in order eventually to support Zipora and her five children. It is clear that their life together started long before their marriage, not only from the early birth of the twins but also from the evidence that before the wedding the couple presented to the pastor a 'royal letter of urgency'. Once again, without wishing unjustly to impugn the fascinating Zipora's honour, her relationship with young Borup is another piece of evidence to suggest that she was the guilty party in the divorce of 1806.

But nevertheless this marriage was happy and lasted until her death. In 1816, Niels Borup passed his examinations, and within a few years he became a highly respected attorney in Danish courts of law at all levels except the High Court. During the early years of the marriage – until 1820 – she continued to run the milliner's shop, and was therefore able herself to help support the new and enlarged family in Købmager-gade.

Niels Borup did not shirk his responsibilities, and in 1820 he adopted the three Wulf children and arranged for their baptism. Zipora's children were therefore gradually drawn into Christianity and fully assimilated into Danish society. Only the Raphael children remained Jewish in accordance with their father's wish.

One of Niels and Zipora's twins died shortly after birth, but the other, Julius Theodor, thrived in the Christian home. Later he gave his mother great satisfaction by deciding to become a pastor in the Danish National Church. Of the three Wulf-Borup children, Carl Wilhelm made a good career in the USA. His brother Gustav became a businessman in Copenhagen, and Wulfine, who never married, died aged seventy-eight in her half-brother Julius' vicarage. Julius had a large family, and Wulfine was the vicarage's indispensable factotum throughout her life. Of the two Raphael children, the son never married and the daughter died childless.

A census taken in Copenhagen at the time of the portrait of sixty-two-year-old Zipora shows that Attorney Niels Borup was then living with her on the Frederiksholm Kanal in a large corner house. Although by 1841 all her children had long since left home, Zipora had a spinster companion, a cook and a parlourmaid. She had thus eventually become the conventional middle-class wife of a well-to-do solicitor, and it was as this, above all, that she hoped to be remembered by her descendants.

Zipora died in 1852, and received a Christian burial. Borup aged rapidly after her death and died in 1860. Throughout her life she appears to have had little contact with her three brothers, but neverthe-less Joseph financed Carl Wilhelm Wulf-Borup's successful emigration to the USA and provided an annuity for his sister on his death in 1848. Indeed, it was she who in 1810 was able to tell her youngest brother Isach how to arrange for his baptism in Fredensborg.

Julius Theodor Borup matriculated at the leading Copenhagen gram-mar school, the Metropolitanskolen, in 1831. He was by no means the first academic in the family. His half-brother, Carl Wilhelm Wulf-

Borup, had already matriculated in 1824, as had his cousin Carl Joachim, Joseph Hambro's only son, and in faraway Bergen most of Isach Hambro's boys also preferred an academic to a business career. Almost all the gifted grandchildren of Calmer and Thobe appear to have been socially ambitious, with a strong inclination towards the intelligentsia. In Denmark and Norway in those days matriculation was a relatively exclusive distinction.

In 1836 Julius became a doctor of divinity. His father had always been deeply religious, and after her baptism Zipora had become an equally ardent Christian so her son's choice was a matter for pride and joy. After a study tour in Germany and Switzerland he taught in Copenhagen, where his natural musical ability led him to become co-founder and first conductor of the Students' Choral Society, still in existence today. A scholarship took him to England in about 1840, just at the time that his cousin Carl Joachim was establishing Hambros bank in London, and afterwards he taught music and English at one of Denmark's best-known old boarding schools, Sorø Akademi, in the

Pastor Julius Theodor Borup (1814–1904), Zipora Hambro's son by Niels Borup, matriculated in 1831, and became a Bachelor of Divinity in 1836. For forty years he was a much-loved parish priest on Zeeland, near Sorø. In 1848, he married Marie Trier (1827–97), grandchild of Mendel Levin Nathanson. Paintings from the 1880s by Johanne Krebs (of Pastor Borup) and Viggo Pedersen (of his wife). Pedersen was their son-in-law, and is best known for his Hans Christian Andersen illustrations. Owned by the Danish family.

Johan Borup (1853–1946), son of Julius and Marie Borup and Zipora's most renowned grandchild, was a pioneer educationalist. In 'Borups Højskole' in Copenhagen he succeeded in transplanting Gründtvig's Folk High School concepts from their original rural environment to the capital. Painting by Ludvig Find, 1924. Borups Højskole, Copenhagen.

most beautiful part of Zeeland. Here he married, in 1848, Marie Trier, grand-daughter of the well-known Jewish reformer Mendel Levin Nathanson. In the 1820's Nathanson had arranged for all his seven children to be baptized. Marie's father, a timber merchant, had also been baptized, and her younger brother, Ernst Trier, was already one of the country's best-known Folk High School principals.

After fourteen years at Sorø Akademi, in 1857 Julius was appointed incumbent of Skamstrup and Frydenlund, two parishes in north-west Zeeland. He spent forty years as a minister before retiring at the age of eighty-three to live with his youngest daughter in Copenhagen. He died at the age of ninety, and became the only one of Calmer and Thobe's grandchildren to survive into the twentieth century.

The vicarage at Skamstrup epitomized the idyllic Danish vicarage of the nineteenth century, a local focus of authority with the popular and industrious minister as the most important figure in the community, wonderfully complemented by his energetic wife Marie. Like all ministers in those days, he also farmed on quite a large scale. The large vicarage household supported no fewer than eight people to run farm and home, apart from the nine members of the family itself and Julius' half-sister Wulfine, who spent her entire life here as a much-loved unmarried aunt.

There may have been some lack of contact between Zipora and her brothers, but the vicarage in Skamstrup became a stronghold for the following generation. Isach's children enjoyed their visits from Bergen, and throughout his life old Isach himself kept in touch by letter with his Danish sister's son.

Only when Marie died in 1897 did Julius consider retiring, and later in Copenhagen he still actively followed events around him. By the time of his death he already had twenty grandchildren, and today the number of his Danish descendants is innumerable. His posthumous reputation, and that of his mother Zipora, stands high among this large body of descendants, to whom Zipora is still better known under her Jewish nickname of Zipperchen.

Johan Borup is one of many fine examples of Danish society's ability in the nineteenth century to assimilate Jews. The progeny of these mixed marriages were often outstanding. Johan had been born while his father was still teaching at Sorø. He attended school there, but matriculated in Copenhagen in 1871. He soon became affected by the pragmatic religious teaching of the pastor and national revivalist NFS Grundtvig, and when Johan became a doctor of divinity in 1877 he preferred a teaching career to the Church. He taught Danish and foreign literature at various schools, and after a study tour in France he added French to his subjects. When later he heard his uncle Ernst Trier speak to the young farm labourers at Vallekilde Folk High School, the concept of the Folk High School gripped him, and from then on he was the inspiration behind the attempt to transplant Grundtvig's ideas to the metropolis so that young people there might share the advantages offered by the adult Folk High Schools. At first he met with many disappointments, but in 1891 he was able to start a 'course for non-matriculated gentlemen and ladies'. From then onwards the Copenhagen Folk High School slowly developed, at first as 'Borup's College', and after 1926 as 'Borup's Folk High School', now well known throughout Denmark. In 1920 the Danish writer Martin Andersen Nexø wrote of Johan Borup: 'As my teacher, he was an ever-inspiring spiritual force. His nature was one of untiring responsiveness, and the source from which so much came is clear to see, for his mind had the industry of a bee, sipping at every flower.'

In 1890, Johan married a minister's daughter, Eline Schousboe, by whom he had two children. Like his father, Johan lived to a very great age; he did not retire from teaching until 1932, and he lived to ninety-three. His son Hans, born in 1893, was for some time principal of the ever-expanding Folk High School.

3   Simon, the Fleet Painter

Calmer and Thobe's son Simon was the elder of the twins born in 1782. Although he was the only one of the four children to display no talent for commerce, he did show marked signs of artistic ability. His humble life as a Copenhagen master craftsman offers little material for a family saga, but his story deserves to be told for two reasons: first, because it represents the prototype of the almost unhindered assimilation of an able and pleasant Jewish family into Copenhagen life; second, because some of Simon's descendants are still remembered for their contribution to the community.

The orthodox Calmer undoubtedly had to consider long and deeply before deciding to apprentice Simon to a Christian house painter. The boy would of course have to live and eat with his master during the five years of his apprenticeship. This would not only mean that he would have to eat food not ritually prepared but also that he would have to work on the Sabbath. Could Calmer take the responsibility of leading his fourteen-year-old son astray in this way? Calmer knew of course that Simon might be allowed to live at home during his apprenticeship, and he also knew of the arrangement by which Jewish apprentices were excused work on Saturdays in return for a cash payment. But this would mean that Simon would have two free days a week, which was almost immoral! The arrangements that Calmer made for Simon are unknown, but the Copenhagen census of 1801 – the last year of his apprenticeship – records him as living at home.

The House Painters' Guild was one of the small and quite congenial Copenhagen guilds. Admission depended merely upon finding a master who would raise no difficulties about taking on a Jewish apprentice under the 1788 Ordnance. Simon completed his five years' apprenticeship without difficulty, and he became a master house painter at the end of 1801. After the mandatory years as a journeyman, he appeared on 8 June 1805 before the guild and presented to an august assembly consisting of the master of the guild, and no fewer than nine assessors and inspectors, a ceiling decoration and a marbled plate. After careful examination they were unanimously approved. Four days later the Academy of Art also accepted his test pieces; he was accepted into the Copenhagen House Painters' Guild and received his licence to trade

Carl Simon Hambro (1782–1831), aged forty-three, a respected Copenhagen master painter and decorator, and captain in the Copenhagen voluntary fire brigade. This portrait was painted by the German-born artist Heinrich Eddelien, who worked for Carl Simon before acceptance by the Academy of Arts. Owned by the Danish family.

from Copenhagen Town Hall. He was then twenty-four, and the town's first Jewish master house painter.

Throughout his twenty-six years as a qualified tradesman Simon seems to have had no difficulty within the guild on account of his Jewish origin. By nature he was friendly, jovial and contented. He had a reputation as a good colleague, and his workshop was recognized as a good place for training and employment.

Like other worthy master craftsmen, he waited to complete his master's text before he married, although he was already engaged to a Jewish girl two years older than himself, Jeanette Nathan, probably one of Thobe's relations. They were married on 30 July 1806, a few months after his brother Joseph married Marianne von Halle.

The couple settled down at Kattesundet, where Simon set up his workshop with £750 inherited from his father. He lived and worked there until 1817, when he bought a large property on Ved Stranden from his brother Joseph. Jeanette gave birth to five children between 1807 and 1812. Their only son died almost immediately after birth, causing the eventual extinction of the Hambro name in Copenhagen.

As a master craftsman, Simon undoubtedly soon developed into what was then called a 'liberal Jew'. In his everyday life he abandoned strict orthodoxy, although he had no intention whatever of formally disavowing the faith of his fathers. This attitude is reflected in the

Jeanette Hambro, née Nathan (1780–1863), married Carl Simon in 1806. Painting, c. 1825 by Heinrich Eddelien. Owned by the Danish family.

Gentile names he chose for his four daughters: Hanne, born in 1807; Henriette, born the following year; Caroline, born in 1811; and Ida born in 1812. They were also, of course, all entered at birth in the Jewish community's register of births and namings.

While still a newly established master and a recently married man, Simon experienced in 1807 the bombardment of Copenhagen and the ignominious abduction of the entire Danish Navy. The British carried off all the ships except one, the ship-of-the-line *Prins Christian*, which was in Norway at the time; however the British sank this ship at Sjællands Odde the following year. The Danish Navy had therefore to be rebuilt from scratch, a large building programme that extended over many years.

The unhappy fate of the Danish Navy led later to an important success for Simon. Like his brother Joseph, he had a happy knack of turning even the most unpromising situations to his advantage. In 1817 the Danish naval dockyard was looking for a master painter to take over the vast amount of painting now necessary, and Simon was awarded the contract. With typical craftsman-like self-assurance, he referred to himself for the rest of his life as the 'fleet painter', and this steady employment eventually made him quite a wealthy man.

For centuries all patriotic master craftsmen had joined one of the town's volunteer corps; either the Civic Guard or the Fire Brigade. As

45

As a young master painter and decorator, Carl Simon witnessed in 1807 the ignominious abduction of the Danish fleet by the British Navy. As shown in this watercolour of that year, they even destroyed ships under construction. The Danish fleet was rebuilt over the next twenty-five years, and in 1817 Carl Simon became the fleet's permanent master painter. Copenhagen City Museum.

was to be expected, the Civic Guard's activities had greatly increased during the troubled years of war, and recruitment to the Fire Brigade had risen sharply following the catastrophe of the Copenhagen fire of 1795 and the bombardment of 1807. Simon had been a member of the Fire Brigade since his apprenticeship years, and he had worked his way up in rank to become one of the town's eight fire captains, which entitled him to wear the Brigade's decorative officer's uniform. The Civic Guard exercised every other Sunday, but the Fire Brigade was not bothered by training; they had to do no more than turn out whenever there was a fire alarm in the capital.

Zipora's baptism in 1808 and Isach's in 1810 appear to have had no effect on Simon's official relationship with the Jewish community; on the contrary, Frederik vi's far-sighted legislation of 1814 gave him pleasure and encouragement. His daughters went to ordinary schools,

46

and his own religious observances gradually became limited to his membership of the Jewish community. During the years without a synagogue, which lasted for the rest of his life, he in fact ceased to be an orthodox Jew; he himself felt that year by year, and imperceptibly he and his family had slipped into Danish society.

The 1819 persecution of the Jews shocked him, as it did hundreds of his liberal co-religionists. Frederik VI's legislation on Danish Jews had deluded them into thinking that they were equal citizens, but religious intolerance, envy and xenophobia still lurked below the surface of the apparently good-natured and progressive Danish people. Simon could not have anticipated an outburst such as this, coming without the slightest warning and with no apparent or tangible provocation.

Simon swept up the broken glass in front of his house and put new windows in the lower floors. Glaziers in Copenhagen were very busy in

47

September 1819. In Simon's home, as in hundreds of other Jewish homes – liberal, orthodox or indifferent – they began to discuss what they should do.

Simon's decision did not cause him much soul-searching. Zipora had been baptized in 1808 and Isach in 1810. If this was the price of future security, he could easily overcome his remaining scruples. If anything held him back it can only have been a certain embarrassed uneasiness that such a step should be necessary for a respectable Copenhagen citizen and captain of the Fire Brigade.

On Sunday 2 December 1819 early-rising citizens of Copenhagen might have seen Simon and his wife Jeanette, dressed in their best, walking with their four young daughters to the church in the suburb of Frederiksborg. They were unknown in this area, and their baptism would not therefore attract attention. Simon had agreed with the minister, Pastor Jens Hansen Freckland, that the baptism should take place that day, when the congregation had left after the service. Simon would of course have been very reluctant to ask any of his guild colleagues or Fire Brigade friends to act as sponsors, so the pastor had kindly offered to act in this capacity himself, with his wife and

Carl Simon's daily workplace from 1817 until his death in 1831 was at Holmen on the most northerly part of Christianshavn, where the navy yards and offices were situated. French lithograph, c. 1835. Royal Library, Copenhagen.

48

Among Copenhagen master craftsmen, to become an officer in the capital's voluntary fire brigade commanded considerable respect. The brigade recruited its leaders from, in particular, craftsmen in the building trade. Carl Simon reached the rank of fire captain, and would have been seen in the uniform shown here not only at fires but also on more festive occasions in Frederik VI's uniform-conscious capital. Coloured print after G. F. Lahde, 1815. Royal Library, Copenhagen.

daughter. So Simon had only to present himself with his accountant and a neighbour.

From that day onwards Simon was to be called Carl Simon. He chose Carl because it reminded him of his father's name, Calmer. Jeanette was baptized Anne Jeanette. The four girls already had Christian first names, but Hanne and Caroline were both given Frederikke as a second name, a choice that may be seen as a propitiatory bow in the direction of Frederik VI. Henriette was given the inexplicable and unusual second name of Axeline, and to little Ida was added the name of Sophie, after her baptized Aunt Zipora. The children never in fact used their new names, which suggests that they themselves were not entirely pleased with the performance. Caroline Frederikke, who had

49

Carl Simon and Jeanette enjoyed one of Copenhagen's most picturesque views from their large house at Gammel Strand. To the right they looked across to the rebuilt Christiansborg Castle; in the centre stood the stock exchange; and on the left the naval church. Just as today,

been named originally after Crown Princess Caroline, refused as an adult to sign herself as anything other than Caroline.

But now that the family had paid the necessary tribute they felt their future in Denmark to be secure. Since birth they had all looked on Denmark as their native land. It was a consolation that the ceremony at Frederiksborg in fact did nothing to alter their day-to-day life, although the parents now had to recognize that the girls could no longer marry Jews, since no orthodox Jew would consider marrying a baptized Jewess. But in the event this was no problem, and the three girls who married found Christian husbands. The first to leave home was Hanne

the city's fish was on sale directly below their windows. His home is today one of the capital's best-known seafood restaurants. Detail of a painting by Wilhelm Pedersen, 1839. Copenhagen City Museum.

Frederikke, who at the age of eighteen married a young and gifted manufacturer, Henrich Leonhard Danchell. In 1827, Henriette married at nineteen a neighbour, a very wealthy young merchant from Bornholm, Andreas Ancker. But tragedy followed when Henriette died in childbirth after eighteen months of marriage. The third sister Caroline never married, and the name of Hambro died out in Denmark on her death in 1892.

In 1831 Simon Hambro died in his large house at Gammel Strand. Outdoor work in all weathers throughout his industrious life had taken its toll, and he died of apoplexy. He was the first of Calmer and Thobe's children to die, although he had been the youngest; he was only forty-nine. Fortunately, Leonhard Danchell was able to carry on the business as guardian of his mother-in-law, Jeanette. In 1836 Jeanette married off her last daughter. Ida Sophie, now twenty-four, became the wife of Pastor Hektor Gyberg. Their eldest son Carl Hambro Gyberg, also became a pastor, and has many descendants alive today. Jeanette survived Carl Simon by thirty-four years. She died in 1865, aged eighty-five, in the same year as old Isach Hambro of Bergen, who had often been an honoured guest at their home.

Denmark's natural transition from crafts to industry following the invention of the steam engine was considerably delayed by the aftermath of the Napoleonic Wars, which had revealed Frederik VI to his impoverished little country as the great loser. Only at the beginning of the 1830s did development get under way, and the point was soon reached when the brand-new circle of Copenhagen industrialists needed to organize themselves. In 1838 they formed the Danish Industrial Association, which later became one of the most influential organizations in Danish industry.

One of the most active founders and uncontested leader during its first few years was Henrich Leonhard Danchell, the enterprising and congenial husband of Hanne Frederikke Hambro. It was Simon who set up his son-in-law in business. In his later days the fleet painter experimented by extending his painter's workshop to manufacture the newly invented oilcloth, which was otherwise imported from England. In partnership with his son-in-law he established the first Danish oilcloth factory in the Gammel Strand house. Danchell's particular contribution was to instal printing presses to print colours and patterns on the new cloth, which could now, like wallpaper, be sold in rolls for cutting into tablecloths, curtains and aprons. After Simon's death Danchell ran the factory very successfully on Jeanette's behalf. He extended the business by setting up a tannery and a department manufacturing lacquered leather for such things as patent leather shoes and handbags. The printing of oilcloth put him into contact with Emilius Bærentzen, a talented and versatile artist who had taught himself the new art of lithography in Paris. In 1837 he and Danchell established Emilius Bærentzen's Institute of Lithography which became the country's leading lithographers.

Danchell, the vice-president, represented the opposition in the Industrial Association's early years. He thought that the other members of the Association's board were far too concerned with industry's technical problems, quite ignoring the questions of marketing many

Caroline Frederikke Hambro (1811– 92), Simon and Jeanette Hambro's third youngest daughter, never married, and at her death in 1892 she was the last Hambro in Copenhagen. She had been baptized, together with her parents and three sisters, in Frederiksberg church on Sunday, 2 December 1819, two months after the Persecution of the Jews. With the money she inherited from Joseph Hambro in 1848, she set up a trust for needy daughters of Copenhagen master painters and decorators. Photograph taken in 1875. Royal Library, Copenhagen.

new products. To make his point he established the Mercantile Industrial Association, with the satisfying result that in 1840 both associations amalgamated, with himself as the first president.

Bærentzen's lithography business naturally consumed vast quantities of paper, and Danchell, always on the alert, turned his attention to paper manufacture. In 1843 he bought two paper mills, Ørholm and Nymølle, at the Mill river in north Zeeland, which until then had been run by British owners. He modernized these two mills by installing steam engines and turbines to supplement the river's increasingly unreliable hydraulic power. He spent his happiest years in the stately old house at Ørholm, in the valley of the little river that is still considered one of north Zeeland's most charming spots.

When Simon and Jeanette's second daughter Henriette died in 1829, a few months after giving birth to her only child Carl, her wealthy, bereaved and already rather reserved husband, Andreas Ancker, was so deeply disconsolate that at first he refused to see the child who had caused his mother's death. To compensate, he immersed himself in his extensive business affairs and made more profit than ever before.

His ageing grandmother, Jeanette Hambro, brought up the little boy until he was twelve. Carl soon showed an interest in literature. He later

53

wrote poetry and translated plays but his interest always proved greater than his talent. When he was twelve his father suddenly, to everyone's surprise, bought the fine columned mansion at Ved Stranden that had belonged to Nicolai von Holten, chairman of the National Debt Commission. He moved into the house with his son in 1840, and for seven years father and son lived a cloistered life there behind drawn curtains. Andreas Ancker never completed furnishing the house, and he himself lived in one room on the first floor, while his son established himself in a small room on the ground floor, beside the shop premises attached to the house. No one ever came to the house except Carl's school friend Emil Møller. The father considered that his odd and awkward son was quite unsuited to commerce, and decided that he should become a farmer. At the age of nineteen Carl was sent to work on a manor farm in north Zeeland, and a year later he went for further training to Germany, Switzerland and Hungary. When he returned home in 1851 his father bought him a very isolated little farm seven miles north of Copenhagen. Here Carl felt himself more abandoned than ever, and he was unable to work up any interest in the farm that had been thrust upon him.

Ørholm paper mill on the picturesque Mølleå, ten miles north of Copenhagen. The factory looked like this in 1845, when Danchell had modernized the undertaking and introduced steam turbines to replace the stream's less efficient hydraulic power. The Danchell family, which still has many representatives in Denmark, lived in the beautiful eighteenth-century house on the left of the mill. Painting by Henrich Eddelien, c. 1840. Owned by the Danish family.

Henrik Leonhard Danchell (1802–71), Carl Simon's intelligent and enterprising son-in-law, first expanded his father-in-law's oilcloth factory and then added a tannery and a patent leather factory. In 1838 he was co-founder of Den Danske Industriforening, and was its chairman from 1840 to 1843. In 1843 he bought the Ørholm and Nymølle paper mills. The first large lithographic institution, Emil Bærentzen & Co. was founded on his initiative. Painting by Henrich Eddelien, c. 1830. Owned by the Danish family.

In 1853 he published a book of poems under the pen-name 'Bebbo' but it earned him no recognition. Then something quite unforeseen occurred; his father suddenly died of a heart attack, aged only fifty-three. This was in 1854, and after the funeral Carl realized in some confusion that overnight, at the age of twenty-six, he had become one of the richest men in Copenhagen.

He immediately arranged for the mansion to be beautifully furnished, and tried to create for himself the role of a rich man, for which he did not have the ability, the strength, nor the stature. On a long journey through Europe in 1855–6 with his only real friend, Emil Møller, he found that he suffered increasingly from attacks of convulsive cramp, which made the last part of the journey something of a trial for them both.

Nevertheless in September 1857 he impulsively married Augusta von Schoutz, the daughter of a Captain in the Swedish Guard. The young couple moved into the mansion, but a month later his health had so deteriorated that he thought he should make a will, in which he ordained that if he were to die without issue half his fortune was to go to his family and the other half to his wife. But if she remarried, half her share was to be used to establish travel scholarships for young Danish

Carl Ancker (1828–57), the philanthropist and grandson of Carl Simon Hambro, was brought up by his grandmother, Jeanette Hambro. In 1850 his father made him become a farmer, although his heart was set on art and literature. When his father died in 1854, the young Carl found himself a millionaire. Before he died, three years later, he had travelled all over Europe, married, and established his subsequently famous scholarship for artists. Painting by J. Jensen, c. 1857. Frederiksborg Castle.

painters, sculptors, writers and composers. Less than two months after his marriage, and with the ink on the will scarcely dry, Carl died.

His pretty young widow did indeed remarry. In the summer of 1860 she became the wife of an elegant young Danish officer – Major, later General, Frederik Stiernholm – and automatically the Ancker Foundation came into being. The Foundation's capital amounted to £8,650, making it the largest Danish private foundation at that time. Its aim has been to distribute sufficient money every year to provide at least one year abroad for a sculptor, a painter, a writer and a composer. However, inflation since 1945 has caused the allocation of funds to be made now only every other year. In the course of more than a hundred years some four hundred Danish artists have benefited from the Foundation.

4 The Practical Isach

Isach Hambro, born in 1782, was the younger of Calmer and Thobe's twins. He became apprenticed to a calico printer at first; this printing technique was relatively new in Denmark, and it benefited from the prohibition on imports of ready-printed calico material. This trade fell outside the orbit of the guilds, and was therefore mainly in the hands of Jewish immigrants who had the necessary skills.

Isach, however, would in fact much have preferred to be a merchant, and when in 1800 his idolized older brother Joseph returned from his apprentice years in Hamburg Isach managed to persuade his parents to allow him also to take a three-year apprenticeship with Calmer's brother in Hamburg, Uncle Mathias. Here he soon proved to be as bright, intelligent and adept as Joseph, and when he returned home in 1803 there was no further discussion about his future. Until his father's death, therefore, Isach assisted him and Joseph in their undertaking, and during this time was able to see something of Europe. Following their father's death in 1806, Isach and Joseph agreed that Isach should settle in Norway, so that, with Uncle Mathias in Hamburg, the brothers could exchange goods among the three countries.

In 1807, when merchants spoke of going to Norway only one town featured in the discussion. This was Bergen, then Norway's largest town, lying on the west coast. It was northern Europe's most important commercial centre, and had enjoyed this position since the Middle Ages.

In those days, to move from Copenhagen to Bergen was not looked upon as a move abroad. Until 1814, Norway formed the northern part of the Danish-Norwegian dual monarchy. The language was very close to Danish, and countless Danish-Norwegian marriages and generations of Norwegian students at Copenhagen University had closely linked the two cultures. Under these circumstances it is understandable that Sweden – the ancient hereditary enemy of Denmark and Norway – was pushed into the background, and it is this which explains the disgrace felt by many Norwegians when in 1814 they suddenly came under Swedish rule. This arose because Denmark, on the losing side in the Napoleonic Wars, was in 1813 ordered under the separate peace treaty of Kiel to surrender its old sister-country. A further bond

Tyskebryggen in Bergen, with St Mary's church on the left. The picture shows an event witnessed by Isach and his wife on 27 May 1814 – heralds proclaim the news that the Danish Prince Christian Frederik has been elected king of Norway at Eidsvoll. Coloured drawing after J. F. L. Dreier, 1814. Historical Museum, Bergen.

Bergen street scene about 1825. This view is from the Nye Alminding square, and to the right is Strandgade where Isach had his general store. The town was dominated by its extensive import–export trade, which was almost entirely by sea. Lithograph after J. F. L. Dreier, 1825. Historical Museum, Bergen.

was the legal systems of Denmark and Norway, which were practically identical. In the 1680s King Christian v had provided both his realms with almost parallel legislation.

Under both legal systems Jews were originally refused entry. This attitude had long been put aside in Denmark, with the result that Danish law had been suitably amended many years previously. In Norway, however, the prohibition had been maintained. Few people were concerned about this, for as yet Norway had seen only a small number of Jews, apart from those shipwrecked and washed ashore on the remote and thinly populated coast.

When in 1807 Isach took passage to Norway with the merchant captain Peter Knudsen he had no knowledge of this singular quirk of Norwegian legislation. But he had scarcely landed on the quay at Bergen and given his name as Isach when trouble began. After selling for some weeks – more or less unchallenged – the goods he had brought with him, an official complaint was lodged against him by the Bergen merchant Claus Svane on the grounds that he had 'illegally infringed the rights of the merchants there residing'. On 2 May the worthy Norwegian judge proposed that Isach should leave the country as soon as possible, but Svane's solicitor demanded that Isach should cease to trade immediately, and that he should also give £20 to the poor of the town. Isach, undismayed, replied that after three weeks he had in fact sold all he had brought with him, and he asked for time to consider the fine until the next week's court-day. The following week he was let off with a fine of £2, but he did not turn for home immediately. In the months that followed he closely reconnoitred the whole situation in Bergen, and did not return to Denmark until November. Shortly before his departure, he put an advertisement into Bergen's local paper declaring that he would not leave the country while any person had an account to settle with him. This advertisement represented the first appearance of the name Hambro in print in Norway. It is interesting that just below this advertisement there was an anonymous, anti-Semitic stab in the back. It is not known how Isach passed the following two-and-a-half years. He may have tested the ground in other countries, where he might perhaps have been more welcome, but in his heart he never gave up the wish to return to Bergen.

In the autumn of 1810 he presented himself to the pastors at Fredensborg who had meanwhile baptized his sister Zipora. Here, at the age of twenty-eight, he was baptized on Sunday 21 September 1810. He took, before Isach his Jewish name, the Christian name of Edvard. This name has been given to so many of his descendants down to the sixth generation that confusion can easily arise. The helpful pastor called in

The entrance to Bergen harbour, on the west coast of Norway. Since the Middle Ages, Bergen had been the country's most important commercial centre, founded by German merchants from Lübeck and Rostock. To the left is the Bergenshus fortress, and behind this Tyskebryggen where the German merchants lived. Lithograph from about 1810. Historical Museum, Bergen.

two local citizens to act, with himself, as godparents. One was the palace gardener; the other the assayer of the Kronborg small arms factory. With his newly acquired and precious certificate of baptism in his pocket, Isach soon sailed again for Bergen, and he remained there until his death fifty-five years later.

Following his return to Bergen, Isach quickly completed the necessary formalities, and on 27 December 1810 he was entered in the Bergen citizens' register as 'the son of Jewish parents, but duly baptized in Denmark on 21 September 1810'. He then took the citizens' oath so that he could receive a licence to trade. He had already found a suitable property to accommodate both his business and his private residence. It was an imposing old corner house in Strandgade, the town's leading business area. It had a shop and seven large rooms. Considering the size of the family he fathered over the next twelve years, he was undoubtedly very far-sighted in establishing himself from the outset on such a large scale. The property included a three-storey warehouse, and brick-built cellars ran under the entire building. From the beginning, therefore, the stage was set for a business to match the high Bergen standards. He was able to pay the £1,000 for the whole complex in cash; as we already know, he had inherited £750 from his father.

After only thirteen months in the town he married on 30 January 1812 a young Norwegian girl, Marie Roggen, the daughter of a haberdasher. She was to be an outstanding wife to Isach over the next thirty years.

Isach directed his activities towards merchandise of all kinds, but in the field of fancy goods he probably offered a more sophisticated range than the people of Bergen had ever seen. Whatever he earned during the early years he invested in further properties. For example, the year after his marriage he bought Nygaard, a beautifully situated country house in Skjold, quite a distance outside Bergen. During his wife's lifetime the whole family spent every summer at Nygaard.

In autumn 1814 Isach witnessed Denmark's surrender of Norway. Like so many other Norwegians in the summer of 1814 he had still hoped that at the last moment the Danish viceroy in Norway, Prince Christian Frederik would declare himself king of an independent Norway. This hope had arisen that spring, when an assembly of Norwegian parliamentarians had adopted Norway's new, free constitution at Eidsvoll. The Eidsvoll constitution was dated 17 May 1814, which Norwegians still celebrate as their National Day. Isach even heard Prince Christian Frederik proclaimed – somewhat prematurely – future king of Norway in the Bergen market square. But nevertheless Sweden succeeded in carrying through the union, which was to last until 1905.

The Eidsvoll constitution, which Sweden wisely respected, became

In 1807, Isach Hambro sailed to Bergen without realizing that Jews had not been allowed to enter Norway since 1684. On 2 November 1807, having been ordered to leave Norway, he announced in the Bergen Adresseavis that if any person had matters to settle with him it would have to be done before his departure. The name of Hambro appears in print for the first time in Norway in this little announcement. But beneath this there was a malicious, anonymous insertion: 'Is a Jew permitted to trade in Norway and remain here until he chooses to leave?' Bergenske Adressecontoirs Efterretninger no. 47, 21 November 1807.

Da jeg nu agter at afreise til Kiøbenhavn: saa bekiendtgiøres dette for Vedkommende, som have noget at afgiøre med mig
J: Hambro.

Spørgsmaal.
Er det en Jøde tilladt at handle i Norge og forblive indtil det falder ham ind at reise bort?

On 17 May 1814 a Norwegian National Assembly, chaired by the Danish vice-regent, Prince Christian Frederik, adopted a constitution in the manor house at Eidsvoll. This step was taken in the hope of avoiding a union with Sweden and of making Prince Christian Frederik King of Norway. He is seen in uniform on the right. Painting by Oscar Wergeland, 1887. The Norwegian Storting's Plenum Hall, Oslo.

known all over Europe as the most free and democratic constitution adopted by any country since the French Revolution. It had indeed scared the absolute Danish king, Frederik VI, because of the great power it gave to the newly established Norwegian Storting. In spite of the constitution's liberalism, Isach must still have read one paragraph with mild surprise, for it was stated in Section 2: '*Jesuits and monastic orders will not be tolerated. Jews are still excluded from entry to the Realm.*' By that time, of course, Isach personally had no need to worry, but he was nevertheless allowed the satisfaction of living long enough to see this intolerant blemish on the Norwegian constitution removed in 1851.

Although economic conditions in Bergen just after the Danish state bankruptcy in 1813 were undoubtedly very much better than in

Copenhagen, the speed with which Isach rose to become one of Bergen's commercial magnates is nevertheless almost incredible. Within a very few years he became completely accepted socially in a town that certainly had no reputation for welcoming even its own native new arrivals. All this was achieved without making any attempt to enter the municipal government and without accepting any other public office. The explanation lies perhaps in his character. Of the four children of Calmer and Thobe Hambro he was the kindest and least complicated. He had no difficulty at all in associating with all levels of society, both in his day-to-day life and on ceremonial occasions.

Once accepted as a Norwegian citizen, he was generous in his support of national ventures. When in 1811 a collection was held in Norway to raise money for its first university at Kristiania, Isach

Isach Hambro (1782–1865), the younger of Calmer and Thobe's twin sons. He was baptized in 1810 in Denmark after being turned away from Bergen in 1807. He became one of Bergen's richest and most highly esteemed merchants, and was the founder of the entire Norwegian line of the Hambro family. Silver wedding portrait, 1837, by the Bergen painter Johan Görbitz. Owned by the Norwegian family.

donated £100, the largest sum contributed in Bergen. By 1816 Bergen considered him good for at least £10,000. In that year he was eighth in the list of the town's contributors to the establishment of the Bank of Norway (Norges Bank).

Within the Hambro family itself it was he who contributed most to its unity. When, during his annual buying trip to the capitals of Europe, he passed through Copenhagen he always stayed with Zipora and her lawyer husband Borup, and he took the same opportunity to visit his twin brother Simon, to whom he felt specially close all his life. But Joseph is rarely mentioned in these encounters, and after 1848, when Isach's sons Johan and Edvard left C. J. Hambro & Son in London in anger, contact between the families in England and Norway ceased for many years.

Isach's wife Marie died of a heart attack in 1841 at the age of fifty. At this time Isach's business was at its zenith, but when she died he lost interest in the undertaking. This perhaps had something to do with his four sons' clear lack of interest in taking over this extensive business. Showing no apparent disappointment, he disposed of his business and his properties in the years that followed, giving his sons £1,000 each and his daughters £500 each. He then moved away to Nygaard, where with one faithful old housekeeper he remained for the next seventeen years.

Marie Hambro, née Roggen (1791–1841), Isach's Norwegian wife. She was a haberdasher's daughter from Bergen, married Isach in 1812 and presented him with seven children during their twenty-nine years of marriage. Silver wedding portrait, 1837 by Johan Görbitz. Owned by the Norwegian family.

He looked after his farming interests and his large garden, and he took pleasure in gathering his whole family there each Sunday. He sold Nygaard when he was seventy-eight and moved back to Bergen, where he spent his remaining five years in a small rented house. He had invested his entire fortune in Norwegian government bonds, and drew heavily on these funds during his long retirement. He died aged eighty-four in autumn 1865, a highly respected old man. He had kept enough capital for each of his seven children to inherit £600.

A last glimpse of the old merchant is given in a letter to his Danish nephew, Pastor Julius Borup, written in 1863, two years before his death. The occasion was Isach's first grandson's recent matriculation with very high grades – although not yet sixteen – at the Latin School in Bergen: 'He is a worthy boy,' wrote the grandfather proudly, 'and if God is gracious enough to preserve him he should sometime in the future grow into a fine man, a joy to us all.' Shortly before this, old Isach and the boy had shared a remarkable experience. The boy had matriculated in classical languages, and had read Hebrew at school. He had been dumbfounded suddenly to discover that his grandfather spoke much better Hebrew than he did. This buried knowledge, stemming from the Copenhagen synagogue, appears to have been the only remnant of his Jewish heritage, and it so impressed his grandson that he

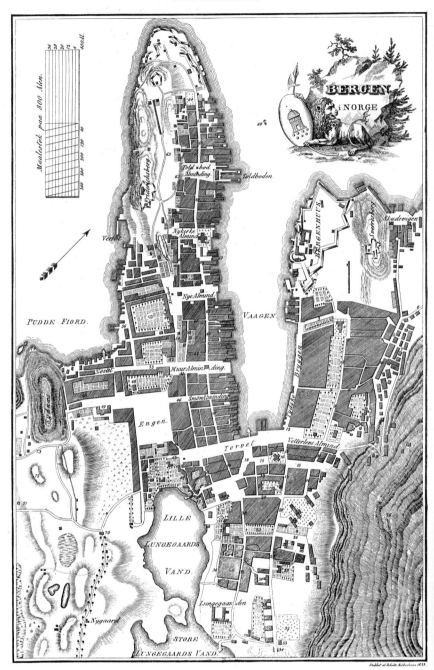

Map of Bergen about 1800. It shows the town's most densely populated area on the long Nordnæs peninsula, with Vaagen, the town's natural harbour, on the right and Pudde Fiord on the left. At the entrance to the harbour towers Bergenshus, the old fortress, and St Mary's church. South of these is the famous Tyskebryggen. At the end of Vaagen is the town's

decided to become a philologist specializing in the Semitic languages.

All the Bergen Hambro children were very gifted. Carl, the eldest, born in 1813, Johan, born in 1816, and Christian, born in 1823, all matriculated in Bergen. Only Edvard, born in 1821, was apprenticed at an early age to Joseph at the Copenhagen bank. All the boys were strikingly blond and Scandinavian in appearance, whereas the daughter, Theodora, born in 1818, developed into a typical Jewish beauty. But in the commercial town of Bergen matriculation had nothing to recommend it. 'Where did old Hambro go wrong, that all his sons want to study?' asked the commercial centre's leading circles. If you were a merchant's son, to study was in fact socially degrading for one's family.

If Isach had indeed made an error, it was perhaps in giving his sons too much money at an early age, so that they were all able to tour in Europe. Naturally, when they returned they found Bergen small and provincial. Although almost all the children married into Bergen's leading families – Carl and Theodora, for example, married a daughter and a son of Bergen's lord lieutenant – it may well be said that the sons started off in the wrong direction. None of them really lived up to the expectations justifiably attributed to them. Indeed, the most notable names among the Norwegian Hambros did not emerge until the third and fourth generations, when the family's hitherto unrealized potential at last blossomed. Whereas the two Copenhagen lines produced pastors, industrialists and Folk High School teachers, and the English line bankers, landowners and officers of the armed forces, it is intellectuals that predominate among the leading representatives of the Norwegian family. Men of letters, humanists and a single politician of world class make up the picture. The amazing adaptability displayed by old Isach in Bergen was to reappear in his grandchildren and great-grandchildren.

Isach and Marie's eldest son, Carl, was in fact named Carl Joachim, but to avoid a confusion of names it is simpler to call him Carl. From his youth he was a friendly and engaging man, who became the first of the Bergen brothers to reveal the pampered second generation's typical uncertainty in their choice of career. After matriculating in 1832, his

---

central space, Torvet. At the bottom left, Fløyen mountain rises as a landmark above the town. By 1823 Bergen had about 20,000 inhabitants. In 1810, Isach Hambro's shop was in the middle of Nordnæs on the corner of Strandgade and Nye Alminding. Royal Library, Map Room, Copenhagen.

preference was to study, but although he left at his death one of Bergen's finest book collections he was not single-minded enough. After spending several years travelling abroad, he returned home in 1836 to go into the clothing and fancy goods business on a large scale. He settled in Strandgade in well-situated corner premises a little nearer to the town centre than his father, with whom he was now blatantly competing.

Carl appears to have been in many ways similar to his English cousin Carl Joachim. Like him, and at about the same time, he tried somewhat demonstratively and ungratefully to make himself independent of his father. But Carl lacked his English cousin's occasional flashes of genius and his own father's diligence and unflagging energy.

In 1838, when his new shop was running well, he married Angelique Bull. The marriage reinforced the respected position the Hambro family now held in Bergen, for the bride's father was the former lord lieutenant of Bergen, Georg Jacob Bull, recently appointed president of the High Court of Norway. For good measure, Angelique's Danish-born mother was the sister of the Danish physicist, H. C. Ørsted. Against this background, the family's great expectations of Carl rose a few more degrees.

Carl J. Hambro (1813–73), Isach's eldest son, was married in Bergen in 1838 to Angelique Bull (1815–99). Photographs from the 1860s. Owned by the Norwegian family.

Carl J. Hambro's general store in Bergen was on a corner of Strandgade. He lived here on the first floor with his wife and ten children until he sold the shop in 1852 to move to his new cotton mill outside Bergen. Painting by J. D. Dahl, 1840.

But the marriage altered nothing in Carl's day-to-day activities, and he followed his father's example by making long buying trips each year to Copenhagen, Paris and London. Rather more impressive was his rapidly improving lifestyle; his extravagance made one of his father's friends exclaim; 'We did not become rich by what we earned but by what we saved.'

During the years 1839–55, Angelique produced no fewer than ten children, three of whom died in infancy. But only Edvard, who matriculated in classical languages and knew some Hebrew, proved to the full that by his own initiative he could live up to his grandfather's expectations.

The large sums that old Isach gave his sons when he sold his business after Marie's death seem to have brought none of them much happiness, especially Carl and his family. At the end of the 1840s he grew bored with the clothing and fancy goods shop, and he decided with the help of his father's capital to make the leap from trade into industry. His ambition was to set up a cotton mill.

The textile industry had established a footing in Norway by the

69

FOTLANDS BOMULDSSPINDERIE

CARL J. HAMBRO

Carl J. Hambro's cotton mill at Vestlandet on the Fotlandsvågen was situated high up on one of the many arms of Bergen Fiord, and relied on water power from a river. Advertisement, 1855.

1840s. The first factories were of course located near small waterfalls, to exploit the water power, and there were already two such factories on Bergen's extensive inner fiord. In 1850 Carl secured the right to exploit a river in the northern arm of the fiord, and there at Fotlandsvåg he established a large, modern cotton mill. The location was well chosen, for the river was supplied by a lake with plenty of water higher up the mountain, and it ran into the fiord over a fairly steep waterfall.

There is no doubt that the new manufacturing plant was carefully planned and produced the right kind of goods, but the expenses of running the large patrician house attached to it for the family's many children made the enterprise too costly. As a result, the working capital available was too limited from the outset. In 1851 Carl sold his general store in Bergen and moved to Fotlandsvåg with the whole family. The factory was quite isolated and totally cut off from the outside world. There were no neighbours for many miles around. All connections with Bergen were by water, and as the inner fiord was usually quite becalmed this meant in practice endless rowing. A trip to Bergen might take at least a day each way, even with the best oarsmen. The result, of course, was that life at the factory could be extremely lonely during the six winter months, but during the summer there was no dearth of friends and relations to spend a holiday and to enjoy the ever-welcoming and superb hospitality of Carl and Angelique.

Carl's venture into industry lasted only seven years. Sales of his cotton yarn to Bergen exporters were at first quite good, but poor liquidity soon caused difficulties, and in the general economic crisis that swept Norway like a tornado in 1858 he had to suspend payments. Only by selling the factory and most of his household effects quickly was he able to meet his debts and avoid bankruptcy. People who knew Carl well said that he showed little distress at this catastrophe. For a friendly man such as Carl, life at Fotlandsvåg was in many ways a voluntary exile from the society in which he and his wife had been reared, and for their children the years at the factory had meant complete isolation from the rest of the world. It was not therefore such a disaster to have to part with the factory, but the fall in social status was hard for his family to bear. It was particularly hard for Angelique, the lord lieutenant's daughter, who had now to allow her older daughters to seek work as domestic helps or governesses with relations and friends. She and Carl moved with the younger children into a small apartment in Bergen.

Old Isach, now seventy-six, said nothing, but he must have been deeply disappointed. He had taken his favourite grandson Edvard into his home, and it was during these years that a close relationship developed between the future educationist and his grandfather. For the rest of his life Edvard was reluctant to speak of his childhood at Fotlandsvåg. He was disappointed in his father, and he thought that Carl should have made better use of his opportunities. He also found it very sad that his mother – who was to survive Carl by many years – should become so impoverished in her old age.

Carl lived for another thirteen years after selling the factory. He took a post at £15 a year as treasurer to the poor relief authorities in Bergen, and he acted as accountant to many of his former business colleagues. His old friends made sure that his last years were the happiest of his life. He was always in the best of spirits, smiling and ready to enjoy a joke, and now at last he had time to read all the books he had collected during the course of his life. He died in 1873, only eight years after his father Isach. Angelique survived him by twenty-five years, and died, aged eighty-six, the dignified grandmother of thirty-one grandchildren.

Of Carl and Angelique's children only Edvard Isach is of real interest. He was three when the family moved to the factory at Fotlandsvåg, and

Edvard I. Hambro (1847–1909), educationalist, philologist and later principal of Hambro's School in Bergen. Photograph taken in 1869. Royal Library, Copenhagen.

at the age of six he was old enough to go to school in Bergen. He lodged with his grandfather Isach, and only spent holidays with his parents when a rowing boat was available for the long trip to the factory. He continued to live with his grandfather after the family's financial collapse in 1858.

After matriculating in 1863 at the Bergen Latinskole, he went to Kristiania University. He stayed with a doctor's family, and from the first day he threw himself into Arabic, Syrian and Chaldean under Professor J. P. Brock, and continued under Professor C. A. Holmboe the Hebrew he had learnt at school.

In 1865, his grandfather Isach died in Bergen. The old man had left his favourite grandson £100, which enabled Edvard to study for a full year at Copenhagen University; here he was able to attend the lectures of Professor J. N. Madvig, the great Latin scholar, and to study Sanskrit, which was not taught at Kristiania. In Professor Madvig's home he was treated like a son, and his Sanskrit studies introduced him to two scholars of similar age to himself, the Danish philologist Vilhelm Thomsen, who later became world-famous, and the orientalist Edvard Brandes, who was to become co-founder of Politiken newspaper and Danish minister of finance. Here Edvard met all the leading Danes of the time, including the ageing Hans Andersen, then at the peak of his fame. In Edvard's opinion Andersen was teased rather too much because of his self-centredness. Andersen was promised two gifts at Christmas 'that he would treasure more than anything else'; he was then presented with his own *Fairytales* in a de luxe edition, and a large photograph of himself.

In Denmark, at the home of his uncle Pastor Julius Borup, he met his fourteen-year-old second cousin Johan, who was able to tell him a lot about the Danish Folk High School movement, which immediately had a great attraction for Edvard. It is interesting to consider for a moment these two of Calmer and Thobe's great-grandchildren, Edvard and Johan, who scarcely ever met again. Against all expectations, each was to abandon at an early stage his planned career – theology for the one and philology for the other – and each in his own way became a pioneer educationist at a popular level. Both were to receive from former pupils testimonials so similarly worded that they might have been written about the same person.

Edvard's year in Copenhagen was happy and instructive, and in 1869, a few years after returning to Kristiania, he took such an outstanding degree that the university was delighted to be able to offer him a substantial scholarship. With this he went to Leipzig for a year to attend lectures in Arabic under the famous Professor Fleicher. The

Edvard I. Hambro, school principal, photographed at the age of forty, when his school had been in existence for ten years and had attained a leading position in Norwegian education. Owned by the Norwegian family.

academic year 1869–70 was in consequence another happy one for him, and he made many new acquaintances who would be of use to a future professor of philology at Kristiania.

But on returning to Kristiania, Edvard chose in the end to teach the common people rather than to follow a university career. A talk with Professor Brock settled the matter:

What kind of a future is it for a healthy and intelligent man of twenty-three like you to wait at least twenty years for me to die so that you can inherit my Chair, only to find that you have one pupil in Arabic every third year, and otherwise spend your time cramming Hebrew into the heads of theological students? It would be no more than letting your brain moulder.

Edvard's preference would have been to found immediately an independent people's university in Bergen, but a more realistic project that occupied his mind was the opening of a Folk High School in northern Norway, taking the Danish Folk High Schools as his model. In fact, his age and his lack of funds decided the matter. He became a teacher at Tank's private school in Bergen: he had hated and despised the outdated and medieval teaching methods at Bergen's Latinskole, and was attracted by the greater opportunities for a more modern type of teaching presented there. He took up his post in 1871, but after a few years he began to compensate for his disenchantment at the lack of opportunity for injecting some life into this already moribund school by arranging lectures, discussions and evening classes in Bergen. One of his students at the evening course 'for young ladies' that he established in 1877 was sixteen-year-old Nicoline Harbitz the youngest in the class. When she became nineteen in 1880 he married her, but even during their engagement she encouraged him to realize his long-cherished plan to start his own school in Bergen.

Hambros Skole opened in Bergen in August 1878, in its own premises in the area to the south of Nordnæs and north of Lille Lungegårdsvand. The programme offered by the school was completely different from that of the town's other schools, which is surprising in the brain-child of a philological scholar. The subjects taught were fewer, but more practical, than had previously been the practice. Because Bergen was a commercial and shipping town, the boys were to be taught where the ships sailed to, what they carried and how the goods were sold. The Middle School was to include lessons in commercial geography, economic history, commercial arithmetic and bookkeeping. The pupils were also to receive physical training. It was the bookish and most unathletic Edvard who introduced gymnastics into the Norwegian school system. Sunday was to be a proper rest day, and

Edvard Isach became a leading Norwegian educationalist, loyally supported by his wife Nicoline, née Harbitz (1861–1926). They were photographed here in 1887 with their two eldest children, Elise and Carl Joachim. Owned by the Norwegian family.

no homework was to be presented on Monday. There were practical courses from 7 to 9 o'clock, mornings and evenings, for clerks and business people who wanted to brush up their knowledge. Emphasis was at first on the Middle School, but later Edvard started a Senior School with a modern approach.

Hambros Skole, of which Edvard was himself the principal for thirty years, was a great success. There were twenty-five pupils in the first year, and six years later three hundred. After eight years the school had already reached its limit, with a steady 400–450 pupils. Numbers at the Latinskole fell so catastrophically that its closure was discussed. Tank's School suffered similarly. Both schools invited Edvard to become headmaster, but he refused. He now had a responsibility towards his own pupils and teaching staff, and he had no intention of deserting them. Moreover, he had no wish to hold a government post.

Nicoline produced four children during the first seven years of their marriage: three girls and a boy, Carl Joachim, who was in due course to become the most famous of all the Hambros. Edvard's marriage was happy from beginning to end, although it is difficult to imagine a greater contrast than between these two strong personalities. They were very dependent upon each other, and they complemented each other in every way possible. 'Neither of them would have become what they were without the other', their son, the president of the Storting, was later to say. And this was in spite of their completely different natures. He was aristocratic by instinct and always reserved; she was homely, boisterous and easily amused. He was quiet and meditative; she was quick and impulsive. She was informal and forthright, but he had such difficulty in using the 'thou' form of address that he often – apologetically – told the story of the member of the Storting who turned aside a colleague's suggestion that they should drop formalities with the following remark: 'Since I reached the age of twenty I have been on Christian-name terms with only one person. This was my wife, and I have regretted this grotesque familiarity for the past thirty-five years.' Behind the grave headmaster's kind and somewhat shy smile lay a ready sense of humour. It was he who once said 'An aristocrat is a man who is bored. A democrat, by contrast, bores others.'

But there were important aspects of life in which Edvard and Nicoline were as one; they were always in complete agreement in their impassioned sense of justice, their indignation at social inequalities and their warm interest in people. Nicoline took part in all activities at the school.

She was known as 'Nico' all over Bergen and became part of the school's image, but she also played an independent and outgoing role

Edvard I. Hambro opened his own school in Stavhusgaten at the southern end of Nordnæs.
The building was completed in 1878. It had been founded as a practical protest against the
outdated teaching methods of the Bergen Latin School, under which Edvard himself had
suffered. Edvard ran Hambro's School until his death in 1909, and was spared seeing it
destroyed in the Bergen fire of 1916. Photograph taken about 1910.

as Bergen's first advocate of feminism. Between 1885 and 1915 she was
the driving force behind Bergen's Feminist Association, and during
those thirty years she travelled far and unravelled many social tangles.
In 1899 she represented Norway in London at the first international
congress called to fight against the white-slave traffic. In her own home
she ran an office to which young Bergen women could turn for advice
and help. It was consequently the most active, alive and sympathetic
home imaginable for a child.

77

Nico Hambro, wife of Edvard Isach Hambro and mother of the President of the Storting. Drawing by the Dutch artist Marie Hübrecht, c. 1915. Owned by the Norwegian family.

Edvard never entered politics, although he was urged to do so. With his unyielding faith in his religious and moral principles and in the constructive powers of continuity, it soon became clear that he was unsuited to party politics. But he was willing to enter into debate on matters close to his heart. His short, clear and direct contributions to the press were always excellently phrased, and demonstrated a personal involvement that could not fail to impress even those who did not agree with all his views. Professor Brock had been right; Edvard was far too deeply concerned with the problems of his time to immerse himself in dead languages. In his thirty years of activity as principal of Hambros Skole his brain had no chance to moulder. In 1902 he had the gratification of seeing his son, Carl Joachim matriculate with splendid grades at the school.

Edvard died in 1909. His death was caused by a painful kidney disease from which he had suffered for many years. As was to be expected, epitaphs by his contemporaries were full of praise and generosity:

He valued highly the impartation of knowledge, but character-building he set higher still. His teaching skills were better than most but his character-building was even better than his teaching.

Any pupil of his gained a lasting impression of a man always developing and growing, who never reached the stage where he became static or dull.

He surmounted the frontiers between town and country, and Hambros Skole was the first in Norway in which boys from town and country met on an equal footing and with mutual regard.

His death in 1909 spared him Bergen's great fire in 1916, which destroyed his school with such short warning that Nico – middle-aged, ill and confined to bed – had to be carried from the burning building. She was sheltered by the Bishop of Bergen. She and her daughters lost all they owned, including Edvard's books, his notes and all the old family documents. But the resourceful Nico did not despair. After the fire she moved to Kristiania, where she was soon elected the first president of the Women's National Council of Norway, an office she held until she retired two years before her death in 1926.

5 The President of the Storting

The President of the Norwegian Storting, Carl Joachim Hambro, deserves a book to himself, and in time one may well appear. Although the greatest deed of his life was most certainly heroic, there was nothing heroic about Carl Joachim as an individual, neither by nature nor by appearance. His most remarkable features were his never-failing sense of duty and his legendary industry, invaluable legacies from his well-loved and much-admired father.

His Bergen childhood in the home of Edvard and Nico left no significant mark. He was to some extent dominated by his strong-willed mother and his three sisters. Throughout his life he could still on occasions appear diffident, almost bashful, and in large gatherings he was noticeably silent and ill-at-ease. In dinner-jacket or tails he was quite out of his element, and in his later years he never accepted evening invitations. As a boy he had refused to attend dancing classes, and he is reported never to have been seen on a dance floor. In general, he was little drawn towards those things in life that other people normally enjoy. He never learned to handle money; it scarcely interested him. He was thrifty by nature, but nevertheless throughout his life he had to struggle against a hopeless financial position. His debts were still uncleared when he died, aged seventy-nine.

Glamour left him quite unmoved, and when he saw his more ambitious colleagues' delight at receiving a decoration, he was amazed that they could not see how inconsequential it was. He never owned a car, and to him it was not a matter for comment that the President of the Storting should travel to work each day on a crowded tram.

In his later days he acquired a gravity and assurance of manner that marked all his actions. On the platform, however, he displayed the whole extent of his personality, revealing his rich temperament ranging from a menacing toughness to astonishing patience. Whatever he wrote or said was always exciting and enthralling. He could appear unbelievably arrogant and malicious, but at heart he was benign; he was unhappy if he gave unintentional hurt.

During the social and cultural debate of the 1930s his position, as might be expected from his education, was on the extreme right wing, and with his ascetic approach to life he rejected the increasingly

The two eldest children of Edvard I. Hambro on the occasion of their matriculation from their father's school in Bergen. Elise and Carl Joachim are both wearing the distinctive, tassel-decorated, Norwegian student's cap. Elise (1881–1966) graduated as a philologist in 1906, started teaching at her father's school in 1907 and ran it shortly before his death. When the school burnt down in 1916 she became Norway's first woman principal at Pihls School in Oslo, and, like her mother, was chairman of the Norwegian Women's National Council. She never married. Carl Joachim's younger sister, Cathrine (born 1880) became a doctor and lung specialist, and for a time was chairman of the National Union of Professional Women. She also remained unmarried. Photograph taken in 1902. Owned by the Norwegian family.

audacious element in literature. In 1933, by a Storting decision, he succeeded in preventing the performance of Marc Connelly's ingenuous play *Green Pastures*, which he disliked. In such areas, of course, his attitude would seem completely out-of-date today. His opponents, knowing of his great burden of work, were critical of his eloquence and repartee, asserting that he frequently concealed a lack of thoroughness with an elegant, satirical remark, brushing aside the point in question.

His capacity for work was in fact almost incredible. He never stayed at the Storting after it rose, but hurried home to his desk to go on working in dressing-gown and slippers. Even in the tram he could be seen reading proofs, and among the members of the Storting it was said that he was well able to write – or translate – a chapter or two of a book if an uninteresting debate was making slow progress. This was recalled by Prime Minister Johan Nygaardsvold on Carl Joachim's seventieth

birthday, but he added that nevertheless Carl Joachim's conduct of the
sittings was better than he himself could have provided. Moreover, he
said, Carl Joachim was the only member who showed no fatigue at the
end of long sittings. 'If one's work gives one pleasure, rest is unneces-
sary,' Carl Joachim used to say. It was in the 'alluring world of the
mind' that he was content. He also said that 'to sacrifice oneself for a
cause or an ideal is one of the most beautiful capacities given to Man,
and from it he derives his greatest strength.' Throughout his life his pen
was his only weapon. When in 1940 the Norwegian military attaché in
Stockholm offered him a revolver for his own protection against
German spies, he shook his head. He knew that he would have neither
the courage nor the heart to use it.

His genuinely democratic outlook coloured his whole philosophy,
although he never tired of emphasizing that 'democracy is not a state of
affairs, but an objective.' He remained a conservative throughout his
life, but his conservatism was more an expression of his attitude
towards the world than towards a party programme. As a result, the
more dogmatic party members and industrialists in the relatively small
conservative party sometimes felt his leadership to be rather an
encumbrance. He saw conservatism primarily as a capacity to evaluate
critically and sensibly the problems of the day, maintaining tradition
and continuity in national life. He took pains to emphasize the importance of respect for the efforts of earlier generations. He was never really
a party man. He had a contempt for dogma, and was always quick to
acknowledge independent thought. All that had meaning for him was
the welfare of his native land and the nation's philosophy of life. He
realized however that the parliamentary system called for a political
affiliation, 'if one is not to act merely as an observer'. For this reason he
became a conservative, but he was too 'artlessly decent' to allow
himself to be hidebound by party politics. Party tyranny was to him a
pest. The conservative party was closest to his philosophy of life, but his
impressive intelligence often made him feel above party politics, which
in turn made him particularly suitable for the office of President of the
Storting.

He was of course conscious of his own remarkable level of intelligence, but he saw this merely as a working tool. One of his own maxims
was that 'intelligence divorced from reality and not controlled by
character is often more of a danger than an advantage', and his strong
sense of religion supported him in this attitude:

Those who have not known belief are unaware that it is life's greatest reality.
They are unaware that, for a Christian, to love God is a reality. Therefore, they
are also unaware of the meaning of asceticism. They are unaware of what it

Throughout his life Carl Joachim Hambro was unhappy about his appearance. 'I am sending you the photograph you asked for', he once wrote to his friend, the author Johan Falkenberg. 'It is not very good, but I never come out well in photographs. But you must do something in return and send me a good picture of yourself. Compared with me, you have the advantage that you look fine in pictures, whereas I am definitely not suitable for decorative purposes.' These photographs of Carl Joachim and his wife, Gudrun, were taken about 1935.

means to sacrifice a wish at God's altar. They believe that God demands self-denial and sacrifice. To him who has known God's reality, everything else is of lesser importance.

Although over the years he became one of Norway's most brilliant debaters, gaining a rare degree of respect and admiration from nearly all his political opponents, throughout his life he remained a somewhat lonely man. He paid the price of his independence. Although he gave colour, warmth and humanity to Norway's political life, there were few he could call his friends; he was so self-reliant in his own convictions that he had remarkably little need of friendship. Although by degrees the Storting became the centre of his life, he was never seen in the Storting's pleasant restaurant, where the members cultivated intra-party contacts during breaks in the proceedings; he had neither the time nor the inclination for this. From all this it follows that, with the almost escapist zest for work that animated his whole life, he was never an ideal family man. He never succeeded in developing with his four sons the deep understanding that he had had with his own father. Neither could he be considered an ideal husband.

As a young student in 1902, accompanied by his sister, Elise, four years his senior and also a student, he went to live at a boarding house in Kristiania. His intention was to study philology, as his father had before him. He knew that his father's greatest wish was that he should succeed him at Hambros Skole in Bergen. But during his early years in the Norwegian capital he was to spend more time in the ancient Students' Association, with its deep traditions, than at the university. It was at the Association that he discovered, to his own amazement, his ability to spellbind his listeners from the platform. Again, it was through the Association's often controversial newspapers and other publications that he first enjoyed the confidence given by the gift to express himself concisely and precisely in print.

In 1905, as a member of the board of the Students' Association, he was a close observer of the dissolution of the union with Sweden and of the reception that year in newly independent Norway of its own royal family. The thirty-three-year-old Danish Prince Carl, now bearing the name of Haakon VII, came ashore at Kristiania accompanied by his British-born wife, Queen Maud. The new king carried in his arms his two-year-old son, later to be Olav V. These were the king and the crown prince that Carl Joachim was to follow into exile in England thirty-five years later.

In 1903, to ease his parents' financial burden, he began to work for the conservative Kristiania newspaper *Morgenbladet* as a relief book reviewer. The fact that he was poorly paid was entirely his own fault; the newspaper paid him the modest sum that he himself had proposed. In his quiet and conscientious way he soon became a valued member of the staff, earning promotion and eventually permanent employment.

His journalism gave him deep satisfaction, but nevertheless he began to take a longer-term view of his future. After benefiting from his ironic and zestful contributions for a year, the editor of Norway's wittiest weekly, the satirical *Korsaren*, suggested to him that he should take over the management of the periodical. To the editor's great surprise, Carl Joachim replied, 'No thank you; I am too good for that!' He had realized that he was in danger of developing into a wit, instead of attending to his neglected studies.

He therefore suddenly put his shoulder to the wheel, and took a degree in philology in 1907, English and French being his main languages. Between 1907 and 1913 he taught at various schools in Kris-

*The President of the Storting became not only the most famous of the Norwegian Hambros;
he was also the only Hambro to have sons to continue the name in Norway. His descendants
now number seven grandsons and numerous great-grandchildren. This is a photograph taken
in 1923 of his and Gudrun's five children. At the back are the twelve-year-old twins, Edvard
Isak and Cato; at the front, from the left, eight-year-old Johan, five-year-old Evelyn and
nine-year-old Carl.* Owned by the Norwegian family.

tiania, and for a year he was a part-time teacher for his father in Bergen.
At the same time he continued to review books, and began to take on
substantial translating commitments. Although he was interested in
teaching, he saw that he was unlikely ever to be able to settle in Bergen.
This realization became a certainty at his father's death in 1910. He
suffered pangs of conscience for some years at having failed to fulfil his
father's wish, and when in 1916 the great fire of Bergen destroyed
Hambros Skole he was tortured by the thought that it might have been
saved had he been there to do his duty.

In the summer of 1910 he married Gudrun Grieg. He was then
twenty-five and she twenty-nine; they had known each other from their
schooldays. Gudrun was the sister of Carl Joachim's school friend

Johan, and the daughter of the parish priest in Bergen, Cato Grieg. Gudrun's mother had died when her daughter was seventeen, and Gudrun had had to manage her father's household from an early age, accepting many of the social duties of a parson's wife towards the sick and the poor. The four years' difference in their ages had made her a young lady while he was still a schoolboy. He had always admired her, and no other woman had ever interested him, but it was some years before they married. Gudrun was intelligent, and as time went by she became a substantial support for her husband, who was always restless and absorbed in his work. When he became President of the Storting, she displayed far greater representational abilities than those of Carl Joachim himself, and as the wife of the President of the Storting she helped to establish a degree of respect for high office that had never before been known in Norway. Between 1911 and 1918 the demands on Carl Joachim's income rapidly increased, although their first home in Eilert Sundtsgate in Kristiania was modest; over this period Gudrun gave birth to five children.

If, during the early years of their marriage, Carl Joachim had been asked what was his ambition, he would probably have said to become a poet; but in spite of his great love of literature he was well aware that he was too down-to-earth and practical ever to become a true poet. For example, the first book he wrote as a young man was a controversial contribution to the Norwegian language dispute, and the second a history of literature for grammar schools.

Even during his early years as a journalist, the scope of his activities beside his literary work was amazing. From 1910 to 1913, for example, he was secretary of the Union of Norwegians, still the major organization of Norwegians abroad. The Union was originally founded for Norwegian emigrants and their descendants, but was later expanded to become a vehicle for Norwegians all over the world. In 1913 he made a successful trip to the USA and Canada in connection with the centenary of the Norwegian Constitution on 17 May 1914, and he had the full support of emigrants at the festivities in Kristiania in the following year.

Shortly after Carl Joachim's return from the USA in 1913, Nils Vogt, *Morgenbladet*'s chief for many years, retired, and Carl Joachim was immediately recognized as his only successor. It therefore fell to him to chart the course of this distinguished daily newspaper during the four difficult years of World War I. With his incisive pen, he defended Norway's neutral interests with equal fervour against all the belligerent powers, condemning Germany's unrestricted submarine warfare as

Carl Joachim Hambro, painted by Axel Revold in about 1928 when he was elected president of the Storting. Norsk Telegrambyrå, Oslo.

strongly as the injustices of the British blockade. His daily leading articles were often little masterpieces of style, which quickly earned him a reputation in political circles. He did not, however, neglect his old literary public, and his book reviews continued to exercise a marked effect upon the literary taste of the paper's readers. The paper's shareholders pressed him to adopt a more friendly attitude towards the British, but this he opposed – Norway was neutral and so was his newspaper! To evade this pressure he borrowed money and, with some friends, secured a majority of shares in the paper. This, however, proved a financial disaster, for after the war the readership fell and the value of the shares dropped accordingly. So at an early age he found himself deeply in debt.

Norway's conservative party soon recognized his political flair. At the end of the war he was nominated for the Storting elections of 1918, and in 1920 he resigned as chief editor in favour of his new political obligations.

87

In 1918 Carl Joachim was elected to the Storting for the first time. It was said that he was elected 'because he had created a name for himself in conservative politics as *Morgenbladet*'s youthful and aggressive editor during the war years', and it was predicted that, 'with his fine brain, his incredible capacity for work and his great eloquence, he would soon capture a central position in Norwegian parliamentary life'.

In the Norwegian *History of Our People*, C. A. Christensen gives the following character study of Carl Joachim as a newly elected member of the Storting:

Rarely has anyone in Norway been better equipped intellectually for a political career. His intelligence was tremendous, both as writer and orator. His historical and political knowledge was most extensive. His debating skills had been refined in the old Students' Association, which knew better than any other Norwegian assembly how to evaluate good repartee, the lightning retort, the apt *bon mot* and the illustrative anecdote. It was precisely this light and scintillating style that perhaps at first made the Storting somewhat sceptical towards him. It was as if he was almost too clever. Perhaps he was superficial? Could he be trusted?

Carl Joachim turned his attention mainly to social policies during the early years, but from 1925 onwards he concentrated increasingly on constitutional matters and foreign policy. In 1926 he became Norway's delegate to the League of Nations' Annual General Assembly at Geneva, where as spokesman for the smaller nations he made his first great speech. In 1925 he became Chairman of Norway's Foreign and Constitutional Committee, in which capacity he was concerned with the two matters that gradually became his main interest – Norway's security and the constitution's inviolability.

Although throughout his life he detested fuss and rarely gave any thought to his personal status, from his first day in the Storting he demanded unconditional respect for this institution, which he considered the most important of Norway's three constitutional cornerstones – king, government and Storting. Later, when he became president of the Storting, he developed into a zealous custodian of the Storting's simple, unceremonial but inviolable rights and obligations.

He went to America again in 1925 to represent the Storting at the Union of Norwegians' celebrations to mark the centenary of the first organized Norwegian emigration to the USA and Canada. His growing admiration for the USA is evident in his book *Glimpses of America*, published in the same year.

In 1926 he was elected chairman of Norway's conservative party, and he also became the party's spokesman in the Storting. This was the true beginning of his political career. In 1927 Carl Joachim deputized

During the twenty years that Carl Joachim Hambro was president of the Norwegian Storting he was a favourite butt of Norwegian newspaper caricaturists. Here he is seen in four versions: top left, a drawing from Dagbladet *in 1928, just after he had been elected, followed by (top right and bottom left) two drawings by Øivind Sørensen from* Aftenposten *in 1930 and 1932, and (bottom right) a caricature by T. Kloumann just before the outbreak of war in 1939.* Aftenposten's Archives, Oslo.

as president of the Storting for G. A. Jahren, who was sick, and in 1928 he was elected president in an exciting contest with the liberal J. L. Mowinckel, fifteen years his senior. Mowinckel had already occupied this office, and soon afterwards became prime minister for the second time. In his *History of Our People*, C. A Christensen writes of Carl Joachim's presidency as follows:

He never became a member of any government, but from the presidential chair he displayed his most outstanding characteristics: not only his clear views on matters of principle, supported by a comprehensive knowledge of constitutional history, but also his efficiency as organizer of the Storting's work. He retained this office of president until Norway's liberation in May 1945, and it was in this capacity that he made his greatest, and now historic, contribution in April 1940.

By the early 1930s he already enjoyed great respect among all parties. It was impossible not to admire his irreproachably conventional but nevertheless highly inspiring conduct of the parliamentary process. His efficiency was such that for several years the Storting's sessions were concluded weeks earlier than had previously been possible. He demanded of the public administration the modesty and thriftiness he displayed in his private life. Tax-payers were not to be burdened with more than was absolutely necessary. The administration should be frugal in managing the funds entrusted to it. It was reprehensible to be careless with money for which others had expended their labour. When, in the 1930s, it was proposed that the Storting's old and uncomfortable seats should be replaced, he said that his president's chair was good enough, and that it would last for many years yet.

Until shortly before the outbreak of World War II, Carl Joachim's name was known only in Norway, but when he was elected president of the League of Nations in 1939 he at once became an international figure. During his thirteen years as the Norwegian delegate, he had put forward his views in Geneva with the same assurance as in Oslo, and his knowledge of English and French was of great assistance to him. The content of his speeches was impressive, and from a linguistic aspect impeccable. As spokesman for the smaller nations, whose rights it disregarded, he considered Chamberlain's 1938 Munich agreement 'disgraceful', and his speech on this subject resounded through the European press.

During these years, his duties as chairman of the Foreign and Constitutional Committee in combination with those as president of the Storting influenced Carl Joachim's conception of his own position within, and responsibilities towards, Norwegian society. Later, when evaluating the 'red letter' day of his life, it must be understood that his resolute action did not result from a sudden surge of genius but was a manifestation of a sense of duty matured over many years. If Norway's security and constitution were suddenly and without warning in deadly danger, there was no doubt in his mind that it was for him, and for him alone, to act immediately.

In the government formed by the Norwegian Farmers' Party in 1931 under the leadership of prime minister Peder Kolstad, an unknown name was to be found as minister of defence – that of Vidkun Quisling. He was a parson's son of good education, had been trained as an officer, and had been Norway's military attaché in Russia. He was a highly intelligent but unrealistic visionary, with unlimited self-assurance and lust for power, chosen by the good-natured Kolstad for lack of greater talents. Quisling quickly became an embarrassment to the government, and on 7 April 1932, during a clash with the leader of the workers' party, Johan Nygaardsvold, the Storting for the first time saw Quisling run amok with rage and hurl frenzied accusations at the workers' party, which he referred to as paid agents of Moscow. The Kolstad government had to make way for a new liberal government in 1933 under the leadership of J. L. Mowinckel and it was expected that Quisling would disappear for good from the political stage. But this was not the case. Before the 1933 election he succeeded in forming a new party of his own, the National Union, which openly acknowledged itself to be a Nazi party. In the following years the party suffered two ignominious election defeats, in which it secured less than 2 per cent of the votes. By the outbreak of war Quisling was completely discredited as a politician, with his party in ruins as a result of internal disagreements and lack of money. In Norwegian eyes, he was finished.

In German eyes, however, this was not so. It was known in Norway that two months after the outbreak of war, in December 1939, he had visited Berlin, and it was also known that he had been received by Hitler. However, it was not then known that he had tried to convince Hitler that there was an imminent threat of Britain establishing itself in Norway, which would be strategically dangerous for Germany. This danger was all the greater because the Norwegian social democratic government and 'the well-known Jew, Hambro' were acting in collusion with the British, and had even entered into a secret agreement to allow the British free access if Norway were attacked by a great power. Such an attack was also possible from the Russian side. All these dangers could be averted if Germany were to arrive first, and Quisling claimed to know precisely how such an advantage could be achieved. The simple answer was for his party to seize power in Norway by means of a coup, and once he and his men were in control German troops could be called in 'for protection against internal and external enemies'.

There is no doubt that what Quisling had to say impressed Hitler, and that the German general staff itself had been toying with such an idea. The first German draft of an operation against Norway was certainly available by 13 January 1940, but it was not until 9 April that Hitler struck.

As late as February 1938, the Norwegian liberal leader J. L. Mowinckel had sought confimation of 'Norway's right as a member of the League of Nations to observe absolute neutrality in the event of a war that did not affect Norway'.

A statement in these terms had been opposed by many people, including Carl Joachim, who saw that any special position for Norway might undermine the collective security for which the League of Nations had always striven. He finally had to be content with a unanimous resolution of the Storting on 31 May 1938 which asserted 'Norway's right to maintain complete and unconditional neutrality in any war which it has not itself approved as an action of the League of Nations'. Carl Joachim of course had no doubts that this resolution left Norway with the old concept of neutrality, and that a similar neutrality had been violated during World War I by both belligerent powers. Norway, incidentally, had not been involved in a war for 156 years.

After the outbreak of World War II in September 1939, both Carl Joachim and the labour prime minister Johan Nygaardsvold were somewhat uneasy about the country's inferior military preparations, but no one in Norway had foreseen the German attack that came without warning during the night of 8–9 April 1940. The attack was such a surprise that only during the previous twenty-four hours had Norway received disquieting reports of perplexing embarkations at German Baltic ports. The first warning had come on Wednesday 4 April from Scheel, the Norwegian ambassador in Berlin, but he had merely hinted at a possible attack on Denmark. On Saturday 7 April Carl Joachim, as chairman of the Foreign and Constitutional Committee and following agreement with Nygaardsvold, asked all committee members to remain in Oslo over the weekend as a precaution. However the foreign secretary, Dr Halvdan Koht, had not considered it necessary to call a meeting of the committee. Nothing of importance was afoot, he said.

In the course of 7 April, however, a firm report was received from Scheel that German ships totalling 150,000 tons had left Stettin two days previously, setting course westwards. At 5 am on Sunday 8 April

Vidkun Quisling (left) *visiting Hitler at the Reich Chancellery in Berlin, 1942. In the centre is Quisling's Norwegian 'home secretary', Albert Hagelin, who had formerly been in business in Germany. In 1945, Hagelin was to share Quisling's fate.*

the British and French ambassadors in Oslo both informed the Norwegian Foreign Office by telephone that they wished to submit a note to the effect that the Allies were obliged to lay mines in certain areas of Norway's territorial waters, and that minelaying had already commenced.

Scarcely had the Norwegian radio broadcast this note on the Sunday morning when the naval staff in Copenhagen reported, at about 1000 hours, that forty-six German warships and forty-eight armed trawlers were sailing northwards through the Kattegat. At three o'clock the Norwegian ambassador in London telephoned to report that a German naval unit was sailing towards Narvik in northern Norway.

During Sunday, 8 April Carl Joachim had on his own initiative summoned the Constitutional Committee to brief its members, and that evening he called the Storting to an emergency meeting, which decided to protest against the Allied minelaying. Later that evening a secret meeting was held to discuss the action to be taken should the policy of neutrality be impossible to maintain. On one point all were

agreed: no one wanted war with England. When the meeting closed at
11.30 many of the members were anxious, but none – including Carl
Joachim – could have foreseen what was to occur in the next twenty-
four hours. As Carl Joachim said later:

Norway and Germany had always had the best possible relationship, and
before the attack on Poland – and later on Belgium and Holland – the
Germans had at least presented an ultimatum. No one in Norway could
conceive that, under the mask of friendship and without warning or declaration of war, Germany would attack Norway like a thief in the night, and
thereby seek to wipe out the Norwegian nation.

After the evening meeting of the Storting on 8 April, Carl Joachim went
home to bed exhausted, not suspecting that during the next twenty-four
hours and with the self-assurance of a sleepwalker he would initiate
action that was to determine Norway's future.

Carl Joachim and his family had lived at Niels Juelsgate 17 since
moving in 1936 from Eilert Sundtgate. It was a picturesque old tim-
bered house, situated more centrally for the Storting, the Foreign Office
and the Palace than his first home. It bore the mark of his literary
interests, with thousands of books on endless shelving.

His daughter, Evelyn, had married a Swedish doctor. The elder of
the twins, Edvard Isak, a lawyer, was now in Bergen. He reached
London in April, and shortly afterwards became employed by the
Norwegian Foreign Office-in-exile. He married in London the following year. On 9 April the other twin, Cato, was employed by a company
at Skien. He eventually reached Scotland via Sweden in 1943, where he
joined the armed forces. Carl was married and lived in Oslo; he was the
centre of German interest during those April days. Showing a somewhat exaggerated concept of Carl Joachim's finances, the Germans
wanted to know in which bank he was hiding his fortune. Carl did not
reach Sweden until 1943. The youngest son, Johan, had been in
America for some time, and he married there before returning to
Norway in 1945. During the night of 8–9 April, then, only Gudrun,
Carl Joachim and two maids were in the house at Niels Juelsgate, and
late in the evening the maids were told to go home. Carl Joachim was
woken by Gudrun at 1 am; there was an air raid alert covering the
whole of Oslo. His first thought was that this was merely a practice, but
when the sirens continued he telephoned the Norwegian press centre,
Norsk Telegrambur\aa, and learnt that foreign warships had been

*King Haakon VII of Norway (1872–1957), originally Prince Carl of Denmark, brother of
the Danish King Christian X. Photograph taken about 1940.*

observed sailing up the southern part of the long Oslo fjord. He immediately telephoned the prime minister, Nygaardsvold, and the minister of defence, Birger Ljungberg. Afterwards, he learnt at 2.15 that five large German warships had been observed near Bergen, and at 3.30 it was reported that large German naval units were sailing towards Trondheim.

That night, most leading Norwegians were in a state of dumb-founded shock. Deeply shaken, prime minister Nygaardsvold said later that this arose 'not only because Norway was in trouble, but from the general feeling that honesty and decency had suddenly and completely collapsed'. Militarily, of course, neutral Norway was quite unprepared to resist a carefully planned attack. In the course of the night this attack proved to be directed against Oslo and all other coastal towns of central Norway, and to involve almost the entire German navy. All the more admirable, therefore, were the emergency arrangements mustered by Carl Joachim during the next three or four hours. Without a moment's hesitation, he grasped the fact that Norway's future as an independent nation would depend upon whether he, from his home in Niels Juels-gate, could instantly devise, set in motion and carry through a plan that would in some way forestall the Germans.

It was clear to him that long before the out-numbered Norwegian army could be even partially mobilized the royal family, the govern-ment and the Storting would probably be overpowered and put under lock and key. If this occurred, Norway would cease to be a sovereign state. Such a situation could not be allowed to arise.

He quickly conceived a plan that was both logical and simple. He had to try to move the royal family, the government and the Storting – a total of 200 people – out of Oslo before the German navy, by now sailing up the most northerly and narrowest part of Oslo fjord, reached the Norwegian capital. Thanks to a successful Norwegian attack on the German navy at Oscarborg in Oslo fjord, which sank among other ships the heavy cruiser *Blücher*, the Germans were delayed for a few crucial hours, and so miraculously, Carl Joachim's plan eventually succeeded.

A report came through at 3.30 that a German naval unit had reached Trondheim. Carl Joachim immediately called the head of the Storting's office to ask him to mobilize the entire office staff and to summon all 150 members of the Storting to meet at 7 am at Oslo East railway station. From there a special train would leave at 7.15 for the town of Hamar. He chose Hamar, 130 kilometres north of Oslo, because it is an impor-tant junction and, if the worst came to the worst, only 50 kilometres from the Swedish frontier, which was heavily armed but neutral. (Carl

Joachim's confidence in Sweden's complete neutrality during these fateful hours proved later to be somewhat over-optimistic.) He then left his home, to which he was never to return, and drove with Gudrun by taxi to the Storting to ensure that his summons had been circulated.

Shortly after 5 am he drove on to the Foreign Office and, with Gudrun still waiting in the taxi, was present at a formal meeting of the government, almost all the members having gathered there by this time. The German ambassador, Curt Brauer, who had presented his credentials to King Haakon nine months earlier, had just left the Foreign Office, having submitted to Halvdan Koht a thirteen-point German ultimatum. The lights had gone out in that part of the city during the meeting with Brauer, but even by candlelight Koht quickly came to the conclusion that the German demand for immediate surrender followed by 'German protection of the kingdom of Norway' must be flatly refused, and in this he was given the full support of the government.

Carl Joachim now presented his plan that the royal family, the government and members of the Storting should transfer to Hamar. The sixty-eight-year-old King, who was in telephone contact with the Foreign Office, immediately agreed, and the government also gave its consent to the plan. Several members felt positive relief in the face of such a clear initiative.

Carl Joachim, still meticulously preserving formality, immediately requested a royal resolution under section 58 of the Norwegian constitution for the next Storting meeting to take place at Hamar. He then asked the minister of labour to confirm the order for the special train at 7.15. He himself had already arranged for buses from the station to pick up those members of the Storting who might be unable to get there in time. During the government meeting, it was also decided to order the general and naval staffs to accompany them to Hamar.

The position of the high court was unfortunately not discussed in this context, and this body of people was not asked to accompany them to Hamar. In consequence the high court became the only institution to which the Germans could turn. In this lies the explanation of the role played in Norway by Paal Berg, president of the high court and former politician, during the following years.

It was agreed with Carl Joachim that Birger Ljungberg, the rather inefficient minister of defence, should try to reach Hamar independently after initiating general mobilization of the Norwegian army and navy. A similar arrangement was made with Adolf Indrebø, minister of finance, who was to take immediate steps to remove from Oslo Norway's entire gold stock of £15,000,000, held in the Bank of Norway.

This was executed with impressive speed and precision. Before the German military could interfere later in the day, twenty-six lorries carrying 2,240 boxes of gold bars had removed this great prize northwards, much to the chagrin of the Germans. From Ålesund the gold was shipped to Tromsø, and from there to England without the loss of a single bar.

Carl Joachim had calculated that the train could not reach Hamar before 9 am. Since no one in Hamar as yet knew anything of the plan, Carl Joachim left the Foreign Office and joined Gudrun in the taxi, in which she had been patiently waiting. Together, they set out for Hamar. He left Gudrun at her brother's farm, about 40 kilometres south of the town, and continued to Hamar, arriving there at eight o'clock.

For security reasons he had told Norwegian Radio nothing of the Hamar plan, and the local chief of police was so surprised that his first reaction was that Carl Joachim was playing a trick on him. But within an hour the ballroom at the Hamar Hotel was transformed into a debating chamber for the Storting, and some 200 beds had been requisitioned in the neighbourhood for the government and the Storting. The royal family was billeted in a large farm just outside the town. Carl Joachim also had the forethought to order lunch for 200 people in the restaurant at Hamar railway station.

The train was very late in reaching Hamar because the line passed a military airfield that was already under air attack from the Germans, and all the passengers had to take cover under a viaduct. It was fortunate that the German pilots did not know of the train's cargo! In the course of the morning the train, buses and taxis brought the royal family, the government and 104 of the 150 Storting members to Hamar. With them came the entire office of the Storting. In the next few hours the staffs of almost all the Allied embassies, which had been put in the picture, also arrived, and Hamar was now teeming with British, American, French, Polish, Dutch, Belgian and Danish diplomatic families, as well as a few Swedes. The radio and the press were also bound for Hamar. By eleven o'clock the plan was known to so many people that the town could not be expected to cope with the emergency for much longer.

At 1 pm the first meeting of the Storting was called in the ballroom of the Hamar Hotel. Carl Joachim had arranged for name labels to be placed in alphabetical order on the long benches. For once, therefore, the normal grouping by parties was suspended; all party differences were set aside. Seven stenographers were in position to record the debate in the normal way.

The first meeting of the Storting in the Hamar Hotel ballroom on 9 April 1940. At this time only 104 of the Storting's members had arrived. The last members arrived by bus after the Germans had begun to enter the Norwegian capital.

The first meeting lasted only half an hour. Carl Joachim called upon Koht, the foreign secretary, to address the meeting, and Koht gave an account of his conversation during the night with the German ambassador. He concluded by stating that Norway was now at war with Germany. Carl Joachim then proposed that this should be noted without further discussion. It was agreed unanimously. The sitting was then adjourned for a few hours. Quisling had already spoken on Oslo Radio at 1 pm as 'head of state', followed immediately by Halvdan Koht on Hamar Radio, presenting to the Norwegian people his version of what had actually occurred.

Carl Joachim had hoped to snatch a short rest before the next meeting, but he had barely taken off his jacket when he was called to King Haakon's quarters. Here prime minister Nygaardsvold, deeply shocked and heartbroken, had told the King that he wished to resign immediately; the King asked for the views of the Storting president on this unexpected request. Carl Joachim was of course in no doubt that Nygaardsvold's resignation would be the worst possible event that could happen after Quisling's radio announcement that he had appointed himself Norway's head of state. Although, as leader of the labour party, Nygaardsvold had of course always been the conservative Carl Joachim's political opponent, Carl Joachim greatly valued this upright, but now despairing, man, and after talking to Nysgaardsvold at his bedside he succeeded in persuading him to stay in office.

The second and final meeting of the Storting at Hamar was called for 6 pm. By now 143 of the 150 Storting members had reached the town, and the minister of finance was able to give the good news that

99

Norway's gold had been removed to temporary safety. It was very depressing, however, to learn that during the day all resistance in Oslo had ceased, and that mobilization was making only slow progress. News had also been received that Denmark had been attacked during the night, and that the Danish government had immediately surrendered to the German ultimatum, submitted, as in Norway, after, not before, the Germans had entered the country.

Because of these events it is understandable that at the second meeting Nygaardsvold expressed his fears that the situation might end with a king, a government and a Storting, but no country or people. Perhaps, therefore, it would be advisable to negotiate with the Germans after all. The King and Carl Joachim, however, both took the view that, in any event, Norway would now become a theatre of war, and that any agreement with the ruthless Germans must be seen as completely valueless.

Just before 6.30 pm, during the second meeting, Carl Joachim was informed that German troops were on their way to Hamar to seize the royal family and the government; the enemy was then only 15 kilometres south of the town. With great composure, Carl Joachim broke up the meeting, announcing that a special train would leave for Elverum, 30 kilometres east of Hamar, within a few minutes.

The unit of German parachute troops on its way to Hamar was under the command of the German military attaché in Oslo, Captain Eberhard Spiller, who had been with the German Embassy since November 1939 and was already well acquainted with Norway's geography. However, by the time he and his 100 men reached Hamar the train to Elverum had left fifteen minutes before. Spiller and his men never reached Elverum. As they continued their advance they were confronted by a group of Norwegian officers who had barricaded the road. An exchange followed in which Spiller was wounded. His men knew nothing of the terrain or the roads, and they decided to return to Oslo without completing their mission. Spiller died the same night in the hospital at Hamar.

The day's third and last meeting of the Storting took place, under even more improvised conditions, at 9.40 in the gymnasium of the Folk High School in the small, totally blacked-out town of Elverum. At this meeting Carl Joachim presented, entirely on his own initiative, the historic 'Elverum Authority', which he had drafted on the railway journey a few hours earlier. The declaration said simply that 'The Storting authorizes the government to take any steps and any measures necessary under the existing state of war.' This formally recognized that the Storting could not function while the Germans were in the

| Stortinget holdtes | Da behandledes | | Stemmetall | Stortingets beslutninger |
	Sakens nr. i ekstraktprotokollen	Sakens nr. på dagsordenen		

År 1940, den 9 april fortsatte Stortinget sitt møte på Elverum.

Møtet besluttedes satt for lukkede dører.

Som forhandlingsutvalg tilsammen med utenriksministeren – eventuelt å drøfte med de tyske myndigheter en overenskomst, ble oppnevnt Lykke, Mowinckel og Sundby.

Regjeringen ble gitt bemyndigelse til opprettelse av tre Londsalaktive statsråder, og presidenten gikk utfra at deri også ligger en bevilgning til å stille til rådighet de nødvendige penger.

Presidenten gikk videre utfra at Stortinget gir regjeringen en general fullmakt til - inntil det tidspunkt kommer at presidentskapet i overensstemmelse med regjeringen innkaller Stortinget til møte igjen å vareta rikets anliggender med Stortingets fullmakt til å treffe de nødvendige avgjørelser og beføyelser på Stortingets og Regjeringens vegne, som må ansees for påkrevd av hensyn til landets sikkerhet og fremtid.

Presidenten anser det også

With a firm hand, the Storting's secretary entered into the minutes for 9 April 1940 the so-called Elverum Authority after its adoption at the third meeting of the day. This brief declaration made it impossible for the Germans to create a legal government in Norway during their five years of occupation. From The Norwegian Størting Through 150 Years.

country. The declaration was adopted unanimously without debate, and at the end of the meeting everyone stood and sang the Norwegian national anthem.

After the war, the minister of supply, Trygve Lie, later to become the first secretary-general of the United Nations, gave his views on the Elverum Authority and its significance:

> By this declaration, Hambro erected his own monument, and in future eras it will take its place in Norway's history. In the face of such an achievement, which only a great statesman with political wisdom, imagination and clarity of foresight could have formulated, any criticism must be stilled. All the practical steps he took on 9 April 1940 – in Oslo, in Hamar and in Elverum – led to unanimous resolutions of the most far-reaching importance. The reality was that this was both Quisling's and Hitler's first serious defeat in Norway. Militarily, the Nazis won the first round, but, thanks to Hambro on 9 April, the 'Quislings' and the Germans suffered the searing agony that always results from a political mistake.

In Denmark, where many people were deeply ashamed of their country's instantaneous capitulation, the Danish newspaper *Information* wrote, shortly after the liberation of both countries in 1945: 'We shall always remember Hambro as the democrat Hitler could not overthrow. We shall remember him as one of the first nails in the Nazis' coffin; a big, strong, hard Norwegian nail!'

Under the Elverum Authority Carl Joachim had created a legal Norwegian government with full constitutional authority to lead Norway in accordance with the law, wherever the government might be forced to move to carry out its duty. No power on earth could contest the validity of this right without amending the Norwegian constitution of 1814. This could be done only by a plebiscite, and 99 per cent of the Norwegian population would vote against it.

Carl Joachim had had only a few hours' sleep during the intensive activity of the last thirty-six hours, but when at last he went to bed on 9 April he slept in the knowledge that he had secured Norway's continued constitutional independence, although he could scarcely have foreseen that the fight against the Germans was to last for five long years.

With a lack of sentiment, he also knew that under the Elverum Authority he had made himself redundant; the Storting had ceased to function and he himself was not a member of the government.

The unfortunate German ambassador, Curt Brauer, was telephoned by a furious Hitler on the evening of 9 April. Brauer had tried to persuade the Führer that Quisling was unsuitable to head the government, but Hitler had roared back that at least he was better than the

President Hambro and the Norwegian General Otto Ruge in conversation at Tromsø on 1 June 1940. Ruge had led the resistance in Norway, and the government wanted him to accompany them to London as head of the Free Norwegian Forces, but Ruge thought that he should stay in Norway with the remainder of his troops. All fighting had ceased by 10 June, and Ruge was taken to a German prison camp where he remained for four years.

obstinate Nygaardsvold, and that next day – 10 April – Brauer must try to reach Elverum and make King Haakon confirm Quisling's appointment.

Brauer's second mission on 10 April was as unsuccessful as his first. King Haakon listened to him for ten minutes in the presence of foreign secretary Koht, and replied that he would rather abdicate than appoint 'that fellow Quisling'. During the subsequent discussion with a government committee, it was repeated that capitulation was out of the question. 'You should be able to see this for yourself', said Koht to Brauer. 'After all, your Führer maintains that a people that gives in to violence does not deserve to survive!' 'Then it will mean a fight,' Brauer replied, 'and nothing can save your country!' To this, Koht quietly replied: 'The fight has already begun.'

Hitler's anger at Brauer's second fiasco resulted in his recall. He was sent to the Eastern Front, where in fact he survived the war. He had, incidentally, advised the German army against 'the Norwegian adventure'.

Carl Joachim left Elverum on the afternoon of 10 April, his mission completed. If there was more for him to do, he must use Stockholm as a base. During the afternoon he reached the little Norwegian town of

Nybergsund. King Haakon and Crown Prince Olav had taken up residence there, and it was there that the Germans tried to annihilate them in an air attack the same evening, shortly after the second refusal given to Brauer. Crown Princess Märtha and her three children had already been taken over the Swedish border. As a Swedish-born princess she was sure of temporary asylum with the Swedish royal family.

The night of 10–11 April, which he spent asleep on two chairs at Nybergsund, was to be Carl Joachim's last night in Norway for some time. Next morning he took coffee with the King, borrowed 200 kroner from the Crown Prince – he himself had not a penny on him – and drove towards the Swedish border in a Norwegian government car, with Stockholm as his destination. The Swedish chargé d'affaires had prepared a visa for him at Elverum. He foresaw that for the time being the Norwegian Embassy in the Swedish capital would be an important point of contact, for example for the recruitment of volunteers, the organization of a refugee office and arrangements for the Norwegian merchant navy to contribute to the Allied cause. Unfortunately his car got stuck in the snow in the wild Norwegian frontier country, but in the British ambassador's overcrowded car, with a typist on his lap, he finally managed to cross the border after some chilly hours on the road.

In Stockholm he put up at the Grand Hotel, but stayed only five weeks in the Swedish capital. He was reunited with his daughter Evelyn, and her Swedish husband, and Gudrun joined him later after succeeding in crossing the border unscathed during April. The few weeks in Stockholm were useful; it was still possible for a long time to telephone anyone in Norway. During this period he was able to establish contact with all the Norwegian missions in Allied countries, and, as expected, the stream of young Norwegian refugees wanting to join the Allied forces began to flow.

Carl Joachim established contact in Stockholm with his distant British cousin, twelve years his junior and later Sir Charles Jocelyn Hambro of Hambros Bank, London. They negotiated the initial agreements for Hambros Bank to finance the Norwegian merchant navy for the time being.

The Stockholm episode was nevertheless a strain. The daily bulletins from Norway reported that the King, the Crown Prince and the government were still being hunted by the Germans further up the Gudbrandsdal, and that the Norwegian army and navy were being systematically overcome in spite of incredible courage and tenacity. The fact that the Germans at first had to abandon using Quisling as head of state might have appeared encouraging, but the truth was that while he was still in office the rage directed against him kept the spirit of

King Haakon hurrying for cover during a German air raid at Nybergsund on 10 April 1940. The following night the Germans bombed Elverum in an attempt to wipe out the royal family. They did not succeed, but forty-five people were killed in the raid.

resistance fully alive. The Germans pressed the high court president, Paal Berg, into setting up an administrative council to provide some form of organization in the country, and the Norwegian people were temporarily rid of their public enemy no. 1 in the person of Quisling. But he was to return in 1943, and succeeded in compromising himself and his Quisling government totally and irreparably.

Carl Joachim came to accept that his personal safety in Stockholm was insecure. The city rapidly became infested with German spies, and the Norwegian minister Bull asked Carl Joachim to move from the Grand Hotel to a more anonymous address. It hurt Carl Joachim that, so far as Swedish officialdom was concerned, he was a most unpopular guest. It could not be concealed that neutral Sweden, impressed by German victories in Holland, Belgium and France in the spring of 1940, behaved more 'neutrally' towards vanquished Norway than towards victorious Nazi Germany, to whom it granted substantial and not very neutral concessions during the first year of the war. Günther, the Swedish foreign secretary, had no wish actually to expel Carl Joachim, but he asked him not to speak on the radio nor to the Swedish PEN Club, an evening to which he had greatly looked forward. On Sweden's part, there was little regret when on 20 May he voluntarily left Stockholm for Tromsø, although Gudrun remained in Stockholm.

As an old advocate of Pan-Scandinavia, he wrote sadly: 'The Norwegian Government never asked for help or support from the Swedish Government – and it certainly got none.'

Under the protection of the British, French and Polish troops that the British had landed in Norway on 18 April 1940, the King and government had reached Tromsø – far in the north of Norway – via Molde by 1 May. During the five weeks that followed Tromsø was the legal capital of Norway, accommodating the King and government and many Allied embassies. It was also the headquarters of the Norwegian National Bank and the centre of Free Norwegian Radio. Carl Joachim set out for Tromsø on 20 May. He had to make a most difficult journey via Kirkenæs and round north Cape to rejoin the King and government.

His stay in Tromsø lasted only a fortnight, however – the town's strange role ceased abruptly when the British had to withdraw all their forces from Norway. Britain herself was now hard-pressed in France, and it was clear that the King and government would have to leave Norway along with the British. On 7 June, less than two months after the German assault, the King, the government and a number of civil servants and foreign diplomats embarked on the British cruiser HMS *Devonshire*: Carl Joachim was among them. It was hard for King

The Norwegian fishing boats which brought some of Norway's gold from Ålesund to Tromsø. From here it was transported to Scapa Flow in the battle-cruiser Enterprise, *taken to the USA in Norwegian ships and then distributed between the Federal Reserve Bank in New York and the Bank of Canada in Ottawa.* Norsk Telegrambyrå, Oslo.

The Storting, Norway's parliament, was established on 17 May 1814 as Norway's legislative assembly under the Eidsvoll Constitution adopted at the time of Denmark's surrender of the country. The present Storting building, seen here, was erected during 1861–6. It was here that Carl Joachim Hambro was first elected a member in 1918, and that during the night of 8–9 April 1940 he successfully initiated his historic action to make it impossible for the Germans to form a legal government. Photograph taken in 1942, with the German Nazi flag flying above the building. Norsk Telegrambyrå, Oslo.

Haakon to leave the country over which he had reigned for thirty-five years. Moreover, the *Devonshire* weighed anchor on the anniversary of the dissolution of the union with Sweden in 1905. The weather was so miserable that this alone was reason enough for tears. However, the proclamation prepared by the government for Tromsø Radio to broadcast to the Norwegian people on that day gave no sign of sorrow; it expressed only a firm belief that the Norwegian government in London would lead Norway back to freedom.

A few days later, King George VI of England received his Norwegian uncle and his large retinue at Kings Cross Station in London. It was a routine to which the British King had become accustomed during recent years. He had already received Wilhelmina, Queen of the Netherlands, and the President of Poland, General Wladyslaw

Sikorski. After King Haakon, King George II of Greece and King Peter II of Yugoslavia arrived, with their governments.

It was no enviable task to establish a government-in-exile in London, although Norway enjoyed the special advantage that, apart from its ability to finance itself, it could also offer the world's fourth largest merchant fleet in the fight against Germany. Free Norway had at its disposal over 1,000 merchant vessels with a total tonnage of over 4,000,000 – a merchant navy surpassed only by the British, the Americans and the Japanese. It was a navy whose owners, captains and crews were in no doubt about which side they were on. It was later said by the British that Norway's contribution of its merchant navy to the Allied cause was equivalent to an army of a million men.

In London Carl Joachim was reunited with his eldest son, Edvard Isak, but here also he began to feel unwanted. Indeed, he made himself rather less than welcome by some very anti-imperialistic speeches, which were not well received either by his own government or by the British Foreign Office. With the approval of Johan Nygaardsvold, he moved on to the USA in early June 1940 to propagate Norway's cause in the press and on the platform. Gudrun joined him there, reaching America after a seemingly endless journey from Stockholm via Siberia, Japan and the Pacific. Here they were reunited with their youngest son, Johan.

Carl Joachim settled in the university town of Princeton in New Jersey, where he took over a house that had belonged to another exiled celebrity, the German writer Thomas Mann. Using Princeton as his base he worked for Norway's cause for the next four years, seeking to create by books, articles and ceaseless lecturing throughout the country an understanding of what was actually happening in Europe. When in 1941, after Pearl Harbor, America entered the war, there was an increasing response to his efforts. His books. *I Saw it Happen in Norway* and *How to Win the Peace*, published in 1940–2, were translated into many languages.

As chairman of the Union of Norwegians since 1923, he had extensive connections with prominent Norwegians in the USA, which were of great assistance to him. The reputation he won in America by his activities during these years is reflected in the honorary doctorates given him by eleven of the universities at which he spoke. Many of the towns he visited made him an honorary citizen.

These four years were, however, fatiguing, and he felt out of touch with Norway and Norway's fate. He could not help occasionally recalling Milton's famous words, quoted by Churchill: 'They also serve who only stand and wait.' Gudrun did not survive the years of exile. She was

Carl Joachim (right) spent almost four years in the USA and Canada during the German occupation of Norway. Norway's crown prince (left), the present King Olav v, also came to the USA from London in 1940 to meet Crown Princess Mårtha and their three children in Maryland. Press photo taken in December 1940. Berlingske Archives, Copenhagen.

suffering from cancer when she arrived in the USA, and she died in their Princeton home on 29 June 1943. Carl Joachim and their son Johan were at her bedside when she died. Edvard Isak, in the USA on a duty trip from London, was also present. Carl Joachim, alone for the last two years of the war, continued his work with undiminished energy, representing Norway at international congresses and meetings in the USA, including the international labour conferences at New York and Philadelphia.

In October 1944, King Haakon and the Norwegian government recalled him to London to assist in the planning of post-war arrangements, which it was now clear would be needed before long. The intention was to ensure that when Norway was liberated there would be a more harmonious transition to normality than many other countries might expect. Of course, to be able to return with a legal government was a sure guarantee that the liberation would be conducted with propriety and an equality of treatment.

Norway was liberated on 8 May 1945. On that day all the German forces in Norway surrendered. None of the exiled Norwegians was able to enjoy this day – a day when Norwegian shops closed 'out of sheer happiness'. Wearing battledress, Crown Prince Olav returned to Norway on 14 May as chief of the Norwegian armed forces abroad, accompanied by a government delegation. On 30 May the remainder of the government arrived, and with it Carl Joachim. The King, now seventy-three, did not arrive until 7 June, when he was received by the entire population with rapturous enthusiasm.

The price paid by Norway for its active participation in World War II had, however, been high. The five years of struggle against the Germans claimed the lives of 10,000 Norwegians. Losses were highest among the seamen, 3,800 of whom were drowned. The army lost 2,000 men, 840 of these during the first months of the desperate struggle in Norway, and the remainder in the service of the Allies. The Norwegian resistance movement lost 2,100 men; 360 of these were executed, 40 were tortured to death, 40 others committed suicide when arrested and 130 died in concentration camps. Of the rest, 1,340 had perished in German prisons, including almost all the 650 Norwegian Jews deported. About 100 were killed trying to flee to England, and 1,900 of the civilian population died in air raids and other acts of war. Of the traitors, 65 informers were liquidated and about 700 young Norwegians were killed serving with the Germans on the Eastern Front.

In 1945, there were probably some people in Norway, particularly among those who had lost their loved ones, who might have preferred a less heroic attitude on 9 April 1940, but at the liberation general opinion was that it had been right to adopt a stance relying heavily upon a final Allied victory.

The transition to normal peacetime was perhaps rather more confused than Carl Joachim had anticipated. The man who had carried the heaviest burden in the country's relations with the Germans was Paal Berg, the president of the high court. Like many others, Carl Joachim's view was that it would be proper to invite him to form the first post-war government to replace the Nygaardsvold government until, following normal Storting elections, a government could be chosen on a parliamentary basis. In the event, however, Carl Joachim was blamed later for not advocating more wholeheartedly the choice of Berg, who in fact finally refused to form a government. This criticism was probably unjustified; it was rather that Berg, a liberal then aged seventy-two, was not eager to become prime minister because he felt that he lacked sufficient support from the returning labour government. In the end, the young social democrat, Einar Gerhardsen, formed a government, having recently returned after four years in a German concentration camp.

As Carl Joachim had hoped, the purge of Norwegian traitors was less bloody than in most other liberated countries. Only twenty-five Quislings were executed, including of course Quisling himself. He was shot at the Akershus fortress on 24 October 1945 after a long trial and a vain

Carl Joachim (left) on his arrival in Oslo after the liberation in June 1945. On the right is Crown Prince Olav in battledress. Norsk Telegrambyrå, Oslo.

appeal against the verdict. Of his ministers appointed by Reich commissioner Josef Terboven in 1943, the minister of trade, Albert Hagelin, and the minister of labour, Ragnar Schancke, shared his fate. Quisling's most notorious henchman Jonas Lie, minister of police, avoided punishment by dying of a stroke on 11 May, the day he would have been arrested. The minister of social affairs, Gulbrand Lunde, was lucky enough to be killed in a car accident before the liberation, and the minister of justice, Sverre Riisnæs, was declared insane. Although during the following years proceedings were taken against over 100,000 people, only some 28,000 received prison sentences, while 30,000 others were merely fined.

Vidkun Quisling in prison at the Akershus Fortress in Oslo in the summer of 1945, shortly before his execution. A British journalist later wrote: 'He added one word – his own name – to the English Language. Quisling has since 1940 been synonymous with traitor.'

The two most hated representatives of the German occupation forces in Norway, Reich commissioner Josef Terboven and his SS chief of police, Wilhelm Rediess, committed suicide on 8 May in the Reich commissioner's bunker in the garden of Crown Prince Olav's home at Skaugum in Asker. The chief of the German Gestapo, Heinrich Fehlis, also preferred to shoot himself when he failed in an escape attempt dressed as an ordinary German soldier. However, of a total of 350 Germans accused of war crimes, only the twelve worst offenders were shot.

In material terms, it was a severely damaged country that was liberated in 1945. Total Norwegian war losses were calculated at over £1 billion.

On his return to Norway early in the summer of 1945, Carl Joachim, now sixty, was not only widowed but homeless. The Germans had first made use of his house, and had then plundered it completely. He therefore gave up any thought of reoccupying the large, empty house he had left on 9 April 1940. In his memoirs, he wrote that the few heirlooms and family documents that had not been destroyed in the Bergen fire of 1916 had disappeared, together with all his subsequent acquisitions.

For five years, Carl Joachim had led an itinerant life in Sweden, Norway, England, the USA and Canada. All five children had long since left home, and he could not bring himself to set up his own establishment once again. So he moved to the Bristol Hotel in the centre of Oslo, where he was given a small suite on the fifth floor. Room

Carl Joachim Hambro, drawn by Øivind Sørensen in August 1947, when he had remarried. His years of exile in London and the USA had left their mark on him physically, but, though he was now sixty-two, his capacity for work and his political involvement were unabated. Aftenposten's Archives, Oslo.

512 became his permanent address for the remaining nineteen years of his life. It was convenient for him to live near the Storting, and he had no wish to run his own household. What was most surprising, however, was that he was not alone in the suite for very long.

During the unforgettable liberation summer of 1945, he had met an

Gyda Christensen (1872–1964), the actress and theatrical manager, married Carl Joachim Hambro in 1946. She died aged ninety-two, four months before him. Photograph taken about 1920.

actress called Gyda Christensen, though not for the first time. He had admired her since his youth, and had been a member of her theatre management in the 1920s. Gyda was now seventy-two; she had been one of Oslo's most popular actresses in the twenties. Her first performance was in 1893 at the age of twenty-one, when Carl Joachim was still an eight-year-old Bergen schoolboy. Their reunion was at a summer dinner party given by Gyda's daughter, Lillebil Ibsen, who had now replaced her mother as one of Oslo's most admired actresses. Carl Joachim proposed to Gyda soon after this meeting. At first she thought his proposal was a joke, but when she realized he was serious she accepted, and they married in 1946. Carl Joachim was reluctant to live in her large house, and she gave way, moving in with him at the hotel. From that day onwards they were inseparable. Carl Joachim resumed his international work before long, and Gyda accompanied him on all his post-war journeys. She was with him at Geneva for the winding up of the League of Nations, in Paris for the peace negotiations, at the

Carl Joachim did not live long enough to see his eldest son, Edvard Isak, elected president of the twenty-fifth UN General Assembly in New York, 1970–1. Edvard Isak is seen here at the opening of the General Assembly on 16 October 1970, flanked by the secretary-general, U Thant, and the deputy secretary, Constantin Stavropaulous. Politiken Archives, Copenhagen.

UN's Constituent Assembly in London and at its routine general meetings in New York. She also travelled with him to The Hague in 1951, when Carl Joachim won his greatest post-war victory in the proceedings at the International Court of Justice involving the delimitation of Norway's maritime boundaries. She was with him on his lecture tours, which once again took him to the USA, but she refused to accompany him on his strenuous electioneering. She brought an enchanting sweetness to his old age. One of his daughters-in-law later said that her husband had never looked at her with such loving eyes as Carl Joachim looked at Gyda.

He continued his Storting activities – now as the president of the Odelsting, a special section of the Norwegian parliament – until his retirement in 1957. That the labour party re-elected him as president of the Odelsting is good evidence of his standing after the war. In complete contrast to previous practice, on the day he retired tribute was paid to him in the Ting in the form of addresses and applause, and, well aware of his ever-precarious finances, the Ting unanimously granted him an honorary pension. There were good grounds for this, one being that he had never in his political life accepted a salaried position; his wish had always been to remain completely independent.

His writings during his last years included a history of his family, welded together by memories of his youth. Much of the information in this book comes from these four volumes. During their last years, Carl Joachim and Gyda were frequently in poor health, and when Carl Joachim was admitted to hospital Gyda moved into an adjacent room. She wanted to be beside him always. Early in 1964, Gyda died at the age of ninety-two. Four months later, the seventy-nine-year-old Carl Joachim died. Some years earlier, King Haakon had decorated him with the rare Borgerdåds medal in gold, which only twenty Norwegians had ever received. The labour party arranged a most impressive state funeral in the presence of King Haakon and the entire government, and the urn containing Carl Joachim's ashes was placed in the grove of honour at the Church of Our Saviour, beside the graves of Ibsen, Bjørnson and other great Norwegians. Later, a cairn was erected over the grave at public expense.

A few years after his death, one of Oslo's old squares was renamed C. J. Hambros Plads. It was the Oslo Municipal Council's wish that the city's young people should see his name every day.

Carl Joachim Hambro was nearly eighty when he died in 1964. His lively face was rarely still, which made him difficult to portray, and the various paintings seldom do him justice. This portrait, painted in 1951 by Haakon Stenstadsvold, is undoubtedly the best. Nordmandsforbundet, Oslo.

See illustrations opposite

Three of Carl Joachim's sons, each in their own fashion, followed in their versatile father's footsteps. Cato alone went his own way. The four brothers have seven sons between them, but among the eight grandchildren there is as yet only one son to carry on the Hambro name in Norway.

Edvard Isak Hambro obtained a law degree at Oslo in *1934* and a doctorate at Geneva in *1936*, and became head of the International Department of the Christian Michelsen Institute in Bergen. He succeeded in escaping to England with the Allied troops in May *1940*. During *1944–5* he was employed by the Foreign Ministry of the Norwegian government-in-exile in London. He married Elisabeth Raverat in *1940*. He was secretary to the International Court in The Hague from *1946* to *1953*. From *1959* he was Professor of Jurisprudence at the Norwegian Commercial University, and *1961–66*, member of the Storting for Bergen; *1966–76*, Norway's permanent ambassador at the UN, and *1970–1* chairman of the General Assembly. He wrote a number of books and papers on international law, and died in *1977* while Norwegian ambassador in Paris.

Cato Hambro, Isak's twin brother, received commercial training in London (Hambros Bank) and in Skien in the years before the war. During *1943–5* he served with the Norwegian forces in Scotland. He married Wencke Petersen in Oslo in *1946*, and received a Master of Arts degree (pedagogics) in *1951*. He was secretary-general of Norway's National Association for Mental Health, *1953–7*; a lecturer at Oslo Teachers' Training College, *1957–9*; principal of the Department of School Psychology at Oslo University, *1965–8*, and psychological adviser to various schools since *1959*. He has written a number of books on psychology, pedagogics and mental health.

Carl Hambro is a lecturer, author and translator. He married Wencke Koren in Oslo in *1939*, and was the only brother to stay in Oslo on 9 April *1940*. He was a teacher at the Oslo Commercial College, *1939–43* and *1945–6*; a lecturer in Norwegian in Sweden, *1943–5*; a lecturer at the Sorbonne, *1946–9*. He was divorced in *1952*, and in the same year married Christine Holter in Oslo. He became cultural counsellor at the Norwegian Embassy in London, *1952–9*, and was chairman of the Norwegian Translators' Association, *1961–5*. Between *1960* and *1967* he published a number of novels and essays, and is considered one of Norway's leading translators, especially of French literature.

Johan Hambro took a law degree in *1939* and went to the USA early in *1940* to study journalism; he was in America on 9 April *1940*. In the following years he was employed by the Norwegian Consulate-General in New York, and here in *1945* he married Lore Aichelin shortly before his return to Norway. From *1946* to *1948* he worked as a journalist for Aftenposten in Oslo. During *1949–53* he was US correspondent for Norsk Telegrambyrå in New York; *1953–5*, press attaché at the UN; since *1955*, secretary-general of the Norwegians' Union in Oslo.

Edvard Isak Hambro,
professor and ambassador,
(1911–77).

Cato Hambro,
psychologist,
(born 1911).

Carl Hambro,
university lecturer and author,
(born 1914).

Johan Hambro,
Secretary-General
(born 1915).

6 Theodora's Grandchildren

The Hambro–Bull combination – begun by Carl Hambro's marriage in 1838 to Angelique Bull – was repeated in 1844 when Carl's sister, Theodora Hambro, married Angelique Bull's brother Johan Randulff.

When she was nineteen Theodora, the prettiest daughter of Isach and Marie, was sent to Hamburg to train as a singer and pianist. She returned from Hamburg in 1838, in time to take part in her brother Carl's impressive wedding to Angelique Bull. It was on this occasion that Theodora first met the bride's brother Johan Randulff, two years older than her. He had begun to study medicine two years earlier at Kristiania, where his father was at the time president of the high court. He qualified in 1841, became a houseman at Kristiania, and then in 1843 settled as a general practitioner in Bergen. In 1844 he married Theodora, and during the next five years she produced two healthy children. In 1845, a son, Edvard Isach, was born, and in 1849 Theodora gave birth to a girl. Sadly, Theodora died in childbirth.

Johan Randulff Bull (1815–94). A lieutenant in the Army Medical Corps, he was attached to the Nordenfjordske Musketeers and became garrison medical officer at Bergen. His father was the president of the Norwegian High Court, Georg Bull, and his mother the sister of the world-famous Danish physicist, H. C. Ørsted. He played an active role in dealing with the Bergen cholera epidemic of 1848–9. He was happily married to Theodora Hambro for five years until her death in 1849. A widower for very many years, he threw himself into social medicine. 'Long Bull' was a well-known and much loved figure in Bergen. This portrait was painted c. 1885. Owned by the Norwegian family.

*Theodora Hambro (1818–49), Edvard Isach and Marie Hambro's youngest and most
beautiful daughter. She was very musical, and in 1836–7 went to Hamburg to study singing
and music. At the age of eighteen she was painted by the Danish artist Louis Aumont, who
was then living in Hamburg.* Bergen Art Gallery.

Johan Randulff and Theodora had been married only five years, and he was now left with a boy aged four and a baby daughter.

Johan Randulff supplemented his income during the early years of his marriage from a lieutenancy in the medical corps, serving two regiments in Bergen. Now that he was alone his public interests widened, and it is pleasant to record that this highly respected family doctor gradually accepted, in addition to the work of his practice, all the less rewarding medical tasks to be found in a provincial town – doctor to the poor, cholera doctor and prison doctor at the Bergenshus. After five years as a widower he married again so that his children might have a mother. His new wife was the daughter of a Tromsø consul. During his forty years in Bergen he became a respected and popular figure, known all over the town as 'Long Bull' because of his remarkable height. He retired in 1885 and moved to Kristiania to be nearer to his son Edvard Isach, with whom he was very close. In the last years of his life he lived with his second wife in the Norwegian capital, and died there aged eighty-one in 1894. His second wife had no children, and died a few years after him. Exceptionally, this female line is

The Norwegian capital's main street, Karl Johan, from a lithograph by Hoffenberg and Trap, c. 1885. It shows Kristiania (which in 1923 changed its name to Oslo) at the time of Henrik Ibsen, when the capital had long outstripped Bergen as the country's major city. At the end of the wide avenue is the palace, then the residence of the Swedish kings, but since 1905 the Norwegian royal palace. Royal Library, Copenhagen.

The same street scene as illustrated on page 122, painted here in 1891 by Norway's most famous painter, Edvard Munch. Bergen Art Gallery.

described in greater detail, since two of Theodora's grandsons became famous professors in Oslo University.

Kristiania had been an insignificant town of 9,000 inhabitants in 1820, but by 1885 its population had risen to 135,000. In spite of this tremendous growth, the Norwegian capital was still no more than a large provincial town. Nevertheless, present-day Norwegians look back with nostalgia to the Kristiania of the 1880s and 1890s. Neither before nor since has Norway boasted such an abundant array of talent in literature, the theatre, art and music. During these decades it was possible to meet at the Grand Café on Karl Johan Street, Henrik Ibsen, Bjørnstjerne Bjørnson, Jonas Lie and Alexander Kielland, the great literary figures of the day. Since Ibsen and Bjørnson were Norway's greatest dramatists, there was of course a remarkable upsurge in the Norwegian theatre, culminating in 1899 in the opening of the National Theatre in Kristiania. The composer Edvard Grieg was also held in high esteem. In the 1890s, the next rebellious generation came on the

Edvard Isach Hambro Bull (1845–1925), aged five, drawn by Siegwald Dahl in 1850. Owned by the Norwegian family.

scene – including the brilliant, but later stigmatized, Knut Hamsun. Among the young painters and sculptors, Edvard Munch and Gustav Vigeland became the most famous.

It was in this talented Kristiania environment that Randulff and Theodora's only son, Edvard Isach Hambro Bull, was later to assert himself. But for the time being, in 1859, he was merely a motherless fourteen-year-old who had to come to Kristiania to matriculate because he could live there with his grandmother. His interest in the arts had been awakened early, and among his modest luggage he brought with him his beloved dolls' theatre.

He matriculated in 1862, and at first decided not to follow his father in his fatiguing work as a doctor. He considered becoming a lawyer. This he abandoned in favour of science, which within a short time led him into medical studies in any event. At this time three Hambro cousins, all named Edvard, were studying at Kristiania University. All three were to become leading figures within their individual fields, a typical feature of the Norwegian family's third generation.

In 1868, Edvard Isach passed his examinations, and a year later married Gina Falsen, the daughter of a Norwegian officer. The same age as her husband, she soon presented him with a son, Theodor. Theodor's excellent book, published in 1932, on the Norwegian line of the Hambro family has provided valuable source material for this book.

Gina died in 1879, and in the following year Edvard Isach remarried. His second wife was Ida Marie Paludan, a girl of only nineteen and the daughter of a Danish parson. The marriage was very happy, and Ida quickly established a good relationship with Theodor, her ten-year-old stepson. She herself produced four children.

In 1870, after a period of study in Austria and Germany, Edvard Isach had settled down as a general practitioner in Kristiania, where he wrote his doctoral thesis in 1875. In 1880 he became chief physician at the Norwegian National Hospital, and began teaching medical students at Kristiania University. A scientific career was now open to him, for his contributions to the Medical Association and to the Scientific Association were at this time of such a high standard that the Storting was expected to grant him a professorship in propaedeutic medicine. With this prospect in mind, in 1879 and again in 1880 he refused offers of a professorship at Uppsala in Sweden because he preferred to stay in Norway. The matter went ahead slowly, however, and in 1887, as part of general economies, the Storting finally refused to

Until Norway was separated from Denmark in 1814, all Norwegians wishing to study had gone to Copenhagen. From 1811 onwards, however, a Norwegian university slowly developed, and Kristiania's university, built between 1841 and 1851, marked a new development in Norway's independent intellectual life. The university was built on the north side of the city's new main street, Carl Johan. The castle, dating from the 1820s, completed the wide avenue beside the university. Lithograph, 1860. Oslo City Museum.

Dr Edvard Hambro Bull's activities as physician to the Kristiania Theatre, and later also to the National Theatre, meant that he and his family knew Norwegian theatrical personalities throughout their lives, and that the dramatists and composers of the golden age of the arts in Norway became his patients. The writers Bjørnstjerne Bjørnson (bottom) and Henrik Ibsen (left) and the composer Edvard Grieg (right), are caricatured here at about the turn of the century by the Norwegian artist O. Guldbrandsen for Simplicissimus, *the German satirical magazine.* Royal Library Copenhagen.

Edvard Isach Hambro Bull, the eldest son of Johan Randulff Bull and Theodora Hambro. As a young man his great interest was in literature and the theatre, but in 1868 he qualified in medicine at Kristiania, wrote his doctoral thesis in 1875 and became chief physician at the Norges Rigshospital in 1880. Painting, c. 1900, by Erik Werenskiold. Owned by the Norwegian family.

establish a chair for him. He took this so much to heart that he resigned his post as chief physician at the National Hospital and gave up teaching at the university, returning to private practice. In the following period, and until his death in 1925, he became Kristiania's best known and most highly respected private physician. In the light of his own disappointment, his pleasure when two of his sons became professors at Kristiania University is readily understandable.

From 1887 onwards he turned his attention away from an academic career towards the enthusiasms of his youth – theatre, art, music and literature. He became chairman of the Kristiania Arts Association, and his home gradually came to reflect the best in the contemporary arts of the period. Later, in 1898, he became a member of the management of the newly built National Theatre, and later its chairman, which brought him into close association with the theatre's actors and playwrights. In the home he created for his children, art and science merged with the utmost harmony, and his large circle of friends and patients were frequently to be found associating there. In time he became doctor and spiritual adviser not only to Ibsen, Bjørnson and Grieg but also to most of the National Theatre's actors. He received the unlimited trust of these people by virtue of his amiable disposition and his unfailing patience.

Ida Marie Bull, née *Paludan (1861–1957), second wife of Edvard Isach Hambro Bull; a photograph taken in 1891 with her four children. From the left, standing, Francis and Edvard Bull; seated, Marie Louise and Johan Peter.* Owned by the Norwegian family.

At his death in 1925, the press obituaries regretted that in the 1880s Norway had rejected his great scientific abilities and refused him a well-deserved professorship. They added, however, that after giving up his post of chief physician his life and work had blended harmoniously with his rich mind and cultivated outlook. Ida survived him by no fewer than thirty-two years. She died in 1957, aged ninety-two.

When at school in Kristiania, Dr Bull's second son Edvard was acknowledged by teachers and fellow pupils as the most intelligent, well informed and assured member of his class, and indisputably the most outstanding pupil of his day. His younger brother Francis said later that Edvard was in fact very sensitive, and saw this sensitivity as a weakness. To conceal his uncertainties he adopted a cool and supercilious manner. During his latter years at school he inaugurated a journal for Scandinavian students, *Scandinavian Youth*, with the co-operation of Danish and Swedish students. In 1898, in one of the early editions, he paid tribute to Henrik Ibsen on his seventieth birthday in the form of an epic poem, calling the great poet 'The cultivator of doubt here on earth'. It was in fact as a sceptic, critical historian and political rebel that Edvard made a mark soon after he matriculated in 1899. He was already deeply concerned at the prevailing social conditions and their historical background.

His career as a historian was rapid and brilliant; this was fortunate, for his life was to be short. After a number of years of inspiring studies in Norway and Denmark, in 1906 he took a degree in history, geography, Latin and Greek at Kristiania University. In 1909 he won a gold medal for a treatise entitled 'Confession and Penance in the Middle Ages', set by the theological faculty. Many were surprised that Edvard of all people should choose to write on this subject, since religion was not the least of his gnawing doubts. But the Middle Ages had always interested him as the era when society began to adopt its present form, and he enjoyed demonstrating that the power of the Catholic church in northern Europe was based exclusively on punishment. In his treatise he asserted that Christianity had never penetrated deeply into the mentality of the people of Scandinavia, and that in fact only a fear of punishment had been assimilated. These were surprising views to present to the theological faculty, and of course his hypothesis gave rise to much discussion; but he won his gold medal.

In the same year – 1909 – he married Lucie Voss. In 1911 a daughter, Karen, was born, and in 1914 Edvard. Edvard senior's doctoral thesis was presented in 1912 under the title 'The People and the Church in the Middle Ages'. In this, his theory that there was a fall in mean

Edvard Bull (1881–1932), son of Edvard Isach Hambro Bull. In 1917 he became Professor of History at Kristiania University. He made no attempt to conceal his strong left-wing attitudes. Drawing by Arnstein Arneberg from the 1920s. Private collection.

temperature in Europe in the fourteenth century caused a mild sensation. He maintained that the decline in northern Europe's development, previously attributed to the Black Death, was probably caused by a fall in mean temperature of $1\frac{1}{2}$ degrees, which affected the whole of Europe over a long period. This had been of no importance in southern Europe and of little significance in central Europe, but it had had catastrophic consequences in Norway and Iceland, where agriculture and cultivation had reached their northern limits. He constructed his theory upon numerous old accounts of years of catastrophe, but he could not of course produce scientific evidence to support it. He often returned to this subject in later years.

In 1913 he became a lecturer in history at Kristiania University. As a teacher, he was widely known and esteemed for his spontaneous charm and his outstanding capacities in discussion with his students. It was important for Edvard that students should think for themselves, and he was proud and happy when he saw that he had really inspired them. Many of his pupils said later that, however much they might disagree with him on a subject, no one had taught them more. He was always more effective in personal contacts than in print, and he was to exercise a great influence on many young Norwegian historians.

Apart from his own literary activities, he took part in the editing of many large works of a national character. For example, from 1921

onwards he was co-editor of the first Norwegian Biographical Encyclopaedia, a gigantic work, still uncompleted, to which he himself contributed many medieval biographies. He later published his *Life of the
Norwegian People*, a two-volume work on the era of the sagas, in which to
the regret of many readers he debunked several old sagas and legends,
discarding them as goods borrowed from other countries. But even the
most disenchanted of his readers were forced to admit that he was
probably right. As a historian, he was Norway's leading representative
of dialectic-materialist historiography; an advantage to him of course
during the years when this form of historiography was fashionable, but
seen as a weakness in later assessments of him as a political writer.

From a political aspect, Edvard's doubts about the justice of the
society in which he found himself were just as crucial to his choice of a
party as his scholastic background. From 1918, therefore, the distinguished professor (he had received this appointment in 1917) was to be
found on the extreme left wing of the Norwegian labour party, and in
that year he published his book, *Karl Marx*. By 1920 the labour party
had become more communist than it had ever been before or has been
since. The Russian Revolution had of course left its mark on Norway,
and in 1920 the labour party was the only socialist party in western
Europe to join – with a great display of exuberance – the Komintern,
founded in Moscow the year before as a focal point for the coming world
revolution. This explains the Norwegian labour party's strident call in
1920 for armed revolution and transfer of authority to a dictatorship of
the proletariat. These discords grated on the ears of the old social
democrats, and the uncritical attitude towards Moscow's rigid dictates
offended the party's centre faction, to which Edvard himself belonged.
With hindsight, the trend of events within the party in the following
years comes as no surprise; developments were of course parallel with
those in many other countries.

As initial enthusiasm for the Russian experiment subsided and
communist progress in all parts of Europe began to run down, the
inevitable occurred: the Norwegian labour party disintegrated. On 15
January 1921 the old and moderate social democratic wing withdrew
and formed a new party, the Norwegian social democratic party. In
November 1923, the residue of the old party split and ejected its most
left wing, Moscow-orientated, elements, who formed the Norwegian
communist party, but this proved too much for Edvard. He stayed in
the labour party that was left, independent of Moscow but still
revolutionary, made up of two-thirds of the former party. In the years
that followed, this new party attracted several members from both the
breakaway groups.

Edvard became vice-chairman of this purged labour party in 1923. He had no wish to stand for the Storting, for he continued to be a dogmatic, class-struggle politician, seeing little virtue in the opportunities presented by the parliamentary process. From 1923 onwards he became the party's theorist and strategist, and to him falls much of the credit that the previously ultra-communist labour party gradually adopted a profile more acceptable to a wide circle of workers. This was reinforced when the Norwegian social democratic party and the labour party came together again in 1927. In the elections of that year, the labour party was returned with the highest number of seats: 56 of the 150 in the Storting. By comparison, the Communists had to be content with three seats.

When the conservative party could do no more early in 1928, the labour party was, on King Haakon's initiative, asked to form a government for the first time. This news caused uneasiness throughout Norway, for the labour party had not yet renounced its revolutionary plans. The report of a coming socialist government resulted in a run on the banks, already beset with other problems.

The party's management was itself doubtful of its chances of success. Although the labour party was now the largest in Norway, two-thirds of the Storting were still against them, and the party had little wish to govern by the grace of the non-Socialist parties. Nevertheless the party at last agreed, and took over on 28 January 1928. In this ministry the party veteran, Christopher Hornsrud, became prime minister, Edvard became minister of foreign affairs and Johan Nygaardsvold minister of agriculture.

Edvard drafted a manifesto that was scarcely calculated to calm the Storting or the people. It read, *inter alia*, that 'the government intends to be guided in all its actions by the interests of the working class and the entire proletariat, and to facilitate and prepare for the transition to a socialist society.' This was soon too much for the opposition, and on 7 February the leader of the liberals, J. L. Mowinckel, moved a vote of no confidence against the Hornsrud government. The following week, Norway's first labour government resigned, having been in office for only eighteen days, the shortest ministry in Norway's history to date. On 15 February 1928 it became clear to the conservative acting-president of the Storting, Carl Joachim Hambro, that his cousin, Professor Edvard Bull, had been toppled as socialist minister of foreign affairs.

However the 'Hornsrud episode', as the eighteen days were later called in Norwegian history, proved a healthy experiment for the labour party. It had learnt that the parliamentary process was more

Norway's first Labour government, 1928. Christopher Hornsrud was prime minister, Johan Nygaardsvold minister of agriculture and Edvard Bull minister of foreign affairs. The photograph shows Edvard in profile on the far left, while Nygaardsvold is third from the left.

advantageous, even to a revolutionary party, than a revolutionary 'all-or-nothing' policy. When the party was returned in 1935, with Johan Nygaardsvold as prime minister, it had acquired more polish as a parliamentaly party and had become well-fitted to govern. In 1935, however, Edward was no longer with them; he had died in 1932.

In 1929, at the age of forty-eight and at the peak of his scholastic and political career, he suddenly fell ill. The brain tumour which caused his death three years later was beyond diagnosis at that time. It first manifested itself by severe fatigue, and later by a distinct sensitivity, which made Edvard, otherwise so kind a man, appear unbalanced. In the final phase he had occasional mental lapses, and the previously razor-sharp thinker would suddenly exclaim: 'Oh dear! Now I'm probably talking nonsense!'

In the spring of 1932, after a demanding series of lectures in Copenhagen, he was ordered to take a holiday to recuperate from overwork. He and his wife were cruising in the Mediterranean when he suddenly lost consciousness. The ship put in to Malta, where he was transferred to hospital. Here he made a surprising recovery, and for a few months was his old self, planning new ventures. Shortly after his return to Norway, however, he again lost consciousness, and on 26 August 1932 he died at the National Hospital in Oslo. His wife survived

Edvard Bull Junior (born 1914), Professor of History at Trondheim University, has followed in his father's footsteps. He graduated in 1939 and married Andrea Rockmann Olsen in the same year. He wrote his doctoral thesis in 1958, and in 1963 he became a professor at the Norwegian Teaching Training College at Trondheim, which in 1968 became Trondheim University. The whole of his substantial body of literary work is concentrated on conditions of work, the trade union movement and social conditions. He is a member of the Academy of Science in Oslo and of the Royal Scientific Society in Trondheim. His son Niels (born 1940) is a graduate engineer. Painting by Arnstein Arneberg. Private collection.

him by thirty-eight years, dying in 1970. Before her death she had the satisfaction of seeing her only son become professor of history at Trondheim University.

Even as a child Francis Bull showed himself to be a far more typical product of his upper middle-class, hospitable and art-loving home than his elder brother Edvard. Francis was not plagued by the unrest that made his brother so critical of society throughout his life. He had been born with a happy disposition, and at an early age he showed gentleness and kindness. He had a marked preference for books, and he could read before he was six. Before he was eight he had ploughed through all the early eighteenth-century comedies of the Danish-Norwegian playwright Ludvig Holberg. When he was twelve his father began to take him to dress rehearsals at the new National Theatre. In 1899 he sat with his father, Henrik Ibsen and Bjørnstjerne Bjørnson watching rehearsals of Ibsen's *An Enemy of the People*. Bjørnson later became his favourite Norwegian writer, for he discovered that Bjørnson had a saving human warmth sometimes lacking in Ibsen. Francis was one of the pall-bearers at Ibsen's funeral in 1908.

He matriculated in 1905, and had no hesitation in deciding to study the history of literature. He took his degree in 1911, and submitted his doctoral thesis, 'From Holberg to Nordal Brun' in 1916. In 1920 he won a competition for a professorship in the history of Scandinavian literature at Kristiania University. Over the next twenty years he became a most popular and admired teacher; his students could not resist his infectious and zestful enthusiasm and the elegant style in which he expressed his views. These qualities made each of his lectures a memorable experience. His extraordinary memory was to influence his entire scholarly approach. He came to occupy a unique position in historical biography – a walking literary encyclopaedia, with a gift of expression that actors might envy. At the same time, his helpfulness and spontaneous kindness to everyone were almost legendary.

The late nineteenth century was the golden age of Norwegian poetry, and it was the last chapter of this epoch, which he had witnessed as a boy, that lay closest to his heart. He was also well-versed in Danish literature. He never forgot that his great-grandmother, Barbara Bull, had been Danish, and that a hundred years earlier, through the Ørsted family, she had known the poets of Denmark's own golden age. In 1924 he married Ingrid Berntsen, daughter of the Danish prime minister Klaus Berntsen. Throughout his life he welcomed any opportunity to speak Danish.

Bjørnstjerne Bjørnson and Henrik Ibsen may be well content to have had Francis to honour their memory. It was said of Francis after his death, that 'he was Bjørnson's proxy here on earth.' He was responsible for the first great collected edition of Bjørnson's works, and he prepared

Contemporary newspaper drawing by Gustav Lerum of a dress rehearsal of Henrik Ibsen's An Enemy of the People, *which was chosen for the opening performance at Kristiania's new National Theatre in August 1899. From the left are Mrs Caroline Bjørnson, Henrik Ibsen, Bjørnstjerne Bjørnson, Edvard Hambro Bull and his twelve-year-old son Francis, later to be called 'Bjørnson's proxy here on earth'.*

135

the centenary edition of Ibsen's collected plays. His own literary contributions were also substantial. As might be expected, he was an industrious contributor to the Norwegian Biographical Encyclopaedia edited by his brother, but his own most important work was *The History of Norwegian Literature*, which he published with Professor Paasche.

Although a century had passed since Norway had separated from Denmark, the old Danish firm of Gyldendal was still the main publisher of Norway's great writers. The works of Bjørnson, Ibsen, Lie and Kielland were still being published in Copenhagen. In 1924 the journalist Harald Grieg expressed the wish that Gyldendal's Norwegian branch should become an independent Norwegian publishing house, 'so that all the great Norwegian writers may be brought home to Norway'. The plan reverberated through the young Norwegian nation that had separated from Sweden in 1905, and Norsk Gyldendal became independent in 1925. Harald Grieg became managing director, and Francis Bull, who had supported the cause with word and pen, became chairman of the board of directors. A lifelong friendship developed between Grieg and Francis, and seldom has any publishing house enjoyed so magnificent a partnership. At Universitetsgaten 16, next door to the house in which he had been born thirty-eight years earlier, Francis was now on the summit of Norwegian literature's Parnassus. With Grieg, he became a member of the National Theatre's board of directors and so further consolidated his position, which now extended to university, publishing house and theatre.

When Germany occupied Norway in April 1940 the industrious Francis, now fifty-four, was working on the last stages of his splendid *History of World Literature*, which he in fact succeeded in publishing in the following year. On 26 June 1941, however, it was rumoured in Oslo that Francis, Grieg and a third member of the National Theatre's board of directors, the banker Johannes Sejersted Bødtker, had been arrested by the Germans and transported, via a prison cell in Møllegade, to the newly established Grini concentration camp, built around a former women's prison outside Oslo. The three friends had been arrested because of their refusal to accept Nazi interference in the theatre's repertoire. This was seen as an 'act against the State'.

Many fellow countrymen were concerned about what would happen to the refined, cultivated and undeniably somewhat unpractical Francis – prisoner no. 480 – among the SS men at Grini. But there was no cause to worry. Rarely has the Hambros' natural ability to adapt to unaccustomed conditions blossomed more convincingly than during the 1,155 days that Francis was to spend in this grim camp. During Norway's five years of occupation, Grini housed no fewer than 20,000

Francis Bull (1887–1974), son of Edvard Hambro Bull, was influenced from early childhood by his father's association with artists, actors and theatrical personalities. He was Professor of Scandinavian Literature at Oslo University from 1920 to 1957, and as chairman of Gyldendal, Norway's largest publishing house, for forty years he was in contact with all the literary figures in Norway. His broadcast talks after the war made him one of the most popular figures of recent times in Norway. This painting by Per Krogh shows him at the age of sixty, in 1948. Gyldendal Norsk Forlag, Oslo.

rebellious Norwegians from all walks of life, and of all political persua-
sions except national socialism. It was not a very exclusive environment.

The concept may appear grotesque, but there are many who believe
that Francis' three years at Grini came to be one of the most profitable
experiences of his life. To his fellow prisoners he soon became their
untiring, encouraging, optimistic and hopeful colleague. Whatever the
hour, he was as spirited as he had been as a young professor. He gave
lectures, recitals and plays; he was a wandering minstrel moving from
hut to hut. He could spellbind his fellow prisoners for hours, perform-
ing complete plays that he knew by heart. At Grini his legendary
memory was invaluable, for no books were available in the camp. His
greatest achievement was a four-hour performance of *Peer Gynt*, in
which he played all the parts. Whenever Norwegians in their memoirs
recall the occupation and mention Grini, Francis is always a central
figure, and his time in the camp has since been poetically represented as
a modern version of the thousand and one nights. After the liberation of
Norway he repeated from memory on the radio – for which his beautiful
voice was particularly well suited – many of the most popular of the
talks he gave at Grini. They were also published in book form.

Francis retired from his professorship and membership of the
theatre's board of directors in 1957 at the age of seventy. He remained
on the board of Gyldendal, and celebrated forty years with them in
1965. His loyal colleague, Harald Grieg, died in 1972.

Francis died in 1974 aged eighty-seven. His wife survived him by
only two years. There were no children. To Norway, his death represented the loss of one of the great and good old Norwegians from the
distant days before World War II.

The last prominent member of the Norwegian family was the youngest
of Edvard Isach and Marie's four sons. Christian was not the most
colourful of the brothers, but he was probably the most reliable. His
wife, Anne Kristine Bødtker, was the daughter of a Bergen merchant.
They married in 1850, and after he died she made it known that she
would much rather have married Christian's older brother, Johan; she
had always considered him 'the most beautiful person in the world', but
he had preferred her tubercular sister and she had to be content with
Christian, and that 'of course could never be the same'.

Christian took a degree in law in 1851, and joined the Swedish-
Norwegian consular service. He was employed for many years in the
Swedish-Norwegian Ministry of Foreign Affairs in Stockholm. In 1865
the Ministry sent him with his family to Bordeaux for a year to study

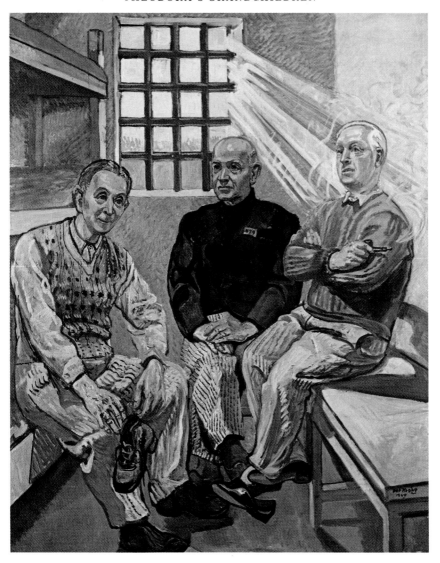

Francis Bull (left) at the Grini prison camp in Norway during the German occupation. He was here for three years and shared the experience with two fellow members of the National Theatre's board: Harald Grieg, its director, and Johannes Sejersted Bødtker, the other two figures in this painting. The three had resisted Nazi pressure upon the National Theatre's repertoire. This picture was painted after the war by Per Krogh, the Norwegian artist, who was also interned at Grini from 1942 onwards. Gyldendal Norsk Forlag, Oslo.

the French consular service. In 1871 he was appointed Swedish-Norwegian vice-consul at Newcastle-upon-Tyne, where he died aged fifty in 1873. Anne Kristine survived him by thirty-six years and brought up the family's two highly intelligent sons, Edvard Isach and Anker.

The elder son, Edvard Isach, became one of Norway's leading lawyers, his special subject being Roman law. He became a high court judge, and many of the finest intellects of the day met in his home. Having no children of his own, he was very hospitable towards young members of the family when they came to Kristiania to study. The president of the Storting, in his memoirs, refers with great respect to his learned, musical and deeply religious uncle. Edvard Isach was foster-father to his wife's nephew, Johannes Sejersted Bødtker, who became well-known as an art collector and banker. In 1931 Edvard Isach and Stine Hambro celebrated their golden wedding with the entire family in their foster-son's large house at Holmenkollen.

The younger brother, Bernt Anker, was just as intelligent as Edvard Isach, and played a prominent and jovial role in the Oslo Students' Association in the 1880s. Bernt Anker had a gift of expression; he was

Young intellectuals in Kristiania, 1887, painted by Edvard Munch. In the centre is Christian Hambro's youngest son, Anker, who died two years later. To the left is the extremist Norwegian author Hans Jæger (1854–1910), whose novel Kristiania-Bohemen *was confiscated in the same year as a scandalous publication. To the right is the author Haakon Nyhus.* Private collection, Norway.

Edward J. Hambro (1851–1936), judge of the Norwegian High Court and jurist, and his cousin and future wife, Stine Bødtker (1856–1937). He was originally a philologist, and for this reason was often confused as a young man with his cousin, the future school principal of Bergen — he therefore changed the spelling of his Christian name to Edward. He graduated in law in 1875, and was a High Court judge from 1910 to 1921. For thirty-five years he was an examiner and lecturer in Roman law at Oslo University. The volume of his legal writings between 1887 and 1924 is so great that it is almost impossible to assess it; half of it concerns Roman law. He is still considered to be one of Norway's great jurists. The couple had no children University Library, Oslo.

musical and a good linguist, speaking fluent German, English, French and Italian. He was a member of Kristiania's bohemian circle, and was painted together with his friend the scandalous author Hans Jæger by Edvard Munch, the circle's famous artist. But his life was to be one of tragedy. As a boy, a shirt button had found its way into his lungs. It always plagued him, and led to his death at the early age of twenty-seven. He took a degree in law in 1887, and enjoyed a brief period in the foreign service at Alexandria. Following periods of convalescence in Italy and Austria occasioned by his damaged lung, he was appointed to a post in Edinburgh, where he died in 1889.

7   The Imperturbable Joseph

Calmer and Thobe's eldest son Joseph has been referred to already, and is one of the most important members of the Hambro family. His brilliant career and patriotic endeavours stemmed from Denmark's difficult financial circumstances following the state bankruptcy in 1813.

Danish history bathes the second half of the eighteenth century in a rosy-glow. Later generations have called the period 'the palmy days of commerce'. Neither before nor since has the country experienced such a great and continuing boom in international trade. During the tremendous conflicts between England and North America and between England and France, Denmark's position as a small, neutral country gave the Copenhagen merchants and shipowners such substantial profits over a period of more than forty years that much of the population was able to share in the benefits. In the 1780s Copenhagen was so affluent that the government had to issue ordinances to restrict luxury.

Names that have left their mark on the period include such merchants as Schimmelmann, de Coninck, Deuntzfeldt, Ryberg, Erich Erichsen and Constantin Brun, names that after two hundred years still conjure up pictures of East Indiamen under full sail, merchants' mansions in Copenhagen, imposing estates in North Zeeland, happiness and pleasure, wit and elegance. The only drawback was that this prosperity lasted so long that it came to be taken for granted, as a way of life that would never end. But the golden age came to an abrupt stop with the turn of the century.

This was the time when Britain could no longer tolerate supplies reaching Napoleon in neutral ships, which were now operating in armed convoys. The attack on Copenhagen by Parker and Nelson in April 1801 was the first warning of harder times to come. The great turning-point came shortly after the introduction of the Continental System. After a three-day bombardment of Copenhagen in September 1807, Britain forced Denmark to hand over the whole of its great battle fleet. This was a national catastrophe that created a hatred of England that was to last for many years.

Much of the flourishing trade that Denmark had enjoyed, and the major part of Danish shipping, had by-passed Copenhagen. Goods

Joseph Hambro (1780–1848), Copenhagen merchant, manufacturer and banker from 1806 to 1848. He probably posed for a portrait only once in his life. The various pictures of him all appear to be copies, of varying merit, of C. A. Jensen's portrait dated 1831, which is reproduced here. It was painted for a circle of friends to celebrate his fiftieth birthday. Although Joseph was never a member of the committee of the Chamber of Commerce, the original hangs today in the conference room of the Copenhagen Bourse, side by side with the greatest names in Danish commerce.

143

The first big assault on Copenhagen by the British was on 2 April 1801, with the aim of forcing Denmark to leave the 'League of Armed Neutrality'. Admirals Parker and Nelson attacked the Danish fleet, but after six hours of fighting the British fleet was in such a sad state that Nelson had to resort to a stratagem. He sent a negotiator ashore with a white flag

were loaded in one foreign country and conveyed to another; only the enormous profits reached Copenhagen. Neutral traffic was now systematically brought to a stop by Britain; Danish merchantmen were seized, their precious cargoes confiscated and their crews interned, exhausting Denmark's reserves. Denmark's exports had always been modest, and before long the great stocks of goods accumulated during the period of plenty had been used up without hope of replenishment.

Economic catastrophe overtook the king and government perhaps even before it was felt by the Danish commercial world. The army permanently stationed on the North German frontier during the last decade of the war against Britain had cost a great deal of money. The

to inform Crown Prince Frederik that if the Danes did not immediately cease fire he would set fire to all the captured Danish block ships, whatever the fate of the crews. The Danish fleet then capitulated. Painting by C. A. Lorentzen, 1801. Frederiksborg Castle.

Treasury was empty and the monetary system disintegrating; silver money now found its way to Hamburg to be replaced for use in Denmark by valueless paper money and poor-quality coins. In 1813 Denmark had no alternative but to declare itself bankrupt. The state bankruptcy, which affected the entire population, is etched vividly on the memory of the nation.

The years immediately following the bankruptcy were, however, by no means the worst. A kind of inertia seemed to keep the country going through 1814 and 1815, but in 1816 a series of business failures began to show how desperate the situation was. Between 1816 and 1821 no fewer than 350 undertakings went to the wall. The list of bankruptcies and suspensions of payments included great commercial houses, merchants and shipowners, as well as small entrepreneurs, artisans and tradesmen. Then, in 1816–17, two catastrophic harvests ruined Danish agriculture, and large farms could be bought at rock-bottom prices. Although their frequency gradually declined, bankruptcies continued until 1835.

In 1813, Frederik VI replaced his minister of finance, Count Ernst Schimmelmann, with the fifty-four-year-old Johan von Møsting, who tackled the seemingly hopeless task with more courage and energy than his capacities had suggested. Treasury funds were by now so low that he had literally to operate on a day-to-day basis. In 1818 it became clear to him that if the country's economy was to be rehabilitated the only solution was to borrow money.

For the last twelve years Denmark had not borrowed abroad. In 1806, the Rothschilds' newly established banking house in Frankfurt had negotiated a loan from their first major customer, the Elector of Hesse. This had been arranged very quietly and smoothly, because the Elector was married to the sister of the Danish King Christian VII. In

Erichsen's mansion at Kongens Nytorv in Copenhagen, built 1799–1802 after the fire. It was located to the right of the Royal Theatre, and was the last of the great merchants' mansions in the capital. Erichsen had planned the magnificent house to please his wife, but she died before it was completed. After Erich Erichsen's final collapse in 1831, the mansion was reduced to the status of a café and later a furniture store. It did not become the head office of Kjøbenhavns Handelsbank until 1888. Anonymous engraving, 1802. Boghallen, Copenhagen.

Erich Erichsen (1752–1837), royal Danish agent, merchant and shipowner. In about 1800 he was Denmark's largest private shipowner, with a fleet of thirty ships. At the time of the state bankruptcy of 1813 he was still able to make very substantial loans to finance ministers Schimmelmann and Møsting, although at that time banking was outside his activities. He had to throw in his hand, as the British were requisitioning more and more of his ships. From 1824 onwards, his increasing difficulties gave Joseph Hambro his great opportunity. Painting by F. G. Gröger, c. 1800. Royal Library, Copenhagen.

other deals, support had come mainly from various merchant houses in Hamburg and Amsterdam.

By 1818 the only member of the distinguished old band of great merchants and shipowners from whom Møsting might expect help was the ageing Erich Erichsen. His cash assets were still substantial, but his merchant fleet had been systematically reduced by the British until Napoleon's final defeat at Waterloo. The only other source of borrowing lay in a number of able Jewish merchants who had established themselves in Copenhagen from the turn of the century onwards. These men with their solid international family and business relationships were able to assist the hard-pressed minister of finance not only by collecting Denmark's debts abroad – they were also in a position to arrange government loans. Smaller loans could be provided in cash, and larger loans by the issue of government bonds, the rate being adjusted to the interest payments, the length of the loan, the borrower's domestic creditworthiness and the security offered.

Even in the years before the state bankruptcy, finance minister Schimmelmann had leaned heavily on wise old David Amsel Meyer, who had been the proprietor of Meyer & Trier, foremost of the great Jewish business houses of Copenhagen. Meyer had been made a privy counsellor by a grateful king in 1812, but had died in 1813. His nephew, the talented Mendel Levin Nathanson, had inherited the business, and by 1821 was acknowledged as one of the most distinguished members of the Copenhagen Stock Exchange. Men like Ruben Henriques were also useful in raising money for the country. Last, but by no means least, there was of course Joseph Hambro. When the worst was over, it was clear that he was the only member of this group to escape unscathed from the vicious financial whirlpool.

The good times had left a few lasting benefits. The bigoted, unenlightened mentality of previous days had gone. The 1780s and 1790s had seen the emergence of a humanism that left its mark in reforming legislation, liberating the country's peasants and abolishing the old, barbaric concepts of justice. This wave of humanism also gradually improved the lot of Danish Jews, although they amounted to no more than two per cent of the population and lived mostly in Copenhagen. From the 1790s onwards the Jews began moving towards legal equality with other citizens. They had the wholehearted support of Frederik VI, who wanted to see the talented Jewish minority integrated into the Danish population. His 1814 legislation on the legal status of Danish Jews was unique in Europe. But although it pleased liberal Jews it greatly worried the old orthodox members of the Jewish community, who of course had reason to fear that their consciously isolated society would now be threatened by defection and disintegration. They foresaw that the legal requirement for Jews in future to be subject to Danish civil law, Danish naming practices, Danish education and other matters would have catastrophic consequences for the Council of Elders' hitherto indisputable and supreme authority.

In about 1800 the Free City of Hamburg, with its individualistic form of self-government, was a wonderful city for a future merchant, for it was a city on the move. As Germany's most important port, at the mouth of one of Europe's largest rivers, Hamburg was an ideal base for numerous merchants engaged in exporting goods from all over Germany. It had good connections with London, Amsterdam and the rest of the world, from which it received a corresponding volume of imports.

Until 1815 Hamburg was a very picturesque town still surrounded by ramparts. With Altona as its neighbour, the town boasted its famous Elbchaussee facing towards Blankenesse, where the rich Hamburg merchants built their grand summer residences with great gardens and parks sloping towards the river. Hamburg was some distance up the estuary, a situation which protected it from the North Sea and allowed it to use the tide for local transport along its many canals.

Hamburg was larger than Copenhagen, and came out of the Revolutionary Wars in a better state than the Danish capital. There could be no better place for a future merchant to serve his apprenticeship;

Until 1815, when the ramparts were demolished, Hamburg was a very picturesque city. Northwards, the fortifications ran across the Alster lake, dividing the Binnen-Alster from the Aussen-Alster. Until 1865 this old windmill stood on the Lombard bridge beside the lake. Coloured etching by Friedrich Rosenberg, 1796. Staatsarchiv, Hamburg.

North of Hamburg on the large Aussen-Alster lake lay one of the city's favourite places for excursions by rowing boat, and the 'Alter Rabe' inn. Coloured etching by Friedrich Rosenberg, 1807. Staatsarchiv, Hamburg.

Hamburg's role in all forms of trade was growing, and its greatest merchants – relatively few of whom were Jewish – soon came to play a major role as bankers to an impoverished Denmark.

Joseph's years of apprenticeship in Hamburg, 1797–1800, set a stamp on him that lasted throughout his life. His father's brother, Mathias Levy, hospitably opened his lavish home to him, and Joseph's own employer, Martin Joseph Haller of the great Jewish trading house of Fürst, Haller & Co., proved an inspiring teacher once he recognized the outstanding abilities of his young Danish apprentice. Joseph had no language problems – as a child he had always spoken German with his parents. He quickly became a great admirer of the Hamburg merchant class, who kept their word and displayed a high standard of business ethics. Their most notable representatives were not only rich, but also highly educated and cultured. Martin Joseph Haller, for instance, was a distinguished art collector.

Nevertheless, Joseph was amused to see how readily a merchant could become narrow-minded and petty, and was determined not to go this way himself. He was only seventeen when he arrived in Hamburg,

Like the Copenhagen Bourse, the old Hamburg Bourse had been built originally as a commodity exchange, and was situated directly on the broad Bourse Canal so that goods could be easily unloaded. This was the picturesque view of the old Bourse from the canal during the years Joseph was in Hamburg. In the background is the old Town Hall. The whole of this part of the town was destroyed in the fire of 1842. Anonymous drawing, 1825. Victoria and Albert Museum, London.

Martin Joseph Haller (1770–1852), the Jewish merchant and banker, was junior manager at Fürst, Haller & Co. of Hamburg and Joseph's mentor in 1799 and 1800. Haller was a highly cultivated man of broad vision, and represented a type of banker unknown to Joseph in Copenhagen. Lithograph by Kitzerow, c. 1830. Staatsarchiv, Hamburg.

fresh from his father's small shop in Copenhagen, but when he returned to Denmark at the age of twenty, equipped with a little working capital from Haller and with good offers of credit from Uncle Mathias, he was already a fully-fledged international merchant, behaving and dressing like a gentleman. His appreciation of art had also developed. As his uncle said, he was beyond the stage of believing 'that true art is to be found only in the royal profiles on silver coinage. Art for 3 marks, 12 pfennigs'.

Joseph's best friend during his early years in Copenhagen was a stockbroker, Ruben Henriques, nine years older than himself. Ruben preferred to call himself R. Henriques jun., since his father's name was also Ruben. In 1801, Henriques had opened the first true stockbroking business in Copenhagen at Amagertorv. This tall and dignified man was of Portuguese origin, and therefore a member of the capital's small, privileged, Jewish upper class, with its own synagogue. Ruben traded in currency and precious stones.

In the course of time Ruben became a well-known figure in Copenhagen. His wife produced no fewer than ten sons, and it was an impressive sight each Saturday when the family set off in procession for the synagogue at Christianshavn. Ruben and his progeny created a dynasty with great powers of survival. In 1976 the stockbroking firm of

*Ruben Henriques Junior (1771–1846),
a Copenhagen bill-broker of Portu-
guese-Jewish origin. In 1801, he became
the first man in Denmark to direct his
business entirely towards trading in currency and precious stones. Each week he
changed the Øresund duty's foreign currency into Danish money for the account
of the government. The Henriques family records describe Joseph Hambro as
the best friend of his childhood years.
Henriques Junior celebrated its 175th
anniversary in 1976 under the management of the family's sixth generation, the
cousins Henrik and Leif Henriques. It is
today Denmark's oldest finance house,
and still plays an active part in the large
bond issues made by Danish banks.
Painting, 1820, by Sally Henriques –
one of Ruben's ten sons.* Henriques
Junior Collection.

R. Henriques jun. celebrated its 175th anniversary in a building not a
stone's throw from its original address, and it is still operating as a
private firm on an equal footing with the great Danish commercial
banks in the floating of Danish government loans. The sixth generation
of Joseph's and Ruben's descendants still maintain both business and
social relationships. Joseph's years in Hamburg had taught him that it
could be just as exciting and very much more profitable to deal in
money as in wool and silk. His friend's lifestyle confirmed this, and even
before his father's death Joseph began to accept and discount his
Jewish colleagues' bills on foreign countries.

On 12 January 1807, soon after his father's death, he married
twenty-one-year-old Mirjam von Halle. In keeping with his long-
standing wish to isolate himself from all that was ultra-Jewish, he

---

*No regular banks were established in Copenhagen until the middle of the nineteenth century.
During the first half of the century all international money transactions were still handled by
private brokers or bankers, who accepted and discounted both commercial bills and foreign
debts of the government. Since such monetary transactions called for reliable international
connections, and were also activities for which Jews did not need a licence, this form of
commerce often became a profitable sideline, and was carried on by many Jewish merchant
houses in Copenhagen. This picture is of the Henriques broking premises at Amagertorv, in
the old Renaissance house which is today the Royal Copenhagen China Factory's shop.
Painting by Sally Henriques, c. 1815.* R. Henriques Junior Collection.

preferred to call her Marianne. She was the daughter of Wulf Levin von Halle, who had established himself as a merchant in Copenhagen in 1779 (the same year as Joseph's father) and was now acting as a billbroker at Amagertorv, just opposite Ruben Henriques. Von Halle was the son of an immigrant gold wire drawer from the German town of Halle. A younger brother had inherited the gold wire business in Købmagergade. Marianne's mother, Priwche von Halle, died shortly after her daughter's marriage. She was born a Goldschmidt from Altona, and was a cousin of Salomon Heine, who later became a great Hamburg banker. Marianne was second cousin to the famous German poet Heinrich Heine.

Joseph had been captivated by Marianne's beauty, her melancholy smile and her gentle, rather helpless, nature. A certain disposition towards ill-health in the Halle family did not deter him. Marianne's elder brother had been very frail and had died young; another brother appeared to suffer from *dementia praecox*, and died early in a mysterious fire.

Ten months after the marriage Marianne gave birth to her only child, a son. Two months earlier she had lived through three terrible nights at their home in Købmagergade – British fire bombs had fallen close to the centre of Copenhagen, and on the third night had set fire to the Church of Our Lady. It was on this occasion that Joseph first realized the nervous and uncontrollable nature of Marianne's temperament. No details exist of Marianne's mental deterioration over the following years. At that time people were reluctant to speak of mental illness, but Marianne was to reveal such a lack of mental balance that, after seven years, Joseph could no longer allow her to care for the little boy. He had been named after his grandfather, Calmer Joachim, but Joseph preferred the Danish form and called him Carl Joachim. Marianne's mental condition was to be Joseph's private sorrow for the next thirty-one years. He never referred to her, and none of his contemporaries had a single word to say of her. His marriage left him a very lonely man, and Marianne's illness gave rise to problems in Carl Joachim's upbringing, not least because it soon became apparent that the son had inherited some degree of his mother's depressive disposition.

To counterbalance this, Joseph applied himself to his business with great enthusiasm. The following story, dating from 1808, the year after Carl Joachim's birth, says something about his precocious commercial talent.

The insane Christian VII died at last in 1808. He had been married to the now long dead Queen Caroline Mathilde, King George III of

*The second and more violent British attack on Copenhagen lasted 'three terrible nights',
from 2 to 4 September 1807. The object of this attack was to force Denmark to hand over its
navy – Scandinavia's largest – so that it should not fall into Napoleon's hands. On this
occasion British troops landed, and surrounded and bombarded the city with incendiary
shells. The British troops were commanded by Sir Arthur Wellesley, later Duke of
Wellington, who acquired at this time the Danish mare that was the dam of Copenhagen,
which carried him at Waterloo. Copenhagen's landmark, the spire of the Church of Our
Lady, had been chosen as a target. When, on the third night, the spire was set on fire and
collapsed, the city capitulated. The entire Danish navy was sailed away to England.
Coloured engraving by G. F. Lahde, 1808.* Royal Library, Copenhagen.

Mendel Levin Nathanson (1780–1864), was a merchant and banker, Jewish reformer and later writer on political economy. The same age as Joseph, he arrived in Copenhagen as a poor ten-year-old boy. At the age of fifteen he spoke fluent Danish and excellent German and French. He was later employed by his uncle, David Amsel Meyer, and in 1806 he became his uncle's partner in the commercial house of Meyer & Trier, which enjoyed the special favour of Frederik VI. Meyer died in 1813, and in 1820 Nathanson had to suspend payments. The firm eventually went into liquidation in 1831. Until then he had been one of Joseph's keenest competitors. Nathanson was far more exuberant, warm and extrovert than Joseph. During his most successful years he did much to provide education and culture for Copenhagen's Jewish community. Painting by J. V. Gertner.

England's exiled sister. His contact with the world around him had been minimal, and during the British bombardment of Copenhagen in 1807 his son, Frederik VI, who had in practice ruled the country since 1784, arranged for his unfortunate father to be moved to safety at Rendsburg in the duchy of Schleswig.

The royal courier took nearly three days to bring the unmomentous tidings of the king's death to Copenhagen. The Danish court spent a further two days drafting a suitable public announcement, with comprehensive rules for the national mourning that would have to be observed by the capital's upper class. In reality there was little to mourn about. Directly he had delivered his message to the court, the courier, on the instructions of the Hambro relatives in Rendsburg, discreetly informed Joseph of the news. He acted immediately. Over the next thirty-six hours he bought up every piece of black cloth and every scrap of black silk in the entire capital. When, next day, the newspapers announced the death, Joseph was the only trader who could supply mourning material of any reasonable quality. In the days that followed, the city's most exclusive citizens queued outside his shop, and Joseph became known as Copenhagen's leading general clothier.

In addition to running the day-to-day affairs of the shop and making a beginning in billbroking, over the next few years Joseph often speculated successfully in currency, earning substantial profits for himself. Given the continually decreasing value of money, he immediately re-invested his money in goods. His interests were soon no longer confined to cloth. Even before 1817 he was trading on a large scale in almost any goods that he considered a good investment. After the end of the Napoleonic Wars in 1815 he specialized in spices and sugar from the Danish Virgin Islands, and later in wool from Manchester, but soon there was scarcely any merchandise in demand in which he did not trade. With foresight and caution he navigated so successfully against the current that when the great bankruptcies began in 1818–19 his wealth continued to grow. By 1815 he was already considered one of the city's wealthiest men, although his international role as government adviser had not yet commenced.

In 1812 he had taken into his business Georg Gerson, ten years his junior. Gerson was the son of a wealthy Jewish broker, and a more unlikely businessman it is hard to imagine. His training had been precisely the same as Joseph's at Fürst, Haller & Co. of Hamburg, but he had divided his time there between business and music lessons; as a boy he had shown quite an extraordinary talent as a violinist. Although his tragically short life left him only thirteen years of co-operation with Joseph, in that time he earned a great reputation as a banker. During

David Amsel Meyer (1755–1813). Through his firm, Meyer & Trier, he was the first Jewish businessman in Copenhagen to work his way up to a semi-official position, becoming Frederik VI's financial adviser in the years preceding the state bankruptcy of 1813. In return, he was unjustly blamed for the Danish economy's catastrophic course during the subsequent years. In 1812 – the year before his death – Frederik VI made him a privy counsellor. Meyer was also an extremely devout and modest man. He distributed widespread charity among the Jewish community, where he enjoyed great respect as a member of the Council of Elders. Relief in the Mosaic School, Copenhagen.

Georg Gerson (1790–1825), banker, violinist and composer, was the son of a wealthy Copenhagen Jewish broker. He trained in Hamburg with Fürst and Haller, 1805–12, but divided his time equally between banking and music. He was employed by Joseph Hambro in 1812, and made his partner in 1816 because of his unique commercial talent and unusual charm. In 1821, simultaneously with Joseph, he was appointed privy counsellor by Frederik VI as a reward for his London endeavours that year in negotiating the Goldschmidt-Haldemann loan. He was one of Copenhagen's most outstanding quartet musicians. He died aged thirty-five after only four months of marriage. Miniature by Christian Hornemann, 1830.

this period he became a leading light in Copenhagen's musical life, and was a prolific composer. Joseph considered him the ablest and most inspiring of his partners. Gerson was the only person who could divert Joseph in his growing loneliness, and in 1816 Joseph made him his partner.

The business soon began to outgrow the shop in Købmagergade. By 1814, Joseph gave up his retail business and moved to a large house at Gl. Strand. His sights were set on the last of the great merchants of the golden days, royal agent Eric Erichsen. In 1817 he sold the house at Gl. Strand to his brother Simon and moved into Copenhagen's most fashionable square, Kongens Nytorv, where he bought an elegant old baroque house only a few hundred yards from Erich Erichsen's imposing mansion. His aim now was to test his strength against the old shipowner, who at that time still had his affairs well under control.

The banking business was now by far the predominant activity, and Joseph established it on the ground floor of the spacious house, creating an elegant home for himself on the first floor. The top of the house was servants' quarters. It was all as well appointed as could be wished, apart from the absence of a lady of the house; there never would be one.

Entering through the great gate, the visitor found himself in a paved courtyard, with a fountain in front of the side wing. Here in the coach-house were Joseph's carriages and his indispensable travelling coach, and beside it the stables. Behind this was yet another courtyard,

The old patrician house at Kongens Nytorv 2, which Joseph acquired in 1817 when he was forced to put Carl Joachim into the care of Professor Reinhardt. His unhappy wife Marianne was then being cared for in Roskilde. His offices were in the lofty ground floor; he himself lived on the first floor, with a large drawing-room behind the four centre windows. Painting, c. 1740, by Rach and Egeberg. National Museum, Copenhagen.

Kongens Nytorv had already become Copenhagen's largest and most exclusive square by about 1700. In this picture the Square is seen from the north, with the Academy of Arts to the left. Then come Harsdorff's mansion and the ordnance foundry, and the Royal Theatre

with extensive warehouses, to which there was also access from one of the side streets leading into the square.

It was Joseph's interest in combining his commercial activities with insurance that brought him to England for the first time in 1815. Such a journey would of course have been unthinkable before the battle of Waterloo in that year, which put an end to the long period of war. Joseph's intention was to learn something of England, and to see whether it could offer goods for him to import at a profit. He also wanted to identify trading houses for future business relationships, so that he might represent them as a banker in Denmark. Finally, he was

which was replaced by the present theatre in 1872. The tall, dark building immediately to the left of Christian V's equestrian statue was C. J. Hambro and Son's Copenhagen premises from 1817 until 1848. Coloured lithograph from P. G. Philipson, c. 1845.

very anxious to become the Danish agent of the already world-famous collective insurance company, Lloyds.

Now that insurance has developed into a specialized form of business, it may appear surprising that Joseph should consider it a suitable new venture for his firm, but at that time British insurance, particularly through Lloyds, was a typical speculative transaction for a merchant. It was common then to give quotations for insurance on offer, accepting the attendant risk of loss or gain. Denmark had a few old licensed insurance companies covering real estate, established in the wake of the Copenhagen fires of 1728 and 1795, but personal property, transport

Count Ernst Schimmelmann (1747–1831), finance minister of Denmark and plantation owner in the Danish Virgin Islands. Although he was already an experienced civil servant when he became minister of finance in 1786, he was forced to recognize in the early 1800s that the Danish economy was about to come to a halt. Between 1810 and 1812 he was in day-to-day contact with the Copenhagen bill-brokers, trying by all conceivable forms of loan to prevent the state going bankrupt. In about 1812 Joseph implemented through him his first minor transactions for the Danish government. Painting by C. A. Jensen. Frederiksborg Museum.

and life insurance were still quite undeveloped. Strangely enough, Danish legislation allowed foreign companies to operate in Denmark. By 1816 he had succeeded in landing the Lloyds' agency in Copenhagen, which provided him with an early and close relationship with England. He also contacted various trading companies, including Adolf Goldschmidt & Co., whose proprietor came from the same Altona family as Marianne's mother. As years went by, Joseph set increasing store by this trade with London, and he probably realized that it might be an advantage to have London as an alternative to Hamburg. He later saw confirmation of his own early perception of the profits to be made in insurance when Nathan Rothschild established his own insurance company in London.

It had been clear to Joseph since 1814 that Marianne's depressions had now reached such unpredictable proportions that it was no longer acceptable for her to have charge of the seven-year-old Carl Joachim. Indeed, it was probably no longer possible for her to live much longer in the family home. After long reflection, Joseph took two difficult decisions that affected the rest of his lonely life and had far-reaching consequences for all his family. First he put Carl Joachim into the care of a family previously unknown to him, and then a few years later he was forced to realize that he could no longer keep Marianne at home, since she now needed constant supervision.

Johan Sigismund von Møsting (1759–1843), privy minister of state to Frederik VI *and Schimmelmann's successor as minister of finance following the state bankruptcy in 1813. The task was almost hopeless, but he tried with honesty and industry to reorganize the monetary system, and during the early years he had more success than had been expected. The king had endless confidence in him, and when Møsting proposed commissioning C. J. Hambro & Son with the large new government loan Joseph's popularity with the king was established. Painting by C. A. Jensen, 1830.* Frederiksborg Museum.

His choice of foster-parents for Carl Joachim demonstrated the complexity of his character and his practical approach to life. He himself no longer lived as an orthodox Jew; he ate what he liked, and he had not said his daily prayers for many years. Nevertheless, he would never for a moment have considered formally deserting the faith of his fathers; he was too proud to do that. The Copenhagen Jewish community looked upon him as one of its most influential members and he wanted to preserve this position until the end. But, on the other hand, he had no wish for Carl Joachim to inherit all the problems of Jews, and he therefore chose a Christian couple to be his foster-parents. He hoped in this way to create a more harmonious future for the boy, although he fully realized that this arragement would involve a great risk of estrangement between father and son.

On Joseph's behalf an acquaintance contacted a Norwegian-born zoologist, Johannes Reinhardt, who is remembered as the founder of the Danish Zoological Museum. In 1814 Reinhardt was about to marry Nicoline Hammeleff, to whom he had been engaged for seven years – because Reinhardt had studied theology for several years before becoming a zoologist they had not been able to afford to marry. In his youth, Reinhardt had spent five years as tutor to the son of a rich merchant, Constantin Brun, and he had lived abroad with the son and Brun's eccentric wife Frederikke, who is well-known in the history of Danish art and literature. It was in the Brun's house that Reinhardt had met Nicoline. In 1814 he was curator of the Royal Natural History Collection in Copenhagen and he had just been appointed professor extraordinary of zoology at Copenhagen University. Here, his salary of under £50 a year would be just enough for them to marry. Joseph informed Reinhardt, through his negotiator, that he was prepared to pay him £50 a year if he would take Carl Joachim into his home.

Their daughter, Mathilde Reinhardt, quotes in her memoirs an enchanting letter written by Reinhardt in the summer of 1814 to Nicoline at Sophienholm, the Bruns' country house. Reinhardt was not on holiday with the others but working in Copenhagen.

Sweet Nicoline, To come straight to the point, your cousin Bang came to see me yesterday morning to suggest that, as soon as we are married, you and I should immediately take a nice little seven-year-old boy into our home. But the boy is – I must say this straight out – from a Jewish family! His parents live in this town, and are among the most respected and liberal of Jews. Incidentally, the boy is said to be very pleasant indeed. The father has refused to employ even the most capable of tutors because he fears the boy will be spoilt by his mother. Very sensible! The boy would stay with us during the week and be allowed home on Sundays only, if this suits us. Such a little boarder would be a great tie to us, and rob us of much freedom and of opportunities for visits to the country. Much of our social life would have to be dropped, because it would not accord with our obligations towards the boy. The proposed payment of £50 is more than my entire present salary!

I am most apprehensive of our great responsibility for the boy's physical and moral development. This will call for a lot of love! I shall first have to see him and his parents. If I don't like them it would be wrong to accept. Unless I feel an interest in him I can do nothing.

But now I must get down to names: it is Joseph Hambro who makes this splendid proposal. Bang adds that Hambro is very liberal in his views, and that if we agree we shall never have reason to regret it. He knows we are about to marry and set up house, and he therefore offers to pay us in advance for the first year. Of course, I don't want to get involved in this, but I have promised Bang not to reject the proposal out-of-hand.

I shall not answer until I know your views. We shall of course be able to marry and set up house even without the £50.

Farewell, my dearest girl.

Reinhardt.

Nicoline replied encouragingly and immediately. The meeting with Joseph must have been a success, for when Reinhardt married Nicoline on 14 January 1815 Carl Joachim moved directly into the beautiful and elegant apartment in Dronningens Tværgade which Reinhardt was now able to rent. Joseph had agreed from the outset that Carl Joachim should attend an ordinary school, and he had no objection to his participating in the school's religious instruction.

Reinhardt and Nicoline were both in their thirties, and the fear that

The newly-married Professor Johan Reinhardt was, thanks to Joseph Hambro's princely payment to him as Carl Joachim's foster-father, able to live in exclusive Dronningens Tværgade close to Kongens Nytorv. The street led directly to minister of finance Ernst Schimmelmann's fine mansion in Bredgade. Drawing by H. G. F. Holm, c. 1840.
Copenhagen City Museum.

they might have no children of their own contributed to their decision to take Carl Joachim into their home. But they need not have worried; in the years that followed Nicoline herself gave birth to four children, who were brought up as Carl Joachim's foster-brothers and foster-sisters. During the early years Joseph often arrived in his carriage on Sundays to take the whole family for a picnic, and in the course of time he became an honoured guest at the Reinhardts. Mathilde Reinhardt wrote that Carl Joachim 'soon proved to be what Hambro had promised: a good little boy, although somewhat spoilt', and added a comment that later proved to be correct: 'He is by nature both melancholy and happy.' Finally she noted: 'With child-like love he became attached to his foster-parents, and he was increasingly influenced by them over the years.'

8 The Government Adviser

Before 1818 Joseph Hambro occasionally assisted finance ministers Schimmelmann and Møsting by collecting foreign debts or negotiating the government's large billbroking transactions. This had of course proved profitable, but he had never had a hand in large government loans – no foreign loans had been raised since the first Rothschild loan of 1806.

Joseph's opportunity came in 1818, when Møsting saw no way out of his difficulties except by taking out a small loan. The finance minister at first asked Joseph to raise quite a modest, but urgent, loan of £30,000 to assist the hard-pressed Danish agricultural industry. The intention was that he and Møsting should then prepare a joint plan to raise a £300,000 loan in 1819. Joseph had no difficulty in negotiating the £30,000 loan in England, which thus entered the picture for the first time. He aimed to use his new British connections when the tenfold loan came to be raised in 1819.

In spite of Møsting's confidence, however, and great sympathy from the chairman of the National Debt Commission, Nicolai von Holten, later to become one of Joseph's most faithful friends and his spiritual adviser, the National Debt Commission was so apprehensive at the size and cost of the loan that the government backed out at the last minute, leaving it to M. L. Nathanson of Meyer & Trier to carry out the negotiations.

This unexpected development was of course a blow to Joseph. His first great opportunity had slipped away at the last moment, but he put a brave face on it. M. L. Nathanson was the jolly, extrovert, spokesman of liberal Danish Jews, and Joseph admired him in many respects, but he knew that Nathanson's position was weak, and that he had probably won the contract by desperate underbidding, which might be expensive for him in the long run.

Nathanson negotiated this transaction in association with the Hamburg firm of Ree, Heckscher & Co., who were the main source of finance, but nevertheless the outcome was as Joseph had expected. Nathanson, speculating far too boldly, fell victim to the violent currency fluctuations of 1819–20, and by 28 July 1820 he had to cease payments. His situation was appalling. His liabilities were estimated at

Christian IV's Copenhagen Bourse, with the dragon spire near the city's port. It was built in the 1620s, and had served originally as a corn exchange, with stocks of grain in all the attics. To unload their cargoes, ships were able to sail right up to the building along the canals on both sides. The ground floor later housed numerous traders' shops. The Bourse became the stronghold of Copenhagen wholesalers and insurance brokers when the shops moved into the town. Later, the stock exchange Bourse also moved into the centre. Joseph was given his wholesaler's licence in 1812, and he came here every day to collect information and to conclude deals. The Bourse retained this central role in Danish commercial life until World War II. It is now the headquarters of the Chamber of Commerce. Coloured lithograph from P. G. Philipson's Publishing House, Copenhagen, about 1845.

£500,000, of which no more than 30 per cent was covered. Both the Treasury and the National Bank suffered losses, but the major losers were Ree and other business houses in Hamburg and Altona. The bankruptcy shook Denmark's general credit rating abroad. Nathanson himself later tried to make a comeback, but in 1831 his business foundered for a second time and then ceased for good.

Early in September 1819 some unpleasant anti-Semitic riots took place. This episode was in such sharp contrast to Frederick VI's humane 1814 legislation concerning the Jews that it had far-reaching consequences

Saturday, 4 September 1819; the prelude to the week-long Persecution of the Jews in Copenhagen. A section of dragoons attacks the crowd in Østergade after a group of anti-semitic provocateurs had smashed the windows of the Brothers Raphael's elegant boutique. One of the two owners of the shop, Lazarus Raphael, had been the husband of Zipora Hambro, but they divorced in 1805. Book illustration by Knud Gamborg.

on the attitude towards Christianity of many cultivated and emancipated Danish Jews. The Hambro family was especially affected.

The 1819 persecution of the Jews is the only 'popular' anti-Semitic demonstration ever to have occurred in Denmark, and it has never been clear who engineered it. Similar disturbances had occurred the year before in many German towns, and the immediate reaction is to view the Danish demonstrations as part of an epidemic. A debate on the Jews in a literary journal a few years earlier may have engendered anti-Semitic attitudes, but the 1819 disturbances in Copenhagen were in fact no more than mob violence, with no intellectual basis whatsoever. The strongest impulse probably came from the continuing fall in the value of money since the state bankruptcy six years earlier. At all events this affected everyone, and the seed of rumour that the city's Jewish stockbrokers were responsible fell on good ground. Nevertheless, the police should not have been taken so completely by surprise.

On 2 September anonymous posters appeared outside the Stock Exchange demanding that on the following Saturday, the fourth, the leading Jewish shops in Copenhagen's exclusive shopping street Østergade, should be destroyed, and that the city's Jews should be attacked in Rosenborg Slotshave, where they always met and strolled together on the Sabbath. It should be added, however, that the chief constable was unusually inefficient, and had taken little notice of the posters. In

Sunday, 5 September 1819; the second day of the Persecution of the Jews. A section of dragoons chases the Copenhagen mob away from Østergade and pursues it down Admiralgade past the ruins of Nicolai church. In the foreground, soldiers of the city's Civic Guard protect an old Jew. Book illustration by Knud Gamborg.

the event, nothing occurred in the Slotshave, for the Jews had warned one another, but in Østergade a large, noisy mob appeared on Saturday evening and quickly put the chief constable's few policemen to flight.

The Raphael brothers' shop at Østergade 67 was the mob's first target. Here Lazarus Raphael (whom Zipora had long since divorced) and his brother Joseph had established the city's most elegant milliners, with plate-glass windows and mahogany fittings, and the firm's name displayed in gilt letters; indeed, shortly before, these very shop fittings had been hailed in Copenhagen as a sensational innovation. All the glass was smashed with cobblestones, and the mob moved on to destroy the remaining but less prominent Jewish shops in the street. The police lost no time in summoning soldiers from the city's main guard at Kongens Nytorv, but they could send no more than a paltry section of six men. Only when a regiment of dragoons appeared was it possible to break up the mob. There were no arrests on the first evening, and the few ringleaders the police and soldiers seized were soon freed by the mob.

Next day the uproar continued in Østergade. Once again, only the military could clear the street, and the mob moved off to parts of the city where Jews lived. Here, as before, all the windows were broken. In Gothersgade a butcher – later arrested – burst through a Jewish stockbroker's door and forced his way into the house, an excited mob at his heels. Once inside, they smashed all the Jew's possessions, shouting 'We have come to get our money.' However, the owner had wisely left his house early that morning.

Monday was relatively quiet, and on Tuesday Frederik vi issued a proclamation, scathingly informing the population of his indignation at the disturbances and of his intention to act with severity if there was any repetition. It was generally expected that the city would now calm down, but this was not to be. All Copenhagen's rowdies and troublemakers were now collaborating, and the mob was flexing its muscles. The next target – which had in the meantime been strongly fortified – was David Amsel Meyer's large establishment at Frederiksholms Kanal 6, where the billbroking firm of Meyer & Trier had its premises. David Meyer had already died, but as Frederik vi's economic adviser during the years leading up to the state bankruptcy the population had selected him – with no justification whatsoever – as the main culprit responsible for the collapse of the Danish monetary system. When in 1812, Frederik vi honoured him with the title of privy counsellor – the first of its kind in Denmark – the old gentleman had replied that such a title could only bring him bad luck. Fortunately for him, he died a year later and did not see his fears fulfilled.

Tuesday 7 September; the fourth day of the Persecution of the Jews. A group of demonstrators on their way through Rådhusstrade to plunder Meyer & Trier's banking house is overtaken by the dragoons. There were no deaths among Jews, demonstrators or soldiers during the week of daily riots, but thirty-two of the demonstrators arrested were sentenced to up to three years' imprisonment. The actual instigators were never found. Watercolour by Peder Klæstrup. Queen's Library, Copenhagen.

On Tuesday 7 September the mob reached David Meyer's house, then occupied by his nephew and successor, M. L. Nathanson. The mob was unlucky in not knowing how little there was to plunder there. Nathanson himself came to no harm – the only casualty was his canary, which was killed when the windows were broken. The dragoons and the Civic Guard were able to prevent large-scale destruction.

Nevertheless the unrest in the city was not yet over, and disturbances flared up at intervals during the following week. Danish diarists of the time wrote of the anger of Copenhagen's leading social circles at the riots, and of how Christian homes willingly opened their doors to Jewish friends who dared not live at home during these troubled days.

The police and the military gradually gained in experience, treating the troublemakers more harshly, and a number of agitators were arrested. These were exclusively artisans, apprentices, sailors, discharged soldiers and common marauders. A few of them were women. Of those arrested between 13 September and 5 October, 32 were sentenced by the military court. The verdicts, against which there was no appeal, were severe. The butcher was sentenced to three years' hard labour, and five others were imprisoned for between one and three years. The remainder were given a bread-and-water diet for up to six weeks.

Joseph's elegant house at Kongens Nytorv was in fact just outside the battle zone, although it was no more than three minutes' walk from Raphael's Østergade shop. No windows were therefore broken in his house, but his brother Simon, who lived at Gammel Strand, had several windows broken in the large, eight-windowed house he had bought from Joseph two years earlier. Zipora was now the wife of a Christian solicitor, and so came to no harm, but her divorced husband's experience undoubtedly disturbed the entire family. Lazarus Raphael had suffered particularly severely; on the third 'quiet' day of the riots he had optimistically fitted new plate glass to his shop, only to see it immediately smashed again.

It was probably at this time that Simon Hambro decided that he, his wife and especially his four young daughters should become baptized. The persecution also persuaded Zipora to arrange for her three children by her deceased husband, Wulf Marcus Wulf, to be baptized and their surname changed from Wulf to Wulf-Borup. It may also have been during these restless days that the taciturn Joseph finally decided that his only son should be baptized and confirmed in autumn 1822.

As for Joseph, it was typical of him that, of the four brothers and sisters, it was only he who never considered baptism. He was no longer a practising Jew, but his personal pride prevented him from allowing anyone to dictate what he should believe and think. In any case, it suited him that the Copenhagen Jewish community should consider him one of their greatest benefactors. He had now reached a common position for successful Jews at the time; his wealth and international outlook had estranged him from the narrow, orthodox, Jewish way of life, but on the other hand he would not allow anyone to force him to turn his back on it.

In 1821, the year after Nathanson's bankruptcy, finance minister Møsting was again in need of money. At this time the Treasury was emptying as fast as loans were negotiated to replenish it. To convert older expensive loans, once again he needed £3,000,000, the first half as soon as possible and the other half in 1825.

This time Joseph was given the assignment, with no competition, but the money market was now tighter, and after Nathanson's bankruptcy Hamburg was out of the running as a source of money. Joseph instead went to London to negotiate with the British firm of Adolf Goldschmidt & Co., which, because of the size of the loan, allied itself with Halde-

Everyday scene before the main entrance to the Copenhagen Bourse in the 1830s. Everyone was allowed on the floor of the Bourse, although, strictly, it was necessary to be accepted as a wholesaler. It is scarcely coincidental that the artist has placed on the right of the picture a couple of Jewish merchants in heated conversation. Throughout the nineteenth century the Jewish element in the life of the Danish Bourse was very marked. Coloured drawing by Peder Klæstrup. Queen's Library, Copenhagen.

mann & Son. For the first time Joseph learnt that an unknown banker who wanted to enlist the aid of other firms in a loan was expected to show his own confidence by taking a share himself. Of the £1,500,000 comprising the first half of the loan, the two English companies sub-scribed £550,000 each, leaving Joseph to subscribe only £400,000. Nevertheless it was an expensive loan for Denmark. Although interest was normally only 4 per cent, the British demanded that it should be set at 5 per cent, and although at a rate of 5 per cent the issue price should normally have been close to par it was fixed at only 75. Moreover, there were exceptionally high expenses. It was therefore clear that, of the nominal £1,500,000, only just over £1,000,000 would reach the Treas-ury, equivalent in fact to a loan at $7\frac{1}{2}$ per cent. By 1821, however, conditions had become so stringent that no exception was taken to this. Neither did it come as a shock that the British demanded security in the form of Denmark's income from the Øresund duty and the Danish Virgin Islands. Joseph sent his two best English speakers – Georg Gerson and a clerk named Andreas Hansen – to London to put the final touches to the agreement. The loan was the most expensive Denmark

173

had ever raised, but Frederik VI was delighted to have recruited a banker who even in those troubled times could raise money for the country.

The King was so impressed by Joseph's efficiency that he wanted to show his gratitude, and shortly after completion of the negotiations, he awarded the title of privy counsellor to him and to Georg Gerson. This title should be considered for a moment: Frederik VI had awarded it only once before – in 1812, to David Amsel Meyer. It is a fundamental misconception to regard the rank of privy counsellor as no more than a convenient title to give to Jews, rather than a proper Danish decoration. On the contrary, the King acted only after much consideration. The 1814 legislation on the Jews had made him fully conversant with Jewish thought, and he knew it would be tactless to offer a Jew a Cross of the Order of the Dannebrog – a devout Jew could never wear a cross, a symbol of Christianity. Although by 1821 that decoration would have been unlikely to embarrass a Jew as liberal as Joseph, the King knew that as a central figure in the Jewish community he still could not accept it.

Joseph did not conceal his pleasure at this appointment, and he appeared with Gerson at the next audience at Amalienborg to thank the King. A verbal exchange is said to have taken place on this occasion between the King and the merchant:

'But my dear privy counsellor, how on earth is it possible to make so much money?'

'Your Majesty, it is no problem. In this country there is gold lying everywhere. You have only to bend down to pick it up from the street.'

'But why do you want all this wealth? You certainly can't take it with you.'

'Oh yes I can, your Majesty; about half of it.'

'What do you mean?'

'Well, Your Majesty, everyone believes I am twice as rich as I really am.'

No one knows how wealthy Joseph was in 1821, but Carl Joachim's foster-mother, Mrs Reinhardt, wrote to her husband at about this time saying that Joseph had made £3,000 on the loan, and that this amount was equivalent to Reinhardt's salary as a professor for sixty years.

By this time Marianne's anxiety state had gradually developed into apathy; having the boy taken from her had undoubtedly aggravated her condition. For some time Joseph considered placing her in the

King Frederik VI of Denmark and – until 1814 – of Norway. He became King in 1808 on the death of his insane father Christian VII, but was in fact Regent from 1784. Painting by C. W. Eckersberg, 1825. Frederiksborg Museum.

Although Frederik VI *considered himself to be an absolute monarch by the grace of God, and is said to have coined the expression 'We alone know what best serves the people', he always tried to act in a kindly and fatherly way towards those he received in audience, which was in fact available to all. In his day, the ceremonial at Amalienborg Castle was very simple, which is confirmed by this illustration of the weekly audience. Drawing by Peder Klæstrup.* Royal Library, Copenhagen.

newly opened St Hans Sindssyge Hospital for the mentally sick near Roskilde, but when he found out more he knew that Marianne should not go to this dreadful place, which did not as yet distinguish clearly between syphilitics and mentally sick, and provided very primitive psychiatric care. When the medical superintendent at St Hans recommended fresh air and as much rest as possible for Marianne, and offered to see her regularly, Joseph found a pleasant widow in Roskilde who was willing to nurse her privately. Here she gradually lost contact with her surroundings, and nothing more is known of her until her death in 1838 after twenty sad years at Roskilde.

At Christmas 1821, when Carl Joachim had been with the Reinhardts for six years and had reached the age of fifteen, Nicoline wrote to her youngest brother:

Have you heard that Carl Joachim is now finally destined for the Christian religion? His father has always avoided expressing his intentions in this matter, and Reinhardt never wanted to force a decision out of him, so the matter has long been left undecided, although he has taken part in the school's religious instruction. But now it is decided. He has begun confirmation classes with our wonderful Mynster, and within a year he will be quietly baptized and then confirmed.

All went according to plan. On Sunday 3 October 1822 Carl Joachim was baptized and confirmed in Trinitatis Church near Rundetårn. Both ceremonies were conducted by the Reinhardt family's 'wonderful Mynster' – J. P. Mynster, who later became a well-known bishop of Zeeland, and had a great influence on Carl Joachim. It must have been a strange experience for Joseph as he followed from the back of the church the Christian ceremony in which he could not participate. The godparents were his foster-parents and Nicoline's brother, with a few of the Reinhardt family's friends. The baptism certainly had a deep effect upon Carl Joachim. Later, in England, he became a deeply religious man who did nothing of importance without first praying for God's favour and protection.

Shortly after his confirmation, Carl Joachim entered the grammar school. The old Borgerdydskole in Copenhagen had always had a good reputation, but in the 1820s it was going through a period of decline. The pupils' manners were poor, and the teaching was not exactly suited to the needs of a future banker. Greek and Latin were crammed to excess, but not one modern language was taught. Carl Joachim's great interest was history. The class of 1825 contained twenty students, and of these three were Jewish-born; apart from Carl Joachim there was his cousin Carl Wilhelm Wulf-Borup whose education Joseph was also paying for before sending him off to America. The third Jewish student was the future Professor Moritz Marcus. Carl Joachim was not very popular in his class. His disturbed mind, inherited from his mother, irritated his friends. He was always oscillating between overbearing and provocative self-assertion and sudden attacks of inexplicable melancholia and depression. One of his school friends said later that Carl Joachim's subsequent career in England was an enigma to all his old school fellows.

9 Joseph's Later Years

In 1814, when Norway was surrendered to unite with Sweden, it had been part of Denmark for four hundred years. In spite of the close relationship between the 'Twin Realms' the legal systems of the two countries had minor differences. One of the more grotesque differences was that since 1686 no Jew had been allowed to enter Norway. This law was not repealed until 1852, and as a result there was not one banker in Kristiania in 1822 able to negotiate on behalf of the Storting for the state's first independent loan. In the autumn of that year, therefore, the Storting was forced to approach Joseph in Copenhagen, who was asked to go to Kristiania, and offered a Jew's safe conduct to enter the country legally.

Frederik vi's newly appointed Privy Counsellor would not consider such a heavy-handed approach. He had no intention of setting foot in Norway under such terms, and demanded that negotiations should be moved to Svinesund, the last Swedish outpost in the wild, mountainous region near the Norwegian frontier. The Norwegians accepted this, and from that time onwards Joseph met no obstacles when he wished to visit Norway. However, their brush with Joseph did not prevent the Norwegian government's lawyers from repeating the gaffe in the case of the Hamburg banker Salomon Heine, who was backing Joseph during the 1830s in further loans to Norway. This wise and kindly banker, respected throughout Europe, found during his first – and probably only – visit to Norway that the country's officials regarded him with as much curiosity as if he had arrived from another planet.

After Norway's cession in 1814 and the new union with Sweden, there followed five years of somewhat embarrassing negotiations with Denmark to establish Norway's reasonable share of Denmark's increasingly substantial national debt, and to arrange for settlement of its share. Following international mediation in September 1819, agreement was reached on a sum of £300,000 (on which Norway was to pay 4 per cent interest), to be paid by instalments to the Danish Treasury over ten years. This arrangement was at least a poultice on the wound for Frederik vi, who had been desperately unhappy at having to surrender Norway and remove the proud, axe-bearing lion from his ancient coat of arms.

Three years later, however, the Storting decided that it would be cheaper to pay over the whole amount to Denmark immediately, if the debt could be substantially reduced. This was by no means improbable, since finance minister Møsting was always on the look-out for ready cash. This arrangement was, of course, suggested, only after seeking Joseph's advice. Joseph secured Møsting's approval, and on behalf of the Danish finance minister he offered a reduction of £40,000, leaving the remaining debt, which by 1822 had fallen to £210,000, at £170,000. Joseph was prepared to lend this money to Norway on acceptable terms and to pay it to Møsting within six months, after which he would become Norway's creditor until the loan was repaid. Joseph raised this large sum in his own name through his Hamburg and London connections, and, like Denmark, Norway was forced to let its customs duties stand as security for the loan. In those days such security was not merely a matter of form. In the following years Joseph had to keep one of his men at Kristiania to check the income from customs duties and to ensure that C. J. Hambro & Son's loan was repaid on time.

Joseph selected for this duty Andreas Hansen, who had carried out his duties so well in London the previous year. Hansen was at that time aged twenty-four and unmarried. He had already proved his self-sufficiency and ability three years earlier when managing a Hambro agency in Guernsey, where European goods were exchanged for South American ones for Joseph's account. Of all the talented men Joseph selected and trained, Andreas Hansen was undoubtedly the greatest. Although he often appeared morose and reticent, he became a leading figure not only in C. J. Hambro & Son but in Danish commerce and banking as a whole.

For the moment, however, he was sent to Kristiania to assume responsibility for control of the loan. He was not a Jew, and had no entry permit problems. Over the next three years he built up – for his own account – a Norwegian branch of C. J. Hambro & Son in Kristiania.

In the 1820s the future Norwegian capital, Kristiania, was still a modest little town of only nine thousand inhabitants – half as many as Bergen. The town's commerce was as yet undeveloped, and young Andreas' firm soon attracted great respect. He felt so much at home there that he even considered settling in Norway.

From 1823 until 1840, when he left Denmark for good, Joseph travelled extensively, and on three occasions he was away from Denmark for nearly a year. His lonely home at Kongens Nytorv was no tie, and later

When Denmark was forced to surrender Norway to Sweden in 1814, Kristiania (Oslo) was quite an insignificant town, and Norwegian commercial life was still concentrated entirely at Bergen on Norway's west coast. The picture shows the approach road to Kristiania from the east along the 400-mile road that still connects Copenhagen with Oslo via Sweden's west

his failing health tempted him to stay in France for long periods. He loved travelling, and took a close interest in political events and their effect on the money market at Europe's stock exchanges. His large private travelling coach took him to Hamburg, Frankfurt, Amsterdam, Antwerp and Paris, as well as to Kristiania and Stockholm and wherever he went he was sure to be found at the best hotel. Sometimes, however, he went further afield, and he was as well informed on Rome and Genoa as on London, Manchester, Edinburgh and Dublin. One journey in 1834–5 took him as far as Algeria, travelling via Corsica, and in 1836 a special mission took him to Bologna, in northern Italy. It is difficult to believe that he could tolerate a lonely hotel life for six months at a time, but at least it gave him the many contacts necessary for the proper conduct of his business. Only in his old age, in just one letter, is a hint of loneliness to be detected. Moreover, he liked to make it known that he slept nowhere as well as in his travelling coach, rumbling over Europe's bumpy roads. Concrete evidence exists about just two of his journeys. The first was a journey to Paris in 1823, mentioned in the

coast. In 1821, after Joseph had arranged Norway's first government loan and sent Andreas Hansen there, they both realized that this was a future, as yet unexploited, trading centre. Coloured print, c. 1830. City Museum, Oslo.

memoirs of Just Mathias Thiele, later a professor of art history. He was son-in-law to Holten, chairman of the National Debt Commission, and therefore well known to Joseph. Thiele had graduated in the summer of 1823, and on 1 October he set out on his first European tour, with Rome as his destination. He wrote:

After a farewell dinner with my friends at Hôtel d'Angleterre, I reached the Copenhagen Customs House and boarded the steamship for Kiel. Here I met Privy Counsellor Hambro, whom I knew through the Holten family. He invited me to accompany him to Paris in his fine travelling coach.

When we reached Hamburg via Kiel, he took me to visit the wealthy banker, Salomon Heine. He was a little, dapper Jew with silver-white hair under his black-silk skull cap. He made a very charming impression when, with a kind but somewhat roguish smile, he introduced me to his cashier with a view to possible future business.

From Hamburg, we journeyed day and night towards Amsterdam over the clinker-paved Dutch roads. At the stages, victuals were handed to us in the coach, and after a few days in Amsterdam, which I spent in looking around, we rolled on until we reached Antwerp.

Hambro was so rich that he had no need to hide the fact that he had started as a merchant by selling pencils and ladies' shoes from France. He was very entertaining, and always willing to explain to a poor fellow like me how to speculate on the stock exchange and make money. One day, as he went on baling-out gold from a leather bag hanging in the coach, I naïvely made a remark about the cost of such a journey. He answered that he had only to be in Paris for a day and the whole journey would be paid for.

We stayed in Paris at the Hôtel des Princes in Rue Richelieu. The Bourse was still open, and Hambro rushed out of the coach, leaving me to take over our rooms, with the words: 'See you at dinner at the table d'hôte.' He hurried to the Bourse, and when he returned he sat down beside me, turned towards me, smiling all over his face, and whispered into my ear: 'Well now, my good Thiele, I have managed to pay for our whole journey.'

'The next day, however,' Thiele recalled, 'we separated amicably, for I was unable to remain at the Hôtel des Princes. It was not the place for the likes of me.'

The £1,000,000, which was Denmark's meagre cash return on the first British loan of £1,500,000 in autumn 1821, poured out of finance minister Møsting's Treasury even more quickly than had been expected. In 1824 he asked Joseph to implement as soon as possible the second £1,500,000 of the loan, which Joseph had, as requested, once more undertaken to negotiate through Goldschmidt & Haldemann in London. This was to be arranged under the same partition arrangements as the first half, and Joseph had therefore to subscribe another £400,000.

Joseph was somewhat ashamed that the first half of the loan should have been so expensive for the Danish government, and his first idea was to raise a £500,000 loan so that at the same time a number of much older and far too expensive loans could be refunded. He also suggested that it should be a 3 per cent loan at an issue price of about 75. This was the kind of loan launched by the Rothschilds, and it had become fashionable because the lower issue prices appealed more to speculators than a loan at higher interest rates offered at close to par.

Meanwhile, the government's former financier, the ageing ship-owner Erich Erichsen, suddenly reappeared with a better offer than Joseph's. A period of brief but intense competition now ensued, and the terms of the loan were tightened up to the advantage of the Danish government. Joseph was prepared to stretch his terms further than Erichsen and won the contest, but he proceeded without ensuring that Goldschmidt and Haldemann in London would accept the new terms.

The National Debt Commission had followed the struggle between Joseph and Erichsen with great interest, and of course it played into

Nicolai von Holten (1775–1850), direc-tor of the Danish National Debt Com-mission. An unusual type of civil ser-vant, he had previously been a successful businessman who had assisted the gov-ernment in numerous broking transac-tions. In 1816, because of his great expertise, he was elected the National Debt Commission's bonds specialist. Later, between 1817 and 1839, he directed the government's bureau for foreign payments. Thus he became Møsting's, and later A. W. Moltke's, right-hand man. From 1821, Joseph's foreign loans for the government were arranged through this very wealthy and highly cultivated man; at the same time, he was Joseph's close and most respected friend. Painting by M. Marstrand, 1846. Frederiksborg Museum.

their hands; the Commission was always afraid that loans would be more expensive than was necessary. The matter ended with Joseph agreeing to divide his £400,000 share of the loan with Erich Erichsen, and to let the British bankers keep their share. The agreement was approved on 6 June 1824, and the King signified his great satisfaction.

The timing of this affair was most inappropriate. In 1824 the City of London had just come through a period of severe difficulty, and when Georg Gerson arrived in London to persuade Goldschmidt and Haldemann to accept the new, stricter terms both Englishmen with-drew. The unfortunate Gerson was forced to make several journeys to London in autumn 1824 to try to retrieve the situation, and on the last of these journeys the recently married banker suffered an apoplectic stroke.

Joseph now had the unpleasant duty of informing Møsting that, while his and Erichsen's share of the loan of course still stood, it was necessary for him to find new partners for the remainder. While the National Debt Commission was considering whether Joseph should be held financially responsible for what was in fact a breach of contract, there was a new and unexpected turn of events; shortly afterwards, Erich Erichsen told Møsting that he could not put up his share of £200,000.

Conrad Hinrich Donner (1774–1854), a Hamburg merchant, was originally a tobacco manufacturer in Altona employing 150 workers, but in 1798 – the year before Joseph began his apprenticeship in Hamburg – he opened his own commercial firm of C. H. Donner, which in addition to trading had interests in shipping and insurance. Lithograph after a painting by J. F. Fritz, Staatsarchiv, Hamburg.

Throughout his life Joseph neither boasted of his victories nor complained of his defeats, but there is one recorded exception. In his later days, at a dinner party, he told the young Danish writer Carl Bernhardt about his difficulties in the cheerless autumn of 1824. In his memoirs, Bernhardt quotes what Joseph had to say. The following narrative is based on Bernhardt's memoirs, with a few additions and corrections for minor lapses of memory.

One Sunday evening in autumn 1824, Joseph was sitting in his house at Kongens Nytorv, sadly contemplating the outcome of his efforts. Not only might he be held responsible for breach of contract because of the withdrawal of his English colleagues, but the channels through which he had intended to raise his own £200,000 were now also failing him; the creditworthiness of C. J. Hambro & Son had hit rock bottom. With a certain grim humour, he recalled that the only cash asset he had was £1,200 in Frankfurt, and he decided that the wisest course was to drive down there, collect the money and start afresh. If it became known that even he could not find his share of the loan, his role as leading banker to the Danish government would be at an end. In the middle of these reflections, his servant announced that finance minister Møsting had called and wanted to speak to him. Although Joseph was on good terms with the minister, Møsting had never visited him at home before.

The Finance Minister went straight to the point. He came direct from the King, whom he had told of Erich Erichsen's breach of faith in the matter of his share of the loan. Erichsen had declared that his business was ruined, and that he owned nothing but his annuity. He had offered to show his accounts to prove the truth of this. Frederik VI had been terribly upset. The following day was posting day for London, and if the British Ambassador, Wynn, was to learn that even Denmark's richest merchant was no longer solvent the position of the Danish economy would be plain to all. The King had therefore ordered Møsting to find a solution immediately, and Møsting now suggested to Joseph that he should instantly accept Erichsen's share of the loan as well as his own. In return, the National Debt Commission would waive their claim to compensation against him for the broken agreement on the British share. Møsting had great respect for Joseph after nearly ten years of impeccable co-operation, and he did not try to conceal that, following Nathanson's failure in 1820 and Erichsen's recent collapse, the National Debt Commission now had no one to turn to but Joseph.

Joseph asked permission to consider this until next morning, and spent much of the night thinking it over. He knew that the great banker Conrad Donner of Altona had shown some interest in the – subsequently abortive – British loan, and that in 1821 he had been hurt when Joseph chose London in preference to Hamburg. Donner had not suffered in Nathanson's bankruptcy, and had not therefore lost confidence in Denmark. Joseph also recalled that Gerson had told him that only a few months earlier Donner had been in London trying to cultivate the Danish Embassy while the British loan was being negotiated. If anyone could rescue Joseph from the difficulties that had arisen it was Donner. Content with Donner's potential as a deliverer, he eventually fell asleep. When he awoke, Joseph decided that he would agree to find the £400,000.

Very early that morning he called on Møsting, and before 7 am they appeared together before the King, always an early riser. He received his privy counsellor with the following words:

'Well, what do you think of all this? Would you have believed it of Erichsen? Ugh! And he tried to convince us that he was an honest man!'

Joseph said calmly that he was willing to take Erichsen's place, adding that before negotiating the details he would have to make a business trip of three or four days. The King accepted this, and exclaimed:

'Well now, I wish to thank you, privy counsellor. This at least is honourable. Now Wynn can write what he likes. Hambro's signature

Martin Johan Jenisch (1760–1827), the Hamburg banker. He was already a highly respected figure in Hamburg's commercial life when Joseph was working there between 1797 and 1800. Generations of the Jenisch family had made their names as merchants in Venice and Hamburg. Lithograph by C. F. Gröger, c. 1820. Staatsarchiv, Hamburg.

should be more than enough for him. Thank God there are still honourable men to deal with in money matters!'

Bernhardt's account continues with Joseph's confession that tears nearly came to his eyes at this royal declaration of confidence, and he was grateful that the King could not know how very fragile was its basis. Joseph planned to catch the paddlesteamer *Caledonia* at 5 am the next day for its weekly trip to Kiel, and then travel on to Altona as quickly as possible. It was vital that no one in Copenhagen should have a hint of his own financial troubles or of his rash promise to the King.

That afternoon he went to a meeting of creditors in Nathanson's estate in bankruptcy, and, as a creditor for £4,000, proposed that his old and respected firm should be treated with the utmost leniency. He was even sufficiently composed to let fall a remark that he himself did not intend to make a fuss about this modest debt.

On the long journey to Altona, he kept turning over in his mind the fact that if Donner had originally been genuinely interested in providing the entire loan himself the present suggestion that he should take over a mere £400,000 would have to be made more tempting. Even though the terms were already the most favourable imaginable, Joseph was prepared to content himself with a minimal commission; indeed he would drop this altogether if absolutely necessary. The over-riding need was to save his reputation as the only remaining banker in

186

Copenhagen who kept his word. This thought calmed him, and he said that he 'ate and slept well on board the *Caledonia*'.

Arriving at Altona, he drove directly to Donner's house, asked for a private discussion with him, and without more ado put all his cards on the table, emphasizing very strongly, of course, that the loan would be of great advantage to whoever could find the money quickly. He added that the question of his own commission was unimportant. 'Donner nearly fell out of his chair,' Bernhardt wrote, 'as if it had never occurred to him that trading in money was risky business.' He could not make up his mind on the spot. Joseph, however, felt unable to rely on Donner's discretion, and was unwilling to leave until he had an answer. 'Donner spent an hour or so making calculations, covering a whole sheet of paper with figures. Meanwhile, Joseph sat down to read a newspaper, although from sheer tension he could not distinguish the letters that swam before his eyes.'

After about an hour, Donner still could not make up his mind. He asked to be allowed to confer with his closest friend and colleague in Hamburg, the great merchant and senator Martin Jenisch. 'Good! Let's go and see him', said Joseph, He took Donner along with him in his carriage, not leaving him for a moment and giving him no chance to

Jenisch's house in Katharinestrasse in Hamburg Altstadt, where Joseph visited him in 1824. The great Hamburg merchant had his headquarters here until 1833, when the firm moved to newly-built premises on Jungfernsteig. After the Hamburg fire of 1842 the firm ceased trading, but continued as a trust company for the large family fortune. Drawing, c. 1830. Staatsarchiv, Hamburg.

talk to anyone in his house. At Jenisch's house Joseph made a clean breast of his position once again, and resubmitted his proposal. Jenisch listened smilingly. He immediately showed more decision than Donner, although Donner was known as a quick and purposeful man of finance. When Joseph had finished his story, Jenisch remarked: 'Well that's the way life goes. Things do work out like this, and there's nothing we can do about it. But I agree to your proposal, and I am prepared to take up the whole amount, if this is what you want.'

Donner had at last regained his courage, and the matter was decided during the course of the night. Jenisch took £300,000 and Donner £100,000, and they promised that the money would be paid over to Joseph with the utmost speed. Carl Bernhardt concludes his account by adding that, on his way home, Joseph 'slept as soundly as a millionaire', and no one in Copenhagen learnt how the remainder of the wrecked British loan had been handled by 'a failure who failed to fail'.

Erich Erichsen had his on-account contribution returned by the minister of finance, less £2,000 for breach of contract, and shortly afterwards Joseph was able to agree on the terms of his promised loan of £400,000 cash. It was not a very profitable transaction, but he had achieved his most important objective – to preserve his reputation as a banker who kept his word.

The difficult autumn of 1824 had barely ended when Joseph suffered a sad blow. On 16 January 1825, Georg Gerson, strained by overwork, collapsed and died in his chair at his desk at the Kongens Nytorv bank. For the last thirteen years Gerson had added an optimistic note to the bank's affairs, as well as to Joseph's private life. He was only thirty-five when he died. It was a serious loss to the bank, but a greater loss to Joseph personally. It was written of the talented Gerson after his death that 'as a banker he always thought and spoke like a Minister of Finance, and as an amateur musician he always played and conducted like a perfect artist'.

It was not only at Kongens Nytorv, however, that his death was mourned. This very popular young man had married only four months before he died. His young widow, Adelaide, *née* David, was the daughter of the wealthy merchant Nathan David. Gerson had known her for many years, for he had been a school friend of Adelaide's brother C. N. David, who later became Denmark's minister of finance. But Gerson's young widow was not to remain long unconsoled. Eighteen months after Gerson's death she became converted to the Catholic faith, to the sorrow of her orthodox father, and a little later made a surprising marriage, to Prince Antonius Pignatelli-Ruffo, who was serving at

Some of Gerson's compositions were published after his death. This is the title page of Six Songs, *published by the Copenhagen Music Association in 1842.* Hambros Bank Archives.

Copenhagen as chargé d'affaires for the Kingdom of The Two Sicilies. She ended her days a welcoming hostess to her former fellow-countrymen in her palace in Rome, and died at the age of ninety-six.

During the nine years that Joseph and Gerson worked together as partners, Joseph was still greatly concerned with goods, while Gerson was almost exclusively involved in banking matters. Joseph now called Andreas Hansen home from Norway and offered him the vacant post. Andreas, however, was a born merchant and not very interested in banking; as a result, roles were reversed. From now on Joseph devoted all his attention to the bank. It fascinated him that, without assistance, he could work out his own plans in matters of the highest importance, that to do this he needed nothing more than pencil and paper, and that it could be done anywhere and at any time provided there was peace and quiet. This working method was inherited by his grandson, Everard, who two generations later controlled Hambros bank in London from his country estate at Milton Abbey or from his villa in Biarritz, with equal assurance. ·

In the event, however, it was difficult to persuade Andreas Hansen to leave Kristiania. Only by making him a partner immediately did Joseph succeed in persuading Andreas, now aged twenty-seven, to return to Copenhagen, and even then only after he had taken the time he needed to marry. It is part of the image of the quiet, always industrious, Andreas that in 1821, while he was managing the Hambro branch in Guernsey, he had become engaged to Emma, the daughter of Thomas Grut, an English clergyman. After his transfer first to London and then to Kristiania, however, he became so wrapped up in his affairs that he forgot to write to his fiancée, and as a result she came to the conclusion that he had forgotten her. When, five years later, on his journey back to Denmark, he made a detour to Guernsey to fetch her, she fainted with emotion at such an unexpected reunion. This was the last time he failed to remember her, for they had eleven children, and he took good care of her sister, Louise, who married an Englishman named Alfred Mansell. In 1830 Mansell entered Joseph's employment as a factory manager.

In 1829 Andreas took out a licence to trade independently as a wholesaler, and in 1836 he left Hambros to run his own business under the name of A. N. Hansen & Co. At Hambros, Andreas had soon realized that he would never be able to establish with Joseph's son the same personal relationship he had had with his father. To put it bluntly, he did not like Carl Joachim. This, however, altered nothing in his relationship with Joseph. As late as 1839, before moving to England for good, Joseph spent his last summer in Denmark with Andreas Hansen and his family, and it came as no surprise when in the same year Joseph sold the factory at Christianshavn to Andreas Hansen's rapidly expanding enterprise.

Andreas' eleven children included six sons, five of whom proved to be of outstanding ability. Many of his descendants have taken the surname of their ancestress, calling themselves Grut. When he died in 1873 – twenty-five years after Joseph – A. N. Hansen, as he was now known, was indisputably the most highly respected personality in Danish commerce, although perhaps not the best loved.

It was not until 1825 that the matter of the abortive British loan was settled, and the manner of its settlement was nothing less than a scandal. Joseph fortunately was not concerned in this, but it was he who had to clear up the mess. The National Debt Commission wanted to avoid paying a commission to Joseph, and chose instead to send Mr Pløyen, a Danish-Norwegian diplomat, to Paris and London to seek the most favourable terms for a loan of £5,500,000. He had been given authority to conclude an agreement on the best offer.

In Paris, James Rothschild was interested, and in London Adolf Goldschmidt once again came forward. Pløyen asked for written bids from both firms, but once the time limit had expired he flatly rejected Goldschmidt's bid, and returned Rothschild's unopened on the grounds that it had been submitted half an hour too late. Meanwhile he

Andreas Hansen (1798–1873) was employed by Joseph in 1813 at the age of fifteen. He became a partner in 1826 following Georg Gerson's death. Some years before Joseph died, Andreas Hansen bought Hambro's Copenhagen factories, and he and his sons ran the Christianshavn enterprise until well into the present century. Andreas Hansen later became one of Denmark's leading merchants, and from 1856 until his death in 1873 he was the authoritative chairman of the Copenhagen Chamber of Commerce. Some of his many descendants have adopted the name of Grut, the maiden name of his English-born wife. The Danish poet and philosopher Piet Hein is one of his great-grandchildren. Painting by C. A. Jensen, 1838. It hangs next to Joseph's portrait in the conference room at the Copenhagen Bourse.

had entered into an agreement with a British-American banking firm, as yet unknown in Denmark, Thomas Wilson & Co., which seems to have bribed him. The ever-trusting Frederik vi had even paid the rascally diplomat £2,000 in recognition of his good work, before Pløyen's old adversary, the Danish Consul General in Paris, Hoppe, revealed the scandal.

The agreement with Wilson was however binding, so Frederik vi took the only course open to him. He dismissed Pløyen and arranged for finance minister Møsting to apologize to Rothschild and Goldschmidt, who had of course protested strongly against their shabby treatment. There is no denying, however, that Møsting drew a sigh of relief six months later when he learned that Adolf Goldschmidt & Co. had failed.

Møsting had great difficulty with Thomas Wilson & Co. in the following years. The extent of the loan was beyond the capacity of the firm; at 3 per cent over 60 years, it was guaranteed at an issue price of 75, but sale of the bonds was slow, partly because of Rothschild's and Goldschmidt's 'bear' activities, which brought the price down to 55 for a time. It was intended that Wilson's should convert a number of older and more expensive Danish loans, but the company found that customers redeemed the old loans without subscribing to the new ones. Møsting therefore did not receive the money as quickly as had been agreed, and in the end he himself had to take over a block of £2,000,000 of the bonds, which he would try to sell as and when the price became reasonable.

During these troublesome years of 1825–7, Joseph was frequently forced to come to Møsting's aid, and at times he played the part of the philanthropist. For example, in 1826 he took over a block of £30,000 of the bonds at a substantial premium; he did this with a view to working his way back systematically into his old position.

In 1826, Møsting's £2,000,000 of the Wilson loan was still a serious and unprofitable burden on the Treasury. It had proved impossible to sell the bonds even at a barely acceptable price, so Joseph established contact with the Rothschilds. In spite of the bad treatment of the year before they probably had an interest in getting back into the Danish market, where they had not appeared since 1806. Rothschilds in London said they were willing to convert the doomed Wilson bonds against a loan of the same amount.

Nathan Rothschild immediately sent his new son-in-law, Amsel Salomon Rothschild, to Copenhagen. The year before young Amsel, the only son of Salomon Rothschild of Vienna, had married his English cousin, Charlotte Rothschild, and Nathan was now employing him as his travelling representative, mostly handling new customers. On 26

In 1824 the artist Richard Dighton published in London an album called City Characters. *It contained about twenty coloured caricatures of important City merchants who might be seen daily in the arcades of the Royal Exchange. Here are three of his personalities; on the top left is Nathan Rothschild (1783–1836), who could be seen every day before his customary column. The other two, from left to right, are Thomas Wilson and Adolf Goldschmidt, both concerned in the Danish loan arranged by Joseph in 1821–7.* Print Room, Guildhall Library, London.

May 1827 Amsel concluded an agreement in Copenhagen for a loan of £2,000,000 at 3 per cent. This loan, however, was expensive, since the Rothschilds, who would have been prepared to guarantee an issue price of 75 in 1825, would now guarantee only 60. Of the nominal amount, therefore, only £1,200,000 reached the Danish Treasury. There were further deductions for Joseph's commission, and for Conrad Donner who had assisted Joseph in the matter. This more modest Rothschild loan concluded an almost uninterrupted decade of Danish loans. Denmark was now again on a reasonably straight course, and no further loans were necessary until 1834. Meanwhile, the Wilson loan staggered on.

In 1829 Møsting retired as finance minister and was succeeded by Count A. W. Moltke. This move was favourable for Joseph. Moltke, for many years a member of the National Debt Commission, was a great admirer of his, and had often spontaneously expressed his admiration of Joseph's ability and loyalty.

Joseph's lonely life in his Kongens Nytorv house remains veiled in mystery. None of his contemporaries who later wrote their memoirs appear to have visited him. The probable truth is that during the early years of his marriage he felt unable to receive guests because of Marianne's mental condition, and that later, without a hostess, he was disinclined to do so. He was also frequently abroad for up to a year at a time. Joseph's official Danish biographer, recounting that 'he lived in grand style', probably meant simply that his large house was luxuriously furnished, and that his horses and carriages were always of the best.

It is clear that Joseph's tastes became more sophisticated during the prosperous 1820s. Through his almost daily encounters with the Director of the National Debt Commission, Nicolai von Holten, he was introduced to one of Copenhagen's most elegant establishments. Holten was an art collector, and had contacts at the Academy of Art through his son-in-law, Thiele, who had become a professor there. It is therefore not surprising that Joseph included Rome in his tour of Europe, which lasted almost a year, beginning in 1829 while Carl Joachim was still under training in Antwerp and Bremen. In Rome Joseph sought out the Danish sculptor Bertel Thorvaldsen. Thorvaldsen employed thirty people in his workshop near the Piazza Barberini. He had lived in Rome for very many years, and had become the focal point of the large and ever-changing community of Danish painters there. When Joseph arrived, the sculptor was engrossed in his memorial to Pope Pius VII, which later became famous, but however busy he

In Rome Joseph made the acquaintance of the Danish sculptor Bertel Thorvaldsen. A relationship developed between them over the following years. Rome was an inspiring inauguration of the great interest in the arts later displayed by Carl Joachim. Lithograph by Emilius Bærentzen after a painting by Horace Vernet, 1835. Royal Library, Copenhagen.

was he always had time for the fellow-countrymen who visited him. When Joseph showed an interest in buying paintings, Thorvaldsen was all the more welcoming – he was always happy to help his impecunious painter friends sell their works. Before long the Danish painters began to call Joseph 'the rich Privy Counsellor Hambro'. This story comes mainly from the many letters Joseph wrote to Thorvaldsen between 1830 and 1835. During his visit, Joseph, with Thorvaldsen's assistance, bought about ten paintings by Danish artists. From 1837 onwards Joseph contributed to the building of the Thorvaldsen Museum in Copenhagen, which was almost complete when the artist died in 1844.

For many years Joseph was also in contact with Thorvaldsen's best Danish pupil, the sculptor H. W. Bissen, who sold him a number of works in marble. Joseph bought from him a bust of the future King, Christian VIII, who had recently visited Thorvaldsen, and also one of Bissen's best-known early works, *The Flower Girl*. In 1838 Bissen carved Marianne's tombstone, and in 1852 he carved a bust of Joseph, assisted only by paintings and his own memory.

Joseph's ambivalent relationship with the Jewish community became in time increasingly affected by his decision to have Carl Joachim baptized. Although he himself never denied his Jewish faith Joseph made several arrangements which indicated that he realized and respected, at least in practice, the consequences of Carl Joachim's baptism. After the death in 1825 of the sadly missed Georg Gerson, he never again employed a Jew in his business. When Joseph died in 1840 there was not a single employee of Jewish origin among the entire staff of the bank, the commercial department and the factory. He had no wish to expose Carl Joachim to criticism from his old fellow-believers because he was an apostate. It was not difficult for Joseph to find young non-Jewish employees. His reputation was high, and the Hambro undertakings were widely considered to be among the best places in the city in which to learn one's trade.

These sentiments came clearly to the fore when, in 1830, the Jewish community at last came to an agreement to build a new synagogue in Copenhagen to replace the old one burnt down in the fire of 1795 and the rather unattractive temporary synagogue in St Kongensgade. As long ago as 1799 the community had found itself a site in Krystalgade, but the difficult period after the bombardment of Copenhagen and the state bankruptcy caused all plans to be suspended. The persecution of the Jews in 1819 halted the project once again. Since then, feelings had run high between the two extreme wings of the community: the old, poor, orthodox Jews and the younger, liberal, businessmen and scholars who, under the 1814 legislation, had long since slipped into Danish society as citizens with equal rights. Joseph had undeniably become a typical representative of the latter group.

When the subscription list for the building of the synagogue was opened the Jewish community had it circulated among its members,

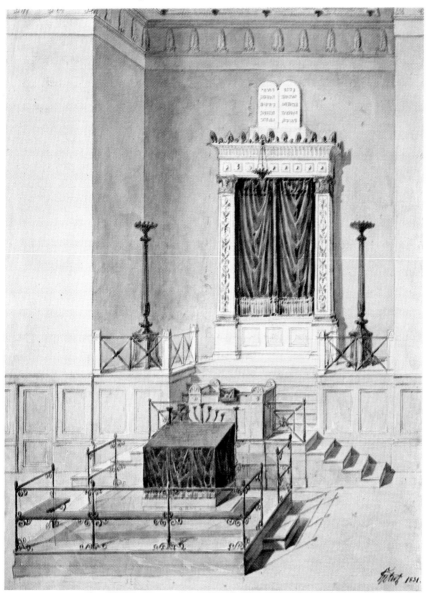

It was not until 1830–31 that the Mosaic Community agreed on the rebuilding of the Copenhagen synagogue, so sadly missed since the fire of 1795, and the richest members were expected to provide the funds to erect an imposing building. The highly respected, non-Jewish Academy Professor G. F. Hetsch (1788–1864) prepared the drawings for the somewhat oriental, classical building that was planned. His drawing of the interior shown here accompanied the subscription list circulated among members of the community. Although as time passed Joseph defended his Jewish faith more from pride than from conviction, he was nevertheless one of the three most generous contributors. Mosaic Community, Copenhagen.

197

accompanied by a drawing of the planned interior by the synagogue's non-Jewish architect, Professor G. F. Hetsch. The subscription list had been prepared with a certain Jewish charm; there were three ways of contributing: (1) by gift; (2) by interest-free loan; (3) by interest bearing loan. Each subscriber could decide the size of his interest and in 1830 £2,800 was collected from 229 contributors – an average of £10 each; £5,000 was made available in loans, and these amounts together were enough for building to start. The driving force behind the subscription was the young, ultra-orthodox wholesaler, Daniel Jacobson, who was a relation of Marianne Hambro. In his memoirs Jacobson recounts the typical reaction of Joseph when he called upon him with the list: 'My dear Jacobson, you know we all have our whims, and a man whose whim is horses will pay more for a horse than another man. It is the same with a man whose whim is paintings. You seem to have a whim for the synagogue. I don't! But if I am willing to pay as much as you have paid I don't think you can claim more of me.' Fortunately Jacobson had himself subscribed £100, so Joseph immediately wrote out an order for the same amount – one of the largest sums subscribed. The synagogue was ready for consecration in 1833. As a donor, Joseph attended this solemn ceremony, but it is not known whether he became a regular worshipper.

In 1825 Carl Joachim, wearing his student's cap, had left the devoted couple who had fostered him for the last ten years, but out of gratitude he kept in touch with the family for many years. He had already become estranged from his own father, but this was not yet very apparent, since for the next few years he was sent to France and Germany, and later America, to learn languages and commerce. The earliest portrait of him is the drawing on the following page, dated 'Bremen 1828'.

Early in 1828 the Reinhardt family was delighted to receive two letters from him. Nicoline wrote to her brother:

We have had the pleasure of receiving two letters from Carl Joachim, who is now 20. Their style and content do him credit. He appears to be developing beyond our expectations. Not only does he write beautifully and elegantly as a merchant should, but he expresses himself affectionately and intelligently. I sincerely hope that the steadiness Reinhardt has always strived to instil into him will take root in his naturally restless character, so that he can become a good and useful man.

During his childhood Carl Joachim had met many prominent people in the Reinhardt home, including artists, writers and politicians. The prime minister, Schimmelmann, whom his father had served merely as a respected banker, became a family friend of the Reinhardts, and the

Danish poet Adam Oehlenschlager was a frequent visitor. There soon developed in Carl Joachim's susceptible mind a strong interest in history, art and literature.

During his five years of practical training between matriculation in 1824 and his return to Copenhagen in 1830, Carl Joachim first worked at Le Havre, Antwerp and Bremen to learn languages. Then he went with Mansell, A. N. Hansen's brother-in-law, to study industry in the USA for nearly a year. This anonymous portrait is from the Bremen period, and is dated 1828. Hambros Bank Archives.

It was intended that on his return in 1829 he should work with his father at the Kongens Nytorv bank, but Joseph was still hesitant. Perhaps he hoped that the impulsive Carl Joachim would gain a little more maturity and polish before allowing him a free hand as his partner. Carl Joachim's growing interest in art and the theatre, especially in actresses, went against the grain. Joseph himself had always led a quiet life and he expected similarly irreproachable behaviour in his employees.

10 The Development of the Business

By the end of the 1820s it was clear to Andreas Hansen that C. J. Hambro & Son's trading in goods was declining, or at least stagnating, and the reason for this was clear to him. After the state of bankruptcy in 1813 and the surrender of Norway in 1814, Copenhagen had in fact run down as a commercial centre. It was as if the capital, with its 115,000 closely packed inhabitants behind Christian iv's two-hundred-year-old ramparts, had lost its vision of the future. In spite of the many vessels in the harbour shipping was declining, and this alone had a paralysing effect on Copenhagen's trade. Hamburg had gradually taken over the Danish capital's trading role. By degrees, Jutland found that it could get its supplies more quickly and cheaply from Hamburg than from Copenhagen. At the same time Danish provincial towns were growing. At the end of the 1820s the British began to relax their duties on corn, and Danish grain exports to England increased. These exports, however, were in the hands of the big provincial merchants, who sailed their own ships to England and returned bearing iron and coal. An equally characteristic development of the 1820s – or rather lack of development – was the fact that the industrial expansion then in full swing in England and America completely bypassed Denmark. All these circumstances were to the disadvantage of Copenhagen's trade, and the ambitious Andreas was forced to think along new channels.

In 1830, therefore, he persuaded the rather reluctant Joseph to send Andreas' brother-in-law Alfred Mansell to America on a one-year study tour, primarily to look at the modern, steam-driven milling industries. Andreas' idea was that what could no longer be earned by trading could certainly be made up by pioneering efforts in the field of Danish industry.

As a merchant, Joseph had become increasingly interested in American goods. Since the 1820s many American merchant adventurers had chosen Copenhagen as a centre for their export trade, leaving Danish merchants to resell the goods to the Baltic towns. This arrangement gave them enough time for two voyages a year to Copenhagen – if they themselves had taken on the Baltic trade they would have had time for only one expedition a year.

Joseph eventually became completely reconciled to the journey when

Mansell agreed to take Carl Joachim with him. Upon their return it was agreed that C. J. Hambro & Son should expand, and establish a steam mill in Copenhagen. The main purpose of the mill was to shell imported rice, but since this was a seasonal trade it was also to be used to grind corn.

In the Copenhagen of 1831 such a plan would have seemed quite sensational. Milling by steam power, already in full swing in America, was unknown in Denmark. In fact, by the end of the 1820s there were only four steam engines in the whole country. Moreover, all Copenhagen's energy demands were still being met by windmills and horse mills. Many picturesque old windmills, sawmills and tan mills, with their murmuring sails turning in the port's fresh winds, towered above Copenhagen's ramparts. Ten miles to the north of the capital, the abundant flow of the idyllic Mølleå combined with suitable damming and a series of millponds, provided a reasonably steady source of power for watermills.

In the summer of 1831, Joseph petitioned for a range of privileges in connection with the establishment of Denmark's first steam mill, and in November he was given, by royal appointment, sole rights for many years to operate a steam mill in Copenhagen. The ageing Frederik VI had not forgotten his invaluable privy counsellor, who had raised so many loans for him.

Joseph was also fortunate in his choice of site for the mill. He had first secured a small site near the harbour, very close to Kongens Nytorv, but shortly afterwards the authorities regretted having given this permission because it interfered with their shipyard plans. He was given, instead, on extremely favourable terms, the Bodenhoffs Plads at the northern end of Christianshavns Kanal, with direct communications to the whole port complex. This gave Joseph five times as much space as the original site, and in addition the little peninsula's situation, with water and quays on three sides, made it possible to cordon off the mainland side of the square. Then, by employing a customs officer and a guard at his own expense, the square was operated as Joseph's private free port, customs duty being levied only on goods carried into the town. At the same time the site was favourable for contact with head office at Kongens Nytorv, since he could sail in his own boat from door to door in less time than by road via Knippelsbro.

The new steam mill was erected and brought into use in 1832–33, and Bodenhoffs Plads soon changed its name to Hambros Plads. The enterprise expanded rapidly in the next few years. Rice husks proved suitable for pig fodder, and pig breeding and a slaughterhouse were added. This soon led to the export of hams. The maritime location of

By about 1830 commercial life in Copenhagen was regaining a little strength, although the golden days were never to return. Danish and foreign ships again arrived at Toldboden, and connections with foreign countries also improved when Copenhagen acquired its first paddle-steamer in 1819. This provided a weekly service to Kiel in Holstein, making it possible to reach Hamburg in little more than a day, compared with the previous minimum of two and a half days overland. Connections with London via Hamburg were also now faster. The time was now ripe to employ steam-power in manufacturing and to show an interest in the production of easily saleable foods. Coloured lithograph from P. G. Philipson's Publishing House, c. 1840.

HAMBRO'S & BODENHOFF'S PLADS.

*Bodenhoffs Plads, or, as it came to be called on nineteenth-century maps, 'Hambros Plads',
had been constructed during the eighteenth century by filling in a very shallow area between
the harbour and Christianshavns rampart. In 1830 Joseph acquired this peninsula, quite*

the undertaking lent itself to the sale of ship's provisions, so Andreas
Hansen installed a large hard tack bakery, which interested Joseph
much more than the rice mill.

A later development stemmed from Joseph's own initiative. On one
of his many visits to Paris he had visited a factory employing the new
preserving technique of 'hermetic sealing'. It had been invented as
early as 1809 by Françoise Appert, the French master cook, but it was
unknown in Denmark. Joseph called in a French specialist, Monsieur
Petit, and installed a large preserving department, primarily for vege-

large but almost bare of buildings, and set up his new steam mill, hard tack bakery and preserving factory. Most of the products could be exported directly from the square, which had quays for loading and unloading. Watercolour by J. A. Rieter, 1847. Copenhagen City Museum.

tables and particularly for green peas. They were popular for ship's provisions, and also sold well in Copenhagen.

Thanks to Andreas Hansen and his brother-in-law Mansell, by 1840 the Christianshavn undertaking was far more profitable than Joseph had ever imagined, and it eventually employed a large number of people. During Joseph's final year in Copenhagen (1839–40), annual exports were 50,000 tons of wheat flour, 3,000,000 pounds of hard tack, 2,000,000 pounds of husked rice and 6–7,000 barrels of salted bacon. Exports from the preserved food department continued to increase.

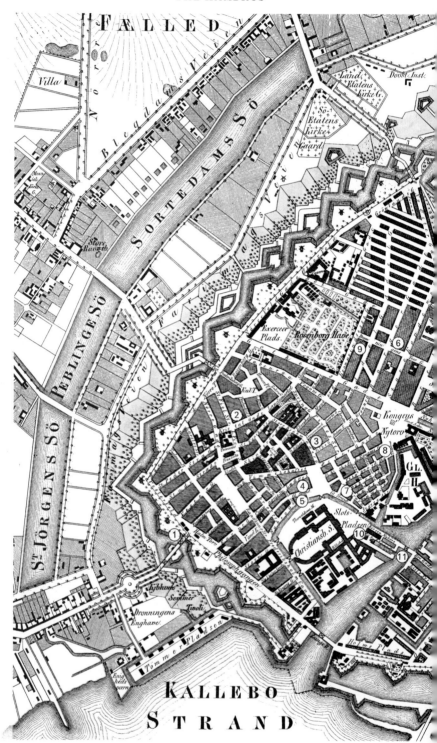

Only 125 years ago Copenhagen was still a fortress town protected by ramparts and moats, although it was becoming increasingly over-populated. The westward fortifications were not demolished until after the cholera epidemic of 1853, after which the city grew to a million inhabitants within a few generations. This map dated 1840 shows Copenhagen as it looked when Carl Joachim, followed by Joseph, moved to London. The numbers on the map refer to the most important places mentioned in the text. (Map Room, Royal Library, Copenhagen).

1. *The Vesterport approach to Copenhagen.*

2. *The new synagogue, consecrated 1833.*

3. *Calmer Hambro's last home in Købmagergade.*

4. *Læderstræde, the Jewish quarter before the fire of 1795.*

5. *Simon Hambro's house at Gammel Strand.*

6. *Professor Reinhardt's house in Dronningens Tværgade.*

7. *Nicolai von Holten's – later Carl Ancker's – mansion.*

8. *Joseph Hambro's bank at Kongens Nytorv.*

9. *Copenhagen residence of Carl Joachim and Caroline, 1834–8.*

10. *The Copenhagen Bourse.*

11. *Knippelsbro to Christianshavn.*

12. *Amalienborg Castle.*

13. *Naval berth, Simon Hambro's work-place.*

14. *Hambros Plads with Hambro's factories.*

207

Luis Bramsen, who worked as a clerk for the firm between 1836 and 1839, wrote in his memoirs of his service with Hambro at Christianshavn:

Each evening, when the day's work was done, it was my task to take the boat to Kongens Nytorv and present myself to the Privy Counsellor at head office for questioning on the day's events. This was not an easy duty, for the Counsellor was a demanding old gentleman. When I appeared before him in the evening, or when once in a while he came out to me, the day's examination began:

'How many barrels of wheat did the Konigsberg skipper unload?' – 'How many barrels of flour did the Englishman take on board?' – 'How many sacks of hard-tack of the various categories?' – 'How much meat; how much bacon?' – 'How many tins of green peas had Petit preserved and sealed; how many tins of herrings in oil?' etc.

It was seldom possible for me to answer all these questions, as it was merely my duty, with another clerk of my age, to keep the day-to-day accounts and to look after the warehouses and the daily 'outside' work of unloading and loading. Some things were my responsibility, but most weren't. On the first occasion I told the Privy Counsellor, with great respect, that the matter was nothing to do with me. He made fun of me next day, telling Mansell that I had replied 'This is not my department', adding: 'Have you got departments out there now too?'

I soon learned to understand, however, that it wasn't the actual figures that interested the old gentleman; he just wanted to see whether his employees were in the picture. Indeed, I believe it actually amused him to try to make me feel embarrassed. I therefore answered up cheerfully and confidently, and as accurately as I could, and this satisfied the Privy Counsellor.

We seldom saw young Hambro. I remember him visiting the mill only once. He seemed to me anything but pleasant.

The plain-speaking Luis Bramsen later turned out to be one of Joseph's most able trainees. In 1864 he founded the Nye Danske Brandforsikring insurance company, which celebrated its centenary in 1964, with some of his descendants still on the board.

It is true that the new Hambro factory at Christianshavn was of little interest to Carl Joachim. He wanted to be a banker and an art collector, not a manufacturer. He appeared only rarely at the factory, and was not a welcome visitor. The staff admired his father, but found the son supercilious and conceited.

In one respect, however, the journey proved to be useful to Carl Joachim. In 1830 he applied for the vacant office of North American consul, and was appointed to the post at the early age of twenty-three. A letter written by Holten, the Chairman of the National Debt Commission, to Joseph in September 1837 shows that he tried to live up to the title. Holten wrote in a postscript: 'Last evening I was at Øregaard for an excellent dinner given by your son in honour of the officers of the

Whatever could not be brought by ship to Hambros Plads on the other side of the harbour entrance had to come by road, and there was only one road leading to Christianshavn. It ran via Christian IV's old seventeenth-century wooden bridge, Knippelsbro, which was not replaced until after Joseph's death. French lithograph, c. 1840.

North-American frigate. It was all very pleasant, and the role of host becomes your son well. I have been told that he is to repeat this pleasant event tomorrow, Saturday.'

Before long, Carl Joachim felt – rightly or wrongly – that his father was disinclined to entrust him with any important duties, and he also noticed that the staff at the bank, who all showed great affection towards Joseph, ignored him. Carl Joachim's over-sensitive and ego-centric nature found this intolerable. After a year, and following his own first successful business trip to Manchester, he asked his father to allow him to establish a branch office in London. He himself would be able to look after it with one or two assistants. By now the bank had so much acceptance business with London on behalf of Danish importers that it would be quite reasonable to take up the other end of the business – imports into England from Denmark – which was otherwise left to foreign banking houses. Early in 1832 Carl Joachim moved to London. He lodged at first in a boarding house, and soon rented an office and warehouse in the south of the City near the Thames. Here he began to build up the enterprise which from 1839 onwards, with the help of his father, was to make his family known the world over. By the

Hambro's manufacturing enterprise at Hambros Plads, photographed in about 1890. Andreas Hansen had long since taken over the business. The illustration shows that even large ships could tie up alongside without difficulty. Royal Library, Copenhagen.

Photograph from the 1890s showing the entrance to the peninsula. Joseph had it declared a free port by paying the wages of a permanent customs officer posted at the entrance to provide a daily guard. Royal Library, Copenhagen.

The great bakery, which supplied hard tack to ships in the harbour, was Joseph's pride. He occasionally sailed out to the factory and would sit for hours watching the baking. Royal Library, Copenhagen.

Even at the time of Andreas Hansen and his sons, travelling to Hambros Plads was always easiest by boat from Kongens Nytorv. Here Andreas Hansen's eldest son is arriving at Hambros Plads. Photograph taken about 1890. Royal Library, Copenhagen.

Øregaard was one of the many beautiful North Zeeland country houses used as summer residences by the wealthy. This property was built in 1806, only four miles from Copenhagen. It was situated in the centre of a large park, with a lawn running down to the Sound. Joseph bought the property in 1833 to please Carl Joachim, who had just returned home with his new bride. Coloured lithograph, c. 1840. Royal Library, Copenhagen.

time of the bank's centenary in 1939 the myth of the gifted young Dane who came to London by accident in 1838 and in the following year set up his world-wide bank was so deep-rooted that it is almost sacrilege to tamper with the legend. But the truth also makes a good story, and it shows quite clearly that it can have been no easy task for a foreigner in England to build up a bank of world-wide ramifications.

Very little is known of Carl Joachim's early years in London, since the British Hambro family never kept records. From later accounts it is clear that from the very first he lost his heart to the England he knew just before Queen Victoria came to the throne. He found the British mentality and way of life much more inspiring than provincial Copenhagen, and his admiration was unstinted for London's great bankers such as Nathan Rothschild and the Baring Brothers, who made his father's undertaking in Copenhagen look like a village shop. But the first report of his other activities comes from his devoted foster-sister, Mathilde Reinhardt:

Carl Joachim, now aged twenty-six, married in London on 12 December 1833! The woman of his choice is twenty-three-year-old Caroline Gostenhofer. She is the youngest daughter of a London merchant of German origin, Theofilius

Øregaard today, quite unchanged even though the suburb of Hellerup has since grown around the park. It owes its preservation to unusually fortunate circumstances. In 1840 Hambro sold the property to Andreas Hansen, whose family retained ownership for the rest of the century. In 1917 the municipality of Gentofte bought the property, and converted the house and park into a local museum. Øregaard Museum.

Gostenhofer. Of course, it is scarcely the marriage his father might have wished, but the old Privy Councillor is nevertheless happy for Carl Joachim's sake, and he impatiently awaits the newly-weds' promised visit to Copenhagen.

Joseph, who had never indulged in any ostentation that might cause offence or envy, now bought Øregaard, a beautiful country house on Strandvejen seven kilometres north of Copenhagen, so that the newly-weds would have a suitable holiday home for their first visit to Denmark in the summer of 1834. Again, it is Mathilde who describes the newly-weds' first visit to Copenhagen, but it is clear that she was disappointed. In her memoirs, she makes it plain that she found Caroline a refined but very neurotic young woman 'whose behaviour was stiff and ladylike, who spoke very affectedly and who in no way tried to hide the fact that she felt very strange in Denmark'. Mathilde added, with some irritation: 'She certainly did very little to make herself at home.' Nevertheless the foster-sister concedes that things must have been difficult for the young bride, since scarcely anyone in Copenhagen spoke English.

Caroline's uneasiness in Denmark disappointed Carl Joachim, who now waited to be accepted into the Copenhagen bank as Joseph's partner, leaving the office in London to lesser functionaries. He wanted to become American consul again, to live in a style appropriate to his position in his own house in Kronprinsessegade, and to spend the summers in the country at Øregaard. Joseph once more gave way; one thing gave him particular pleasure – Carl Joachim's love for Caroline was deep and sincere. A further gratification was that before the end of 1834 she presented him with his first grandchild. This was Charles, born on 2 October at Øregaard. On 29 January 1836 followed another son Percival, and on 13 July 1838 a frail little daughter, Caroline Marie, whose failing health increased Caroline's neurosis.

But the renewed collaboration between father and son was still unsatisfactory. Caroline felt alien and lonely in Copenhagen, and the three small children were a great burden to her. At Øregaard – one of north Zeeland's most idyllic country houses – she felt even more lonely than in Copenhagen.

In the autumn of 1834, Frederik VI discovered that he needed to raise a new loan of £2,000,000, a so-called reserve fund loan, to draw on if the need arose. This more or less corresponded to what would today be called an international credit. Finance minister Moltke immediately passed the matter over to Joseph. However, Rothschilds had written a very pleasant letter to Moltke, and he gave Joseph to understand that, without wishing to put pressure on the highly respected banker, he would welcome it if the Rothschilds were once again to act as lenders.

This time of course there was no urgency about the loan, and the negotiations were fairly relaxed; the money was not to be made available by any fixed date. Moltke wanted either a 4 per cent loan at an issue price close to par or a 3 per cent loan at an issue price of about 75. Joseph might deduct a commission of $\frac{1}{2}$ per cent of the loan's nominal amount, equivalent to £10,000. This was of course a substantial amount, but Moltke had gradually come to realize the advantages of having a shrewd agent to negotiate in London's harsh financial climate; an increase in the selling price of only 1 per cent would cover the commission twice over. In his instructions to Joseph, he wrote as usual that he relied on Joseph's 'skill, ability and devotion to His Majesty'. As security for the loan Joseph was authorized to offer once again the proceeds from the Øresund duty and the Danish Virgin Islands, and if this proved insufficient he could also offer security on a number of Crown properties. Joseph went to London in October 1834 to make preliminary enquiries. Moltke had also commissioned him to go to Spain to try to collect a large Danish debt, and so he made preparations

Caroline Gostenhofer (1810–52) married Carl Joachim Hambro at St George's, Blooms-
bury, in London on 12 December 1833. Soon afterwards they went to Copenhagen where
over the next four years she gave birth to three children – Charles, Percival and Caroline.
Her youngest son, Everard, was born in London in 1842. Hambro Family Archives.

for a long absence. The visit in fact lasted nearly a year, since during intervals in the negotiations he took the opportunity to regain his health.

He had no objection to negotiating with Nathan Rothschild personally, although he had never done so before. He knew that he had to take his time and thoroughly consider all the details, for the Rothschilds had a reputation for being quicker and more able than the British houses he had negotiated with in the past. He did not delay in inviting Nathan Rothschild to lunch at his hotel, and the famous banker, by now only two years from the end of his active life, appeared with his nephew and son-in-law, Amsel. Nathan had never used his Austrian title of Baron, conferred in 1821, but his young Viennese son-in-law liked to call himself Baron de Rothschild, like his own father and his other uncles.

It was soon clear that it was a particularly inappropriate time for raising a new loan. There was a marked shortage of money in London, and even against security Rothschilds were asking as much as 4–5 per cent for short-term loans. Nathan told Joseph that his brother, James Rothschild of Paris, had recently lost millions on French 3 per cent bonds, and that he was in a bad mood, not so much because of the money he had lost but because of his competitors' ill-concealed delight at his losses. However, Joseph believed that James Rothschild would be able to cope with this situation: 'It is said that his annual income by way of interest exceeds the French civil list, which at present amounts to 11 million francs,' wrote Joseph to Holten with awe. Joseph also listened with interest to what Nathan had to tell him of James' worries over the large debts owed to him in Madrid. Following King Ferdinand VII's death the year before, the Spanish throne had passed to his infant daughter Isabella, but her uncle Don Carlos also claimed the throne. A fierce struggle had arisen between the rival parties, which had rapidly led to a state of complete lawlessness. At that time, to travel to Spain was to risk one's life. All strangers were robbed and manhandled, and only mounted couriers had any chance of slipping through, since the robbers were not interested in documents. For the time being, therefore, Joseph put aside the matter of the loan, and decided to postpone his trip to Spain until the situation there improved.

He eventually succeeded in raising the Rothschild loan in the summer of 1835, but meanwhile the situation had changed. There was less need for the money in Denmark, and Copenhagen was expressing a general disinclination to raise loans abroad. The Rothschilds pressed for permission to supply the agreed amount, but Joseph quietly let the matter drag on. Denmark took an advance payment of 10 per cent, but the remainder of the large sum remained untouched. Young Amsel S.

Count A. W. Moltke (1785–1864), Danish prime minister and scion of Denmark's most wealthy and influential family. Drawing by J. V. Gertner, 1848. Frederiksborg Museum.

Rothschild bombarded Joseph with letters right up to 1837, urging him to implement the loan; the Rothschilds could not keep such a large amount available for an unlimited period, and Joseph must understand this. Very naturally, Amsel's many letters were impatient, but over and above this they were frequently ingratiating, patronizing and finally rather condescending. All this Joseph took in his stride. Later, when Carl Joachim learned of this correspondence, its intolerant tone inspired his enmity towards the Rothschilds.

The loan was never completed. At Joseph's suggestion the advance was repaid to the Rothschilds at the end of 1837, plus £20,000 for the inconvenience caused. Of this compensation Joseph paid £10,000, equivalent to his own commission. As recently as 1832 one of Joseph's men at the Christianshavn factory had quoted him as having said: 'No merchant should let a shilling run through his hands unless there is a penny stuck to it. As far as I am concerned, the business we are running isn't a charitable organization!' Within five years, however, he appears to have turned his back completely on this attitude. By degrees he had become so wealthy that his greatest problem was to find good investments for his capital rather than to make more money. This explains his remarks in a letter of November 1837 from London to Count A. W. Moltke, giving his opinion on the now apparently superfluous loan:

A loan of this kind is the wrong way to go about things today. In our day and age, the word loan has become detested. I need hardly emphasize my concern for my Fatherland. It would be unpleasant for our good and gracious King to hear the comments this loan would provoke. I want to avoid this with all my heart, and I will willingly contribute my mite to avoid such criticism.

A. W. Moltke was dumbfounded at Joseph's high-minded gesture, and replied warmly:

I have repeatedly assured you how much I appreciate the unselfish patriotism and wisdom with which you execute the transactions and assignments I placed in your hands with such confidence. As the person to whom His Majesty has entrusted the country's finances, it is very pleasing to have as a banker a man who on so many occasions has proved that he puts his own country's interests before his own.

The Rothschilds were not, however, left empty-handed. In the middle of the negotiations that preceded the cancellation of the loan, a long-feared catastrophe occurred. Thomas Wilson & Co. ceased payments in 1837, and thereafter Moltke dared not use this firm to distribute Denmark's half-yearly interest and repayments to bond-holders. With immense industry and painstaking care, Amsel S. Rothschild arranged for the London house to step into the shoes of the Wilson firm, which soon after went bankrupt. Rothschilds took over the loan for the remaining forty-six years of its sixty-year life.

Joseph had contrived in various ways to arrange for the 1835 loan to be called off, and for Rothschilds to take over the Wilson loan on acceptable terms. For example, Moltke had given him permission to hold out to young Amsel the prospect of a Cross of the Order of the Dannebrog if matters were resolved satisfactorily. 'This would please his old parents in Vienna,' wrote Joseph to Moltke. When matters were settled in March 1838, both the King and Moltke thought it equally important for Joseph to receive the Cross of the Dannebrog to mark the occasion. It was typical of developments among liberal Jews in Copenhagen over the previous two decades that Joseph no longer

Carl Joachim Hambro, painted in this miniature by an unknown artist, as a newly married man in Copenhagen in the 1830s. Hambros Bank Archives.

hesitated in accepting this honour from his King. It was in fact the last honour, for Frederik VI died a year later.

It took longer for Joseph to make a mark in Sweden than in Norway. One reason for this was that Sweden itself had a number of excellent bankers, many of whom were Jewish. Since 1782 Sweden had allowed Jews to settle in Stockholm, Gothenburg and Norrköping. A charitable

'Gamla Stan', the oldest part of Stockholm when Joseph first visited Sweden in the 1830s. In the middle of the picture is the royal castle, where Joseph was received by the King. The

observer of these new arrangements might have seen them as a modernizing and humanizing extension of the 1781 Swedish Ordinance on religious freedom, but it was probably equally an expression of the wish to attract initiative and capital to Sweden. The Ordinance of 1782 did not extend as far as might have been expected. Although it had been drafted on an Austrian model, it was stricter. Jews in Sweden were not allowed to marry Christians nor to employ them. They were excluded from the crafts, and, as in Denmark, most of them were forced to trade in money, precious stones and other goods not reserved to the guilds. Denmark accepted the principle of equality in 1814, but in Sweden the struggle for full equality continued throughout most of the nineteenth

castle is situated on a small island between the present north and south parts of the city. Lithograph, c. 1840, probably by Johan Henric Strömer. Stockholm City Museum.

century. The greatest advance came in 1838, with King Carl xiv's Johan full approval. Like Frederik vi, he had no prejudice against the Jews.

Joseph's first contact with Sweden was in autumn 1834, just after his return from a year's journey abroad. On this occasion he and his good friend and colleague Salomon Heine of Hamburg negotiated a 4½ per cent loan of £500,000 for the Federation of Swedish Mine-Owners. Joseph visited Stockholm with Heine in 1836, and returned for the last time in 1843, when he was received by the ageing King, who appointed him Swedish-Norwegian privy banker. Joseph said later that the King had displayed the ultimate in French courtesy, embracing him heartily upon his appointment. Even Frederik VI had never done this, and it was an unforgettable experience that Joseph always enjoyed recounting.

Nevertheless it was later generations of Hambros in London who reaped the great harvest of these contacts with Sweden. In 1876, the penultimate year of Carl Joachim's life, a long series of loan transactions, which has continued up to the present day, was initiated with Sweden.

In the years between 1834 and 1837 Joseph was abroad with scarcely a break. In 1835 he was in Bordeaux questioning the many Spanish refugees about the situation in Spain and the possibility of a journey to Madrid. King Ferdinand's former minister of finance, Don Julian a Perez, himself a refugee, urgently warned him against travelling to Spain. Even at that time he could not expect to come out of such an expedition alive. The minister of finance was well aware of the Danish debt, and advised him to bide his time. The two men, both of whom obviously had time on their hands, met each day in Bordeaux and discussed the European situation.

Joseph, now aged fifty-seven, gradually had to give more consideration to his health and was troubled by his growing loneliness. In a letter from Paris to Holten dated October 1837, he wrote:

You ask about my health. It is only so-so. I keep to a strict diet, stay at home when it rains, but I feel that my 57 years of effort to get on in the world are beginning to show their consequences. I doubt whether I shall remain here in Paris for the entire winter, and I am seriously thinking of going further South, especially if the cholera there is over. If I can avoid my gout this winter my knees will probably get better, and with God's help I shall then be able to stay at home with my son and his family and my friends. As I get older, I find it trying to be alone. Even in Paris I'm not happy – only with my family. Otherwise there is absolutely no news from here. I am sorry to hear about your nasty toothache.

In January 1838, Joseph was still in Paris pampering his health, so it was Carl Joachim who on 11 January received a message from the widow of Counsellor Herholdt at Roskilde, who was now looking after his mother, that Marianne Hambro had died quietly and peacefully the day before at the age of fifty-two, and it was Carl Joachim who had to make arrangements for the funeral at the Jewish cemetery in Copenhagen, which he had never before seen. There were few mourners, for not many of the family friends had known Marianne.

Many years before, Joseph had reserved a large plot at the cemetery for his family, a display of foresight which for once proved misplaced. When he himself arrived home he commissioned the sculptor H. W.

King Carl xiv *Johan of Sweden, seen here aged forty-three in general's uniform and wearing the Order of the Seraphim. He was a solicitor's son from the little town of Pau in France who won fame as Marshal Jean-Baptiste Bernadotte in Napoleon's army. In 1806 Napoleon created him Prince of Pontecorvo. Between 1807 and 1809 he earned a reputation as an able administrator and a most liberal French pro-consul in the occupied North German Hanseatic towns. In 1810 he was chosen to succeed to the Swedish throne, since Carl* xiii, *the Swedish king, was old and childless. In 1814 Denmark, at Bernadotte's suggestion, was forced to surrender Norway to Sweden. Therefore, on his accession to the throne in 1819, Carl* xiv *Johan also became king of Norway. The present Swedish king, Carl* xvi *Adolf, is his great-great-great-great-grandson. Painting by Françoise Gerard, c. 1810.* Royal Castle, Stockholm.

223

No portrait exists of Joseph's unfortunate wife, Marianne (1786–1838).
Neither is there any account of her isolated life for nearly twenty years in various nursing homes near St Hans Hospital at Roskilde. She seems to have been
obliterated from all family records. Only
H. W. Bissen's tombstone in the
Copenhagen Jewish cemetery now bears
silent witness to her existence. Joseph
had reserved a large plot in the cemetery
so that he himself could eventually be
buried beside her, but he died ten years
later in London and was buried in the
Jewish cemetery there.

Bissen to carve a tombstone for Marianne. He did not request a
Hebrew inscription, but had Marianne's name carved into the stone,
calling her the privy counsellor's wife although she had scarcely ever
grasped – let alone used – the title. Although she played such an
insignificant role in the lives of Joseph and Carl Joachim, she had cast a
heavy shadow over them. Her death marked a turning point. Joseph's
homecoming did not lead to a happy reunion with the family. After a
few months he quarrelled with Carl Joachim, who soon afterwards left
Denmark for good. A year later his best friend Nicolai von Holten,
Director of the National Debt Commission, was appointed to supervise
the Øresund duchy and moved to Elsinore; and Joseph's benefactor of
many years, Frederik VI, died in 1839. These events help to explain why
Joseph, even at his age, was able to adapt so easily when he moved to
London in 1840. There was in fact very little to keep him in Denmark.

In 1838, shortly after the return of Joseph from his long journey, there
had been a clash between father and son. After four years in Denmark
Carl Joachim announced that he wanted to return to London with his
wife and children, to take up the London end of the business again, but
this time under his own control. If his father would make over to him

£50,000 he would show what he could do. As ever, Joseph gave way; after all, Carl Joachim was his only son. But he must sometimes have wished that this son was as pleasant, talented and amenable as his Norwegian cousin Edvard Hambro, who, now that he was employed by the Copenhagen bank, was living with Joseph. At that time Joseph undoubtedly saw far greater potential in him than in his own son. Late in autumn 1838, Carl Joachim returned to England with Caroline and the three children. From that day he returned only rarely to Copenhagen.

Carl Joachim had certainly chosen a very inopportune time for setting up an independent banking enterprise in London. In spring 1839 a crisis was already ravaging the British financial world, and in the period that followed several banks and bankers in England and the USA collapsed. During the summer in 1839 there were alarming reports about Carl Joachim's circumstances in Old Broad Street, where he had established himself early in the year.

Between 1834 and 1838, when Carl Joachim tried to act as his father's right-hand man in C. J. Hambro & Son at Copenhagen, he lived with Caroline during the winter in the highly fashionable Kronprinsessegade. This street had been built up thirty years earlier on the edge of Kongens Have. It is still one of the city's most desirable addresses, and commands a fine view over the great park surrounding Rosenborg Castle. Watercolour by H. G. F. Holm, c. *1840.* Copenhagen City Museum.

That summer, Andreas Hansen and his large family had been Joseph's guests at Øregaard. During a pleasant summer luncheon news reached Øregaard that Carl Joachim had taken on immense commitments, was said to have lost all the funds he had brought with him, had suffered a nervous breakdown and was confined to bed. Travel in 1839 was not as easy as it is now, but Joseph had always made up his mind quickly in an emergency. The same evening he was on his way, and three days later he reached London via Calais and Dover. He moved into the north London house of the bedridden Carl Joachim, together with the panic-stricken Caroline and their three children. The atmosphere soon became unbearable. Carl Joachim did not want to make a clean breast of his difficulties and Joseph, normally so restrained, probably allowed his anger to get the better of him. Not long after this, Carl Joachim disappeared to Hamburg with his entire family. He had refused to discuss matters with his father, who was left to form his own impression by enquiries among the staff in Old Broad Street. He soon grasped the situation, although we do not know the extent of the loss. He now called in one of his trusted Copenhagen staff, so that he might have at least one able man on the spot. After some time Carl Joachim and his family returned to London, but he was in such a disturbed mental state that he had to enter an English clinic, where the doctor, Alexander Sutherland, ordered complete isolation and absolute quiet for an indefinite period. The unhappy Caroline had to travel back to Denmark alone, spending the rest of the summer at Øregaard with her children.

Carl Joachim was forced to spend almost a year in the clinic, and Joseph now made preparations to take up permanent residence in England. Everything in Copenhagen was in good hands, and able men were occupying all posts in the bank, the commercial department and the factory. In autumn 1840 he sold Øregaard to Andreas Hansen, whose descendants kept it in the family until 1901. At the same time he made over the Christianshavn factory to Andreas, getting an excellent price for it.

In London, Joseph first rented a flat in Upper Portland Place; later he bought Bransbury House, a beautiful country house at Roehampton, then a few miles south-west of London. From here he could go by a carriage to the centre of London whenever he wished.

His only communication now with poor Carl Joachim in the clinic was through the tactful and understanding Dr Sutherland, and a few letters that Joseph wrote to him in autumn 1840 have been preserved. Carl Joachim was tortured night and day by the obsessions that he would no longer to able to support his wife and children, and that as a

After his earlier visits to London in 1832 and 1833, Carl Joachim was able in 1838 to approach with confidence the question of a location for his own bank. The site had to be in the City near the Royal Exchange, the Stock Exchange and the Bank of England. He chose 70 Old Broad Street. This is a view along the street from Threadneedle Street. The bank opened in 1839 and remained here until 1926, when it moved to 41 Bishopsgate. Lithograph, c. 1840. Print Room, Guildhall Library, London.

result his whole family would be destroyed. At the doctor's suggestion Joseph drew up a contract committing the interest on £30,000 to Carl Joachim's future maintenance, but Carl Joachim would sign the document only if the doctor signed first. Joseph trod with more caution than ever before, but to his great sorrow he recognized in Carl Joachim's symptoms an obsession similar to Marianne's in the early years of their marriage.

Carl Joachim slowly recovered. By 1842 he was himself again, and although he and Caroline had the sorrow of losing their delicate little two-year-old daughter, Caroline Marie, there was great happiness when on 11 April of the same year Caroline gave birth to the family's fourth and last child, the only one to be born in England. He was christened Everard.

Although Carl Joachim had recovered his health, he took no significant part in the business during the years that followed. Joseph attended to everything. He was at Old Broad Street every weekday and often on Saturdays, which it must be remembered was not a working day for Jews. Carl Joachim, by contrast set himself the task of writing a history of Denmark for his children. This occupied him throughout 1842, and in 1843 and 1849 the book was published in English in two handsome volumes. The concentration needed helped him to regain his equilibrium. In 1843 he became a British citizen, and in future he signed himself Charles Hambro. Relations with his father gradually improved, perhaps because they did not see each other every day, since for large parts of the year Carl Joachim was convalescing at seaside resorts or in his beloved Scotland. In the event, the gradual deterioration of the neurotic Caroline's health became as pressing a problem as his own earlier indisposition.

The striking lack of information about the strained relationship between father and son in England makes it all the more refreshing to be able to turn to Hans Christian Andersen, the Danish writer of fairy tales, as a witness to the harmonious relationship that eventually existed between Joseph and Carl Joachim during the closing years of Joseph's life.

In the summer of 1847 Carl Joachim, with Caroline and the three boys, spent a long holiday in Scotland. As usual, old Joseph was left looking after the business. One Saturday he was alone at the bank when a customer arrived to draw out a few pounds. Joseph recognized him as the Danish poet Hans Andersen, then aged forty-three. Andersen was on his first visit to England, to negotiate with his publisher Mary Howitt, perhaps to bask a little in his own fame, and also in the vain hope of being received by Queen Victoria. To compensate, he had a

Charles and Percival Hambro, the two elder sons of Carl Joachim, painted by a Danish artist in 1836. Hambro Family Archives.

happy reunion in London with the idol he had admired for so many years, the Swedish singer Jenny Lind, who now held him in sisterly affection. That summer, the whole of London was at Jenny Lind's feet; her concerts at Covent Garden were always oversubscribed. Andersen, impractical, helpless, timorous and worried, was delighted to find in Joseph an admirer and a fatherly protector. Joseph looked after his financial affairs in England, negotiated with the publisher on his behalf, criticized his poor English and invited him for long, peaceful weekends at Bransbury House. Andersen found everything as charming there as in one of his fairy tales. His diary entry for Monday 26 June 1847 runs as follows: 'Hambro arrived in his own carriage and took me into the country. It was as if London was buried behind me. Cheerful countryside, velvety grass, beautiful sunshine. Most of Hambro's people spoke Danish. Sheep and horses ambled in the meadows as if on show. A bluish haze lay over distant London. I feel healthier here than in the town.'

Jenny Lind, 'The Swedish Nightingale' (1820–87), She was beautiful and had unusual charm. In the summer of 1847 London was at her feet. In 1852 she married her pianist, Otto Goldschmidt, and soon afterwards retired from the stage. Nevertheless, she still performed on special occasions, for example at the marriage of the Prince of Wales (Edward VII) to the Danish Princess Alexandra at St George's Chapel, Windsor, in 1863. Swedish lithograph, 1840. Royal Library, Copenhagen.

Andersen was a great admirer of Sir Walter Scott, and wanted to see the country he had immortalized in his books, so Joseph invited him to come on a trip to Scotland, where they could visit Carl Joachim and Caroline, who were on holiday in Scotland at the time. Carl Joachim, Andersen's diaries and letters inform us, met the two travelling companions in his elegant carriage at Edinburgh Station and drove them to his imposing house, where Andersen was given a fine, sunny guest room. Carl Joachim told Andersen that once, in Copenhagen, he had seen the poet come into the bank, but did not have the courage to speak to him. Now he was all the more pleased to meet him as a guest. Caroline was a charming hostess, although Andersen found her very frail and somewhat neurotic; she joined none of their trips during Andersen's visit. Andersen was enchanted by the three boys, especially five-year-old Everard, already big for his age, whom he called 'Goliath'. Andersen was impressed that Carl Joachim said grace at

Hans Christian Andersen was already well known over most of Europe when he visited the Hambro family on his first journey to England in 1847. He is seen here in 1836, just after he had published his first collection of fairy-tales, including The Tinderbox, Big Claus and Little Claus *and* The Princess and the Pea. *Painting by C. A. Jensen, 1836.* Odense City Museum.

every meal, and that the whole family went to church on Sundays. He himself devoted Sunday mornings to letter-writing and to his diary.

Carl Joachim was vicariously proud to see the poet's portrait displayed in all the bookshops, often beside that of Jenny Lind. He asked an unsuspecting bookseller whether Andersen's books sold well, and this was eagerly confirmed. When he asked the bookseller whether he had ever met the famous writer, the man said that regretfully he had not. There was great merriment when Carl Joachim asked him to meet the gentleman he had brought with him! At one museum there had been a rumour that Andersen would arrive, but it was Joseph who was mistaken for the important visitor – the handsome old man was the only member of the company who looked like a real poet.

Carl Joachim was infinitely generous towards Andersen. He was most anxious to give him a present, but Andersen modestly declined; however, when the poet lost his umbrella he was persuaded to take Carl Joachim's. Joseph returned to London after a week, and Andersen accompanied the rest of the family to other parts of Scotland for a few days' visit to Walter Scott's countryside. The friendship between Carl Joachim and Andersen continued for ten years, and later Andersen dedicated to him the English edition of one of his books.

It is pleasing to catch a last glimpse of father and son together under such harmonious circumstances. It was indeed not before time, for Joseph died the following year.

In 1834 Joseph's nephews Edvard and Johan Hambro – the sons of Isach Hambro – had been sent to Copenhagen to work for their uncle in the Kongens Nytorv bank, and Edvard soon became very close to Joseph. He saw in the young Edvard, fourteen years younger than Carl Joachim, a potential future head of the bank if Carl Joachim proved too unstable. In Copenhagen Edvard lived with Joseph like a son of the family, and this continued in London. Joseph remembered his nephew in his will, leaving him a substantial sum of money. Edvard's brother Johan, five years his senior, was even more gifted than Carl Joachim but just as impulsive and restless, although Johan was more sociable. Johan had often broken off his banking training; in 1841 he had become a doctor of divinity, and then began to study law. He was widowed after six weeks of marriage to a young tubercular Norwegian girl, whom he had loved and would not forsake. 'He was the most noble person ever to have lived in this world', said one of his sisters-in-law later.

Some time in the 1840s Johan returned to London and once again became actively involved in the bank. Joseph felt that with these two clever Norwegian cousins in control the bank would be able to carry on,

Johan Hambro (1816–80) was the second son of Isach Hambro, the Norwegian merchant. He was the most intelligent, and also the most charming, of the four Bergen brothers. Drawing by Siegward Dahl, c. 1840. City Museum, Oslo.

if Carl Joachim chose to withdraw to the family estate that Joseph had decided Carl Joachim was to buy after his father's death.

Carl Joachim was very fond of Johan, and admired the easy charm the elegant Norwegian displayed at all levels of society. He was prepared to welcome him as his future partner at the bank, but he hated and detested Edvard. He had for years looked upon Edvard as Joseph's spy, reporting on his son's initiative or lack of it. At his death in 1848, Joseph in fact believed that Carl Joachim, Johan and Edvard would together form the future management of the bank. But this did not come about. In autumn 1848 Carl Joachim did in fact offer Johan a partnership, but on the express condition that Edvard should be immediately dismissed. Johan replied that, if Edvard was thrown out, under no circumstances would he stay on. He had no wish to pay for his promotion by agreeing to such an injustice towards his own brother.

In the event they both left the bank in anger, and for good measure they settled in Newcastle where they established an agency and banking business. This they provocatively called 'Hambro Brothers', and they began to compete keenly with Carl Joachim in London for Danish and Norwegian customers. This dispute meant of course that the old family contacts with Norway nursed by Joseph for nearly forty years were suddenly completely severed, and all mutual dealings ceased from

233

Edvard Hambro (1821–84), third son of Edvard Isach of Bergen. He is photographed here in 1850 with his English wife, Mary Ann, née Blackburn (1821–85). He died childless, a Lloyd's agent in Antwerp. In the family's ownership.

one day to the next. Johan and Edvard now hated and scorned Carl Joachim from the bottom of their good Norwegian hearts, and they did not conceal their feelings from their father in Bergen.

But Carl Joachim won the contest. After a few years the two brothers could no longer carry on, and were forced to close down the business in Newcastle. Johan moved to London, where for many years he ran a chemico-technical factory with no great success. He died in London in 1880, three years after Carl Joachim. During his final years young Everard Hambro had supported his impoverished Norwegian relation, who wrote him charming letters of thanks for the assistance he so sorely needed. Johan had remarried in 1856, but life became no easier for him. His new English wife, Cecilia Hamilton, bore him no fewer than seven daughters, but he could not provide for them. Six of them took to nursing in England, and died unmarried. Edvard married in Newcastle in 1850 and managed somewhat better financially, since his English marriage remained childless. He died in 1884, a Lloyds agent in Antwerp.

The wrecked relationship with the Norwegian family undoubtedly worried Carl Joachim in his final days. He never came to terms with Isach in Bergen after the outbreak of the family dispute. It was typical of Carl Joachim that reconciliation was postponed for almost thirty

After Joseph's death, Carl Joachim came to realize how much he owed to his father. In September 1851 he asked the sculptor H. W. Bissen, who had known Joseph since his visit to Rome in 1829, to come to London to model this bust. It was prepared from the few pictures available, supplemented by Bissen's memory of meetings with Joseph in Copenhagen. The model was completed in October 1851, cast in bronze and carved in marble in Copenhagen in 1852–3. The bronze bust was sent to Hambros bank in London, where it still stands; the marble bust was ordered by Smidt and le Maire, who took over Hambros bank in Copenhagen in 1848. In 1916 Smidt's son presented the Copenhagen copy to the Frederiksborg Museum's collection of famous Danes. It is still to be seen there. Frederiksborg Museum.

The elegant old Hambro house on Kongens Nytorv, built in 1736, stood for 156 years. In 1892 it fell victim to the reconstruction of Magasin du Nord, the still-flourishing department store. Hambro's house, which now looks remarkably small, has been drawn in where it stood before demolition.

years until his death in 1877. In his will he set aside £5,000 for distribution among the numerous descendants of his long-dead Uncle Isach. A descendant of one of the lucky heirs, Carl Joachim Hambro, President of the Norwegian Storting, told the story of Johan and Edvard in his memoirs. As a child, he wrote, he was often told that the piano in his home had been bought with the money his father had suddenly and unexpectedly received from Hambros Bank in London.

Joseph would have turned in his grave had he known that Carl Joachim would disown his Norwegian cousins. In any event it was now clear that there was nobody to manage the bank but Carl Joachim himself. The most surprising aspect, however, is that he proved that it was not beyond his capabilities.

11 Carl Joachim, the Baron

Joseph died on 3 October 1848 at his Roehampton country house in south-west London. Although at the time of Marianne's death ten years earlier he had reserved a space for himself by her side in the Copenhagen Jewish cemetery, he was now, at his own wish and for practical reasons, put to rest in the Jewish cemetery at Whitechapel, east of the City. But his tombstone is no longer to be found. With his usual care he had instructed Carl Joachim in his will to ensure that 'as soon as the Almighty has called me from this world, I am properly buried according to the Jewish custom, quietly and without undue ceremony, and as early in the morning as the Jewish rules will permit.'

Death did not take Joseph by surprise. His will had been prepared in 1844, and nothing had been changed by the time of his death. Its whole content was centred on one intention – to safeguard the future of Carl Joachim and his family in the best way possible. Shortly before his death he made over the bank in Copenhagen to Smidt and le Maire, and Andreas Hansen had long ago taken over the factory at Christianshavn. All the available assets were now therefore concentrated in England. Joseph had remembered with generosity many of his Danish relations; Edvard, his favourite Norwegian nephew; his servants; the Jewish communities in London and Copenhagen; and he had established in Marianne's name large scholarships for young Danish merchants. Nevertheless, there remained nearly £300,000 for Carl Joachim. Even in England this was a very considerable sum, particularly since at that time there were no such thing as death duties.

But, as was to be expected, the will also clearly reflected Joseph's concern for Carl Joachim's fortitude and mental balance. When the will was prepared in 1844 it was directly influenced by Carl Joachim's harrowing period in hospital. It therefore provided for his future not to have to rest upon the bank, which was to be carried on only for the benefit of Carl Joachim's son, Percival. Carl Joachim himself was to take £90,000 of the inheritance immediately and invest it in securities. Thereafter, 'at the earliest opportunity and without acting rashly', he was to use this money to buy landed property which 'on the basis of sound judgement and knowledge' would provide yearly interest of at least 2 per cent. Joseph added that the country house, which was to remain in the family in perpetuity, was never to be mortgaged for more than one third of its purchase price, and that the family's eldest son, Charles, was to inherit it. As to the bank's future, he urgently recommended that Carl Joachim should liquidate it 'if it caused him too much mental anxiety', and he added that if Carl Joachim should ever lose more than £50,000 in one transaction it would be wiser to liquidate both the commercial house and the bank immediately rather than to attempt to make up the lost money!

Joseph's will certainly showed little faith in his son, but Carl Joachim, now forty-one, eventually realized that everything in it had been drafted with the best of intentions. He had found it difficult to understand his father's patronizing arrangements and solicitude, but now that Joseph was dead he came to realize what he owed to his father, for without Joseph there would have been no London bank at all, and therefore a Hambro country house would have been unthinkable in the foreseeable future. It is true that it was Carl Joachim who had originally moved to London, but his share in the creation of the Old Broad Street business he now inherited had been very small.

In a letter Carl Joachim wrote a few days after Joseph's funeral to the Scottish doctor, Professor Simpson, he makes no attempt to conceal the debt he owed to his father:

All the kind words we now hear about my father cannot console us in our sorrow. It was of course my father who managed our entire business, so that my new duties already weigh heavily upon my shoulders. His undertaking was known and respected all over the Continent for the simple reason that his abilities were so unique. I must now honestly do my utmost to maintain the reputation of the Hambro name. And that will not be easy, as in this my self-chosen new country which I love dearly – perhaps more than many of its own sons – I still find myself in a rather isolated position.

People who had known Carl Joachim as a young man in Copenhagen would probably have had even more reason than Joseph to expect the rich heir to drop into the life of the idle rich. His father had given him an opportunity for this by requiring him to buy landed property. But Carl Joachim would have been misjudged. During his remaining thirty years he was left to stand on his own feet. He was certainly never a happy man, and few of his contemporaries would have said that he was good company, but he managed to live up to the Hambro standards, often in spite of the most appalling difficulties. Moreover, he succeeded in leaving the bank in good shape for his youngest son Everard, whom posterity may well consider the most far-sighted banker of the family.

In March 1848 rebellion in the two Danish duchies of Schleswig and

Emile le Maire (1814–1912), wholesaler and banker, and his partner, Wilhelm Smidt (1801–84). When they were quite young they both entered Joseph's employment, and remained his eminently able and loyal assistants until his death. From 1840, when Joseph finally decided to settle permanently in England, they shared in the management of the bank. Shortly before Joseph's death in London, in 1848, they bought the premises and the banking undertaking and operated it for their own account as 'Smidt & le Maire' – as Hambro's firm link with Denmark. The relationship continued until Wilhelm Smidt died in 1884. Le Maire was a very wealthy man when he retired. Before he died he had assisted in founding Privatbanken in 1857, Kjøbenhavns Handelsbank in 1878 and the Burmeister & Wain shipyard. The premises on Kongens Nytorv were sold in 1884. Painting and lithograph from the 1870s. Royal Library, Copenhagen.

Holstein led to war against the rest of Denmark. The cause was a dispute that centred on the complicated right of succession to these two partly German-speaking provinces in the south of Denmark. During the closing months of his life Joseph, although confined to bed, anxiously watched developments. He contributed to a voluntary fund for equipping the Danish army, sending the Danish war minister, Orla Lehmann, a cheque for £1,500 – the highest donation from any one individual. When Prussia decided to support the rebels in 1849, the situation of the Danish army suddenly became critical. Money was now needed so that the war could be continued.

The Danish minister of state, Joseph's old benefactor Count A. W. Moltke, was very reluctant to impose a war tax on Denmark, and preferred to raise a foreign loan. He soon learnt, however, that war loans were no longer popular in international financial circles, and that

Denmark's war against Schleswig-Holstein was very unpopular indeed. It was seen as no more than a dispute over the dubious interpretation of old agreements and treaties, exaggerated by nationalism. Since Joseph's death Moltke had looked upon C. J. Hambro & Son as no longer in the running, and he first approached bankers in St Petersburg and Amsterdam. In both places he was rebuffed. His agent then met with the same reaction in London at both Rothschilds and Barings. When rumour of the Danish enquiries spread in the City, *The Times* wrote in a leading article that 'the best way to prevent war is to bring it home that no money can be raised in England for this sort of adventure'.

Faced with this emergency, Moltke's representative in England finally approached Carl Joachim. This was in the spring of 1850, and for the first time since his father's death Carl Joachim found himself at the centre of events. Moreover, it was a matter near to his heart because

The Danish war against the duchies of Schleswig and Holstein, 1848–51, was founded on an old ambiguity about the right of inheritance to these provinces. Schleswig had a predominantly Danish population, whereas Holstein was wholly German and a member of the German Confederation. The war dragged on, interrupted by several armistices, after Holstein had received military assistance from Prussia. General opinion in England was that Denmark did not deserve to be helped. The war, which ended with the intervention of the Great Powers, was seen as a Danish victory, and as a consequence Carl Joachim's bold loan made him popular in Denmark. The picture shows the battle at Dybbøl on 5 June 1848. Painting by Jørgen V. Sonne. Frederiksborg Museum.

of his Danish background. At about this time he wrote to Dr Simpson: 'The Germans want war and the impoverished Danes must raise money somehow. I shall have to lend them £800,000.'

This was in fact the amount, at 5 per cent interest, that the Danish lawyer and politician Frederik Treschow was seeking when he finally contacted Carl Joachim. Carl Joachim had no doubts about the Danish government's security, but the question was, of course, whether British bond buyers would look at a war loan after the comments in *The Times*, and whether Denmark would consider a selling rate of 90 as too high. Carl Joachim was anxious that it should never be said in Denmark that he had tried to make a lot of money out of the misfortunes of his old country, and when the agreement was concluded he himself took responsibility for half the loan, which he intended to offer in England at a rate of 90, leaving Denmark to take over the other half at a selling rate of 84. He expressly asked Treschow to publish the terms in the Danish

Frederik Treschow (1826–1869), solicitor of the Danish High Court and politician. The Danish government sent this highly respected lawyer to London in 1850 to seek a loan of £800,000 from Carl Joachim to finance the war against Schleswig-Holstein, which had begun in 1848. This loan was Carl Joachim's first large independent transaction after his father's death. Although the war was unpopular in England, he succeeded in issuing the Danish government bonds. Painting by M. Marstrand, 1846. Royal Library, Copenhagen.

press, so that his old fellow-countrymen might see that he was acting with fairness.

Of his own £400,000, he very soon sold £250,000 worth, but it looked as if the remaining £150,000 would be a drag on the market. He therefore approached Barings, who were willing to accept the bonds only at 77½; this of course would have ruined the transaction. Instead, he then issued scrip of Hambros bank to the same amount and at the same rate of interest. This was immediately over-subscribed. In fact, it appeared that the name Hambro meant more in London than the name of Denmark. Within a few days the Danish-British bonds reached a rate of 100, and so the Danish loan became a first-class deal in spite of Carl Joachim's unpretentiousness. What thrilled him specially was that he had dared to take on a transaction that both Rothschilds and Barings had refused. A further pleasure was the public declaration by the Danish minister of finance, Count Wilhelm Sponneck, that nobody

King Frederik VII of Denmark, the last and childless king of the old Oldenburg stock, which was replaced in 1863 by the present Glücksburg line. On 6 October 1851 he created Carl Joachim Hambro a baron. It was a remarkable gesture, for the new Danish Constitution of 1849 had in principle abolished such creations. The king, however, wished to express to Carl Joachim his gratitude for the 1850 war loan. Painting by J. V. Gertner. Frederiksborg Castle.

Count Wilhelm Sponneck (1815–88), Danish finance minister during Denmark's war against Schleswig-Holstein. He was a distinctive personality in Danish administration and politics, respected for his indisputable ability and ruthless will, but at the same time his unbelievable arrogance and self-assertion made him very unpopular. It can be said to his credit that he appreciated that Carl Joachim was risking personal ruin in 1850 in negotiating the great war loan. He ended his career as director of the Danish National Bank. Drawing by F. G. Gertner, 1850. Frederiksborg Museum.

could blame Carl Joachim for earning a substantial profit from his patriotic action. Count Sponneck was tactful enough not to mention the amount, which was probably between £30,000 and £40,000. Such was the outcome of Carl Joachim's first independent transaction as a banker; Joseph could scarcely have done better.

One fortunate feature of Carl Joachim's first large issue transaction was that Denmark won the war, or at least was able to claim that it was about to do so. In fact, fighting ceased early in 1851 as a result of the very welcome intervention of the Great Powers. Denmark at least retained sovereignty over the duchies for another thirteen years until in 1864 Bismarck, with Austria's help, conquered both provinces; later, in 1866, he annexed them to Prussia, having put Austria out of the running.

During the euphoria in Denmark after the war the minister of finance, Count Sponneck, felt that Denmark should show her gratitude to the only man who had been willing to help his old fatherland in its distress. Early in 1851 the Danish ambassador in London, Count Frederik Reventlow, was instructed to discover what form of appreciation the helpful banker would prefer. This presented no difficulty to Carl Joachim. All five Rothschild brothers from Frankfurt had been made Austrian barons in 1821, and although Nathan Rothschild of

There are remarkably few pictures of Carl Joachim. This photograph shows him in 1862 aged fifty-five, just married for the second time after ten years of often deeply depressive loneliness. Royal Library, Copenhagen.

London had never used his title it had later been adopted by his eldest son, Lionel, only one year younger than Carl Joachim. Similar ennoblements had taken place within the Baring dynasty. If Carl Joachim was to aspire to the social level of his two keenest competitors, he needed to ask the Danish government for the hereditary Danish title of baron. But he was fully aware that this was not the most favourable time for such a nomination, since under the new democratic constitution of 5 June 1849 future ennoblement in Denmark had been abolished in principle. Nevertheless the ambassador forwarded Carl Joachim's request to Copenhagen. After discussion by the Council of State, the king was recommended – not without some opposition – to grant Carl Joachim's wish. A week later Carl Joachim received a most friendly letter from Count Sponneck, informing him that:

It had been a pleasant duty most humbly to present to His Majesty his views on Carl Joachim's patriotism, energy and skill during his first transaction in the interests of Danish finance, and he had therefore recommended that His Majesty should show his most gracious satisfaction in the form of the very highest favour, in accordance with the Council of State's resolution of 4 April 1851.

On Sponneck's recommendation, therefore, on 8 April 1851 the King had most graciously agreed 'that the head of the C. J. Hambro & Son trading house in London, Carl Joachim Hambro, be elevated to the Danish rank of Baron, the title and rank of Baron to be inherited by whoever of his true male issue is considered head of the family, and in descending order thereafter'. This was followed by Sponneck's personal congratulations and his express hope 'that Carl Joachim's descendants to the last generation may preserve the memory of his merits and of His Majesty's satisfaction'. Never in his life did Carl Joachim experience such pleasure in receiving a letter.

Two weeks later he received a letter from minister of Justice Bardenfleth asking for a sketch of his proposed coat-of-arms. Carl Joachim had in fact already arranged for the Royal College of Arms to design his civil coat-of-arms. He had chosen three rings as the main device, and there is little doubt that these rings were to symbolize the three great world religions, Christianity, Judaism and Islam, as equal concepts. This device is to be found in the coat-of-arms of other baptized Jews. As a British subject since 1843, he had with filial respect added the British lion, and above the close helmet he had retained the vigilant falcon which Joseph had used for many years on his seal. Under the escutcheon he had inserted his own device: '*In Deo*'.

This design he sent to Copenhagen, and by autumn the royal patent at last arrived, signed by King Frederik VII on 6 October 1851. For this patent, the Danish herald had designed another coat-of-arms. By special royal permission, the sinister of this coat-of-arms displayed the savage of the Danish national arms, while Joseph's vigilant falcon was enlarged on the dexter. The escutcheon itself remained virtually unchanged, although a *Dannebrog* (Danish flag) was placed in the centre. The escutcheon was surmounted by a seven-pointed, pearl-studded, baronial coronet. The close helmet above was doubled, and

Carl Joachim's commoner's arms, prepared for him by the Royal College of Arms when he became a British citizen in 1843. The rings symbolized the world religions, the falcon originated from his father's old seal, and the lion symbolized his British citizenship. The motto, 'In Deo', was his own.

an axe-bearing lion in startling red was added above the sinister helmet. The lion is inexplicable, since it resembles the Norwegian lion that had been removed from the Danish national arms when Norway was lost in 1814.

In 1852, Carl Joachim sent the original Danish version to the Royal College of Arms for them to approve its use in England, but the College made no attempt to conceal the fact that they found the Danish arms somewhat primitive, and the arms were then compressed. In this process the savage was becomingly rejuvenated, and the details were given better dimensions and a more attractive balance. This is the form in which the arms exist today. Carl Joachim had them on his furniture and in stone, and as late as 1926 his descendants had them painted over the fireplace in the bank's new Bishopsgate conference room.

Carl Joachim's elevation to baron in 1851 remained unique. He was the first and the last to be so honoured in Denmark following the constitution of 1849. Another unique feature of the title was that it was not to pass to the eldest son but to whoever was considered head of the

On the basis of the commoner's arms, Frederik VII's Copenhagen heraldists designed the new arms of nobility with the seven-point baron's coronet and a savage from the Danish national coat of arms, adding the Danish flag. Joseph's falcon acted as supporter on the dexter side.

family. This variation had been urged by Carl Joachim himself, because he could not as yet see clearly whether the title would go to the bank's future chief or to the heir to the country estate he was about to purchase.

Neither the title nor the coat-of-arms is now used to any extent. The coat-of-arms' use in a modest and simplified form as shown on the following page typified modern attitudes. Several generations of Hambros have been knighted in England, and the foreign title of baron now sounds rather strange. When today, the Hambro family speaks of 'the Baron', the reference is always to Carl Joachim.

Carl Joachim's elevation to the rank of baron had an amazing effect upon his self-assurance. No doctor or psychiatrist could have exercised so incredible an influence upon his mind as the royal patent of 6 October 1851. From that day, he became fired with intense energy, and

When Carl Joachim wanted to have his arms licensed in England, the Royal College of Arms simplified his Danish arms and substantially rejuvenated the royal savage. In this form, Carl Joachim used the arms on furniture and on Milton Abbey's facade.

1851 was the most active and happy year of his life. Not only did he begin to search for his future country estate and to enter into co-operation with the statesman Cavour in Italy, but thanks to Denmark's participation in the Great Exhibition at the Crystal Palace in London his old interest in Danish artists was revived. The Danish sculptor Adolf Jerichau had executed a marble bust of Hans Andersen, which

Andersen asked Carl Joachim to arrange to be shown at the Exhibition. This led to Carl Joachim's acting as intermediary for those Danish artists who participated, and afterwards the grateful Jerichau presented him with Andersen's bust. After Carl Joachim's purchase of the Milton Abbey estate in 1852 Jerichau and his painter wife assisted Carl Joachim in the choice of paintings. In the years that followed, Carl Joachim became almost obsessed with an urge to equip Milton Abbey with furniture, works of art and rare books to match his position in society.

Symbols are simpler today than in the nineteenth century, and noble arms are now scarcely suitable for a company. Carl Joachim's colourful old arms have been modified to produce this logo, which appears on almost all printed matter emanating from Hambros Bank Limited.

Since Joseph's death in 1848, Carl Joachim had been preoccupied with the issue of loans which Sponneck and Cavour respectively had needed for Denmark and Italy. Only now, four years later, was he able to turn his mind to the provisions of his father's will. With the profits he had made from the two transactions it had become possible to consider larger estates, befitting his new title of baron and his position as one of the City's prominent bankers.

The delay was also assisted by the declining health of Caroline. She was proud of all the honour bestowed upon Carl Joachim and proud as well of her new title as baroness, but now she had to rest most of the day and the idea of moving to new and much bigger surroundings made her nervous. She died on 8 March 1852 at only forty-two, and left Carl

Joachim with the three boys – Charles, now seventeen, Percival, fifteen, and Everard, ten. Considering the enormous and lasting depression Carl Joachim developed soon after Caroline's funeral, it is amazing to see that he was able within two months to make up his mind and buy the Milton Abbey estate, a property which included four villages and covered 8,000 acres in the heart of Dorset, just over a hundred miles west of London. The last owner had been the Sixth Earl of Portalington.

Milton Abbey was due to be sold at the end of June that year. There was no time to waste and on Saturday 29 May 1852 Carl Joachim paid his first visit. As he looked from his horse-drawn carriage, he could not fail to have been impressed with the Dorset countryside. The main approaches to the Hall were lined with a thick carpet of bluebells, a vivid hue against the first flush of green leaves and fern. He could look over the tree tops as he descended the steep hillside beyond the village

View of the Milborne valley with Dale Cottage in the foreground. The lake was part of Capability Brown's plan to landscape the park, and in its creation part of the old town was drowned. To the far right, above the trees, can be seen the rooftop of Milton Abbey. The photograph, found in one of Princess Victoria's photograph albums, was taken during her visit to Milton on 31 May 1909. Reproduced by gracious permission of Her Majesty Queen Elizabeth II.

251

A view of the North Lawn front of Milton Abbey and Hall showing the Gate Tower which provided the main entrance to the courtyard within. The Hall was designed for Lord Milton by Sir William Chambers, and built between 1771 and 1776. The site he chose was that of

of Milton Abbas, and catch a fleeting glimpse of the Hall and Abbey as they stood side by side in the Milborne valley, surrounded by an amphitheatre of beechclad hills. It was a glorious, heart-warming sight made perfect by the Abbey, a monument to his religion. He decided to buy it and within six months the conveyance had been signed. The price he paid was nearly three times as much as his father's original estimate, since the Milton Abbey estate cost £240,000.

Beneath the beauty of the buildings, however, there was much sadness. Just a hundred years earlier, the Abbey had been at the centre of a busy market town which had now vanished. When Lord Milton had purchased the estate in 1752 he brought about irrevocable changes. He had destroyed many of the old monastic buildings so that only the Benedictine Abbey itself and, immediately to the north, the Abbots Hall built in 1498, still remained. At the same time he commissioned Sir William Chambers, one of the most renowned architects of his day, to build a new house. Ingenious harmony was the result.

the old monastic buildings, which had once been associated with the Benedictine Abbey and of which only the Abbots Hall remained. This he cleverly incorporated into the South side of the Hall. Dorchester Record Office.

Chambers managed to incorporate into his design the lovely old Tudor hall which was over fifty-three feet long and had a wonderful hammer beam roof, recognized as one of the finest specimens in England. It formed the south wing of the new building which he had constructed around the courtyard. In the three new wings local tradition had been continued by the use of flint and Portland stone. The result was impressive, one of the finest examples of eighteenth-century Gothic architecture.

The park landscape had also been changed; this was the work of the famous Capability Brown. Extensive beech woods were planted on the surrounding hillsides, while in the valley the stream had been dammed and a lake created, a beautiful view to delight the new landlord, Lord Milton. Yet the enhancement of the valley had led to the destruction of the town, once one of the largest settlements in Dorset, for now part of it was flooded by the lake and the rest was removed. Only one cottage survived. A complete new village was constructed beyond the hill, out

An aerial view of Milton Abbey and Hall taken in 1950. Bought by Baron Hambro in 1852, the family remained here until 1932 when it was sold for less than half the original purchase price. Subsequently it has become the home of a boys' public school. Reproduced with kind permission of the University of Cambridge. (Cambridge University Collection: copyright reserved.)

of sight of the new Hall. Along both sides of the broad, winding village street, Milton Abbas was built with its thatched, uniform cottages lining the valley, open lawns to the front and steep gardens behind. In the centre, on the south side, Lord Milton had raised a new parish church with the original almshouses from the old village sited opposite. Today Milton Abbas appears as one of the most picturesque villages in the country but to the new inhabitants in the eighteenth century it epitomized the disruption of the old order and provided the basis of deep hatred towards Lord Milton.

This was the estate to which Carl Joachim now came with his three sons. The local tenants might have mistrusted him too, for he still had a heavy Danish accent, he knew nothing of country affairs and his melancholy air did little to enhance his image. The previous family had been hated so vehemently, however, that the small acts of kindness which he initiated came as a great surprise and slowly he won their affection. He started in 1853 by building a new school at the east end of the village. Within a decade there were four teachers and 130 pupils. Another act of generosity came just before Christmas in 1857 when his eldest son, Charles, was married. He gave a great dinner to the farm tenants in the Hambro Arms Inn, and presented to every labourer and cottager, regardless of age, a pound of beef, two pounds of bread and one pint of beer. The gifts were warmly appreciated and did much to heighten his local standing.

Perhaps the most important aspect in his role as landlord was the restoration of the Abbey which had been so badly neglected by his predecessors. The local newspaper recorded that 'It was Baron Hambro's way to do things in the best possible manner.' He employed Gilbert Scott, the well-known ecclesiastical architect, and gave him *carte blanche* to carry out the work. It was an enormous task and cost £50,000. Scott first saw the Abbey in March 1862 and he began work late that summer. All the plaster was stripped off the interior stonework, the floor was dug up and for a time the inside became a mason's workshop. The tower piers and vaults were stabilized and defective masonry renewed. The work lasted three years. One of the additions included a font inspired by the baron himself, and executed by a celebrated Danish sculptor, Adolf Jerichau. Another addition was the

Although the origins of Milton Abbey may be traced to a Benedictine foundation in the tenth century, the present building dates mainly from the fourteenth and fifteenth centuries. Gilbert Scott was employed by Baron Hambro to restore the fabric in 1865, a commission which is reputed to have cost £50,000. Dorchester Record Office.

west porch which still bears Carl Joachim's initials, CJH, and those of his second wife, EFH. This became the main entrance to the Abbey.

Of equal importance to the restoration itself was the gift which the baron then made to the local community. Under Lord Milton and his family the villagers had been excluded from the Abbey for they had their new parish church in Milton Abbas. Now Carl Joachim decreed that the villagers could attend the services there again. He did not want to keep the splendour of the Abbey to himself, and felt that others should enjoy it as well. His religious commitment had not wavered with the passing of time and it made his loneliness more tolerable.

It is interesting to speculate whether Carl Joachim might have found himself able to live up to his new role as baron and feudal lord if he had had Caroline by his side, and whether with Caroline's help he might have given his two older sons a more sensible upbringing. At Caroline's death his energy was suddenly deflated, and remained so for five years. He did not fully recover until he remarried in 1861. A victim of his congenital depression, after Caroline's death he isolated himself from his surroundings and his few friends. One of the few people with whom he occasionally corresponded then was the beautiful Polish painter Elizabeth Jerichau Baumann, wife of the sculptor Adolf Jerichau. He often bought paintings from her, and she had always fascinated him. His letters to her throw light on his frame of mind following Caroline's death.

[August 1852]: The Lord has taken from me the angel for whom I have worked and whose smile was more precious to me than anything in the world. It is difficult therefore for me to say 'Thy will be done.'

Baptismal font in the Abbey church at Milton Abbey, carved by the Danish sculptor Adolf Jerichau in 1861–2. Its origin is recorded in a very typical letter from Carl Joachim to Jerichau dated 3 November 1860: 'Today is my birthday, and I want to give myself a present. Having thought over carefully what I would like, I have agreed with myself to spend £300–£400 in commissioning you to carve a font for my beautiful abbey church, whose aisles are as high as Roskilde Cathedral. It must interpret the words of St. John's Gospel, Chapter 3, verse 5: "Unless one is born of water and the spirit, he cannot enter the Kingdom of God". My idea is that the text might be represented by a dove – the Spirit of the Lord – rising from a rock – the Rock of Eternity – with an olive leaf that could hold the necessary water. This is only my suggestion. I am sure you have a much more beautiful conception of the subject. Please send me your drawing and tell me how I may expect this commission to be carried out.' In the lively correspondence about Jerichau's drawing that followed, Carl Joachim wrote: 'I like the angel with the cross, but I am not so happy about the praying angel, for it is praying in sorrow. I would prefer this angel to stand with upturned countenance and a palm branch in one hand, like the angels in heaven singing hosanna for every true child of God who at baptism is admitted to the heavenly, holy, Jerusalem with God.'

This country house on the edge of Putney Heath was an hour's drive southwest of the City. Carl Joachim Hambro much preferred it to his town house and enjoyed many summers there with his family. After his death, it became the residence of his youngest son, Everard. Photograph from the 1860s. Owned by the English family.

[February 1853]: I spent a miserable Christmas Eve at Milton Abbey, and saw in the New Year alone in my large house by the fire in my bedroom, thinking of happier days.

[May 1854]: I have taken on so many responsibilities in this country that I could never renounce them; neither would it be right to do so, as in spite of all I am happier in England than I have been anywhere else. My liking for the English temperament and thought strengthens me in my efforts to find peace in Christ, without Whom I should be completely lost.

[November 1854]: I have had to pay for my position and my ambition with a thousand sorrows and anxieties. My pleasure in my career now seems like so many soap bubbles. I am deeply worried about my children's future in this country. Since my wife's death I have lost the will to work, and today there is scarcely sufficient work to occupy my clerks at the bank. For this I have only my own passivity to blame.

[Summer 1856]: I am suffering under an apathy that makes it almost impossible for me to answer a letter. I try to meet my obligations as best I can, but since my wife passed away real pleasure has become wholly foreign to me. I try humbly to acknowledge my Saviour's goodness, and to understand that He is good whatever He may give or take. But nevertheless I cannot regain my peace of mind.

He was soon so overwhelmed by loneliness at the vast Milton Abbey that he moved to a smaller property on Putney Heath, where he was closer to London. He now visited Milton only to set in motion the restoration of the very dilapidated abbey church or the repair of his tenants' cottages in Milton Abbas. In a letter to Hans Andersen dated 1855 he wrote, in his usual rather high-flown language, that he was seeking to build a posthumous reputation with bricks, whereas Andersen was so privileged that he could do the same merely with the written word.

Although he repeatedly claimed to be very concerned about his sons' future he was soon in deep conflict with his two elder sons; and only Everard, his youngest son, was able to appreciate his depressive father's good intentions. In the domestic field also Carl Joachim was not very successful in adapting to the role of widower. In the year after Caroline's death he arranged for his ageing mother-in-law, Mrs Gostenhofer, to act as housekeeper, but this was not a success. He wrote to Elizabeth Jerichau Baumann: 'I myself was not at ease with her, and she did not get on with the children.' Next, the American widow of Caroline's brother became a kind of housekeeper – Caroline's brother had died in New Orleans three weeks after Caroline. An earlier letter reads: 'I don't know her, but descriptions lead me to hope that she and her three little children will fill my empty house, and that she will become the good spirit that the children and the home need.' The

Carl Joachim aged sixty, drawn in 1867 when he had grown a beard. The anonymous picture is from the little museum at Milton Abbey, and it is said that in the last century a reproduction of the portrait hung in many of his tenants' cottages.

children liked her, but Carl Joachim did not, and eventually, probably a short time before she returned to America – he wrote callously: 'I myself am now as good as alone, for my brother-in-law's widow is more repulsive than attractive to me.'

In 1853, the lonely Carl Joachim wrote to Professor Jerichau in Copenhagen asking him to sculpt Caroline from a picture he was sending. A few months later the preliminary, gypsum version of the bust reached London. Carl Joachim wrote back enthusiastically:

The bust of my wife is quite excellent and gives me immense pleasure. Words cannot express it. I kiss the cold gypsum many, many times with my warm lips, and think of happier days until tears come into my eyes. It is unbelievable that you have been able to create such a likeness, although you have never seen her. How I look forward to seeing the completed work in marble!

The marble bust was not ready until 1856, but it gave Carl Joachim 'happiness and heartfelt pleasure'. The bust has now been lost.

Carl Joachim wrote rarely about his finances during these sad years, but some remarks to Elizabeth Jerichau Baumann show that the restoration and maintenance of Milton Abbey was expensive. In 1856 he wrote:

At this time I must exercise great self-denial for at least a year, as I am engaged in building schools for my tenants' children in the villages, which will cost me £2,000. Undeniably a large sum of money. But I hope that someone will bless my memory some time in the future. In fact I seek my pleasure in this kind of expenditure, as I use hardly anything on myself.

In two letters to Percival, he wrote in February 1855: 'In business I am dreadfuly dull; my own fault for losing my head and sending my customers away', and in May 1855: 'As for my business, I feel like one awakening from a dream, and feel that the last three years' neglect have put me back very much from a financial aspect, although not in actual loss of money. The world has moved on quickly and left me behind.'

Carl Joachim's apathetic existence brightened a little in 1857 when Charles at last married the wealthy girl his father had selected for him. The young couple moved into Milton Abbey in the same year, and the size of the property became a little more justifiable.

Carl Joachim slowly regained his equilibrium, and began once again to take an interest in the bank.

The new Carl Joachim, full of initiative, is undoubtedly associated with his remarriage on 2 April 1861. At the age of fifty-five he chose as his new partner in life a thirty-five-year-old widow. His bride was the childless Eliza Greathead, née Turner, who had been married to a British official in India. She was a nurse, and had cared for Carl

Eliza Turner (1825–1919), the second wife of the Baron. The marriage only lasted sixteen years, for he died in 1877. She remained a widow until her own death forty-two years later.

Joachim when he was in hospital in 1860. To his closest friends Carl Joachim somewhat shyly quoted the old German saying: '*Alter schützt vor Torheit nicht*' (age is no protection against folly), but with Eliza at his side the fifteen years of life still left to him were reasonably happy.

The correspondence with Elizabeth Jerichau Baumann ceased quite abruptly when he remarried. It is evident that the new baroness was jealous of her, and certainly had no wish to be painted by her. In 1861, when the painter announced that she would visit Carl Joachim, as she often did when she came to England, there was suddenly no room for her. She was hurt, and this is probably reflected in the impression she gave of Carl Joachim's reawakened social life in a letter to her husband the year after the marriage:

Last night I dined with the Hambros. These are my impressions of the unnatural life of the rich: At 8.30 p.m. dinner was served. Earls and barons inside, and the most beautiful landscape outside behind drawn curtains! Everything imaginable – *ad nauseam* – in the way of delicacies was offered: melons, strawberries, grapes, figs, etc. etc., and with them the inevitable champagne. And this against a background of thousands of poor starving children lacking the merest necessities. I had place-of-honour at the table, but I would much rather have eaten porridge and cod with you and the children in our country cottage.

12 My Friend Cavour

In spite of Carl Joachim's depression the firm of C. J. Hambro & Son progressed steadily in the 1850s. The number of acceptances increased, not only with Denmark, where Smidt and le Maire were now functioning as independent but very loyal colleagues, but also with Norway and Sweden. The map on which the older British merchant bankers had divided up Europe showed that none of them was as yet displaying the slightest interest in Scandinavia. From the beginning this was Hambro's territory.

But of course it was large international loans that most fascinated Carl Joachim. A banker was able to display his personal skills and create a name for himself only by the successful negotiation of large bond issues for creditworthy countries under acceptable market conditions. Other branches of banking were more anonymous. Joseph's shining example must have been a daily challenge to Carl Joachim, and his rank of baron, he felt, now called for justification.

Making large sums of money became in time a kind of consolation to the depressed man. It was some compensation for his unending self-reproach, and as an achievement he did not regard it as conflicting with his religious, social and patriotic convictions. Yet it is probable that he never felt at ease with his growing wealth. The astounding capacity to abandon oneself to the enjoyment of wealth that seemed to be inborn in almost every member of the Rothschild clan was not present in Carl Joachim. It was his son Everard who became one of the City's great and well-adjusted pillars of Victorian society, displaying a genuine and guiltless *joie de vivre*. During Carl Joachim's twenty-nine years as an independent banker he in fact negotiated several large international loans, some of them for Denmark. He financed railway extensions on Zeeland in the 1850s, and gave financial backing for Denmark's next war – this time disastrous – against Bismarck in 1864. He arranged government loans for both Norway and Sweden, and he was later to open up connections with Greece in a most untraditional way. But none of his great loans has caused so much comment so often as his audacious dialogue with Cavour in Italy. Ultimately, the relationship between the two men had such far-reaching historical consequences that in his old age Carl Joachim justifiably asserted that in being the first to

Camillo Cavour (1810–61), Italian statesman and the great driving force in the unification of Italy. Hambros Bank portrait collection.

finance the unification of Italy he had inspired Bismarck to unify Germany a few years later.

The Cavour affair began in the summer of 1851. Communication with the kingdom of Sardinia's new minister of finance, Camillo Benso di Cavour, began when Carl Joachim's Italian banking colleague, Emile de la Rue of Genoa, visited him in London in the spring of that year to discuss the possibility of raising a large loan for Sardinia. The amount involved was in fact no less than £4,000,000. De la Rue did not conceal the fact that Sardinia's ambassador to London had just met with a refusal from the Baring Brothers, and that in the face of this Cavour had contemptuously remarked: 'These gentlemen are reluctant to enter into a struggle with the House of Rothschild.'

This was probably an accurate judgement, since the City's unwritten law and the merchant bankers' invisible map showed that the Italian peninsula had been 'Rothschilds country' since the Napoleonic Wars. Baron James Rothschild of Paris had provided finance for the small north Italian provinces for many years, and since 1821 his brother, Baron Carl Rothschild, had run the family's bank in Naples, the capital of the kingdom of the Two Sicilies. Again, when the authorities in Austrian-controlled Lombardy lacked money, the third brother, Baron Salomon Rothschild, had been at hand in his bank in Vienna. The Baring brothers thought that it would pay them in the long run to respect these facts of life.

On this occasion, however, there were special circumstances. Cavour no longer wanted to borrow from the Rothschilds because he planned to break their Italian monopoly. At the same time, he probably welcomed a new financier who could offer him more favourable terms than had the Rothschilds in the past.

The idea of ousting the House of Rothschild from Italy appears to have attracted Carl Joachim. During his very early days in London, while Nathan Rothschild, the second of the five famous brothers, was still alive, the powerful family had made a tremendous impression upon Carl Joachim. But in 1837, during Joseph's last great Danish loan negotiations, Carl Joachim had observed the condescending and patronizing attitude of the London Rothschilds towards his father, and he had become increasingly resentful of the family. Dare he now make a stand against them? And was he in fact qualified to assess Sardinia's value as a borrower? After all, the amount was five times greater than his recently negotiated loan for Denmark, and he had then had the advantage of knowing more about Danish circumstances than anyone in the City.

Like any well-informed banker at the time, Carl Joachim knew no more of Sardinia than that it was a small kingdom in the north-west corner of Italy near to France, that it consisted of the regions of Piedmont and Savoy with the large island of Sardinia, that it had five million inhabitants and that its capital was Turin. He also knew that Sardinia was alone among the Italian peninsula's twelve regions – kingdoms, duchies, the Papal States and the Austrian provinces – in

The popular Italian satirical journal Fischietto *originally had its doubts about Cavour's chances of uniting Italy. This drawing from the 1850s bears the text: 'It is difficult to sew a boot that doesn't fit and makes you use crutches for the rest of your life.'* From Storia d'Italia.

265

having an Italian ruler, and that as a consequence a strong, democratic Italian patriotism flowed from this one kingdom, which two years earlier had warred against Austria, though unsuccessfully. After paying reparations, the little kingdom had been left with a national debt of £3,000,000, and as a result all work on extending the railways, education and industry had come to a hopeless standstill. After the disastrous war the old king, Carl Albert, had been forced to abdicate, leaving the throne to his twenty-nine-year-old son Victor Emanuel II. But the strong man in the country was the new minister of finance, Cavour. His reputation was high, not only because of his ability but also because of his far-sighted ideas concerning Italy's political future, which he had often expressed as a journalist before entering politics.

After the usual soul-searching Carl Joachim convinced himself that he should take up the challenge, and Cavour sent his personal representative Count Thaon de Revel to London to negotiate the details of the loan, including the ever-sensitive matter of the opening price. If interest was to be fixed at 5 per cent, buyers would of course be tempted by a relatively low initial price, but the lower the price the more expensive the loan would become to the borrower, since he would receive the proceeds less expenses but at maturity would have to redeem at par. For a 5 per cent loan the market rate at that time was about 85, but Cavour wanted to arrange the loan on specially favourable terms, and suggested that Carl Joachim should offer the bonds at as much as 90.

Carl Joachim was uncertain what to do. The precept that old Joseph had passed on to his son in the last years of his life had been 'Experience, knowledge, common sense and calm'. Carl Joachim knew that in this matter he met none of the four essentials. He proposed at first to take on the loan without himself subscribing for a personal share, but it was soon brought home to him that in such transactions the banker must always show customers his own confidence in the deal by personally subscribing for a large share.

He later declared that he was willing personally to subscribe £400,000 – 10 per cent of the loan – well aware that he was staking not only the whole of his recently inherited fortune but also his newly acquired prestige and his entire future credit. If this transaction failed he might as well close the bank. However, they agreed at last on an opening price of 85. Even this was a little higher than the Rothschilds' most recent loans to Sardinia. This alone would be enough to anger James Rothschild in Paris. Another hitch occurred when Cavour found himself in temporary trouble with his own parliament, which suddenly took fright at borrowing more money. Rumour of this did nothing to increase Sardinia's creditworthiness in the City, and for a time Carl

King Victor Emanuel II *of Sardinia, painted in 1849 at the age of twenty-nine when he succeeded to the throne of his little north-west Italian kingdom, which included the island of Sardinia. The artist was Gerolamo Induno.* Museo del Risorgimento, Milan.

Joachim lost courage and put the matter aside, until a thundering letter from Cavour called him back into line.

Cavour had been impressed all along by his new banker's realistic approach. Carl Joachim was of course fully aware by now that Cavour's intention in negotiating the loan was to put his country on its

267

When Cavour succeeded in raising his Anglo-Sardinian Loan from Carl Joachim in 1851,
Fischietto *published this drawing of the overjoyed finance minister swinging the English
money bags in a merry dance with the war minister, the rest of the government providing the
music.* From Storia d'Italia.

feet again, so that he could move on to realize his lifelong dream of a
united Italy. But Carl Joachim also knew that serious investors in
England preferred profit to political slogans. It would be better therefore for it to appear to be a railway loan. Indeed, buyers should be able
to convert the bonds into railway shares when, as was planned, Sardinia made over its extensive railway network to a private joint stock
company. The right title for the loan also deeply concerned him. Bonds
should have a name that gave real confidence. He therefore rejected
The Sardinian Railroad Loan in favour of The Anglo-Sardinian Loan,
which he thought would sound more impressive not only on the London Stock Exchange but also on other European stock exchanges where
the bonds would be marketed.

The £4,000,000 loan was offered in London in May 1851. By August,
only £2.2 million had been subscribed at the agreed price of 85. This
meagre result quickly brought sarcastic comments from James
Rothschild in Paris, and Carl Joachim began to realize that the
Rothschilds intended to thwart him. This they set out to do, quickly
and efficiently. The bonds were marketed in London, Berlin and Hamburg, but by manipulation they were suppressed in Amsterdam and

Brussels. 'The Rothschilds are keeping them off the market,' Carl Joachim reported furiously to Cavour in summer 1851. In Paris, James Rothschild directly advised his customers not to buy the bonds until the price had substantially fallen. In September they fell temporarily to 80, and Cavour watched the price of the Rothschilds' older Sardinian loans suffer a similar fall. These loans were undoubtedly the subject of 'bear' activities by James Rothschild, and it is clear that he wanted to prove to Cavour that it was better to have him as an ally than as an enemy. Carl Joachim was on tenterhooks and working up a persecution mania, but Cavour encouraged him to hold on to the original price.

Soon after this, rumours circulated in London that the price of unsold Anglo-Sardinian bonds was to be reduced to avoid a catastrophe, and Carl Joachim was forced to take emergency action without delay. He now allied himself with a bold British speculator named Lewis Haslewood, who subscribed for £400,000 at just under 85. Carl Joachim did not like having to accept this outsider as a partner, but he felt he had no choice. Haslewood's younger brother Edward was sent to Turin to investigate the Sardinian railways, and he reported that they were so secure that orphans and widows could safely invest in them.

To the weekly Fischietto, *Cavour's activities in 1850–61 were a constant source of incredulous mirth. He is seen here in 1851 as both finance minister and foreign minister to King Victor Emmanuel, and in 1861 when he was eventually able to cock a snook at all those who had not believed in his amazing ability.* From Storia d'Italia.

Nevertheless, in October 1851 Anglo-Sardinians fell in London to a rock-bottom price of 79½. Early in November Cavour told Carl Joachim that he would probably have to sell the remaining bonds at the best price he could get. Fortunately Carl Joachim had now regained his composure, and he was able to reply to Cavour with calm and dignity: 'Such a step would finish Sardinia's credit in London, and this credit must be as dear to you as your own honour as an individual.'

This brave answer won Cavour's heart once and for all, and at last Carl Joachim's stubbornness was to be rewarded. In mid-November Cavour became Sardinia's minister of state. At this time, when his own and his country's popularity were growing in England, the foreign secretary, Lord Russell, launched the slogan: 'Italy for the Italians'. At the end of the month Anglo-Sardinians were being quoted at 82½, and just before Christmas they passed their original opening price and went as high as 87.

Cavour was happy and relieved, and although Carl Joachim could now expect an additional profit on his own £400,000 he nevertheless expressed his admiration for Cavour: 'I am still not content with the price. If people knew you as you deserve to be known, your funds would be quite at another price.' He continued with this prophetic statement: 'I am united heart and soul and fortune with Sardinia, because I believe that your country is destined to be yeast for the regular progress of humanity, and that neither despots or anarchists can stop it.'

Carl Joachim's reaction to the six or seven nerve-racking months of crisis made such an impression on Cavour that, shortly before Christmas 1851, he wrote this letter to Carl Joachim:

My dear Baron,

Although I commissioned my friend, Mr. de la Rue, when he passed through Turin, to express to you the entire satisfaction of the King's government on account of the skilful and courageous way in which you performed the mission you had undertaken, I feel the need for expressing to you directly, my dear Baron, my personal feelings of esteem and gratitude.

I sincerely congratulate myself on seeing the financial interests of my country in your hands. They could not be better served. What you have already done for us is to me a sufficient guarantee of what you will do in the future. I am convinced that once our loan has overcome the difficulties that our adversaries have placed in its way, it will follow a steady rising course. That will be a glorious result for you and for us. I am counting on this with certitude, and I believe that I should soon have to congratulate you on the constant progress of your credit on the London Stock Exchange.

Yours sincerely,
Cavour.

In the autumn of 1858 Cavour persuaded Emperor Napoleon III to act as protector of the divided Italian people against powerful Austria-Hungary, which dominated the entire Po basin. In return, Piedmont-Sardinia agreed to give up Savoy and Nice to the Emperor. In April 1859 Cavour engineered an attack by Austria on Piedmont-Sardinia. Napoleon III immediately led a large French army across the Alps into northern Italy, where the Austrians were defeated, first at Magenta on 4 June and then at Solferino on 24 June. Museo del Risorgimento, Milan.

France and Austria quickly agreed to an armistice at Villafranca, where the young Emperor Franz Josef of Austria and Napoleon III met. Austria had to surrender all Lombardy to Sardinia. Soon after this the duchies of central Italy joined voluntarily. The unification of Italy had begun. Coloured lithograph by Pedrinelli. Museo del Risorgimento, Milan.

Cavour proved to be right. Early in 1852, Anglo-Sardinians rose to 90, and Carl Joachim not only emerged with credit from the great transaction but in the end he made a substantial additional profit on his own £400,000. Had Joseph been alive, he would certainly have acknowledged Carl Joachim's flair and ability, although he himself would not have embarked on the Italian venture.

A friendship developed between Cavour and Carl Joachim, although they did not meet until 1856 when Cavour, visiting London, presented Carl Joachim on the king's behalf with Sardinia's Order of St Mauritius, and also gave him the portrait of himself which still hangs in the bank. During the intervening years, Carl Joachim had repeatedly sent Cavour constructive suggestions designed to improve Sardinia's finances and monetary system, and although Cavour was not the kind of man to welcome advice he always replied, and sometimes followed the advice.

Carl Joachim was able to follow at a distance Cavour's brilliant strategy between 1859 and 1861 during the struggle, no longer clandestine, to unite the entire Italian peninsula, and Cavour's realization of his dream that his own king, Victor Emanuel II, should occupy the throne of the great new realm. He must surely have been delighted to learn that the Rothschilds in Naples had closed their bank and fled with the Neapolitan royal family in 1860. The Rothschilds never again opened a bank in Naples.

At Cavour's death in 1861, Hambro's business relations with Italy ceased for a number of years, but on many occasions after Carl Joachim's death Everard was able to harvest what his father had sown in Italy.

When Victor Emanuel II was acclaimed king in spring 1861, many of Carl Joachim's colleagues had jokingly called him 'the kingmaker'. In 1862 the title was revived, but this time the Greek throne was the subject. The Great Powers – England, France and Russia – were experiencing difficulty in selecting a new king for Greece. The Greeks had rebelled against the German-born King Otto after thirty years of unpopular reign. The Greeks now wanted Queen Victoria's second son, Prince Alfred, and he had in fact already been acclaimed in Athens. But Queen Victoria had very firmly turned down Prince Alfred's candidature. First, there was an old agreement that the candidate should not come from one of the Great Powers; second, Alfred would be needed in England should anything happen to his eldest brother Edward; and, finally, this insecure Greek throne was being offered to him by a gang of rebels, and in Queen Victoria's

Further to the south of Italy, King Victor Emanuel himself led his army against his opponents, but at first the Papal States were carefully bypassed. Here the Piedmontese army is shown in action at Martino on 24 August 1859. Museo del Risorgimento, Milan.

On 5 May 1860, Giuseppe Garibaldi, the Sardinian champion of liberty, sailed with his red-shirted army of liberation from Genoa to Sicily, where he was victorious over the unpopular King of the Two Sicilies. By 7 September Garibaldi was in Naples, and coming from the south was able to meet up with Victor Emanuel on 7 November 1860. Rome was not incorporated into the new Italy until 1866. Painting of the Battle of Calatafimi. Museo del Risorgimento, Milan.

273

The beautiful old Danish baroque church in Wellclose Square, London, was built between 1694 and 1696. It was at this time that the Danish Prince George became consort to Queen Anne of England. The church was consecrated on 15 November 1696, but the indolent Danish prince could not be persuaded to preside. He excused himself because of the distance and the short period of daylight. Following Denmark's repeated clashes with England

opinion it did not offer the proper prospects for an English prince.

Queen Victoria's negative attitude was a serious blow to the Greek delegation, which arrived in London in anticipation of King Otto's imminent abdication. Carl Joachim's Greek banking colleague, Dionysos Katenakis, expressed one day at luncheon his regret at the embarrassing situation in which his country now found itself, since the Greek delegation simply did not know where to turn.

Carl Joachim of course knew of the negotiations then in progress

between 1801 and 1814, the church was rented out as an English mariners' church. Carl Joachim was therefore sure of a large attendance when, in July 1862, he unexpectedly invited all the Danes in London to a service at the church, without revealing its true purpose. The old church was demolished with very little respect seven years later. Anonymous watercolour, c. 1840. Print Room, Guildhall Library, London.

aimed at marrying Alexandra, the eldest daughter of the heir to the Danish throne, Prince Christian (IX), to the British Prince Edward (VII), and he now began to think constructively in his characteristic and often surprising way. Yes, he said, of course he could help the Greeks.

The Danish Navy was due to visit England between 11 and 18 July 1862, and it was planned that the frigate *Jylland* should sail up the Thames and anchor at Gravesend. On board the frigate was a party of young naval cadets which included the Danish Prince Vilhelm, younger brother of Princess Alexandra. Carl Joachim now made this young prince his candidate for the Greek throne, since he seemed to be the obvious choice. Although the Greeks had been disappointed not to get Prince Alfred, they could scarcely be less than delighted if he were replaced by Edward's future brother-in-law. He passed his suggestion to the Greek delegation via Katenakis. The Greeks were attracted to the idea, but of course they wanted to see the young prince. Could Carl Joachim arrange this?

Carl Joachim now devised a stratagem which showed how effectively and untraditionally he could act when his nerves were steady. To mark the naval visit he invited the entire Danish community to a service in London's two-hundred-year-old Danish church ensuring that the captain of the *Jylland* would be present with his officers and cadets. He then invited the Greek delegation to witness the ceremony from secluded seats behind the organ.

In the eighteenth century the Danish community in London had been quite numerous, but during the Napoleonic Wars it had shrunk almost to the point of extinction. Since the repeal of the British corn laws in the 1840s the community had increased substantially, but the beautiful Danish church in the Port of London, close to the Tower, had not been used since early in the century. It had been rented out and was later used as a British seamen's church. No Danish service had been held there for the last fifty years. It was therefore something of a *coup* for the deeply religious Carl Joachim to secure the old church for one Sunday only. He was certain that the Danish community would support him and fill the church to capacity. His greatest difficulty was to find a preacher; there had been no Danish priest in London for many years. He eventually found a young Danish theologian who agreed to conduct the service.

On 15 June the church was filled, and so that everyone could see the seventeen-year-old Prince Vilhelm a golden chair had been placed for him directly in front of the altar. He was escorted to the chair by the Danish churchwarden, Johannes Grønlund, but he modestly seated himself on an ordinary chair beside it. He was quite unaware of the real purpose of the service. It is clear that Carl Joachim, who knew his Bible well, had thoroughly briefed the priest, who preached on a text from the Acts of the Apostles: 'He persuaded Jews and Greeks.' No one noticed the Greeks watching from the organ loft. As expected, they formed a very good impression of the Danish prince.

Two days later Carl Joachim gave the finishing touch to his surprising initiative. Although as a British citizen he was no longer a frequent visitor to the Danish Club, his title as a Danish baron bound him in some degree to it, and the members were always proud to see him at their annual festivities on 6 October, King Frederik VII's birthday. He now showed his gratitude to the club by inviting the entire membership to a farewell supper for the *Jylland*'s officers and cadets. He hired a complete wing of the Crystal Palace, which had been moved to Sydenham, about six miles from London, after the closure of the Great Exhibition of 1851. If Prince Vilhelm eventually became king of Greece, no London Dane was to be left in any doubt about Carl Joachim's role in the affair.

Seventeen-year-old Danish Prince Vilhelm (left) at the time when he unsuspectingly attended the exceptional service for Danes at the Danish church in London. He was then a Danish midshipman taking part in a visit by the Danish Navy to London. On the right he is seen in the following autumn as the Hellenic king, bearing the title of George I, leaving for Athens via London with a letter of credit issued by Hambros bank. He had meanwhile become brother-in-law to the future King Edward VII of England, who had married his sister Princess Alexandra in spring 1863. Royal Library, Copenhagen.

The last picture of Carl Joachim, showing him shortly before his death in 1877. In his later years his sight became very weak, and his letters had to be read to him. The picture is a xylograph published in the Danish Illustreret Tidende. *In the year of his death, this paper paid tribute in a long and handsome obituary to the British banker who had never forgotten his old fatherland.* Royal Library, Copenhagen.

With Eliza by his side and in splendid spirits himself, he received three hundred Danish guests at the Crystal Palace on 17 June. They had been invited for a full day's outing with a visit to the famous building's permanent exhibition, followed by supper. One young guest was the future permanent under-secretary, C. F. Ricard. He had been invited through the Danish Embassy, and in his memoirs he wrote of the wonderful evening given by the baron and of the thirty courses and select wines they enjoyed, two orchestras alternating in providing the music. The only disappointment was that the *Jylland* had to sail from Gravesend the next morning, and the captain and his party left rather early. As a consequence the speeches that should have been made during the dessert had to be abandoned, and Carl Joachim was not therefore given the thanks he deserved. Three months later, King Otto and Queen Amalie left Greece, never to return. There is no doubt that the Greek delegation's action in coming to London had been timely.

The following spring, all the pieces fell into place in the most accommodating way. The British foreign secretary, Lord John Russell, had an opportunity to inspect for himself the red-cheeked Prince Vilhelm when on 10 March 1863 his sister, Princess Alexandra, married Prince Edward. Negotiations with Denmark soon began, and that autumn the young prince travelled to Athens to assume the throne of Greece. Carl Joachim did all he could to smooth the path of his Danish candidate. He was well aware that the prince's father, Prince Christian, was a somewhat impecunious Danish officer before he became king of Denmark, and he immediately offered to finance Prince Vilhelm's journey to Greece with letters of credit on C. J. Hambro & Son. The journey would be expensive; the new king of Greece had to pay his respects to Queen Victoria in London, Tsar Alexander II in St Petersburg and Napoleon III in Paris, to express his gratitude for the support given him by the Great Powers. Only when this was out of the way did he join at Toulon the Greek warship sent to take him to Piraeus. Fate even willed that the Danish minister of finance, Count Wilhelm Sponneck, who in 1851 had been instrumental in making Carl Joachim a baron, was selected to accompany Prince Vilhelm on his journey as his permanent Danish adviser. It was therefore Sponneck and Carl Joachim who together drafted the letter of credit for £10,000. This document was tactful enough to state that the money was to be repaid when Prince Vilhelm – now 'King George I of the Hellenes' – had arranged his financial affairs in Greece.

Apart from Carl Joachim's personal satisfaction at the success of his patriotic new plan, he was probably in no doubt about what he had achieved as a banker. Naturally, little Greece had no place on the

One of Carl Joachim's many and often surprising benefactions to his native city of Copenhagen was the establishment of its first two public hot-water baths for the community. For the construction and operation of these baths he provided £6,000 between 1849 and 1860. In 1864 the first Hambro Public Baths, shown here, were opened in Borgergade. There were fourteen bath-tubs for men and six for women, with twenty wash-houses with drying-, mangling- and ironing-rooms. The baths were in use until shortly before World War I, when the Copenhagen municipality itself began to take over this social duty. Illustration in the Danish Illustreret Tidende, *1864.*

bankers' map of Europe, either as Rothschild country or Baring country; it was an entirely new market. As the new King's personal banker, Carl Joachim could expect to be invited to float any loans the Greek government might need. Greece was a very primitive country, and in 1863 there was as yet not one railway.

Carl Joachim's candidate for the Greek throne proved to be highly suitable. He ruled Greece for forty-nine years and, with brief interruptions, his many descendants succeeded in retaining the throne until very recently. Greece floated its first foreign loan in 1881, and as expected it was negotiated by C. J. Hambro & Son, then headed by Carl Joachim's gifted son.

Since the turn of this century an important thoroughfare beside the port of Copenhagen south of the Tivoli Gardens has been known as Hambrosgade. It was named after Carl Joachim to express Copenhagen Corporation's gratitude for the gifts and foundations with which he had endowed his birthplace in his old age.

He was as surprising in his choice of endowments as in many of his business transactions. For example, he presented his native city with its first hot-water public baths. Working on the Victorian concept that a clean mind can thrive only in a clean body, he thought it right that the poor of Copenhagen should have facilities for a cheap hot bath, and at the same time be able to wash their clothes conveniently and inexpensively. From 1849 onwards he contributed a total of £6,000 towards this project, and the first public baths were opened in 1864. In 1870 they were followed by more baths.

Carl Joachim's second public baths in Copenhagen were built in about 1870 in Købmagergade beside Trinity Church, where he had been baptized in 1822. The temple-shaped baths can be seen in the centre of the picture. Although this institution was also intended for Copenhagen's poorer classes, its visitors were in fact quite exclusive. It was in use until 1918, and was not demolished until about 1970, when this whole quarter of the city was rebuilt. Detail of a drawing by Des Asmussen, 1968.

Gilbert Scott's monumental sarcophagus, with an effigy of Carl Joachim, in Milton Abbey, erected a few years after his death in 1877.

From the mid 1860s Carl Joachim was well supported at the bank by Everard, always his favourite, who was in sole control during his father's declining years. Carl Joachim never completely gave up his literary interests, and shortly before his death he republished his history of Denmark in a new, illustrated edition. In the last year of his life his sight was so poor that Everard had to read his correspondence to him. On 17 November 1877 he died, aged seventy. The obituaries that appeared in Denmark would have pleased him, for Denmark had indeed lost a worthy son. He had given directions for his burial in his will. A marble monument to the memory of Baron Milton and Lady Caroline, who had built the Hall at Milton Abbey in the 1770s, had been erected in the abbey church in 1775, and Carl Joachim saw no reason why he, as a later patron and protector of the abbey, should not be buried with equal dignity in his beloved church. Although on many occasions during his life he had doubted his own capacity and fortitude, these frailties are not reflected in the imposing monument erected over his burial place a few years later by Sir Gilbert Scott.

Eliza, who had dutifully tended and nursed Carl Joachim during his last fifteen years, bought a house in Bournemouth where she lived until her death in 1919 at the age of ninety-six.

It would be an exaggeration to say that Carl Joachim's death left a void among a wide circle of friends; he had been too odd and anti-social. But his deep and genuine admiration of the British character and way of life so influenced his descendants that today all the Hambros give a remarkable impression of extreme Englishness. Carl Joachim's role in the family was most difficult and thankless. Indeed, to overcome not only a change of parents but also of religion and nationality is to expect much of such a vulnerable temperament.

13 The Baron's Two Elder Sons

Charles Joseph Theophilus was born in Copenhagen on 2 October 1834, the eldest of Carl Joachim's three sons. His name, Charles, was significant as it represented the first anglicized use of his father's name and it has since been passed down to each generation of the family until, even today, it is the name of the chairman of the bank and his elder son. Although born in Denmark, Charles spent only his first four years in Copenhagen. Then his father moved to England permanently and the new Hambros bank was established in London.

Charles felt very close to his mother, Caroline, and often referred to her in later life, but he found his father difficult to understand and their relationship was never easy. Carl Joachim's dark moods of the 1840s and utter depression after Caroline's death in 1852 meant that communication with his sons was almost impossible. With Charles' growing independence tension mounted to a climax in the winter of 1853, when Charles was banished to India. He was to spend two years abroad with a tutor called Botcherby, a miserly, miserable man whom Charles loathed with vehement intensity.

The official purpose of Charles' long voyage was to restore his health. Secretly, however, Carl Joachim was more concerned for his son's mental health than for his physical condition as he recognized in Charles some of his own troubles and those of his Danish mother, Marianne. He confessed to his second son, Percival:

I fully believe it was a most merciful dispensation for us all that Botcherby took him away. Discipline is not pleasant, but under a really pious man restraint can never be injurious. I know how much I have erred in the education of my children. I praise the Lord that you have turned steady and with His blessing Charles may become so likewise and all will yet be well.

Already starved of family affection, Charles was now to be imprisoned with a religious, sickly old companion. The young man's mental endurance was soon stretched to the utmost.

Charles, meanwhile, interpreted his father's motives quite differently. At nineteen he had fallen hopelessly in love with a girl called Ella Chapman and just before Christmas that same year he had asked her to marry him. He had not had the opportunity, however, to ask formal permission of either Mr Chapman or his father before he was told to

284

The three sons of Carl Joachim Hambro were keen fishermen and in 1863 they were photographed wearing costumes from Trondheim in Norway. From left to right, standing: Montagu Guest from Canford Hall in Dorset; Charles Hambro; and his wife, Susan. Seated: Frank Smith, son of the banker Martin Tucker Smith; Percival Hambro, then working for his father at C. J. Hambro & Son; Miss St Quintin; R. Yorke, brother of Susan; and Everard Hambro, who had just come down from Trinity College, Cambridge. Hambro Family Archives.

pack his trunks and leave the country. He did not even say goodbye to Ella. As he sailed away from England he was convinced that his father had discovered his intention to marry her, and that he strongly disapproved. In this respect at least, Charles was correct. Carl Joachim confessed later that he had no desire to see his eldest son marry a girl whose father had no great reputation in the City.

Ella and Charles wrote to each other frequently, but letters sometimes took many weeks to arrive and replies often took months. After a year's travels Charles had still failed to approach Mr Chapman or his own father. Absence made the problem increasingly difficult. He explained the unhappy situation to his younger brother Percival who was then up at Oxford:

Charles Hambro, the eldest son of Carl Joachim, was banished to India where he travelled for two years with a miserable tutor called Botcherby. It was a lonely period for the young man, who felt heartbroken at the loss of his beloved Ella. Hambro Family Archives.

I had a letter from dear little Ella who was in trouble. She wrote to ask me (if I thought good) to tell the Governor of my love to her, for her position was a very difficult and painful one. I love her so much that I cannot tell you how unhappy this made me . . . and I promised to write to my father and to tell him my love for her though how I can do it, I do not know . . . If the Governor should be hard and get in a passion and positively refuse his consent what could I do? My dear fellow I feel in a fix I assure you, if the Governor says *yes* I am all right and happy to the last extent but if *no* then thousand times worse off than now, what are the odds? I thought of saying that if he would consent I would read like a horse and then get through Oxford and then think of Ella but I do not fancy that and, after a roving life for 3 years, I never could sit down to books again.

In May 1855, Charles eventually made up his mind. He had tortured himself long enough – apart from Percival, he had no one in whom to confide. In the distant lands of northern India he had resolved that he would rather face life without Ella than risk disinheritance. As the eldest son he would inherit his father's country estate, which now meant more to him than the girl he had not seen for eighteen months. He wrote to Percival: 'I would rather lose a hand than lose Milton, I cannot tell you how fond I am of it, or how I have looked forward to the enjoyment of it.' Whether Carl Joachim had originally known of the affair or not, the long absence had finally brought it to an end and now the 'engagement' was broken.

All the troubles over Ella grew distant compared with the problems of life with Botcherby. His tutor had obviously been instructed to keep a close rein over his charge, and in this letter to Percival, Charles described a typical day in his life in Simla where normal social intercourse was strictly denied to him:

I will tell you what I have done today and it is no unusual day at all. This morning got up at $6\frac{1}{2}$ and at 7 went out with B. for a walk. He was so weak that he has a pony to ride up any little hill. Home at $8\frac{1}{2}$, prayers. Breakfast, dull as possible, for the tea was bad. After breakfast I went to my own room. Got up 5 sections in the fourth chapter of Xenophon, sent them to B. Went and had lunch by myself at 2 and from 2 till now at $6\frac{1}{2}$ I have seen nobody and have amused myself drawing etc. as best I could. Now all the fashionable are out but I must stop at home and cannot even go to the reading room in the Hotel without telling him. Nor can I play billiards. We shall have dinner at 7, tea at $8\frac{1}{2}$ and at 9 to bed. What the devil he does all day I don't know. But that is how I spend mine, and day after day it is the same. There is a great deal of fun here if I could enjoy it. A cricket match yesterday, an archery meeting on the 3rd etc. but the devil excuse the old fellow, I shall be glad to go away into the wild hills again. I have no tobacco or cigars, and no money to buy any, nor any books.

When Charles complained to his father, he was told to settle his 'little differences' by himself and 'not mind his will being ruled by that of another'.

On the question of money, Botcherby was particularly mean. Charles wrote: 'I am dreadfully badly off for money and wish the Governor would take compassion on me and fix me an allowance as I have not even the 1£ [a week] I had in England.' Charles was given his old allowance eventually, but if Botcherby thought he had misbehaved it was immediately stopped. His only resort was to entreat Percival for help. Clearly, Charles had much greater expectations than Botcherby could ever have imagined: 'Many, many thanks for the tin you sent. I have received one 5, 10 and 20£ notes. B. has managed so that we have no money again and he has not paid me the 1£ a week he usually does now for 5 weeks. I have told him nothing about the money except that I received 10£ in a letter from England.'

Although Charles sometimes found his life extremely hard to bear, there were numerous occasions when he was able to appreciate the richness of the areas through which he travelled. He wrote long descriptive letters – marked 'public' – to his family, which were to be read aloud by his father to the family gathering at Roehampton or Milton Abbey. There were also the private ones which were written for Percival's eyes alone. The family learnt of the general scenes in the towns and countryside, while Percival would read vivid descriptions of bear-hunting expeditions, pig-sticking and hawking, of pipe-smoking and the pretty Indian women. Charles asked Percival: 'What would you give for a native, with a gold ring in her nose? Some of them are very handsome and really desirable, most of them wear trousers, very convenient things, as they have only to be unfixed at the top and let down.'

Above all, however, Charles enjoyed wandering in the mountains. Perhaps it was the sheer majesty of the Himalayas which he loved so much, or perhaps it was the sport which they offered. Perhaps it was the test of human endurance, the will of the individual against the trials of nature. All these qualities were discovered, in October 1854, on his tortuous journey to Leh, a remote city in the mountains of Kashmir. Botcherby's careless planning meant that they were still among very high peaks even in the middle of November, which meant dressing in a tent 'with the mercury at zero' and waking in the morning with 'our breath hung in ice on the blanket before our faces'. Fifty years later Charles' nephew, Percival Hambro, conquered those same mountains around Leh. Both of them had restless spirits and here they could find solace and inspiration.

Even in those distant places, and in spite of his father's dictatorial attitude, Charles often thought affectionately of home. He wrote: 'When I am alone I think I see you all at Roehampton as I remember it, perhaps at tea and all around the table or the Governor in his large armchair.' In one letter to Percival he concluded with the pitiful plea: 'God be with you and may he bring me home some day safe and welcome.' His sensitive nature made him feel like an outcast; he needed the warmth of his family, not the isolation of India. Over the two years his letters to his brother had expressed elation, depression, humour and forbearance. His reactions to the unusual circumstances had been those of any normal young man. In view of his own troubled mind, Carl Joachim had not been the best judge for his son. Although his remedy had been well intentioned, it had also been misguided.

When Charles at last returned to England in the spring of 1856, he once again obeyed his father and went to Trinity College, Cambridge. As he had anticipated, he did not find it easy to concentrate on books after his long travels, but he still had the prospect of the Milton Abbey estate to look forward to, so he felt bound to co-operate with his father's demands. He was not up at university very long, however, before he met his future bride, Susan Yorke. She was a very beautiful girl, whose father was The Hon. Henry Yorke, Archdeacon and Canon of Ely; her uncle was the fourth Earl of Hardwicke, of Wimpole Hall, Cambridge-

The Great Court of Trinity College, Cambridge, *by R. B. Harraden. After his travels in India during the early 1850s, Charles was admitted to Trinity College where he was followed by his brother Everard. Later Everard's sons, Eric and Olaf, and his grandson Jocelyn also studied there.* Reproduced with kind permission of the Master and Fellows of Trinity College, Cambridge.

shire. No doubt Carl Joachim was relieved that Charles had found a god-fearing wife whose family were so well established.

Charles and Susan were married on 15 December 1857 by her father in the small church beside Wimpole Hall. After the magnificent reception they left for Dorset where they spent the first part of their honeymoon. From Blandford Station to Milton Abbas they had a dark seven-mile journey and it was 11 o'clock at night before they arrived, but then, as they descended the hill into the village, they were met by an extraordinary sight. Milton was ablaze with candles burning brightly in every cottage window, and torches flaming at intervals down each side of the village street. They drove slowly through the cheering crowds which had gathered since early evening to welcome them, and eventually came to the top of Luckham Hill where a great bonfire had been lit, made of no less than ten wagon-loads of furze and timber. Around the glowing embers the tenants had assembled after their dinner at the Hambro Arms Inn. Then, in a speech, Charles and Susan were formally congratulated and welcomed to the estate. They stayed at the Hall until Christmas was over and then left for Italy.

A view of the West Lawn front of Milton Abbey and Hall, c. 1852. This was the Hambro family home for eighty years. Hambro Family Archives.

On their return, Charles was able to lead the life of an English country squire. Earlier, Carl Joachim had been much opposed to the idea and in May 1855, when Charles had been travelling in India, he had confided to Percival: 'May the Lord give that Charles may take to something steady. Not merely to be the fine gentleman. We were put into the world to work.' But Charles was never interested in City affairs, and besides, in his absence Percival had been chosen as Carl Joachim's successor to run the family bank.

Charles was far more content with Milton Abbey than he could ever have been in the City. Here he could be master of his affairs, free to enjoy the countryside, his Hall and the gardens. The Hall itself could sleep a hundred people, so there was plenty of scope for entertainment. Although Charles and Susan had only two daughters – Caroline born in 1859 and Agneta born in 1864 – they employed nine male and fifteen female servants to run the domestic household and another fifteen men to look after the grounds and stables. Apart from the shooting parties, one of Charles' favourite pastimes was foxhunting, a sport which gave him the opportunity to meet old friends such as Montagu Guest from nearby Canford Hall. In his youth Montagu had also travelled in India, and subsequently they both entered Parliament. The hills and vales of central Dorset offered delightful countryside over which to ride,

and Charles, Susan and Montagu often hunted together with both the Portman and the South Dorset hounds.

Charles' position as one of the foremost squires of the county led him to take an active interest in various local affairs. He served for more than thirty years in the Queen's Own Dorset Yeomanry. During his command, it is recorded that 'he gained the respect and esteem of every man who served under him.' On his retirement he was made an Honorary Colonel, and a photograph of him in uniform is shown on page 292. As a mason, he was Deputy-Provincial Grand Master for the Province. He was also a magistrate for the county, an active member of the Melcombe Regis District Council and, in 1882, High Sheriff of Dorset. He was influential in all these roles, but particularly so during his years as a Member of Parliament.

In 1868 he was elected to represent the Borough of Weymouth as a Liberal Conservative and remained with that constituency until 1874. Once the Redistribution Bill had been passed he stood for the County seat and in the election of 1885 he was defeated by only thirty-two votes against H.P. Sturgis, the Gladstonian candidate. The following year, however, he fought the same opponent again and on this occasion won by a substantial majority of nearly a thousand votes. He then held the seat until his death in 1891. He was an advocate of all constituency

Colonel Charles Hambro (1834–91) served in the Queen's Own Dorset Yeomanry Cavalry for more than thirty years and on his retirement in 1890 was made Honorary Colonel. As the owner of the Milton Abbey estate he followed the tradition started by Lord Milton, who became colonel of the regiment at the time of its foundation in the Napoleonic Wars. Charles' nephews, Harry and Angus, also joined in later years. Dorchester County Library.

interests regardless of party considerations, and whenever he appeared at political gatherings he was welcomed with enthusiasm by opponents and supporters alike.

While his father had restored the Abbey and built a new school and cottage hospital in Milton Abbas, Charles was responsible for enlarging and improving the parish church, essential now that the population of Milton Abbas had grown since the village had been built a century earlier. The work was done in memory of Susan, who died in London on 9 July 1887. Through her he had won the happiness which had eluded him as a boy, and he never fully recovered from her death. He organized a church collection among his friends and although the total came to nearly two thousand pounds he contributed well over half that amount himself. As a result a new chancel, organ, vestry and south aisle were added. It remains almost unchanged today.

In 1891 Charles fell ill just before the Easter parliamentary recess and went to Monte Carlo to recover; but on Saturday 11 April he died of pneumonia. He was only fifty-six. His last moments were spent with his youngest brother Everard, his daughter Agneta and his lifelong friend Montagu Guest who had travelled to the Riviera to be with him at the end. His body was sent to Southampton and from there by rail to Dorchester. Local respect was so great for him that on the day of his funeral all businesses were closed, the streets were lined with mourners, and a long procession of carriages followed the hearse from the station to Milton Abbey, eleven miles away. A Union Jack was draped over his coffin, and beside it lay the hat and sword which he had worn as Honorary Colonel of the Dorset Yeomanry.

The coffin was taken into the Abbey and laid to rest at the chancel steps for an hour while sorrowful music was played on the organ and the solemn watch ensued. During the slow march to the parish church the Abbey bell tolled. Charles was buried in the family vault in the churchyard next to the ashes of his beloved Susan. He had no wish to be buried in the splendour of the Abbey.

Among the many hundreds of mourners was a crippled lad wearing a dark blue uniform. At his own cost he had travelled from London and had walked the seven miles from Blandford on crutches to attend the funeral of his benefactor. He had been a bootblack outside the House of Commons where Charles had noticed his disability and secured his admission to a cottage hospital. The deed was worthy of Charles' character. He had been a gentle, generous person and much loved by those who knew him. Throughout his life he had apparently drawn all

Described in the family album as 'The Cut. Triumph of Woman over Man', c. 1864. It shows Charles Hambro and his friend Montagu Guest being snubbed by Susan Hambro and Miss St Quintin outside the Hall at Milton Abbey. Hambro Family Archives.

The photograph above is taken from the family album and dates from the 1860s. It is called the 'Beauties' and shows the fifteen men working in the stables and kennels. Note the chimney-sweep on the right-hand side.

The photograph below is described as 'one or two servants', but actually there were fifteen female and nine male domestic servants working in the Hall during the period when Charles and Susan were in residence. Hambro Family Archives.

classes to him. The hard lessons of tolerance, humility and compassion which he had learnt in India had remained with him for the rest of his days.

Percival was the second of Carl Joachim's three sons, born on 29 January 1836 in Copenhagen. As a youth he was thought to be a much stronger character than Charles, and enjoyed a closer relationship with his father who wrote him many letters in the mid-1850s confiding his worries over the family and bank. At the time Percival was an undergraduate at Merton College, Oxford, where smoking parties, dances and sport often distracted him from his studies. Persistently troubled by a throat infection, he struggled hard to pass examinations. His father was disappointed but not unkind: 'You need not have the slightest alarm regarding me for I reproach myself quite as much as you that I have impeded your education by various measures of the harm of which I am now aware. The Lord will help us all and yet bring a satisfactory result.'

In April 1857 he decided to enter the bank. Carl Joachim was particularly pleased as it meant that they would live and work in the office together, but he warned Percival that the path of commerce would be difficult:

Your ignorance of French German Spanish and Danish will daily make you feel humbled but if you determine to begin by the beginning and so master the subordinate parts of the craft you will by degrees through your good abilities take a leading part and by employing your morning and evenings in the study of languages particularly French and Spanish you may get on altogether . . . you will need all your spare time to master difficulties . . . Even such as handwriting will be of moment.

A City Life and sport and easy idle life will not go together and you must buckle up to stem in the office if you expect to get on. The clerks have three or four weeks in the year, that you will have also, but better terms than Rawlings or myself enjoy you will not have as you might end your commercial life even more sadly than your academical.

Take care of your health and when a few weeks fresh air have restored you come back to your loving and affectionate father.

Percival enjoyed a few weeks' fishing in Norway, but once he started work in the bank his life changed as dramatically as his father had predicted. He worked long hours, and when Carl Joachim suggested that he went to stay with one of his old friends in Hamburg to improve his German and knowledge of foreign banking, he considered leaving the bank and going to the Bar. Susan, his sister-in-law, was furious and told him: 'The fact of the matter is, you are intensely idle . . . I declare if you leave the office – Charlie shall go into it.'

His health had frequently caused problems in the past. Then in 1868 he discovered that he had cancer of the foot and in the summer of that year he explained his condition to his beloved Grace:

3 swells are going to come and sit upon me. I am to have my foot cut, and they hope a simple cut will do, if not they may have to take away part of the bone. I am to have Paget who is a very safe man. At present I have no pain in it but I have a soft lump which grows bigger and bigger and so it had best be done . . . Paget has another swell to help him and my own man, Clover, gives me cloroform.

Fortunately, Percival made a good recovery from his operation and by Christmas 1868 he was able to pursue his relationship with Grace in earnest. By then he was nearly thirty-two. Their endearing letters show that they had been deeply in love for more than two years. Again, however, Carl Joachim did not approve. Grace was just seventeen and her father, Henry Otway Mayne, was merely a major in the Indian Army. He wanted his son to marry a wealthy City gentleman's daughter instead. On 9 February 1869 Percival wrote to Grace from Weymouth that he would ask his father's blessing when he next went to London. He said that he had intended to ask the week before, but 'My father was laid up with gout . . . so all things considered I found it best to wait.'

On 24 February 1869 the forthcoming wedding was reported in the local newspaper and on 13 March they were married. Everard, Percival's youngest brother, and his wife Mary wrote warm letters of congratulations. Such short notice, however, can scarcely have been satisfactory for either family. Perhaps the timing of Carl Joachim's announcement on 1 March 1869 was significant, for he said that Percival had been advised to retire from the bank for medical reasons. By then, Everard, who was six years younger than Percival, had grown up, and at twenty-six his turn had arrived to be made a partner in his father's firm.

Percival and Grace lived at Wallop House, a modest country mansion in Hampshire. Before the end of the year Grace produced her first child, Henry, and within another year, on 10 December 1870, she gave birth to twins. She survived only a few hours and then died. She was only nineteen. Their marriage had lasted twenty-one months – a fleeting period of utter devotion. Percival was left with three motherless children all in the first year of their lives. He named the twins Percival and Grace.

Four years later, on 4 February 1875, he married again and was able to provide a mother for his children. His second wife was Arabella

Percival Hambro (1836–85), Carl Joachim's middle son, was born in Denmark, educated in England and studied at Merton College, Oxford. He joined C. J. Hambro & Son in 1857 and retired in 1869. At the age of thirty-three he married Grace Mayne who was then eighteen. Within twenty-one months of marriage she had given birth to three infants, first Harry and then twins, Percival and Grace. She was only nineteen when she died and all her children were less than a year old. Hambro Family Archives.

Norman of the eminent banking family from Bromley, Kent. With the births of Dorothy, Norman and Bertram his family grew quickly and by 1880 he had a total of four boys and two girls. Five years later, however, his health failed again, and he died at Brigmerston House in Wiltshire at the early age of forty-nine. His children and their descendants were to perform important roles over the next seventy years. His eldest son, known as Harry, inherited the Milton Abbey estate and pursued a lifelong career in the family bank. The second son, known as Percy, became a general in the army. Norman died heroically in the Boer War and Bertram died during World War I.

14   Everard, the Youngest Son

The youngest of Carl Joachim's three sons was born on 11 April 1842 and christened Everard Alexander. Although his parents had been married in London eight years previously, he was the only member of the family to have been born in England – both his brothers, Charles and Percival, seven and six respectively, had been born in Denmark. By 1842 his parents had been established in London for three years and although the family bank had experienced initial difficulties, the help and able guidance of his grandfather Joseph had ensured its permanent place amongst the City finance houses. The foundation had been laid on which Everard one day would build a bank of international repute on a scale quite beyond the dreams of his predecessors.

Everard's capabilities far excelled those of his brothers. Even as a boy of thirteen his poise and confidence were considered outstanding. On a particular occasion at Milton Abbey he was required to give a vote of thanks, which he did so uncommonly well that the estate steward told his father the next morning that 'Evie' would one day be Lord Chancellor. The remark may have been incidental, but future events were to show that this was an astute judgement of Everard's character. Although he never became Lord Chancellor, within the next thirty-five years he did become one of the pillars of the City.

Everard was educated at Mr J.P. Clover's school at Roehampton and then, like Charles, went up to Trinity College, Cambridge. His fellow undergraduates in the college represented many other banking houses; they included Yarbrugh Lloyd, Charles Barclay, Nathaniel Rothschild, Francis Smith, Edward St Aubyn, Frederick Leslie Melville and Joseph Gibbs. The Prince of Wales was another notable contemporary. The Prince's friendship with the banking fraternity became widely known, and many years later, as Edward VII, he was Everard's guest at Milton Abbey.

One of Everard's closest friends was Martin Ridley Smith, the elder brother of Francis Smith with whom Everard had been at university. Their father, Martin Tucker Smith, was a senior partner in the prestigious private banking house Smith Payne and Smith which had been established in 1758. In Everard's lifetime the Hambros and the Martin Smiths enjoyed an extremely close relationship, one originally based on friendship but soon cemented by marriage.

Everard Hambro (1842–1925), the youngest son of Carl Joachim, became the most notable banker in the English family. He was educated at a private school in Roehampton and was then admitted to Trinty College, Cambridge, where he was a contemporary of the Prince of Wales, Nathaniel Rothschild, Yarbrugh Lloyd, Charles Barclay, Frederick Leslie Melville and Joseph Gibbs. Hambro Family Archives.

299

Everard met his wife while yachting in the Western Isles of Scotland with his friend Martin Ridley Smith. They called at Rothesay on the Isle of Bute which was the home of Martin's wife, Emily Stuart. Everard fell in love with her sister Mary, whom he married in 1866. Hambro Family Archives.

One summer in the early 1860s Martin and his wife, Emily, invited Everard to join them on holiday, sailing in the Western Isles of Scotland. They called at Rothesay on the Isle of Bute, which was Emily's childhood home – her father, Henry Stuart, was a grandson of the 2nd Marquess of Bute. The holiday was to be a memorable occasion since Everard, then dark, handsome and bearded, fell in love with one of Emily's younger sisters, Mary. Carl Joachim approved of his choice, and on 23 October 1866 Everard and Mary were married with great ceremony at St George's, Hanover Square.

Everard and Mary lived at 70 Princes Gate, a fashionable London address just south of Hyde Park. Next door to them were Colin and Constance Hugh Smith, cousins of Martin and Emily. Colin was a successful wharfinger and in 1863 had started the famous Hay's Wharf in Tooley Street. He and Everard became lifelong friends and at the end of the 1870s they were both elected directors of the Court of the Bank of England; in 1897 Colin became Governor. The friendship of the two families extended to the next generation, and in 1927 John, Colin's youngest son, became a managing director of Hambros Bank.

While retaining their town house for the winter, Everard and Mary liked to spend the summer out of London so in 1871 they rented Mount Clare, a beautiful Georgian mansion which had been built by Adam a century earlier. It stood in thirty-five acres of grounds overlooking the treetops of Richmond Park. For three years they shared it with the Hugh Smiths, but in 1874 they decided to join Carl Joachim at Gifford House, a fine villa on the edge of Putney Heath. The old gentleman was now almost blind and had only a short while to live.

Everard's new move to Gifford House brought him into close contact with his neighbour, J. Pierpont Morgan, who in the summer months used to spend many weeks at Dover House, his English country seat. In the 1870s Pierpont was a partner of the New York bank, Drexel Morgan & Co., but his business was intricately linked with that of his father, Junius Spencer Morgan, whose firm J. S. Morgan & Co. was based at 22 Old Broad Street, London. Everard was associated with both the London and the New York Morgan banks, frequently becoming involved in the same foreign loan syndicates and the issue of American railroad securities. Over the years Everard and Pierpont became firm friends, as their sons and grandsons were to do later.

Everard and Mary's three youngest children, Angus aged six, Violet aged five and Olaf aged four. Hambro Family Archives.

Junius Spencer Morgan (1813–90) was chief of J. S. Morgan & Co., 22 Old Broad Street. He was a banking ally of Everard Hambro whose bank was at 70 Old Broad Street. Junius and Everard were both responsible for providing part of the initial £20,000 with which to start the Royal National Pension Fund for Nurses in 1886. Reproduced with kind permission of Morgan Grenfell & Co. Limited.

Although Mary produced five children in the 1870s only two sons survived: Eric, described as 'young Hercules', who was born on 30 September 1872, and Harold, born on 25 January 1876. Two died as infants: Maurice as a six-month-old baby, and a twin of Harold's who died at birth. The third tragedy occurred with the death of Hermione, the only daughter, who died soon after her eighth birthday. Undoubtedly the death of the little girl caused the greatest anguish. For several years Mary suffered badly with thyroid trouble and for a while no more children were born. By the early 1880s, however, she had recovered and gave birth to three more babies in three successive years. Angus was born on 8 July 1883, Violet on 24 September 1884 and Olaf on 1 December 1885. Thus Everard established his family: he now had four strong, healthy sons from whom to find a successor, and to carry on the Hambro name.

In 1873, meanwhile, the combination of Everard's love for children and his philanthropic nature had encouraged him to buy a modest house in Roehampton overlooking Putney Heath, where he started an orphanage. He ran it entirely from his own resources until 1879 when he allowed another children's home to become incorporated. Thus it grew much larger, and with Mary as the patroness it became known as the Hambro Orphanage for Girls. Throughout the hectic years of the

1880s Everard still found time to pay regular visits to the children, usually calling at half past eight in the morning. After supporting the home for thirty-six years he finally presented it to the Waifs and Strays, the forerunner of the Church of England Children's Society. The home then cared for eighteen girls.

Everard's philanthropic nature showed in other areas, too. In 1886 Sir Henry Burdett realized the need of a scheme to give financial protection to retired nurses. One of his major problems was to find the necessary £20,000 which had to be deposited with the Court of Chancery before a pension fund could be started. Everard was one of four bankers who generously donated the sum; the others included his friend Junius Spencer Morgan, Lord Rothschild and Henry Hucks Gibbs. Their joint efforts meant that the scheme could begin and by the end of the decade the Royal National Pension Fund for Nurses was fully established with over a thousand proposals for annuities. Indeed, within ten years nearly 40 per cent of the nursing population held policies in the Fund. The Hambro interest has continued into the twentieth century with the chairmanship of Everard's grandson, Sir Charles Hambro, from 1947 to 1963 and his great-grandson, Charlie, from 1968.

John Pierpont Morgan (1837–1913) was the son of Junius and worked in the United States for Drexel Morgan & Co., bankers, and then in 1894 established his own bank, J. P. Morgan & Co. Meanwhile, on the death of his father he had become chief of J. S. Morgan & Co. in London. He spent a large part of each year in his house at 13 Prince's Gate in London, and in his country home, Dover House in Roehampton, which was next to Everard Hambro's Gifford House. The two men were close friends throughout their lives. Reproduced with kind permission of Morgan Grenfell & Co. Limited.

In the early 1880s Everard had moved his permanent home away from Putney Heath to Hayes Place, near Bromley in Kent. Here he lived in a large country house which had once been the home of the Pitt family. It had extensive gardens, a tennis court, and a farm where he kept a herd of pedigree Guernseys. Nearby lived his friend and brother-in-law, Martin Ridley Smith. Other members of the banking fraternity were also close at hand, such as the Lubbocks, the Martins and the Normans. Through the experience of family, university and neighbouring friends an intricate pattern of contacts had begun to emerge. Gradually Everard was being drawn to the very centre of the City's web.

Everard first entered C. J. Hambro & Son in 1864 and then, on the retirement of Percival five years later, he became one of the bank's four partners along with his father, Edward Rawlings and Robert Heriot. After the death of Carl Joachim on 17 November 1877 Everard became senior partner. He had complete, unquestioned control of the bank, since he then owned the largest share of the assets. He inherited all his father's capital in the bank which, in addition to his own share, amounted to nearly half a million pounds. This meant that he held 75 per cent of the bank's total capital which then stood at £650,000.

In 1878, at the age of thirty-six, Everard's earnings from the bank were £52,000. The figure was calculated on the basis of a 4 per cent interest payment on his capital and then a 75 per cent share of the remaining profits in line with his proportion of the total bank capital. In that same year, Edward Rawlings received about £9,000 and Robert Heriot about £8,000. A great contrast clearly existed between the partners themselves, but an even greater gulf emerged between them and the staff. The two managers both earned approximately £800 a year and of the twenty-seven clerks over a third received £300. In addition, there were five 'boys' who were each given £120 a year. The thirty-five staff salaries came to approximately £10,000, while the profits which the three partners shared amounted to £69,000. These disparities were, of course, by no means unusual in the 1870s, and the Hambro banking house was always considered a generous employer by the standards of the time.

During the 1880s, Everard's income rose dramatically and during 1886–9 it averaged £150,000 a year. This sum enabled him to enjoy a luxurious standard of living. But, significantly, he still took care to reinvest, on average, 55 per cent of his income annually. Within ten years he managed to double his capital from £500,000 to £1,000,000, and increased the total capital of the bank to £1.3 million by 1 January

By the time Joseph and Carl Joachim Hambro founded their London bank in 1839, the Bank of England had already been established for 145 years. Its original Royal Charter declared that it was to be governed by a Court of twenty-six directors. With only a four-year gap, Everard and Charles Hambro served as directors for eighty-four years from 1879 until 1963, during which time they were intimately involved with the Bank's affairs and became central figures on the Court. Guildhall Library.

Although the site of the Royal Exchange dates back to the mid-sixteenth century the present building was constructed after the fire of 1838 and opened by Queen Victoria in 1844. From 1720 it was the home of the Royal Exchange Assurance Corporation which began with Marine Insurance and soon after added Life and Fire. Guildhall Library.

Map of London showing the locations of various banks in 1881. Source: Post Office Directory 1881.

1. Bank of England.
2. Smith, Payne & Smith.
3. N. M. Rothschild & Sons.
4. Robarts, Lubbock & Co.
5. Martin & Co.
6. Glyn, Mills, Currie & Co.
7. Barclay, Bevan, Tritton & Co.
8. David Sassoon & Co.
9. William Brandt's Sons & Co.
10. Nathaniel Cohen & Co.
11. Baring Brothers & Co.
12. Antony Gibbs & Sons.
13. C. J. Hambro & Son.
14. Samuel Montagu &' Co.
15. Lazard Brothers & Co.
16. J. S. Morgan & Co.
17. Hay's Wharf.

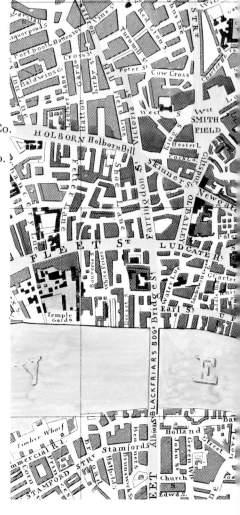

1890. Thus he quickly built up his reserves for the years of depression which, one day, might follow.

As the capital base expanded, the scope and size of the bank's activities grew enormously. Acceptances which were the bread and butter element of the banking business doubled from just over £1,000,000 at the end of the 1870s to over £2,000,000 by the mid-1880s. A peak of £2.6 million was reached in 1889. This tremendous rise was largely the result of Everard's American policy. He began to finance trade across the Atlantic and also the intercontinental trade between North and South America. He relied on an extensive network of corres-

pondents based on the three New York banks, Phelps, Stokes & Co., Drexel Morgan & Co., and Heidelbach & Ickelheimer & Co. As his contacts grew, his American operations mushroomed and from the basis of acceptances he became involved in many other areas such as bullion dealing and the syndication of American railroad loans.

Everard's greatest delight as a banker was to arrange the issue of foreign loans, a task which required enormous skill and patience. Although he raised money for private companies such as the Great Northern Telegraph Co. in Denmark, the Trans-Caucasian Railroad Co. in Russia, the Southern Mahratta Railroad Co. in India, and the

Marietta and North Georgia Railroad Co. in the USA, he was much more attracted by the larger government loans. These dwarfed the private issues both in size and excitement and also, of course, in the profits which they generated.

At this time London was the centre of the world capital market, and in the 1870s Everard issued four loans totalling £6,500,000. These were required specifically by Norway and Sweden to finance the development of their railways. By contrast, in the 1880s, he was involved in the issue of loans totalling approximately £85,000,000 not only for Sweden and Norway, who borrowed £13,000,000, but also for Denmark, Greece, Russia and Italy. While the market grew, competition intensified, and as larger sums of money became involved the syndication of the loans became more frequent. Everard drew a friendly circle of French, Scandinavian, American and British bankers around him to support his issues. Hoskier in Paris, Tietgen in Copenhagen, the Morgans in New York, and Smiths in London were all important allies, but towering above them all was E.C. Baring, who in 1885 became Lord Revelstoke. He was chief of Baring Brothers & Co., the oldest and one of the most respected banks in London, whose capital base of about £2,000,000 during the early and mid-1880s was three times that of C. J. Hambro & Son. The alliance added enormous weight to the Hambro syndicate.

In 1881, Everard became involved in one of the fiercest battles of his life. In the middle of May that year secret letters and coded telegraphs arrived on his desk at 70 Old Broad Street, through which he learnt that the Italian government had approved the issue of an enormous loan worth £29,000,000. The proceeds would be used to buy silver and gold which would be circulated as normal coinage, while part would be retained as bullion. Thus the government hoped to establish a strong national currency. It would be one further milestone along the road of Italian development.

In strictest confidence Everard learnt from Count Maffei, an old friend and an Italian politician, that the issue had already been offered to a rival bank, the Rothschild Brothers of Paris. Magliani, the Italian

---

E. C. Baring, chief of Baring Brothers & Co., was created Lord Revelstoke in 1885. His support over the £29,000,000 Italian loan in the early 1880s was of vital importance to Everard, just as Everard's help in November 1890 was of great significance to the house of Baring. Throughout the 1880s these two figures worked closely together in many aspects of banking. Reproduced with kind permission of Baring Brothers & Co. Limited.

finance minister, had felt obliged to ask them first since they had dealt with the last Italian loan in 1863 and, even more important, because they could take advantage of the Paris Bourse which was traditionally thought the best market for Italian securities. The response had been extremely slow, however, for trouble was brewing in North Africa which would cause serious tension between France and Italy. Already, the annexation of Tunis by the French had been expected for several weeks. Under these conditions the Rothschild Brothers were not prepared to face the unpopularity of a new Italian loan.

The hesitancy of the Rothschilds gave Magliani an excuse to offer the loan to C. J. Hambro & Son. He welcomed the opportunity of 'shedding the Rothschild yoke' just as Everard, of course, was pleased to win Italy back as Hambro territory. Everard had dealt with the Paris Bourse on many occasions before and, unlike the Rothschilds, he did not think French politics would be a serious problem. Anyway, he had much more faith in the London market. On 10 June 1881 the formal invitation arrived and Everard accepted the challenge.

The prospect was almost overwhelming for, apart from issuing such an enormous loan, Everard was also expected to purchase the bullion which involved £16,000,000 in gold, and the rest in silver. Approximately 4,000,000 ounces of gold had to be bought on an extremely unpredictable world market. A great debate developed in the newspapers and the City as to whether such large quantities of gold could be purchased without raising the price. Much depended on the immediate requirements of the USA. Until 1879 it had been a net exporter, but in 1880 the situation had changed. Its demands in the next two years would be vitally important. If there was a balance of payments deficit gold would again flow out in large quantities and, in these circumstances, the Italian demand might be satisfied. Everard took the gamble.

The resources of C. J. Hambro & Son alone were quite inadequate to control the flotation of such a large issue on both the London and the Paris markets. Everard decided to form a strong syndicate. His main allies were Baring Brothers & Co., who were old rivals to the Rothschilds and experienced in large loan issues. For obvious political reasons he also invited an Italian group which included the National Bank of Italy and the Credit Mobilier of Italy; in order to take full advantage of the Paris Bourse he also asked the Banque d'Escompte. He trusted in the combination of these five banks, together with all their friends, to provide the strength to combat any opposition.

The next step was to simplify the operation. He arranged for the loan to be split so that the first half would be issued within the next few

Cartoon by Lib, 1888, showing three of the most important City characters of the day. From left to right: Lord 'Natty' Rothschild (1840–1915), chief of N. M. Rothschild & Sons, Lord Revelstoke (1828–97), chief of Baring Brothers & Co., and Everard Hambro (1842–1925), chief of C. J. Hambro & Son. Hambros Bank Archives.

weeks, while the remainder should be dealt with whenever the syndicate thought appropriate. By avoiding one enormous issue he hoped to spread the collection of gold and, at the same time, prevent the markets becoming saturated by Italian bonds. The plan was agreed by the Italian government, and on 13 July 1881 the subscription list for the first issue was opened. The price had been fixed at 90, the interest rate was 5 per cent and the amount to be sold was £14.6 million.

He had been careful to prepare the path beforehand by winning support from his banking friends at home as well as those in Copenhagen, Stockholm, Hamburg, Paris, Lisbon and particularly New York. Despite adverse press comments and some opposition in the market, the results were highly satisfactory. Applications poured in and it rapidly became clear that the loan had been oversubscribed. When the allotments were made, however, the syndicate took care to reserve £900,000 for themselves so that they could make a profit when the price rose.

Morale remained high and in the new year Everard began to feel the time had come for the second issue. Rumours began to appear in the press. Then catastrophe struck. It was the first of many which haunted him as the year dragged on. The Paris market had been in a feverish state for many months, and now it collapsed. When the bubble burst in the middle of January many banks and companies suffered tremendous losses. Particularly relevant was the fate of the Banque d'Escompte. Its shares plummeted from 700 to 500 francs in only two days, and in order to meet its obligations elsewhere it was forced to sell its portion of the Italian loan syndicate. So the syndicate lost its Paris partner.

The Rothschilds had been carefully planning the Paris crisis for months. The apparent victim of their attack was Monsieur Bontoux and his bank, the Union Générale, which he had started in 1876 in order to oppose the Jewish banking fraternity. His idea had enormous appeal and the price of his bank shares had risen beyond all expectation. Outwardly the Rothschilds had appeared unruffled by the project, but throughout 1881 their tentacles had begun to accumulate shares of the Union Générale and its associated companies. Suddenly, in January 1882, they had sold them all, causing a collapse in the price on the Bourse, and thus 'obliterated' the Bontoux empire, the public

The Baron Alphonse de Rothschild (1827–1905) was head of the house of Rothschild in Paris and brother-in-law to Natty Rothschild in London. He was Everard Hambro's main opponent in the great Italian loan which he was intent to spoil. But, after a long struggle, Everard triumphed. Guildhall Library.

credit of which never recovered. The Paris and London markets qui-
vered for weeks under the strain, so that a second Italian issue was out
of the question.

The loss of the Paris representative meant that the syndicate would
either have to rely on the London market alone or find another bank to
replace the Banque d'Escompte. The Italian banks made a formal
request at the end of March that an invitation should be sent to the
Rothschild Brothers of Paris. Obviously such a step would have been
quite abhorrent to Everard. He was sure that the second issue could
survive on the London market alone, particularly now that it had just
begun to show signs of improvement. Two factors were in his favour:
first, the earlier Paris troubles had receded and the market was
steadier; second, there had been good results from the Italian budget,
and on Everard's own advice Magliani had been able to reduce some of
his country's wealth taxes. This encouraged English investors and, as
Everard had predicted, demand for Italian bonds increased and market prices picked up.

Everard's views prevailed and the Rothschilds did not receive their
invitation. Now, more than ever before, the strain fell on C. J. Hambro
& Son and Baring Brothers & Co. and their joint control of the London
market. The second issue had been delayed long enough and at the end
of April new prospectuses were sent to the same friends as before. Only
the date and the issue price were left blank. This information would be
sent in code later when the precise details had been agreed – such
decisions could only be taken at the last minute, since they had to suit
the temperament of the market at the vital moment of the issue.

'April' was the code which meant 88 was the price. Wednesday
3 May was the date for the subscription list to open. Another loan of
£14.6 million was to be issued. This time, however, the result was
disastrous. By the end of the afternoon a mere £1,000,000 had been
subscribed. By 11 am the next day only another £500,000 had been
applied for. At 3.30 pm Everard informed Grillo of the National Bank of
Italy that the loan would be far from covered. He wrote: 'I greatly
regret . . . that a better success has not crowned our joint efforts, but
you must admit that it was pure chance that we fell upon a bad moment
for the second issue . . . our market has completely lost life.' At another
vital moment the ghost of misfortune had appeared again, this time in
the form of an Egyptian crisis. Political tension suddenly mounted as
the threat of a Nationalist revolt became imminent, bringing into
question the whole future of British power over the Suez Canal. Naturally the London Stock Market was highly nervous. The final allotment
had been only £3,000,000, leaving more than £11,000,000 in the hands

of the syndicate, a ruinous burden for the four banks to carry alone.

Again the Italian group wanted to send an invitation to the Rothschild Brothers of Paris and so gain access to the Paris market. And again Everard dismissed the proposal. He wrote to the Italian ambassador in London: 'The position of our two houses, that of Baring and mine – being what it is – would make it quite impossible for us to allow anyone to say that we had undertaken something which we could not carry to a good end.' Whatever the opposition, however great the pressure, the Italian loan had to succeed, and Everard could not give way. The Rothschild yoke should not burden him as well.

The only alternative was for the syndicate to remain loyal and each subscribe for their share of the remaining £11,000,000, in the hope that the market would eventually rally and investors would then buy bonds from the syndicate. Fortunately, by the middle of May Italian securities were in good demand, and extremely large amounts were being sold. For some reason or other, Louis Cohen & Co. of London seemed to have an insatiable appetite. Then correspondence from France showed that the Rothschild Brothers of Paris and G. Cohen of Paris were willing to form a second syndicate to relieve the pressure on London! This was the third time the membership of the Rothschilds had been suggested and for a third time it was refused. Everard was not interested in their help. He still had confidence in the Italian stock and loyalty to the London market.

Steady buying continued, and by 12 June when the price stood at 90 Everard saw his chance to sell the balance of the loan. He wrote to the other banks in the syndicate asking them how much they wanted to keep for their own account. By one o'clock the next day, however, the opportunity had vanished as the price lost its firmness. Once more the Egyptian troubles were to blame. Alexandria had been sacked and fifty Europeans massacred. Yet again a ghost had appeared to unnerve the market. Another month passed, and on 13 July Everard wrote to Commander Balduino of the Italian bank, the Credit Mobilier: 'The total unsold today is £8,036,840 – capital. Had it not been for the Egyptian business there would have been little left.' August came and the price was only $86\frac{3}{4}$, far below the issue price. Unless the syndicate was willing to accept a big loss there was no question of selling the balance.

Five weeks on a grouse moor in Scotland was a powerful antidote to the trials and tribulations of City affairs, and on his return to London Everard was determined to bring the loan to a rapid conclusion. On 22 September he decided to sell the remaining balance of just under £6,500,000 to individual banks, at $87\frac{3}{4}$, a price slightly below par.

C. F. Tietgen was the founder of Privatbanken in Copenhagen and the Great Northern Telegraph Company. He was Everard's closest associate in Denmark and together they were involved in the issue of many foreign loans including the great Italian loan of 1881–3.

Baring Brothers & Co. agreed to take £2,000,000, his own bank took £1,000,000 and the rest was divided among various other British, French and Italian banks. The price meant that on the second issue the syndicate lost money, but it was a minimal loss and in the circumstances there was no hope of obtaining a profit. Moreover, Everard had been particularly shrewd in arranging that a large part would pass into safe hands which would hold the stock firmly until higher prices could be acquired.

The last deed which remained was to secure the final shipments of gold and silver. Since July 1881 bags, barrels and boxes of coins and bars had been arriving at the Italian ports of Genoa, Naples, Venice and Livorno and by train at Milan and Turin, all bound for Rome. A web of gold had been cast far and wide from Europe to the New World. London, Paris and Berlin had been major suppliers, but New York had beaten them all, sending £3,000,000 worth across the Atlantic. The bullion had poured into Italy steadily throughout the period, and even as early as April 1882 Everard had been sure of a satisfactory outcome to this side of the venture at least. By January 1883 the last shipments had been received and he could boast that the task which people had said was impossible had now been successfully accomplished. During the past eighteen months the price had remained relatively stable at

£3 17s 6d to £3 17s 10d per ounce. His gamble with American gold had paid off. His good friends, the bullion dealers Heidelbach & Ickelheimer & Co. of New York, had been an invaluable source of assistance throughout the whole operation.

In February 1883 Everard drew up the final syndicate accounts. It had been a most complicated affair, not only because of the two issues, but also because of the hundreds of extra calculations which surrounded the numerous purchases of gold and silver. It transpired that at the end of this long operation a net profit of £335,000 had been achieved. It represented 1.14 per cent of the total loan, no mean feat in the face of such determined opposition and difficult market conditions. Far from being disappointed, Everard felt triumphant, and published the result in the press. Those banks such as Drexel Morgan & Co., J. S. Morgan & Co., Brown, Shipley & Co., Heidelbach & Ickelheimer & Co., Norddeutsche Bank, Privatbanken, E. Hoskier & Co., Fosters & Co., and Scandinaviska Kreditaktiebolaget, with whom Everard had shared his portion of the loan, were both pleased and grateful. Hoskier wrote: 'Allow me to congratulate you most sincerely on the successful

Sunset over Genoa Harbour, *by Giuseppe Sacheri. Great shipments of gold arrived at the port of Genoa in the early 1880s, purchased with the proceeds of the Italian loan which Everard Hambro issued on the London market.* Reproduced with kind permission of Archivio Storico di Milano.

A Scene on Change, Pillars of the City *from* The Graphic, *9 May 1891. Inside the Royal Exchange Everard Hambro, centre right, is whispering to Lord Rothschild. On the far right other well-known bankers, Alfred Cohen and Samuel Montagu, are talking to one another. In the aftermath of the Baring crisis these were depressing days for the City.* The British Newspaper Library.

winding up of a business which must have cost you enormous labour and which reflects so much credit on your management.'

The financial rewards of C. J. Hambro & Son were small in proportion to the immense worry which had been caused and the large amounts which had been pledged. Everard's profit from the syndicate came to only £9,143, while his one per cent commission fee amounted to £35,433. But there was a good chance that he made considerable gains on the balance of the £1,000,000 which he had purchased at 87¾ on 22 September 1882. The Stock Exchange Year Book quoted 88¼ in 1883, 89⅝ in 1884 and 95½ in 1885. After all the difficulties, Everard's confidence had been well founded.

The financial gains, however, were as nothing compared with the battle which had been fought. It had been a headlong campaign, Hambros and Barings against Rothschilds. Even a one per cent profit meant victory. To have conceded at any stage would have meant immeasurable loss of prestige. The Rothschild yoke over Italy had been lifted and the name of C. J. Hambro & Son lived on. Everard's reputation was strengthened and his nerves steeled. He had launched himself as one of the greatest bankers of his era and he had succeeded.

Lord Revelstoke's unfailing support in the early 1880s had enabled Everard to weather his great Italian storm. In 1890 the time had come for Everard to repay the favour. In 1888 Baring Brothers & Co. had undertaken a capital issue for the Buenos Aires Water Supply and Drainage Company. The sale of stock had been bitterly disappointing and even two years later large unsaleable blocks of it weighed heavily on the bank ledger. At the time of the issue Lord Revelstoke had agreed to pay the Company its capital in three instalments, but as the payments became due he found himself paying out far more than he was able to collect from the sale of stock. Other liabilities were also pressing, and by the beginning of November 1890 his bank was facing a liquidity crisis. He needed funds at once but in recent weeks former sources of credit had withered completely. Lord Revelstoke was desperate.

Everard was aware of the impending disaster long before the news broke in the City. He was deeply involved as well. At the end of the year his ledger recorded a 'doubtful debt' of nearly a third of a million pounds owing from S. B. Hale & Co., the Argentinian managers of the Buenos Aires company in question. Everard had helped Baring Brothers & Co. to issue the stock and had subsequently lent money to S. B. Hale & Co. Thus C. J. Hambro & Son was in trouble too – the difference was merely a matter of degree.

As the crisis reached its climax, Everard took decisive action. One report claimed that he and Lord Revelstoke had spent the long hours of Friday night, 7 November deep in consultation trying to find a solution. By eight o'clock on Saturday morning Everard was already outside Lord Rothschild's house in St Swithin's Lane. Lord Rothschild, however, was quite sure that Barings could not be saved. Everard's next move was to consult Lidderdale, the Governor of the Bank of England, who was shocked by the news, which was the first intimation he had received of Baring's problem. Quickly he sent a note to the Chancellor of the Exchequer, Goschen, to come to the City on Monday morning. Then, at Everard's request he agreed to meet Lord Revelstoke and his cousin, Francis Baring, that same afternoon at three o'clock in Everard's own offices at 70 Old Broad Street. There, all four of them could meet in strictest secrecy.

When Barings presented their accounts that afternoon the picture was totally confusing and it was impossible for the Governor to discern whether Barings was insolvent or otherwise. He ordered that more precise figures should be calculated without delay. One point was clear:

the firm was in dreadful trouble and required money immediately. Yet the Bank of England's 'Reserve' was less than £11,000,000, adequate in normal times but not enough if the Bank was to rescue Barings.

On Monday the Governor saw Goschen who promised government support only if Barings was proved to be solvent. Everything thus depended on the revised figures which were eventually presented on Wednesday. They showed assets of nearly £25,000,000 against liabilities of £21,000,000, of which £15,000,000 was in the form of acceptances spread widely throughout the City. If Baring Brothers & Co. collapsed the effect would be enormous. As the Committee of the Stock Exchange pointed out: 'What securities would have been saleable, what bills would have been discounted?' Clearly, with the scale and diversity of the bank's interests, the disaster would have had overwhelming results both in London and abroad. After all, the bank was the oldest, and one of the largest and most prestigious houses in the City.

By Thursday afternoon the figures had been verified by two directors of the Bank of England, and the next day Goschen agreed to lend the support of the government. The Governor now played his trump card and started a massive rescue operation which took the form of a guarantee fund. This was not a new idea since the Bank of France had used a similar device to help the Comptoir d'Escompte the previous year. What was so remarkable, however, was the speed with which it was brought into operation on the following day.

The Bank of England pledged £1,000,000 which was doubled by a joint offer from Glyn, Mills, Currie and Rothschilds. The guarantee of just over another million was given by a combination of ten other banks including C. J. Hambro & Son who offered £100,000. By 5.30 pm £3,250,000 had been pledged. Later that evening the five main joint stock banks joined the effort and the total reached £6,500,000. The minimum requirement was thereby achieved. Next day, Saturday 15 November, various country, Scottish, colonial and foreign banks pledged more money, as did several merchants and individuals, so that the final figure came to just over £17,000,000. The confidence of the City had been shaken but its unity had been strengthened, and Barings, although badly bruised, was able to survive without dishonouring a single bill of exchange.

During the week only a few people had known of the impending crisis, but by Saturday the news had crossed the Atlantic and New York had been alerted. The guarantee fund provided the safety net, however, and although there was surprise and fear there was no real danger of panic. Robert Heriot, one of Everard's partners in C. J. Hambro & Son,

Everard Hambro, KCVO *(1842–1925), chief of C. J. Hambro & Son and later chairman of Hambros Bank Ltd, 1877–1925. He was described as a giant not only in stature but in character, in ability and in talents. In the 1880s he became a leading figure in the City and established his bank as one of the foremost in London. Portrait by Sir John Lavery,* RA, *c. 1915.* Hambros Bank Archives.

'Villa Espoir' was Everard's home in the fashionable resort of Biarritz on the coast of south-west France. He used to visit it each year during Febrary and March from the early 1890s until the outbreak of World War I. The mild climate and golf on the links were two of the main attractions, while sketching and playing cards, sometimes with the Prince of Wales, later King Edward VII, were other frequent diversions. Hambro Family Archives.

wrote to Mr Ickelheimer, who was one of their best customers in New York. The letter was brief and ended thus: 'I have not time to write [more] now, as I have been very busy, Mr Hambro having been much occupied in perfecting the plan to secure the required assistance by which alone the crash could be averted.' This was just one of the tributes paid to Everard's endeavours which had shown his loyalty and timely perception.

A new public company, Baring Brothers & Co. Limited, was formed with a capital of £1,000,000 to take over the business of the old firm. Everard bought forty of the shares which were valued at £500 each. It was one of his last efforts to help his old friend, for although the new company survived, Lord Revelstoke never recovered from the shock. He retired in 1891 and died six years later. Thus Everard lost one of his most valuable allies.

The frenzied years of the late 1880s came to a shattering climax in the autumn of 1890. Many bankers suddenly found themselves in very different pecuniary circumstances from those which they had recently enjoyed. Lord Revelstoke had not been alone in his sufferings; Lord Rothschild too was worried. He commented in the middle of November 1890 that the year's accounts would not be pleasant reading, and that he should have to live more quietly.

C. J. Hambro and Son was also seriously affected. Profits which had ventured over £200,000 in 1886, and had remained near that level until the end of the decade, now plummeted to only £57,000 in 1890. In addition Stock Exchange quotations, particularly for South American stocks, had been falling headlong, and Everard found many of the firm's investments to be 'dubious' or 'valueless''. On 31 December 1890 debts from companies which had failed that year reached £31,000, the sum for doubtful debtors amounted to more than £340,000, and the original worth of 'stocks not valued' came to over £550,000. Nearly £1,000,000 was at stake. Drastic steps had to be taken. Everard was grateful that he had been cautious during the past few years and he was able to create a special reserve fund of £250,000. He took it from the main capital of the bank so that just over £1,000,000 remained.

Business slumped further, and the immense strain of the previous autumn was beginning to show its mark on Everard. In order to escape the gloom of the City, he decided early in 1891 to take Mary to Biarritz to celebrate twenty-five years of married life. The fashionable coastal resort in south-west France was frequently visited by the Prince of Wales. Although they stayed there in February and March, before the main English season, they found the air so warm and congenial that they were away much longer than anticipated. Often they went sketching together, sometimes over the Spanish border where Mary found herself transfixed by the picturesque villages and snowcapped Pyrenees. At other times they played 'le golf', which Mary was just beginning to learn but which Everard played very well. After the worries of the past four months Mary was relieved and thankful that she could write to her nephew, Harry: 'It has done Uncle Evy *such* a lot of good.' They both enjoyed themselves so much that soon afterwards Everard bought a house in Biarritz called the Villa Espoir, which the whole family used to visit every year until the outbreak of World War I.

When Everard returned to London nothing had changed to remove his pessimism that even darker days would yet enshroud the City. For the rest of the year business remained slack, and so it continued into 1892. In addition to all the bank's monetary problems, Everard became seriously ill and throughout the spring and summer of that year he suffered from severe attacks of malarial fever. He was forced to retire from work for long periods, and was often delirious, and quite incapable of holding a pen. These bouts occurred frequently at first but gradually, as the summer wore on, they became less regular. Instead of travelling to Biarritz, Everard convalesced near Edzell in Scotland where for many years he had rented the Gannochy estate from the Earl of Dalhousie. It covered 17,000 acres of upland moors, and was a highland paradise of heather and grouse. As the hills gave way to the lowlands, the North Esk flowed through a long gorge where salmon struggled hard against the racing current as they sought the tranquillity of the higher streams. Beside the gorge stood Gannochy Lodge where Everard slowly regained his strength, reflecting that when this year's 'glorious twelfth' arrived he would be unable to participate in his favourite sport.

Though his health returned, worse financial conditions ensued and the nadir of the depression was not reached until 1893. By this time the level of acceptances, commissions and interest had all been halved since the peak of 1889. Moreover, the balance sheet total of £6,500,000 had, within those four years, fallen by 44 per cent. Profits had sunk to a mere £18,000, so that even the basic 4 per cent interest on partners' capital could not be paid. Business in general was dreadfully dull. British trade was suffering from persistent lethargy, confidence had not returned to the City, and overseas securities in particular were regarded with great mistrust. Although in the last two years Everard had raised capital for Russia and Greece, new stocks were rarely being issued and few opportunities arose for Everard to use his great flair for this type of business. Furthermore, he had lost the support of Lord Revelstoke. Without the backing of the former Baring Brothers & Co., Everard was in a much weaker position to enter the fray of the foreign loan market.

By the mid-1890s the dawn of a more prosperous era was just beginning to break. More foreign loans were being issued, and though they were all for comparatively small amounts Everard was able to raise money for Norway, Sweden and Denmark. In addition new developments in the gold and diamond mines of South Africa, and a revival of the railroad development in North and South America, all brought many new investment opportunities. British exports were increasing at last, and with the consequent growth in trade the volume

Gannochy Lodge together with 17,000 acres of moorlands near Brechin in Forfarshire, Scotland, was rented by the Hambros from the Earl of Dalhousie. The whole family enjoyed excellent grouse shooting. Everard, Eric and Olaf, in particular, were keen deer stalkers, while Percival and Charles loved salmon fishing. Hambro Family Archives.

While the men went shooting on the grouse moors the ladies sketched and read books. Here Mary Hambro is sitting beside the North Esk river as it flows through a steep gorge not far from Gannochy Lodge. Violet, her daughter, is lying by the water's edge. Hambro Family Archives.

of acceptances was rising once again. A more promising future awaited the new generation of Hambros who had recently joined the bank.

Everard had been without family support since the death of his father in 1877. Ten years later he had lost his most experienced partner, Edward Rawlings, and from then on he worked with the two Heriots – Robert, who had joined the bank as a partner in 1869, the same year as himself, and his son Walter who became a partner in 1887. Now the time had come for his nephew, Harry, and his eldest son, Eric, to learn the business of banking. Harry started in the traumatic years of the early 1890s, while Eric, three years younger, began his career during the better years of the mid-1890s.

Harry was the eldest child of Everard's brother, Percival, who had worked in the bank for a short and unsuccessful period which had ended in March 1869, the year of his son's birth. Harry experienced a sad and turbulent childhood. His mother, Grace, had died just before his first birthday, and although his father had remarried in 1875 he never felt a great affection for his stepmother. He was only sixteen when his father died and left him responsible for his five younger brothers and sisters. For one so young he faced a difficult task and often turned to his Uncle Everard for help and guidance.

When he left Eton he travelled to France and Spain where he learnt the languages and became acquainted with foreign banking methods. In Paris he worked for Emile Hoskier & Co., one of his uncle's oldest allies. This gave him direct contact with the Paris Bourse, an important capital market on which to sell foreign securities, experience which was to prove useful in later years. After eighteen months Everard wrote and asked him whether he would like to return to London and join C. J. Hambro & Son: 'We will try and teach you our way of doing business and when you understand a little more about it I shall be most willing to let you into a share of the profits and do what I can to advance your future.'

Harry accepted the invitation but did not leave Paris until the following year when, on the death of his uncle Charles in April 1891, he inherited the Milton Abbey estate. Just at that time, however, a severe agricultural depression was causing great hardship for the tenant farmers and, instead of being a joy, the estate proved to be nothing but a relentless burden. The additional responsibility weighed heavily on the young man's mind and he became quiet and introverted. Despite his immediate troubles, his inheritance meant that potentially he had become an extremely wealthy bachelor, and in 1896 he married Edith, the daughter of Cosmo Bonsor who was a politician and well-known

Everard Hambro and his family gathered at Gannochy in 1898. Standing, from left to right: Eric; Everard and his wife, Mary; Angus; and Harold. Seated, from left to right: Sybil, Eric's wife; Charles, her baby; Olaf; and Violet. Everard, Eric, Olaf and Charles were the first four Chairmen of Hambros Bank. Hambro Family Archives.

City figure, being a director of the Court of the Bank of England from 1885 to 1928. Harry married well and Everard, who was a friend of his father-in-law, thoroughly approved.

As a banker, meanwhile, he was both capable and diligent, and his sense of duty made him an invaluable asset to C. J. Hambro & Son. His serious, shy manner explained why Everard once said of him that 'he wrote very good letters, better on paper than with people'. He developed a keen eye for detail, a methodical approach to his work and a thorough understanding of the business, and although he lacked the humour and charm which his cousin Eric exuded, he was not so easily led astray. As the twentieth century unfolded, his tenacity and obvious ability were to prove of great importance to the bank.

Eric Hambro was a great contrast to Harry. He had no family problems to colour his childhood or early youth. His grandfather and parents had doted on him as a baby and he had been raised in luxury among a warm-hearted and happy family. He had irresistible charm and boundless good humour, and was always extremely popular. After Eton he followed in his father's footsteps and went up to Trinity College, Cambridge, where he developed an interest in politics and became an avid sportsman. Golf was his favourite game and he was immediately selected to play for the university. This was an honour well earned since he established a new record by going round the Cambridge course in only seventy-two strokes.

His closest friend at Trinity was Walter Burns, whom he had already met at Farnborough where as young boys they had both played in the school cricket XI. During their undergraduate years they used to join shooting parties every Saturday throughout the winter in various parts of the country, and in August they would both travel north and shoot on the grouse moors of Scotland. Walter was the nephew of Everard's friend, J. Pierpont Morgan, who since the death of his father, Junius, in 1890 had become the senior partner of the London bank, J. S. Morgan and Co. Walter's own father had been made a partner in 1878 and now, like Eric, he was destined to join his family bank. The London alliance between C. J. Hambro & Son and J. S. Morgan & Co. was destined to continue into another generation.

Soon after Eric left Cambridge he became engaged to his cousin, Sybil, who was the daughter of his father's best friend and brother-in-law, Martin Ridley Smith. For many years the two families had lived on either side of Hayes Common in Kent, and the children had practically grown up together. Eric had been tall as a boy and now, at 6 foot 6 inches, he stood an inch above his father. He was dark, handsome and full of life. He was a good match for the attractive Sybil with her strong character and striking personality. Everard was delighted, of course, since it meant that the two banking families would once more be joined in marriage. This marked another stage of the Hambro-Smith dynasty which, in that generation alone, was to be reinforced another three times.

After the wedding Eric and Sybil sailed to New York where Eric gained valuable experience in American banking. For much of the time they stayed with J. Pierpont Morgan Junior, whose father was, by this

Eric Hambro (1872–1947), the eldest of Everard's sons, pheasant-shooting on the Milton Abbey estate in October 1909. His loader is carrying a 'Gannochy', a device with a capacity for 100 cartridges arranged so as to facilitate quick reloading. Hambro Family Archives.

time, reaching the zenith of his career with J. P. Morgan & Co. in Wall Street. Many useful contacts were made; it was nearly a year later that Eric and Sybil returned to London, where Eric's stormy career with C. J. Hambro & Son began. As the eldest son he would naturally inherit Everard's position in the bank, but almost thirty years were to pass before his father died and during that time Eric remained very much under his control, rarely being given the chance to take any real responsibility in the firm.

By the end of 1897 the future of C. J. Hambro & Son looked much brighter, and now that Eric and Harry had both gained a little experience in the business and had made successful marriages Everard thought it appropriate that they should each begin to receive a 4 per cent share of the profits. On 1 January 1898 a new agreement was signed which included himself and Robert Heriot as the senior partners and Walter Heriot, Eric and Harry Hambro as the three junior partners. By this time Walter had married Audrey Martin Smith, the elder sister of Eric's wife, Sybil. Thus the Smith element strengthened and all the partners became closely interconnected.

The business of the bank was still highly geared to acceptances which had regained their level of the 1880s, and formed 39 per cent of the total balance sheet which in 1898 came to £5,000,000. A further 8 per cent was lent at call, and nearly 20 per cent was invested in stocks and shares with a small amount being lent on the Stock Exchange to brokers for funding their operations. Apart from an allowance for bad debts, the rest was almost entirely correspondence business with foreign bankers.

In view of the recent traumas caused by investment operations in the Americas, where wild speculation had led to overinvestment and widespread default on loans, it is surprising to find that of the £1,000,000 which Everard had currently invested in stocks and shares over half were heavily weighted towards this part of the world. North America claimed 30 per cent of the total and South America represented 22 per cent. Of the two main types of investments most of the money was attracted towards the further extension of the railway network, which after the doldrums of the early 1890s was beginning to claim new interest. The secondary but nevertheless significant area of investment was in municipal development such as water supplies, gas facilities and new harbours all of which were desperately needed by the quickly expanding towns of the New World. Even after the recent problems Everard was still anxious to pursue his American policy, encouraged, no doubt, by his friendship with the Morgans and Eric's recent visit.

The bank ledger clearly demonstrated that Everard looked for his investment opportunities outside the Dominions and Empire and not within them. Mining shares, mainly relating to South African gold and diamond companies, amounted to £86,000, while British and colonial securities which were shown jointly in the accounts only came to another £86,000. A mere 18 per cent of the whole portfolio, therefore, was connected with the financial development of these areas with only a minute amount filtering through to British securities. The Manchester Ship Canal and the Channel Tunnel Company provide two of the rare examples.

One of the bank's main functions still was to act as an issuing house, but only £50,000 out of the total portfolio of £1,000,000 was actually invested in foreign state bonds. This underlined the fact that, under normal circumstances, C. J. Hambro & Son did not underwrite its own issues, nor those of other houses. For short periods it may have held stocks, but as a rule Everard preferred to keep his relatively small sum of capital for other investment purposes.

Over the next fifteen years the balance sheet totals doubled from £5,000,000 to £10,000,000 as the boom years of the pre-war era reached their peak. World trade figures had revived from the sleepy years of the early and mid-1890s and the volume of acceptances rose dramatically from £2,000,000 to £5,500,000. They formed an ever-increasing percentage of the balance sheet, and from 1907 onwards they maintained a level of 50 per cent or more. The old description of the acceptance business as the bread and butter of banking operations was even more true in the early years of the twentieth century than it had been twenty years earlier.

The bank still acted as an issuing house but the enormous currency loans of the 1880s had disappeared and far more business was being undertaken for city corporations. C. J. Hambro & Son issued bonds for Kristiania in 1900, Rome in 1904, Rosario in 1907, Gothenburg in 1909, and Copenhagen in 1898, 1901 and 1908. They all involved small amounts, however, generally less than £2,000,000, so although they swelled the profit figures they did not account for the same proportion of the profits as they had done in the earlier days of Everard's supremacy in the bank. Some railway loans were still being raised, including, for example, one for Greece in 1902 and another for Finland in 1909, but even these were small by former standards. When the rest of the world had begun the process of industrialization, London had provided the capital, but as the movement gathered pace foreign countries began to look to other markets for their money. From that moment the position of London as the prime source of capital began to decline, and although World War I was the real watershed the change could be detected already.

The years 1907 and 1911 were very bad for the City in general but, apart from these years, bank profits maintained a consistently high level of about £150,000, reaching a pre-war peak in 1901 of £233,000. The good times which had last been seen in the 1880s had returned, and Everard was again able to earn large amounts; in 1901, for example, his income reached the princely sum of £168,000. Normally, however, it hovered around £100,000. As more of the family joined the partnership his share of the profits fell from 75 per cent to 60 per cent; in practice this made little difference to his standard of living as he still rarely withdrew more than £60,000 a year. By contrast, Robert Heriot's earnings usually approached £20,000 and the juniors frequently earned up to £6,000 each.

In 1909, Olaf Hambro, the youngest of Everard's four sons, joined the partnership. Like Eric, he had left Eton to go up to Trinity College, Cambridge, after which he began his career at the bank. The similarity of their paths ended there, however, for the two brothers were strikingly different. Although Olaf enjoyed a round of golf, or a day stalking stags on the moors or shooting pheasants at Milton, he did not attain the prowess of his eldest brother who excelled as a sportsman and who, on one occasion in Scotland, claimed nineteen grouse with one shot, while on another occasion, in India, he destroyed two tigers in succession – the first with his right barrel, the second with his left! Olaf certainly had some of the charm and good nature of his elder brother but he was a much steadier character, less extravagant in his manner, more cautious in money matters, far more capable of rational assessment and, like his father, he was an exceptionally able banker.

Olaf began to learn the business at a time when Everard's physical presence at the bank became much less constant and so he did not suffer the same dominating apprenticeship that Eric had experienced in the later 1890s. His father only came into his office for a little of January, most of May, June and July, part of October and all November; the rest of the time was spent at Biarritz, Gannochy, North Berwick and Milton Abbey. Although during these long absences his father insisted on being informed of the bank business every day, Olaf was able to learn his way about the operations of C. J. Hambro & Son in a manner which had been denied to Eric. Olaf made a valuable beginning before the onset of World War I which held him in good stead for the difficult post-war years. He, not Eric, was to be the great banker of his generation, but his time was yet to come.

One of the crowning events of Everard's life was his election, at the age of thirty-five, to the Court of the Bank of England. As a director his service remained almost unbroken from 1879 to 1924, and throughout this long period he was able to enjoy direct and regular contact with many other leading merchant bankers. The appointment of relatively young men had been the practice of the Court for a long time. It meant that after some twenty years they could be elected Deputy Governor and then Governor, having already gained many years' experience of Bank affairs. Although, in theory, the appointment as Governor was no longer a matter of rotation as it had been earlier in the nineteenth century, in practice the system had hardly changed. In Everard's case, however, the pattern was quite different, and throughout his forty-five years of service he was never appointed Deputy or Governor of the Bank.

In the early 1890s Everard was convinced that there should be major reform in the Court. Recent events had shown that the affairs of the Bank had been seriously mismanaged. Mr May, the chief cashier, had allowed unauthorized overdrafts. This situation, which had been completely overlooked by the Governor, had caused enormous embarrassment to the Bank and the chief cashier was asked to resign. As a result, in November 1893 an internal committee was formed to investigate the

A Dirty Crossing, *cartoon by John Tenniel in* Punch, *January 1894. The Old Lady of Threadneedle Street lifts up her skirts disdainfully as she picks her way across the road of mismanagement. Frank May, the chief cashier, had allowed unauthorized overdrafts and an internal committee including Everard Hambro was established to report on his case. It marked the beginning of Everard's heavy criticism of several aspects of the Bank's internal organiza-tion.* Guildhall Library.

A DIRTY CROSSING.

whole question of 'Advance and Overdrafts and the safeguards which were deemed necessary for the restoration of proper control'. Everard was one of the members, but for him this inquiry was just the beginning. He wanted to attack the system of management itself.

His main contention concerned the identity of the Committee of Treasury. Its membership was composed of those directors who had passed 'the Chair', and had been at some time both Deputy Governor and Governor. Thus it consisted of a very experienced group of individuals who had once had control of 'the Old Lady' and who were, in theory, the best advisors to the Governor. Everard questioned the infallibility of this exclusive group. He argued that while ex-Governors might have great experience, they were an ageing sector of the Court, out of touch with current market trends, and retaining membership of their 'City club' for as long as they possibly could. He wanted to inject into it some of the junior members who, like himself, had not yet become Governor. More particularly he wanted to include those members who served on the Committee of Daily Waiting, the body which managed the everyday affairs of the Bank. This would give the junior members more status and, at the same time, break down the aura which surrounded the seniors' committee.

He also wanted to change the system of ex-directors. Most years, one or two directors would be forced to go out of the Court in order to allow new directors to be elected. This meant that there was a reserve of two or three ex-directors to be called upon if one of the current directors

The Court of directors of the Bank of England, 1903. Samuel Morley was the Governor and the second on his right was Everard Hambro, who served the Court from 1879–1924. Also directors at this date were Henry Cosmo Bonsor, Edgar Lubbock and Hugh Colin Smith,

suddenly died. As a result, there would always be twenty-six voting members. In due course the ex-directors would be re-elected but, as they were all juniors, their turn to go out came round very quickly. Everard wanted the system to apply to seniors as well, so that the juniors would be forced out less frequently. Everard, for example, had been a director of the Court for fifteen years and a member of his family bank for thirty years. It would be absurd to consider him an inexperienced banker and there were many other juniors in a similar position.

Everard caused a great stir amongst the seniors when he put his resolution before the Court on 1 February 1894. Henry Gibbs, outstanding amongst past Governors, was emphatically against the proposal. He described Everard as 'being antagonistic unlike anything he had known in his forty-one years at the Bank'. He condemned the juniors for their silent votes and general disinterest and even accused

whose families were by then all inter-related with the Hambros. The weekly Court meetings
meant that these City figures were able to enjoy direct and regular contact with one another.
Reproduced with kind permission of the Bank of England.

them of neglecting their duties. David Powell, the Governor, and
Benjamin Greene, another of the Court's leading figures, were also
wholly unsympathetic. After all, it was in the interests of the seniors to
maintain the status quo, so defending their power and the yearly
income of £500 which went with it.

Many of the juniors fully supported Everard, including the Earl of
Leven and Melville, who felt so strongly about the issue that in 1894 he
resigned. Support also came from Hugh Colin Smith, Everard's old
friend from Mount Clare, and Cosmo Bonsor, father-in-law of
Everard's junior partner and nephew, Harry Hambro. When Colin
became Governor in 1897 the proposals were at last given a sympathetic hearing, but although some minor changes were agreed, the basic
principles remained the same. There were too many seniors to oppose
the change.

Dividend Day at the Bank of England, *1850, painting by G. E. Hicks. Originally there were over 1,200 subscribers to the Bank's capital and the distribution of the dividend became a famous City event which brought crowds of people to the Bank's Dividend Office. Payment by attendance was enforced until 1910.* Reproduced with kind permission of the Bank of England.

In 1897, according to seniority, it should have been Everard's turn to be Deputy Governor, but for another thirteen years he remained a junior, an outcast from the Committee of Treasury. However, in 1910, tradition was broken and the doors to the seniors' committee were finally opened to him. The old order was beginning to change and at last his sagacity was recognized. From then onwards he was fully involved with Bank affairs, and though he was in his seventies he rarely missed the weekly Committee of Treasury meetings. His intimate knowledge of international affairs meant that he became of very great importance in the war years, particularly in dealing with exchange rate problems. He came to be acknowledged as one of the central figures of the committee. Everard had finally won his place at the heart of the City's web.

15   Changes at Milton Abbey

When Charles Hambro died in 1891 the Milton Abbey estate passed to his 21-year-old nephew, Harry, who was just about to begin his career in the bank. The country estate with its wonderful Abbey and impressive Hall should have been a marvellous inheritance for the young man, but instead its burden increased remorselessly as the nineteenth century drew to its close. Agriculture was in an impoverished state as supplies of grain, wool and meat flooded into Britain from the New World, swamping the home market and causing prices to fall headlong. Wheat had cost an average of 55 shillings per quarter during 1870–4, but it had fallen to an average of less than 30 shillings by 1890–4, a reduction of 45 per cent. While those on fixed incomes could buy more food, those farmers with fixed outgoings could no longer meet their expenses.

The tenants on the estate found it impossible to pay their rents, and arrears mounted dramatically. They were already high in 1892 but within two years they had jumped to 27 per cent of the rental and by 1894 Harry was owed nearly £1,900 in arrears from farm rents alone. Eviction would not solve his problem, since it would be hard to find suitable and willing replacement farmers in these difficult times. He was trapped by circumstances which left him no choice but to reduce the rents and thereby his income. Between 1892 and 1894 they fell from £8,000 to almost £6,500.

Harry's financial situation would not have been nearly so desperate if the estate had not been encumbered by two large jointures, one of £3,000 per annum due to his step-grandmother, Baroness Hambro, and one of £1,000 due to his stepmother, Mrs Percival Hambro. By 1894 the nose-dive in rents and mounting arrears meant that the combination of the two jointures accounted for 66 per cent of the annual farm rents which he actually received. They were fast becoming intolerable. Up to Michaelmas Day 1893 he managed to pay the charges in full, but as his financial situation grew worse he found it difficult to respect such an onerous commitment. He managed to continue the smaller payment which was due to his widowed stepmother who relied on the income to support her four teenage children, but the payment to the Baroness proved much more of a burden. Instead of paying her the

337

Harry Hambro (1869–1933). In 1891 he inherited the Milton Abbey estate and began to work for his uncle Everard in C. J. Hambro & Son. He joined the Queen's Own Dorset Yeomanry Cavalry but left when he was forced to sell the estate in 1900. Hambro Family Archives.

full £3,000 which was the original rent from the lands in her jointure, he only paid her the current income which, because of the fall in rents, came to substantially less.

The seventy-year-old Baroness was furious and threatened Harry with court action, but he would not succumb. In December 1895 she took her case, Hambro v. Hambro, to the High Court of Justice where the judge, Mr Justice North, held that Harry owed her £3,895. The young man found himself in an embarrassing position. At only twenty-five his earnings from the bank were a pittance compared with this sum, his father had left him little money, and the estate income was dwindling rapidly while the outgoings remained relatively stable. He was forced to borrow capital from his cousin Eric, thus placing him on the slippery slope to disaster. Each year he paid the old Baroness the amount raised from rents of the lands in her jointure, while Eric made up the difference. By 1899 Harry owed his younger cousin over £10,000.

If the impoverished tenants and the Baroness thought they were suffering from hard times, the situation for Harry was fast becoming disastrous. As well as the jointures, there were many other charges such as taxes and tithes, poor rates, church rates, money for the school and the almshouses, fire insurance cover and heavy repair bills for the estate. Each year he paid out 15 per cent or more of his farm rental on the maintenance of the farmsteads providing 'new leading for windows', 'cementing barn floors', 'whitewashing dairies' and 'repairing piggeries' to name just a few examples. In 1894 these bills came to over £600, and the cost of fencing, drainage and roads came to another £300. In this respect he was doing no more than his duty but other landlords, endowed with less foresight, might have adopted a far more miserly attitude.

His uncle Everard, however, had made it quite clear to him in the first year of his inheritance that it was always a good policy to be generous with maintenance costs, especially in times of falling rents. He had argued that heavy investment would arrest further decline and ensure a higher base for the moment when agricultural fortunes turned and rents could be raised once more. This was sound advice and may have been instrumental in preventing rents falling as fast as they had done from 1892 to 1894 when they had plummetted by about 19 per cent. Despite a further decline in agricultural prices during the second half of the decade, by 1899 the rents were just over £6,000 which meant

Carl Joachim bought the Milton Abbey estate in 1852 and the following year built a new school in the village of Milton Abbas. When Harry inherited the estate in 1891, Everard wrote to him: 'It is clearly your duty to see that the children of the people committed by God to your care should have as good an education as possible.' Photograph c. 1900. Hambro Family Archives.

The old town which had grown up around the Abbey was destroyed by Lord Milton who insisted that it should not be seen from the windows of the new Hall which he built in the 1770s. It was rebuilt in a neighbouring valley and provides an early example of a model

that over the last five years they had fallen by no more than 6 per cent. Nevertheless in only seven years Harry had been forced to accept a reduction in his income of £2,000 per annum. It is not surprising that he could not afford to live at the Hall and usually let it, together with the shooting rights on the estate, to a Mr Drucker for £830 a year.

For the first few years of the decade Harry rarely visited the estate except to preside over the rent audit dinners which were held at the Hambro Arms Inn. On other estates there may have been bitterness and animosity between tenants and landlord, but at Milton his gener-

village, each side of the curving street being lined with thatched cottages which provided dwellings for two families. It remains much the same today except that the chestnut trees have gone and the inn on the left has taken the name The Hambro Arms. Hambro Family Archives.

ous and sympathetic attitude towards the rents and maintenance of the farm buildings meant that a relationship had developed based on trust and respect. This became patently clear at the end of June 1896 when Harry brought his young bride Edith home to the Hall at Milton Abbey where they intended to spend their honeymoon.

At Milton Abbas crowds of villagers waited expectantly as the bridal carriage rolled into sight and the brass band started to play. A large number of mounted tenantry rode out to escort Harry and Edith into the village which was gaily bedecked with bunting and banners and arches of evergreen. They stopped beside the school which Harry's grandfather had built. All the children were standing outside, dressed in their prettiest clothes, holding branches of ivy and colourful flags. After several songs, one of the little girls presented a bouquet of wild flowers to Edith, a gesture which touched her deeply. The children waved goodbye as the bridal couple proceeded through the village and then onwards to the lower Lodge where the two horses were taken out of the shafts and the carriage was pulled by the tenants through the Abbey grounds to the front of the Hall. The Abbey bells were pealing merrily and a cannon was fired from the village as they arrived.

On the following Tuesday a grand luncheon was given in the Abbot's Hall for all the farm tenants. A band played in the conservatory while the eighty-six guests tucked into a feast of salmon and cucumber, sole in aspic, lobster mayonnaise, lamb cutlets, veal, roast chicken, ox tongue and roast beef; to follow there were ice creams, raspberry and redcurrant tart, Genoa pastry, trifle, meringues *à la Chantilly* and Crème Montmorenci. Friday was the turn of all the cottagers on the estate, and over 1,200 of them arrived at the Hall for tea in a huge marquee where, in spite of its size, several sittings had to take place in order to cope with the numbers. Unfortunately it poured with rain just before the first sitting and everyone had to run for shelter in the Abbey. The storm soon passed, however, and the festivities continued. Swings and roundabouts had been erected for the children and later that afternoon cricket was played on the lawn. To crown the day's events, as it grew dark, a splendid display of fireworks was given by Messrs Brock of London.

Despite his financial difficulties Harry had been generous with the celebrations and the occasion was remembered for a long time by young and old alike. The bond between his family and the villagers, which had already grown steadily over the past forty years, was now strengthened further. Harry admitted in one of his speeches that Edith 'is already insisting that I shall come here a great deal more . . . and it is my wish some day to live among you, when I shall know everyone of you here by name as I do now by sight.' Sadly, the words proved to be nothing more than a vain hope for, as the years passed by, the financial burden of the estate became increasingly impossible to bear.

By June 1900 Harry found he could no longer continue as landlord and he was forced to sell the estate. Current agricultural prices meant that the value of land had fallen by a third since his grandfather's time, and instead of £240,000 he only managed to obtain £152,000. The family story still persists that Harry had no idea who the purchaser had been, so it must have come as a great surprise to learn that it was none

The two gentlemen. Everard Hambro on the left, tending his beloved plants, and Martin Ridley Smith on the right, having 'difficulties with a new toy', were great friends from the early 1860s until Martin's death in 1908. Between them they married three Stuart sisters. Martin married Emily in 1861 and had five children, Everard married Mary in 1866 and had five children who survived to adulthood, and then, two years after Emily's death in 1882, Martin married another sister, Cecily, who added three more children to his family. In turn three of Everard's children, Eric, Violet and Olaf married three of their cousins from Martin's family, Sybil, Everard and Winifred. Hambro Family Archives.

other than his Uncle Everard. At least this meant that the estate would stay in the Hambro family but whether Harry was really pleased or not is difficult to judge. It must have been very hard for him to accept that his extravagant cousin Eric would not only inherit the senior position at the bank but would also, one day, become the owner of the Milton Abbey estate.

If the estate had been free from encumbrances, Harry would have instantly been a rich man but, after payment of debts and the formation of a guarantee fund against the two jointures, he was left with little more than £23,000. He had to wait until the end of 1922 before he could claim his full inheritance, and only then was he able to buy the 800-acre

Hyde Estate in Bedfordshire which is still owned today by his grand-son, David.

On purchasing the Milton Abbey estate in 1900, once again Everard could live in his childhood home and restore it to its former glory. He dispelled the gloom which had hung over the Hall for the last ten years and with his wife and young family recalled warmth and merriment and comfort. With his capital of £1,000,000 and income that year of £110,000 he could easily afford to meet all the estate expenses and the cost of maintaining the grand style of a country squire. He was there several times a year: when the pheasant season opened on 1 October, when the family gathered at Christmas, and when the bluebells were flowering in the middle of May, acres of them carpeting the surrounding woodlands. On each occasion there were large house parties of family and friends and marvellous festivities, particularly at Christmas. Over the next twenty-five years Milton enjoyed its heyday.

Everard's new role brought him immense happiness, something which Constance Hugh Smith recognized immediately on her visit with her husband, Colin, in December 1903: 'All the old easy Mount Clare days are revived here. . . . We went to Church in the beautiful Abbey. Evy Hambro looked very handsome and splendid in his Stall. Life must seem to be complete to him, Milton his, huge means to keep it perfect, two sons very happily married, a very nice daughter and two more sons, and Mary well again. What more can he want?'

His happiness was shattered in June 1905 by the death of Mary at the age of fifty-seven. She was buried next to the graves of her two little children in Hayes Churchyard near Bromley in Kent. One of the mourners described the occasion: 'It was a drenching day. The dark Hayes Church was as dark as night; only the crowds of black grieving people were to be seen . . . so ends that happy Milton life where she enjoyed so much and where she was the centre of happiness and kindness.' One of her many pleasures had been to visit all the local village schools at Christmas time, taking Christmas trees and presents for the children. Over the past four years she had won the hearts of

---

Violet Hambro MBE *(1884–1965), the only surviving daughter of Everard Hambro, married her cousin Everard Martin Smith in 1906 and gave birth to six children. The first three are shown here: Mary, the eldest, is the mother of Peter Hill-Wood, executive director of Hambros Bank Ltd. Violet ran a convalescent home in World War* I *and during World War* II *she was chairman of the* WLA *and co-organizer of the* WVS *in Hertfordshire. Another of her grandchildren, Andrew Martin Smith, also works in the bank.* Hambro Family Archives.

many families on the estate. Mary and Everard had been happily married for almost forty years, and now the partnership had come to an end. From then onwards Eric's wife, Sybil, assumed the role of hostess at the Milton gatherings.

For many years the Christmas visit to Milton lost much of its former charm and seemed empty without the presence of Mary in the midst of all the festivities. The main attraction became the various shoots, whether for pheasants rising from the woods, roe deer wandering in the thickets, or wild duck flying over the two ornamental lakes below the Hall in the Milborne valley. In 1904 *Country Life* reported: 'There are not many Estates in the Kingdom where the shooter can have sport of such various kinds and of such fine quality.' Everard himself was described as one of the best shots in the country. He had a steady arm and a wonderfully quick eye. His sons were all masters of the sport as well, but Eric, in particular, outshone the others. For many years they had all been trained on the grouse moors of Scotland and long ago shooting had become one of their favourite sports.

In 1908 King Edward VII bestowed a great honour on Everard by creating him Knight Commander of the Victorian Order. The following year Sir Everard invited him to shoot at Milton, an estate which years before had been considered for the Prince of Wales before

The royal shooting party at Milton Abbey, December 1909. There were ten guns which in three days shot nearly 3,000 pheasants. From left to right the group consisted of: Lord Gerald Granville, Sir Frederick Ponsonby, Eric Hambro, Captain Lang, Cosmo Bonsor, Lord Savile, Sir Everard Hambro, Sybil Hambro (Eric's wife), King Edward VII, Miss Thornwick, Lady Savile, Mrs Bonsor, unknown, Colonel Streatfield, Angus Hambro and Olaf Hambro. Hambros Bank Archives.

Sandringham had finally been chosen. The King, no doubt, had heard of Milton's excellent reputation and was delighted to accept the invitation. The morning after the King's arrival, on Tuesday 4 December, the shoot began. The party consisted of ten guns and at 10.40 they set off from the Hall. Since the King and Sir Everard were both nearly seventy they could no longer stand a full day of strenuous walking, and rode on horseback. Thirty-one gamekeepers and loaders assisted them. In addition, there were forty-six beaters, all wearing white smocks with distinctive red fur cuffs and collars, which had been introduced by Sir Everard as a safety precaution several years previously. By mid-afternoon over 1,300 pheasants had been shot. They covered the various beats on the estate until Thursday and then, on the Friday, they visited a neighbouring estate at Bryanston. In three days at Milton alone they had shot nearly three thousand pheasants, and when the King returned to London on Saturday he was quite satisfied that the estate had lived up to its reputation. Unfortunately he never returned, for he died the following May.

By 1910, Sir Everard was spending far less time at his offices in 70 Old Broad Street, and his visits to Milton would often last several days or even weeks. He insisted on being kept up-to-date with news from the bank and received a daily letter from one of his partners. A young boy

The forty-six beaters all wore white smocks with red fur collars and cuffs. This uniform was remarked on as 'being a very good example in safety precautions as the beaters could be clearly seen'. Both this photograph and the one opposite are reproduced with kind permission of C. Fookes, Esq., Brewery Farm, Milton Abbas.

was sent to the village post office to pick up the mail, telegrams and newspapers. If Sir Everard ever met him when he was out walking he would call out 'Here, boy.' He would then take *The Times*, scan through the financial pages, and afterwards hand it back with the remark: 'Shares are up, boy', or down, whichever was the case. One of his favourite haunts on the estate was the blacksmith's shop where he used to sit and muse for long periods at a time. If anyone asked where he was, the usual answer would be: 'Blowing the bellows, blowing out the news'. Far removed from the City, no doubt, he found it a reassuring place to contemplate new policy and ensure his bank's survival.

After 1911 new life returned to Milton when Sir Everard decided in his seventieth year to marry a pretty young girl called Ebba Whyte, then in her early twenties. He had met her while on holiday at his villa in Biarritz. Only the previous year a contemporary had described him: 'Cast like a heroic mould on a colossal scale, one of the handsomest men even at sixty-eight . . . a giant not only in stature, but in character, in ability, in talents . . . he overwhelms while he fascinates'. Even though he was growing old he was still an immensely attractive man both in looks and character. Although initially his family was very cautious, particularly Sybil and his only daughter Violet, they soon grew very fond of Ebba. She was a marvellous organizer, full of spirit, and always ready to join in the fun and games with Sir Everard's growing flock of grandchildren, great-nephews and -nieces. Christmas regained its vib-

The thirty-one gamekeepers and loaders attendant at the royal shoot. Mr Waight, weighing 18 stone, was the head gamekeeper on the estate and is sitting in the centre. Note his broad-checked tweed suit material which can be recognized on several of the other game-keepers in the picture.

rancy and all the family gathered with their various offspring, followed by troops of nurses, nannies and governesses.

Patsie Tapley, the twin daughter of Percy Hambro, vividly recalls her childhood days spent at Milton:

Christmas was magic and the Christmas tree a great surprise with wonderful presents for everyone. One Christmas the five-year-olds had fairy bicycles which we played with up and down the passages by the nursery. I remember Grampy with his long white hair and beard and his smiling face. He used to sit in a huge chair by the log fire in the old Hall whilst we played cards around the footstool at his feet. There was always this wonderful smell of flowers, carnations and lillies I think, and grapes known as Black Hambros. I remember a general feeling of richness and warmth and comfort. I felt very secure.

Sir Everard turned Milton into a great family home and during the first quarter of the twentieth century it undoubtedly became the focal point for almost the entire family.

16 Military Warfare

The excitement of life in the British Army with its opportunities to travel throughout the Empire, to hunt big game and enjoy other sports proved an attractive alternative to a career in the City under the watchful eye of Everard. Percy, Harry's brother, followed in the footsteps of his maternal grandfather, Major Henry Otway Mayne, and became the first member of the Hambro family to be commissioned as a regular soldier. A keen horseman, he was drawn instinctively to the cavalry and after leaving Eton in 1889 he went to Sandhurst and then joined the 15th Hussars. Thus began a distinguished career in which he eventually rose to the rank of Major-General. His cousin Harold, who was Eric's brother, was the next Hambro to be given a commission. He decided to train as a gunner and so entered the Royal Artillery at Woolwich. Norman, half-brother to Harry and Percy, was the third and last of his generation to join the regular army. He chose the infantry and was commissioned in the Kings Royal Rifle Corps.

By the autumn of 1899 these three young men were scattered throughout South Africa defending the British Empire against the Boers. While Percy and Harold were fighting under General Roberts, Norman, then twenty-one, was stationed in Natal under the ill-fated command of Sir Penn Symons. Within nine days of war being declared he found himself in the midst of a bloody battle which was his first and only experience of fire. At 6 am on 20 October 1899 the Boers were found to have taken possession of Talana Hill, a small settlement just two miles from the British camp at Dundee. Although the hill was so close Symons had made an 'unpardonable error' by leaving it unguarded the previous night, and when the Boers opened fire he decided immediately to make a frontal attack on it.

Second Lieutenant Hambro was in command of the left half of his company and found himself in the centre of the firing line throughout the attack. He advanced with his men until he reached the trees at the bottom of the hill and then, just as Captain Wortley was giving him orders, he was wounded by a bullet which broke his jaw. Although he was gravely hurt he refused to succumb to the pain and after being bound up by his captain he insisted on climbing the hill. He managed to reach the wall half-way up, where his company gathered until the final

Lt Norman Joachim Hambro died at the age of twenty-one on active service during the Boer War. His captain wrote of him: 'Although he was such a young officer and it was his first experience of fire, the most experienced veteran could not have borne himself more gallantly.' Reproduced by gracious permission of Her Majesty Queen Elizabeth II.

orders to advance were given. When he heard the command he was the first to scale the wall and, amid the deafening roar of the guns he led his men to within ten yards of the crest where he fell, riddled with bullets. He was killed only twenty yards from the enemy.

Captain Wortley, who was himself badly wounded in the battle, wrote to the young man's mother, Mrs Percival Hambro:

Although he was such a young officer and it was his first experience of fire, the most experienced veteran could not have borne himself more gallantly, or set a more noble example to his men than he did. He behaved in fact as a thorough rifleman and I know no higher praise. I need hardly tell you that he was most beloved by all his brother officers, and in my, and the opinion of all his seniors, he would have made a splendid officer.

The victory at Talana Hill was a Pyrrhic one; many had died, and the next day the survivors were forced to abandon their camp at Dundee and only just escaped being surrounded. In London praise of Symons was unceasing. Crowds gathered in Trafalgar Square likening him to Nelson. He was promoted to general and hailed as the great saviour. The details of his 'mad' attack were not revealed until February 1900, until which time many of the officers who had survived the battle were besieged at Ladysmith, confined to the town for four months with no means of escape, all telegraph wires cut, and just bread

Major-General Sir Percy Otway Hambro KBE, CB, CMG *(1870–1931). Following Eton he joined the 15th Hussars and served in India for many years where he was a skilled horseman and at one time an instructor at the cavalry school. He later served with distinction in the Boer War, World War 1 and subsequently in Mesopotamia. In 1925 he was appointed major-general in charge of administration at Aldershot and in 1927 was given command of the 46th Division of the Territorial Army.* Hambro Family Archives.

and horseflesh for food. Finally, in March 1900 after the town was relieved, Percy learnt from one of the officers, H. R. Blore, the circumstances of his half-brother's death but even then, the story was not fully told. As Blore wrote: 'The poor general is dead now, so we do not like to say too much about it.'

Percy's first major encounter with the Boers was in February 1900 on the eastern border of Cape Colony at the diamond town of Kimberley, where 45,000 civilians and members of the British Army had been besieged for 124 days. Food was scarce, disease was rampant and the town's surrender was imminent. Relief came just in time when long lines of cavalry, with Percy amongst them, approached from the south-east leaving a cloud of dust in their trail. The Boers were defeated and the people of Kimberley freed. Percy then moved north with his regiment to the Zand river where another victory was gained, and from there the regiment went into the heart of the Transvaal and saw action near Johannesburg. Percy had given distinguished service in the various campaigns and was awarded the Queen's Medal with three clasps.

For the two young Hambros who survived the war in South Africa the peacetime army held many opportunities. Between 1902 and 1914 Percy spent most of his time in northern India where he held several staff appointments and later became an instructor at the Cavalry

Lady Hambro, née Marjorie Bingham (1890–1965) wife of Sir Percy Hambro, with her three children, Susan (at the back) and the twins, Patsie and Evy, in 1922. On Sir Everard's seventy-ninth birthday he wrote to his nephew Sir Percy: 'I was allowed to have your three children down to lunch with me [at Hayes] and I can assure you it was a treat and they all behaved as well if not better than three grown-ups would have done.' Hambro Family Archives.

School. As a keen horseman this was a job he loved dearly, but there was also ample scope outside his work to use his skill with horses and, besides becoming a brilliant polo player, he took part in the Kadir Cup. This was a pigsticking championship in which wild pigs were hunted in the bush by contestants on horseback carrying long spears. In addition to being a team player Percy's restless, independent spirit inspired him to go on great hunting expeditions in the mountains. In 1902 he trekked 1,200 miles northwards across the Himalayas and over the sand desert of China to the high mountains of the Tienshan which straddled the Russian-Chinese border in the heart of central Asia. The purpose of his journey was to shoot ibex and one of his trophies, a 53¾-inch head, was the largest recorded in his day.

Percy remained a bachelor for the whole of his youth but, at forty-one, he fell in love with a girl of twenty, called Marjorie, the daughter of Brigadier-General Bingham of Bingham Melcombe in Dorset. They had known each other in India and were married in London on 2 August 1911; the reception was held at 70 Princes Gate, Everard's former town house, now occupied by Eric and Sybil and their three children, Charles, Richard and Zelia. After honeymooning at Milton Abbey they returned to India, but before long Marjorie found that she was expecting a baby and, being unwell, she came back to England. In 1912 their first child, Susan, was born. Three years later, family history repeated itself when she gave birth to twins, Everard and Patricia – always known as Evy and Patsie. Percy, who was of course a twin himself, wanted the boy to be named after his uncle, Sir Everard, 'who has been more than a father to me since my own died and more I cannot say of any man'.

His cousin, Harold, who was six years his junior, had found his bride much earlier in life. In April 1902, after returning from the Boer War, he married Katherine Scott, a 'graceful pretty' girl whose uncle was Lord Avebury, of the Lubbock banking family. They stayed at the Villa Espoir for their honeymoon, where Harold could pursue his favourite sport on the links at Biarritz. Like his elder brother he was a keen golfer, and one of the original members of the Army Golfing Society. His best stroke was his drive and on at least one occasion he recorded a drive of 360 yards from the tee. He played for the army team in England and also in India where he was stationed soon after his marriage.

At the end of 1905 he was transferred for two years to Rhodesia where he and a team of other officers were given the task of mapping the Zambezi river eastwards from Livingstone. A vast tract of land north and south of the great river had been administered by the British South Africa Company since 1889 but only now, sixteen years later, was it

354

Harold Hambro, Everard's second son, joined the Royal Horse Artillery and in 1905 went to Africa to map part of the Zambezi river. This photograph was taken on a six-week safari in north-west Rhodesia in 1906. Hambro Family Archives.

properly defined. Katherine joined her husband in the rough conditions of the bush where they lived in a covered waggon pulled by a long team of oxen. One of their greatest joys was to have observed the stately Zambezi cascading over the Victoria Falls; Katherine is reputed to have been the first white woman ever to have witnessed the sight.

No one in the family escaped the turmoil of World War I. Everard, although in his early seventies, returned full time to C. J. Hambro & Son and gave invaluable service to the Bank of England by his distinguished membership of the Committee of Treasury. Eric and Harry, meanwhile, were both involved deeply in economic warfare while, as regular officers, Percy and Harold found themselves immediately stationed in France, where they were joined shortly afterwards by the other young Hambro men who now offered their services to their country.

Percy was stationed at the headquarters of the British Expeditionary Force in northern France. After the long hard winter of 1914–15 he tired of static warfare and craved for action in the Dardanelles, but he was destined to remain in France for the rest of the war, becoming

Captain Angus Hambro (1883–1957) married Vanda St John Charlton on 29 April 1916. The wedding took place at Holy Trinity, Sloane Square, London. Vanda, born in 1885, is the last member of the family to live at Milton Abbas today. Hambro Family Archives.

assistant adjutant and quartermaster general. He was mentioned in despatches on various occasions and received the brevets of lieutenant-colonel and colonel. His distinguished service earned him several awards, including the Croix de Guerre and the Portuguese Order of Avis, First Class. He was made CMG in 1918 and CB in 1919.

Harold was also in France at the beginning of the war where he learnt of the birth of his only child, Nigel, in January 1915. Like Percy he was mentioned in despatches several times and promoted to brevet lieutenant-colonel, but later that year he was forced to retire from active service owing to a duodenal ulcer. After a period of convalescence he went to Swaythling near Southampton where he joined the remount service. Hundreds of horses were being wounded in battle and in order to avoid congestion in the veterinary hospitals at the Front, after they had received treatment, many were shipped back to England where the remount service ensured that they were farmed out and well cared for during a period of three or four weeks' convalescence. Horses were then a vital part of the 'war machinery' and Harold was responsible for making sure that as many as possible were sent to France for active service. His orders in February 1917 indicated the massive scale of the operation. He was told to increase the numbers exported by two hundred per week.

On 1 March that year he travelled to France to inspect the condition of horses at the Front, to discover whether any improvements in their welfare were possible and to assess which breeds were best suited to survive the various types of war operations. On 6 March he joined Percy who was stationed near Bretennoux, only a short distance from the battle zone of the Somme. They spent a day together which Harold recorded in his army book: 'Saw the sea of mud which the men and horses had to live in . . . the whole country was one mass of shell holes, the Germans were busy and the roar of artillery incessant with the screech of shells and the bursting of high explosives . . . saw our aeroplanes, a flight of 5 at about 12,000 feet'. At the end he wrote: 'a day always to be remembered'. He left Percy in the dismal atmosphere of the Somme and returned to Swaythling where he continued his own essential work. In recognition of his valuable efforts he was made CBE in June 1919.

Angus, Everard's third son, always desired a country life rather than that of the City or Army. For several years he helped to manage his father's affairs on the estate at Milton Abbey and in 1910 he became MP for South Dorset. Shortly before the outbreak of war, in January 1914, his wife Maud died aged twenty-eight of tuberculosis. She left three young children, Alec, Michael and Peggy. Later that year Angus joined the Queen's Own Dorset Yeomanry; being declared unfit for active

Lt-Colonel Harold Hambro was invalided out of active service in 1915 and went to join the remount service at Swaythling near Southampton where he was responsible for the shipment of war horses to France. This caricature was drawn by Captain Richard. Hambro Family Archives.

357

Angus and Olaf Hambro often visited the links at Biarritz. Angus was the outstanding golfer in the family and, as a scratch player, he was one of the leading amateurs of his day. He was a member of the Royal and Ancient Golf Club of St Andrews from 1908, and became captain in 1928. He was also Chairman of the Rules of Golf Committee. Hambro Family Archives.

service, he was sent with his regiment to Suffolk to guard the east coast where he was soon promoted to captain. In April 1916 he married Vanda St John Charlton, a sweet, good-natured girl whom he had known before war had broken out. Although he remained with the territorial army reserves until 1922, early in 1918 he decided to return to his political career and was appointed parliamentary private secretary to the secretary of state for air, Lord Stonehaven. The Air Ministry had been formed on 1 January that year to take over control of the Royal Flying Corps and the Royal Naval Air Service. In April 1918 the two were united to form the Royal Air Force.

Olaf, the youngest of Everard's sons, had been working in the bank before the war but, in 1915, he too joined the Army and was commissioned in the Coldstream Guards. He served near Percy at Arras in northern France for a long period, interrupted in February 1917 by his marriage in London to Winifred, daughter of his father's close friend, Martin Ridley Smith. After Emily died, Martin married Cecily Stuart who was the sister of his first wife and Mary Hambro. Winifred was the youngest child of his second marriage and so, like Eric, Olaf married a cousin. She was a girl of rare beauty, whom he had known all his life and of whom his father thoroughly approved. Shortly after they were married Olaf had to return to active service in France, leaving Winifred to share the same unhappy fate as many other brides of her day. Before long he was promoted to captain and twice mentioned in despatches.

Harry had already lost one half-brother in the Boer War and as soon as World War I broke out his other half-brother, Bertram, left his job as a stockbroker in the City and joined the Royal Horse Artillery in France and Flanders. He had suffered from tuberculosis as a child and therefore was not passed as fit for active service, but being a very good linguist, particularly in French and Spanish, he became an interpreter. He survived at the Front until the end of February 1915 but then, after the long and cruel first winter of the war, his health failed and he was forced to relinquish his commission. Following his convalescence in Dorset he agreed to visit Argentina to raise money for the British government. By the end of the outward voyage, however, his 'trench fever' returned; he became unconscious for several days, and eventually died in hospital at Buenos Aires, where he was buried at the British cemetery. He left a young widow called Marjory who was the daughter of Sir Neville Lubbock, and two small daughters, Diana and Faith.

Towards the end of the war the Army took two more Hambros, Val and Charles; being the first sons of Harry and Eric respectively, they were the eldest members of the next generation. Val, born in 1898, left

Bertram Hambro was described as a great-hearted man who made a valuable contribution to philanthropic organizations in the poorer parts of London. He died on 25 April 1915 of trench fever, which he contracted while serving at the Front with the Indian Expeditionary Force. Hambro Family Archives.

359

Val Hambro, the elder of Harry's sons, died in 1918 on active service in France, aged only nineteen. This photograph was taken when he left Sandhurst to join the 60th Rifles. Hambro Family Archives.

Sandhurst to join the 60th Rifles. He was the cheerful extrovert of his family and only nineteen when he died on 22 March 1918 during active service in France. Charles, Val's second cousin, left Eton in 1915 and followed his uncle, Olaf, by being commissioned in the Coldstream Guards. His father, Eric, was in Sweden at the time and was horrified when he heard the news. He wrote to his wife, Sybil: 'It is wicked to think of sending a boy aged eighteen to lead troops, neither fair to the men or to the boy.' Charles nevertheless served with distinction in France, Flanders and Germany, and was awarded the Military Cross for conspicuous bravery. He risked his life several times by swimming across a canal under open fire to rescue wounded men from the far bank. He too was wounded, but survived. He was destined to perform an even more vital role when the call came again in the 1940s.

17 Economic Warfare

Eric's role in the war was very different from the military campaigns of his relations. At the end of June 1915 he set sail from Edinburgh in a Royal Navy cruiser, HMS *Inconstant*. He was bound for Bergen and then Stockholm as part of a four-man British delegation whose aim was to persuade the Swedish government to allow the free transit of goods across Sweden to Russia. He had been recommended by his childhood friend, Launcelot Hugh Smith who in peacetime worked for Rowe & Pitman, brokers to C. J. Hambro & Son, but who, at present, worked for the Board of Trade. Launcelot had been appointed as head of the mission and since the Hambro family had been bankers to the Swedish government for several generations, he thought Eric would be one of the most acceptable choices to the foreign negotiators and, therefore, most likely to produce the best results. Robert Vansittart, from the Foreign Office, and Hugh Cleminson, a celebrated commercial lawyer with close Scandinavian contacts, made up the delegation.

Their main problem was that although, in theory, Sweden was neutral, in reality the court and army were violently pro-German and were constantly in fear of Russia invading the country's eastern borders. Within commercial circles, however, the attitude was different. Here at least there was room to manoeuvre, since restoration of the normal trading pattern was greatly desired. Sweden had just imposed licences on British goods bound for Russia, insisting that equal quantities should be allowed to pass to Germany. As a result of these prohibitive measures, Britain had been forced to take drastic steps and reduce her trade. Commercial relations were in danger of breaking down altogether, which would have dire consequences for each of the three countries.

Of the five Swedish delegates, two were extremely pro-German, while the others were very pro-Sweden, that is to say, neutralist. Their chief was K. A. Wallenberg who, at the onset of war, had temporarily given up the chairmanship of the Stockholms Enskilda Bank and taken the post of minister for foreign affairs. He was thought to be the most powerful man in the country. The Wallenbergs and Hambros had been friendly since 1879, and the relationship between Knut and Eric proved to be an important factor in these negotiations. Eric admired Knut

Knut Wallenberg (1853–1938), from a painting by E. Stenberg. He was Swedish minister of foreign affairs during World War I and was a key figure in the Anglo-Swedish trade negotiations. Eric described him as 'a splendid type of man with a head very like a mixture of father's and Natty Rothschild's'. He was the eldest son of A. O. Wallenberg who founded the Stockholms Enskilda Bank in 1856, of which Knut was chairman from 1911 to 1914 and from 1917 to 1938. He was also a director of Hambros Bank from the time of its merger with BBNC *until his death.* Reproduced with kind permission of the Skandinaviska Enskilda Banken.

immensely and described him as 'a splendid type of man with a head very like a mixture of father's and Natty Rothschild's'. The respect was fully reciprocated; soon after Eric had arrived Knut went to see Esmé Howard, the British minister in Stockholm, and referring to Eric said: 'The British Government could not have made a better choice or one more acceptable to the Swedish Government.'

The British delegates attempted to put pressure on the Swedish government through commercial interests, but the task of persuading them was far from easy. German propaganda made life very uncomfortable for the British team, who were continually followed and publicly criticized. Even from the outset Eric was aware that the mission might have arrived too late. Originally they had expected to stay two weeks, but their work dragged on much longer. It was a period of endless meetings, proposals and counter-proposals. There were interminable discussions with the Russians and continual liaison with the British government, while the Swedish delegates made their approaches to the Germans.

During the first four weeks in Stockholm the British delegates uncovered several 'pro-German plots', and by the end of July the Swedes were beginning to tire of the Germans and show more signs of friendship to the British. The longer the delegates stayed, moreover, the better known they became and the more their personal popularity increased. This was particularly true of Eric, whose numerous contacts through C. J. Hambro & Son, combined with his irrepressible good humour and willingness to join in all Swedish customs, were a considerable help in winning favour and respect. On one occasion he arranged a secret meeting with a person whom he was informed would be influential in changing 'the temper of the Swedish government'. Eric was driven forty miles outside Stockholm to the country house of the individual in question. He recorded: 'We were quite alone. At the end of dinner he poured out his woes to me. "Why are not all Englishmen like you?" he said. We talked and talked and ended up by health drinking, and I was sent back to Stockholm with the feeling that though my stomach was ruined I had captured the stronghold to the eventual advantage of our work here.' In addition, Eric seemed to have possessed a natural instinct for 'deals'. Over a casual dinner one evening he managed to purchase the total output of Sweden's largest iron and steel manufacturer, agreeing to provide him with coal in exchange. Eric thought, quite rightly, that, if the goods were earmarked for Britain, then at least the Germans could not use them.

Negotiations see-sawed throughout August. No sooner would the British think they had found a compromise when the Swedes would

Sir Everard Hambro (on the left), his daughter-in-law Sybil and his son Eric outside the Gate Tower of the North front of Milton Abbey. In the summer of 1915, Sir Everard was anxious that Eric should return quickly from Sweden to help in C. J. Hambro & Son as affairs at the Bank of England came to demand more and more of his own time. Reproduced by gracious permission of Her Majesty Queen Elizabeth II.

suddenly turn on them, wrangle over minor details and use various other delaying tactics. At the end of the month, however, Eric received an urgent message to return to London. The British government wanted to conclude the negotiations as quickly as possible and to have a first-hand account of the proceedings in Sweden. In early October he went back to Stockholm with the government's final proposals. The Swedes were proud, still afraid of Russia and much too heavily involved with the Germans for the British delegation to have complete success. Nevertheless by 26 October Eric was able to write that they had managed to clear all vital materials which hitherto had been held up in Swedish ports, and so free them for use by the Russians. Already, Russia's situation had improved immensely. Quite apart from formal negotiations, moreover, the delegation had played a decisive role in combating German influence in Sweden and, above all, in keeping the Swedes out of the war. Furthermore it had prevented the breakdown of commercial relations between Britain and Sweden, a situation which had appeared most probable in the early summer. His Majesty's government stated that 'they desire to express their appreciation of the ability and zeal with which the delegates coped with the extraordinarily complicated problems encountered in the course of the negotiations'.

During these four months Eric played a prominent role in the delegation which, far from being merely commercial in nature as he had originally envisaged, proved to be of the highest political consequence. Launcelot wrote to his mother that Eric's presence 'has been everything to me in every way', and in a letter to Sybil he wrote: 'One day I will try and tell you what he was to me in Sweden and how splendidly he worked and succeeded. I am enormously impressed by him. Don't tell him but being on his own and away from Uncle Evy must have made all the difference. Of course he was much loved by everyone, but it was much more than that.'

The part Eric played in the Swedish delegation was widely recognized and only two months after his return to England he was co-opted, again by Launcelot Hugh Smith, on to the three-man Norwegian committee established under the auspices of the Board of Trade. With a budget of £5,000,000 its aim was to purchase 75 per cent of the Norwegian fish caught during the main harvest between February and April 1916. This would deprive Germany, normally Norway's largest fish export market, of a valuable food supply and, furthermore, of fish oils from which glycerine was obtained to produce high explosives. Britain was certain that the Germans would try hard to buy large quantities from Norway. Time being of the essence, Henry Maurice from the Board of Agriculture immediately took John Irvin, a fish trader from Aberdeen, to talk to the Norwegian suppliers. After protracted negotiations the basis of an agreement was eventually reached.

Eric's role on the committee was that of banker. His contact with financial circles throughout the world, but particularly with Scandinavia, was obviously significant, and his experience of buying large quantities of foreign currency without upsetting the equilibrium of the market was another vital consideration. In January 1916 C. J. Hambro & Son was instructed to act as agent for the British government in the purchase of Norwegian kroner. Eric was informed that over the next three months approximately 85,000,000 kroner would be needed. Yet he knew that usually the market only dealt with a maximum of 500,000 kroner each day. In addition, he was warned that on particular occasions less than a week's notice might be given even for very large purchases of currency.

Eric feared that the purchase of such considerable amounts, in so short a period, would immediately alert interest in the foreign exchange market. This was to be avoided at all costs, since the longer the Germans remained ignorant about the whole business the better it would be for Norway and Britain. Eric proposed that he should be authorized immediately to start buying kroner and discreetly place it in

Eric Hambro (1872–1947) was the eldest son of Sir Everard. After Eton he was admitted to Trinity College, Cambridge, and then joined C. J. Hambro & Son. A public-spirited man, he was MP *for Surrey from 1900 to 1907, and closely associated with Scandinavian trade negotiations during World War* I. *He succeeded his father as chairman of Hambros Bank in 1925.* Hambro Family Archives.

an account with the State Bank of Norway, using the name of C. J. Hambro & Son and not that of the British government. In this way a pool of currency would build up and with the regular purchase of only moderate amounts, the market price would not be greatly affected. The Treasury agreed to his suggestion and authorized him to purchase, in the first instance, up to £1,000,000 worth of currency. Anything over that amount would require special permission. Eric reacted quickly and began making various purchases. He was already well prepared when a secret and urgent telegram arrived on 25 January asking him to buy the equivalent of £1,000,000 – about 15–16,000,000 kroner – before 1 February when a major contract for Norwegian fish would be signed. By 26 January he claimed to have already purchased 75 per cent of the requirement and stated that he would obtain the remainder within a few days. The first hurdle had been overcome without any problems.

In the weeks that followed more currency was required and buying continued in the traditional manner. Eric conceived a clever plan, however, which would secure kroner at a most reasonable price but, at the same time, would avoid attracting attention from the open market. Through one of his banking friends in Buenos Aires he arranged the purchase of nearly £500,000 worth of gold from the Argentine government which was held at the time in Stockholm. He persuaded his

Sybil Martin Smith (1874–1942) married her cousin Eric in 1894 and produced four children of whom the eldest was the distinguished Sir Charles Hambro. She was a lady of immense character who spoke many languages, is reputed to have smoked cigars, and often sailed her yacht to the Seychelles and other distant places. Hambro Family Archives.

contact to agree to the transaction by impressing upon him that it was in the national interest. Instead of costing the quoted price of 16.85 kroner to the £ he managed to obtain 17.40 to the £. He was doubly anxious to secure the deal for, apart from the cost advantage, he knew that the Germans were endeavouring to procure the same gold. He won, therefore, on both counts.

By 16 March 1916, Eric was confident that the remainder of the 85,000,000 kroner could be purchased without difficulty. The Norwegian operation had been so successful, however, that the government decided to extend the programme to 1917 and new estimates showed that 138,000,000 kroner would be needed. Instead of buying such large quantities on the open market, the government considered it far more appropriate to borrow the sum over a two-year period. On 1 June, C. J. Hambro & Son, together with the British Bank of Northern Commerce Ltd, were authorized to negotiate the loan with various Scandinavian banks giving the government the option to repay the money in either gold or currency. By this means the government aimed to defer purchases of kroner for at least two years, by which time it was hoped that easier conditions would prevail. Meanwhile, the operation brought Eric into direct contact with the British Bank of Northern Commerce Ltd, a recently established Scandinavian orientated bank which was based in London, and which before long was to have still closer links with C. J. Hambro & Son.

With all his Scandinavian contacts Eric had been well placed to act on behalf of the government in the crisis years of World War 1. At no time before or after did he excel at his work to the same extent. He enjoyed the excitement of the tasks with which he was presented, and executed them with an enthusiasm and vigour which had been absent from his previous banking days. He had lived too long in the shadow of his father's reputation. In his efforts for the war, he was free to act on his own behalf, and blossomed as a result. In 1919 he was made a KBE in recognition of his valuable contribution.

Following the 'glorious days' of the bank's Edwardian period, the outbreak of war heralded a new era. The traditional role of merchant bankers was to finance the international movement of goods, but suddenly in 1914 the old trading network disintegrated because former contacts were found to be in enemy territory and lines of trust were broken. Merchant bankers were forced to adapt their operations as essential foods and materials for war came to dominate the dwindling volume of trade. Alternative contacts had to be made and new credit facilities arranged. For those who were heavily involved in northern European trade the war years were bleak and the financial effect was disastrous. The acceptances of C. J. Hambro & Son dropped from £5,000,000 in 1912 and 1913 to an average of only £2,000,000 between 1914 and 1918.

Political instability inevitably made the Stock Exchange nervous. Many of the bank's existing investments now became heavily depreciated and the total value of the bank's portfolio dropped by 33 per cent. On 19 November 1914 a guarantee fund of £250,000 was established by all the partners in anticipation of future losses which they feared might occur. A major problem, of course, was the loans made to debtors who were now in enemy territory. By 1918 unpaid interest on the debts had grown to £161,000 while the capital outstanding was over £600,000, 40 per cent of which was due from Germans and the rest was owed by Austrians.

There were a few compensations, however, since C. J. Hambro & Son with all its Scandinavian connections was particularly well placed to act as agent on behalf of the British government in arranging credits, purchasing currency and effecting payments for the products which Norway, Sweden and Denmark offered to Britain. As this was Harry's main area for concern he became involved with shipments of carbide, hides, pickled eggs, butter and bacon from Denmark; timber, bar iron, steel ingots, ball bearings and munitions from Sweden; as well as timber and ships from Norway. C. J. Hambro & Son was also involved in the purchase and movement of cereals from Argentina and Australia on behalf of the British government as part of reciprocal trade agreements with Norway and Sweden. Since Eric had been appointed a member of the Royal Commission on Wheat Supplies in January 1917 the responsibility of these operations fell on him. By the end of the war the Treasury's account with the bank had grown to £23,000,000 thus accounting for the dramatic increase in the balance sheet total from £10,000,000 to £44,000,000 between 1913 and 1917.

Even with earnings from these government operations, the war years were, on balance, exceptionally lean ones so far as the profits of the bank were concerned. They had exceeded £100,000 in the boom years of the Edwardian era, but the dismal reality of the period from 1914 to 1917 was a continual deficit. The worst year was 1915 when the ledger recorded an overall loss of £58,000. As a result of the financial position, the six partners were forced to exercise severe restraint. Their total average withdrawals fell from £104,000 in 1912 and 1913 to only £32,000 in 1914 and 1915. Eric seemed to be the worst hit. Even though he had been receiving a share of the profits for fifteen years, on 31 December 1914 his capital was only £12. Tiger hunts in India, holidays in North America, a wife who was 'smothered in diamonds', and four children partly explained his position. He faced an embarrassing situation in the three years which followed and had to receive substantial support from his father who gave him presents of £10,000, £5,000 and £3,000 from 1915 to 1917. Olaf, who was more careful by nature and, as yet, had no children to provide for, received only one gift of £5,000 and otherwise managed on his own income.

18 A Break with the Past

In the immediate post-war era banking once more became a prosperous business. By the end of 1919 the volume of acceptances had regained their pre-war level of £5,000,000 and profits had returned to the respectable figure of £130,000. C. J. Hambro & Son had weathered the crisis of the war years, although the bank had not emerged totally unscathed. Nearly £600,000 was still locked up in German and Austrian debts which the six partners were forced to carry themselves. In the event Sir Everard shouldered the main burden, but there was strong feeling that it would be far safer to form a company with limited liability rather than continue as an old-fashioned partnership. If the tide turned completely against them every last penny which the partners owned would be liable to be called.

When the British Bank of Northern Commerce Ltd (BBNC) approached C. J. Hambro & Son in the summer of 1920 with a proposal to amalgamate the two banks, the Hambro family looked upon it as a welcome gesture. Apart from the practical angle of the added security of becoming a joint stock company, the family already knew many of the personalities involved since the people who founded the company in 1912 were mainly Scandinavian bankers. For example, the powerful Knut Wallenberg, who was chief of the Stockholms Enskilda Bank and one of the founders and largest shareholders of the BBNC, was known particularly well by Eric through his wartime experience in Sweden. Moreover, through the large kroner loan which had been arranged on behalf of the British government in 1916, Eric had gained a valuable insight into the BBNC internal operations and had got to know several of the directors.

The family was aware from the published accounts that the BBNC was undoubtedly an efficient organization with a modern accounting system, good management and an excellent growth record. In only eight years, the balance sheet total had grown to nearly £22,000,000, and by 1920 had reached almost the same figure as C. J. Hambro & Son! In addition, helped by the support of many of its shareholders, much of its business originated in the Hambro territory of Scandinavia. So it seemed wiser to take the opportunity to nip the new bank in the bud rather than let it continue as a rival. Here was the opportunity.

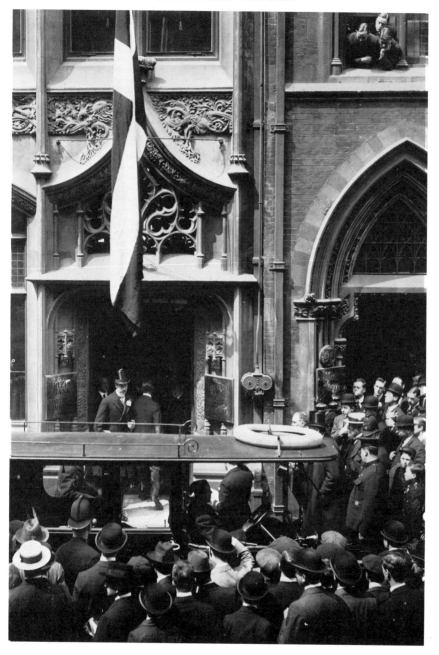

Christian x of Denmark leaving the offices of the British Bank of Northern Commerce at 41 Bishopsgate, the bank which merged with C. J. Hambro & Son on 31 October 1920. The new bank was originally called Hambros Bank of Northern Commerce Ltd, and the first chairman was Sir Everard Hambro. Hambro Family Archives.

371

The BBNC, meanwhile, wanted to share the prestige of a first-class banking name such as Hambro and at the same time shed its foreign image. Although it had been established at 41 Bishopsgate, London, its capital was predominantly foreign – 78 per cent came from Denmark, Norway and Sweden, just over 8 per cent from Russia, and tiny proportions from France, Portugal and Canada, leaving a mere 13 per cent from England. Only by enlarging the British interest would it come to be seen as a British bank, an image which the directors coveted. Without doubt, a merger with C. J. Hambro & Son would achieve this aim overnight.

Hambros Bank of Northern Commerce Limited was born on 31 October 1920, representing the conversion of one of the great merchant banking houses into limited liability form. The new issue of 200,000 shares was entirely taken up by the six partners of the old private company, thereby doubling the paid-up capital to £1,000,000. The subscribed capital was £4,000,000 and the reserve fund totalled £1,050,000. Sir Everard was the new chairman, and H. Bendixson, the former chairman of BBNC, became vice-chairman jointly with Sir Eric Hambro. Harry and Olaf Hambro were managing directors. Psychologically, the Hambros immediately dominated the new operation, although the former general manager of the BBNC, Gerard d'Abo, played an extremely valuable role over the next 40 years. He too was appointed a managing director.

Only ten months after the amalgamation, in August 1921, the name was abbreviated to Hambros Bank Limited, since the retention of the words 'Northern Commerce' was felt to be prejudicial to business in southern Europe and the Americas. At first the thirty members of the staff at the BBNC stayed in the Bishopsgate offices, while the fifty-one clerks (eighteen of them women) and nine messengers of C. J. Hambro & Son, then earning a total of nearly £30,000, stayed at 70 Old Broad Street, content with their 10 per cent salary bonus which Sir Everard gave them when the merger was agreed. Although the two addresses were only a short distance apart, the inconvenience involved meant that plans were soon afoot to concentrate the whole operation under one roof.

The Bishopsgate site was chosen as more appropriate and the architects Messrs Niven and Wigglesworth were commissioned to design new premises. While the building was in progress the former BBNC staff were removed to 3A London Wall. On 23 February 1926 the new offices of Hambros Bank Limited were opened. The dignified late seventeenth-century-style frontage and the rich mahogany interior provided a characteristic warmth and solidarity in keeping with the

On 23 February 1926 the new premises of Hambros Bank Ltd were opened at 41 Bishopsgate. It combined the old offices of C. J. Hambro & Son in 70 Old Broad Street and the former offices of the British Bank of Northern Commerce. Since then the bank has expanded along the street into 51 and 55 Bishopsgate. Hambros Bank Archives.

Hambro image. Today, half a century later, the same building houses the main office and heart of the bank.

Sir Everard did not live to see Hambros Bank installed in its new offices in Bishopsgate, for he died on Thursday 26 February 1925. He was nearly eighty-three and had remained active almost to the end of his life, until finally, after a heart attack, he had been forced to rely on an electric wheelchair. The old gentleman passed away peacefully at Hayes Place in Kent and four days later he was buried in the parish churchyard beside the grave of his first wife, Mary, and their two little children, Hermione and Maurice.

A large number of people well known in banking and business circles were present at the funeral, while many others attended the memorial service held at St Michael's Church, Cornhill, in the City. Another service was held in the ancient Abbey at Milton, where a great assemblage of Sir Everard's Dorset friends and tenants gathered to offer their last respects to the man who had brought so much colour and life to the estate. For them, 'the old order' at the Hall had changed for ever. In Sir

374

Christmas at Milton Abbey, 1919. Sir Everard, aged seventy-seven, is standing beside his second wife Ebba, to his right. His five children and twelve of his grandchildren are also present, the youngest being Jocelyn who is the baby sitting on the knees of his mother, Winifred. After Christmas Sir Everard wrote to his nephew Percival: 'We had a very good Xmas party at Milton, all went well, and by killing a heifer and a bullock I was able to feed them. I think we all enjoyed it very much and of course Milton is a grand house for the children with its long passages. We had a ball, a show from London. . . .' Hambro Family Archives.

Everard's pew Mr Perkins, who had been head gardener for over twenty years, placed a magnificent wreath of amaryllis lilies, white azaleas and violets which had been nurtured in the hall gardens. It was a touching tribute to a man who had appreciated nature's simplicity and beauty so much.

Death marked the end of a fifty-year reign during which time Sir Everard had ruled with exceptional ability. Even in his youth he had been acknowledged to have remarkable powers of perception, a quick and penetrating insight and a broad knowledge of financial affairs. Then, after his father died, he had been able to work with complete freedom and excel beyond all expectations. He had encouraged the bank's rapid growth in the formative years of the 1880s, pitting the name of Hambro against that of Rothschild. Through his caution he had shielded it from the waves of panic which had regularly engulfed the City. Finally, he had ensured its entry into the modern era as a public company, strengthened by the powerful support of many influential Scandinavian shareholders and bankers.

His personal charisma was immense. The family were all drawn closely together beneath his protective wing and those who worked under his command respected and loved him deeply. One man who served him for forty-four years said: 'It was not service but friendship.' Even as a director to the Court of the Bank of England, where he had caused such dissension in the 1890s, he had become a central character, and eventually had been welcomed to the Committee of Treasury. In March 1925 a formal tribute was paid to him:

The Court desire to place on record their high appreciation of his conspicuous abilities and wide knowledge of affairs which, throughout this long period, have always been at the service of the Bank. They also wish to express their feelings of personal regard for one who, by his unvarying kindliness and courtesy and by his personal charm has won the esteem and affection of every member of the Court.

Sir Eric now became the second Chairman of Hambros Bank. Following the recession of the early 1920s, business was beginning to expand and, in 1925, the bank could look forward to a new era of prosperity. At last there was a sound basis for true revival of trade as reconstruction of the post-war economies began to gather momentum. The northern European and American economies were booming, and although Great Britain was left behind the London merchant bankers were in a strategic position to take full advantage of foreign resurgence and reap the ensuing benefits. The rise in the acceptance figures reflected the

Gerard d'Abo was born at Arnhem in 1884 and worked for the Société Général in Le Havre and London, and for Lazard's, before becoming manager of the British Bank of Northern Commerce. On the merger with C. J. Hambro & Son in 1920 he became a joint managing director of the new bank and retained this position until his retirement in 1957. When he died in 1962, Sir Charles Hambro wrote: 'All men instinctively trusted him and respected his good judgement, while his international upbringing gave him the knowledge of people and countries so valuable for his work.' Hambros Bank Archives.

growth in trade, and between 1922–24 and 1925–31 they rose from an average of £7,000,000 to nearly £10,500,000, an increase of almost 50 per cent.

Another factor which accounted for growth in the bank's operations was the additional business introduced by the BBNC in 1920. Its relationship with Finland is one of the most interesting examples. Although C. J. Hambro & Son had floated the first foreign loan for the country in 1909, after Finland declared its independence of Russia in December 1917, the BBNC, and not C. J. Hambro & Son, had offered to finance the trade of the new republic. By then it was torn by civil war with its economy completely disorientated, having lost its traditional export customers to the east. BBNC's courage was well rewarded, since the forestry industry of Finland quickly found a new market for its products in western Europe, particularly in Great Britain. As Finland's economy expanded and stabilized so its banking requirements increased, and after the merger in 1920 Hambros Bank found that the Finns were extremely active customers. Indeed, even today the Finnish forestry industry is one of the bank's major sources of acceptance business.

Important side effects emerged from the initial relationship between the bank and Finland. The bankers were careful to nurture the new republic through the difficult years of its early development. When external capital was needed to finance new harbours, industry and other projects, Hambros Bank was the London issuing house which was asked to float the loans. Olaf and Gerard d'Abo, formerly at the BBNC, were mainly responsible within the bank, and in 1923 the first issue of £1,000,000 was arranged, followed by another of £2,000,000 in 1927. Two years later a corporation loan of £500,000 was floated for The City of Abo (now Turku) which then had a population of 60,000 and was the second largest port in Finland. This was followed in 1930 by an important industrial loan of nearly £1,750,000.

Since 1914 many changes had taken place in the political geography of Europe as former boundaries dissolved and new nations emerged. In common with the bank's policy towards the new republic of Finland, it also offered its services to Iceland which, since 1920, had been recognized by Denmark as an independent sovereign state. During the course of the decade the island's development began to accelerate. In the summer of 1923 Sir Eric's son, Charles, spent a few weeks there. The following February the bank undertook to issue a small loan of £200,000 on behalf of the Landsbanki Islands (the National Bank of Iceland), and this was followed in 1930 by a loan of just over £500,000 for The Kingdom of Iceland. Charles maintained a continuing interest, becoming involved again in the 1930s.

Charles Hambro at Camp Vigholt in Iceland in July 1923, where he enjoyed several days of excellent salmon fishing. Hambro Family Archives.

During the early years of the 1920s the Bank of England had informally restricted the issue of foreign loans in London, but, as demonstrated by the Finnish and Icelandic loans of 1923 and 1924, a few exceptions were permitted. Once the Bank had given its tacit approval again, however, the London capital market flourished and the Hambros were eager to resume their pre-war interest in this area. Just as the bank had helped Finland and Iceland, it also offered its services to Hungary and Romania, both torn apart by their experiences during the war. The first loan for the Hungarian Land Mortgage Bank was floated in 1926, followed by another in 1928, and in the next year £500,000 was raised for the city of Budapest, which then had a population of nearly a million. The Romanian loan of £2,000,000 in 1929 specifically aimed to stabilize the currency and was therefore, like the great Italian loan of 1882–3, of basic importance to the country's economy. All these issues were the responsibility of Olaf who, to his credit, showed great eagerness to pioneer new areas of influence.

From 1863 to the mid-1890s Greece had been one of Baron Hambro's and Sir Everard's most important customers. In the 1920s it again became a major source of business, the main concern of Sir Eric. In August 1923, as a result of war between Greece and Turkey, the Treaty of Lausanne was signed which led to a mass expulsion of Greeks then living in Asia Minor. The Greek government made a free transfer of 1,250,000 acres of land to the refugees, together with buildings and land around Athens and Piræus, but there remained a desperate shortage of capital to finance the resettlement. In December 1924 a loan of £7,500,000 was raised by Hambros Bank in London.

This marked the beginning of a series of issues for Greece which, apart from a small railway loan in 1926, were much larger than any of the other loans which the bank issued in the 1920s. Between 1927 and 1928 the sum of £3,000,000 was raised for the National Mortgage Bank of Greece to spend on extensive drainage schemes; then in 1928 two loans which totalled nearly £8,000,000 were floated to stabilize the Greek currency, to provide capital for three government agricultural and public works contracts, and to allow further funds for the settlement scheme. Sir Eric developed a close relationship with Drossopoulos, the Governor of the National Bank of Greece. Through him he became very optimistic about the future of the economy and personally invested a great deal of money in various Greek ventures.

Fortified by the new level of activity which the bank had been able to

From 1897 onwards J. Pierpont Morgan Junior used to stay with the Hambros at Gannochy, and when Everard gave up the tenancy in 1913 Eric and J. Pierpont Morgan took it jointly. 1921 was an excellent year with over 9,000 birds (including grouse, pheasants, partridges and woodcocks) being shot and on one day alone, 25 August, over 1,000 grouse were shot. From left to right: Harry Morgan, W. Steele, W. Paton, Lord Elphinstone, J. Pierpont Morgan Junior, Eric and Angus Hambro. Hambro Family Archives.

reach during the prosperous years from 1925 to 1928, the board of directors voted to increase the capital of the bank from £1,000,000 to £1,400,000 by capitalizing reserves and issuing 400,000 'A' shares at £1 each. At about the same time, the family, which had acquired half the capital of the new Hambros Bank in 1920, was now able to increase its holdings to a majority of shares and so take formal control of the bank. In March 1929, The Hambro Trust Limited was established to ensure that the divergent family interests should remain cohesive, and so keep the power vested within the family.

At the end of March 1929 the balance sheet of Hambros Bank reached its inter-war peak of nearly £34,000,000, whilst acceptances reached the unprecented level of £12,500,000. In his annual speech Sir Eric explained that high interest rates in the USA had caused great uneasiness, and there was an additional threat that the Federal Reserve Bank would increase them further to curb speculation. As a result the demand for London acceptances had grown immensely in the last few weeks 'and one can say that practically the whole of the pre-war acceptance business is now back in London'. By the summer of that year the US economy was already in decline, and on 24 October a momentous panic swept through Wall Street. On that day alone 13,000,000 shares were sold, precipitating the resounding crash of hundreds of firms and worldwide depression. The initial results in Britain were not as traumatic as in the USA or Germany, and so long as the volume of world trade remained high the London merchant bankers were not unduly hurt by the immediate effects of the American disaster.

Indeed, until the Christmas of 1931 the bank continued to prosper. Seven years of Sir Eric's chairmanship, aided by meticulous support from Harry, the thrusting and shrewd attitude of Olaf, and the influential help of Gerard d'Abo, had witnessed a period of increasing activity in a world which was still severely torn by the tumultuous events of the war. Within a few months, however, the situation changed dramatically. Already, beneath the icing, deep cracks had begun to appear. In March 1932, Sir Eric found himself and the bank to be the unfortunate victims of the grim depression which then dominated the financial affairs of the whole world. He was already sixty and decided to retire from the bank completely, giving up the chairmanship to his youngest brother Olaf, who was then forty-five.

The depression of the early 1930s was an extremely sad period for the whole of the Hambro family. Already, in the previous November, Major-General Sir Percy Hambro had died aged sixty. After World

This photograph, taken on the occasion of a royal visit to Kidbrooke, is headed 'Queen Mary and Captain Olaf Hambro at Kidbrooke Park, June 5th 1934'. Reproduced by gracious permission of Her Majesty Queen Elizabeth II.

War I he served at the army headquarters in Baghdad, and was awarded the KBE for his distinguished sevice there. Then he returned to India for a period of four years. In 1925 he ended his career overseas and was appointed major-general in charge of administration at the Aldershot Command. He introduced the Military Tattoo which has been held there ever since. In May 1927 he was given the command of the 46th Division of the Territorial Army, which carried with it the

Winifred Martin Smith married her cousin Olaf Hambro on 17 February 1917. She was a marvellous golfer and an enthusiastic skier. Her life came to a sudden and tragic end when she drowned in Loch Ness on 28 August 1932. Hambro Family Archives.

command of the North Midland area regular troops, a position he held until May 1931 when he retired with Marjorie and his three children – Susan, Evy and Patsie – to Queen Camel House in Somerset. Only six months later, on 25 November, he died. He was buried in the parish churchyard, but, befitting his long and noteworthy career, an army memorial service was held for him in the Chapel at the Royal Hospital, Chelsea.

Sir Eric's retirement the following March was a great disappointment to his son Charles, who soon suffered his own personal tragedy when on 16 April his wife Pamela died after only twelve years of happily married life. She had been out riding near their country home at Delcombe Manor in Dorset when she had been caught in a severe rainstorm. She contracted pneumonia and never recovered. She left three daughters, Cynthia who was 11, Diana 10, and Pamela 7 years old. Charlie, the present Chairman of Hambros Bank, was only twenty-one months old at the time. Pamela Hambro was buried near Loch Rannoch in Scotland, on an estate belonging to her family.

The next disaster occurred only four months later, when on 28 August Winifred, who was Olaf's beautiful wife, died after an accident on Loch Ness. The family were out in their speedboat when the engine caught fire and everyone except for the old nanny decided to jump overboard and swim towards the shore. Olaf looked after one of his sons while Winifred, who was known to be a very strong swimmer, followed behind Jocelyn, the eldest of the children and the present Chairman of Hambros Limited, who was then only thirteen. When he reached the edge of the loch, he looked back for his mother, but she had disappeared. No trace was ever found of her body and the dark, formidable depths of Loch Ness became her burial ground. Ironically, the nanny remained on the boat and drifted safely ashore.

Winifred's death left a deep scar on Olaf and he never remarried. He sold his Scottish house at Glendoe with its terrible memories and direct view over the loch. Clearly the year 1932 was a turning-point in his life – in March he became chairman of the bank and in August a widower. The tragic events of the year forged a lasting bond between him and his nephew, Charles. Although they were totally different in character – the elder an introvert, the younger an extrovert – these two men were able to work in harmony at the bank throughout the next thirty years.

Six months later came the death of Harry Hambro, remembered by one young man who was then in the bank as being 'very prim and proper with a big white moustache'. This was the man who had experienced such a difficult childhood and later, when he was only thirty-one, had been forced to sell the family estate at Milton Abbey.

Pamela Cobbold married Charles Hambro on 22 October 1919 and gave birth to four children, Cynthea, Diana, Pamela and Charlie. She died of pneumonia on 16 April 1932 and was buried near Loch Rannoch in Scotland. Hambro Family Archives.

He had already lost his two half brothers in war when, in 1918, his elder son Val was also killed. Thwarted by his uncle's and his cousins' positions at the bank, he was very pleased when his younger son, Jack (1904–1965) was appointed as a director in 1931, an appointment which, thirty-two years later, led him to the position of chairman.

During his long career in the bank Harry had made connections with many other City firms. Just before World War I, he was appointed a director of the Westminster Bank, and he was also on the boards of various telegraph companies such as the Eastern Telegraph Co., Eastern Extension Australia and China Telegraph Co., and Marconi's Wireless Telegraph Co. In addition he was involved with insurance companies, being a director of the Indemnity Mutual Marine Assurance Co., and Chairman of the Northern Assurance Co.

Soon after buying a country estate known as The Hyde, in Bedfordshire, he became involved in local county matters. He was elected a member of the Bedfordshire County Council, appointed High Sheriff in 1929, and President of the Luton Bute Hospital in 1931. In 1932, however, his health began to fail and soon after Christmas he had a heart attack, followed by pneumonia. He died on 14 February 1933 and was buried at East Hyde near his home in Bedfordshire. A memorial service was held at St Michael's Church, Cornhill, in the City.

Cricket on College Field, *by William Evans. Since the latter half of the nineteenth century all the Hambro sons have been educated at Eton, where several of them have been keen cricketers. Both Charles Hambro and his son Charlie played for the Eton cricket XI.* Reproduced with kind permission of the Provost and Fellows of Eton College.

19 The Depression

Charles Jocelyn Hambro inherited the high-spirited, sport-loving nature of his father, together with his good looks, physique and charm, but these qualities were mixed with the shrewd, more cautious attitude of his grandfather. As a result he enjoyed one of the most successful careers of his generation. Even at Eton he had excelled himself, by captaining the school cricket XI. Then before he was twenty-one he had distinguished himself in the Army and had been awarded the Military Cross.

After the war he joined Hambros Bank and in 1924 he was appointed a director. Before settling down to his City career, however, he went to America and worked in the Guaranty Trust Company of New York where he gained valuable knowledge of American financial affairs. During this time he and his wife Pamela lived with Harry Morgan, who was the son of John Pierpont Morgan Junior, then chief of J. P. Morgan & Co., New York. Since 1913 John Pierpont and Sir Eric had jointly rented the Gannochy moors in Scotland from the Earl of Dalhousie, and so for a few weeks every summer the families had met. Charles' friendship with Harry was a lasting one which proved of the utmost significance in later years.

Soon after he returned to England his grandfather died and, as the chairman's son, Charles quickly began to take an active role in the bank, visiting Greece and other countries in order to expand its business. In April 1928 a great honour was bestowed upon him when, at the early age of thirty, he was elected a director to the Court of the Bank of England. His appointment was especially notable since new recruits were no longer being drawn exclusively from the traditional merchant banking families as they had been before World War I. Before the end of the 1920s the emphasis had shifted radically, so that the Court now included industrialists and other businessmen. However, the Governor, Montagu Norman, recognized Charles' unusual ability and realized that he was one of the few bankers with first-hand experience of American finance. By then the role of New York and the dollar had become of major importance in the international monetary system and, in Norman's view, Charles' knowledge was extremely valuable.

There were, however, two other reasons for Charles' appointment.

J. Pierpont Morgan Junior (1867–1943) became head of J. P. Morgan & Co., New York, on the death of his father in 1913. He was a close friend of Eric and Charles Hambro and proved a useful ally to Charles during his early years as a director of the Court of the Bank of England. Reproduced with kind permission of Morgan Grenfell & Co. Limited.

Sir Everard had given exceptional service to the Court, so the renewal of the family representation was particularly welcome to all those members who still remembered the old gentleman. Moreover, Charles' age suited Norman's plans admirably, since young directors presented no immediate rivalry to his own succession. His lengthy stay as governor was unprecedented, and by the mid-1920s his position had become the centre of a major controversy. The very basis of the appointment was rotational yet, in spite of long absences through illness, he managed to retain his position until 1944.

Charles' election came eighteen months before the Wall Street crash. Soon enough, however, London was facing its own crisis, one which resulted in a decisive change in the financial affairs of the City. Following the New York fiasco, late in 1929 'hot' money had poured into London which then became a financial haven against the turbulent storms elsewhere. Once confidence in London began to falter, however, these foreign funds rushed out, leaving the City with a liquidity crisis of major proportions. £200,000,000 was withdrawn between mid-July and mid-September 1931. Even the August credits of £130,000,000 which had been arranged in Paris and New York had not been able to halt the loss. Money was being taken away in ever-increasing quantities.

Early in September the situation became extremely serious, and on the ninth the Bank established a Foreign Exchange Committee to deal with the day-to-day decisions concerning the spot rate and the forward exchange market. Since Charles was one of its original members he was soon drawn to the very centre of the sterling arena and, amidst all his family worries, his role at the Bank of England during the next two years was of enormous importance.

By Friday 18 September the decision to take Britain off the gold standard had become inescapable. A currency which was freely convertible into gold was no longer practical, since the reserves were now almost exhausted. The pound had been much overvalued since the return to gold in 1925, and the fixed rate of US $4.86 was to be abandoned so that sterling could find its own level without automatic readjustment by the Bank of England. Two of its representatives met the Prime Minister, who was called back from Chequers to attend a meeting that Friday evening to give his approval to the Bank's proposal. As yet only a small band of people knew, but on the following Sunday the Court of Directors gathered to be informed of the decision and to raise the bank rate from $4\frac{1}{2}$ per cent to 6 per cent. Later that evening the government issued a public statement. Within eight days the currency had depreciated by 26 per cent, and soon much of the confidence in sterling had been restored.

Although the image had changed, nevertheless sterling still had an extremely important function in the world monetary system, and the shedding of one means of regulation did not infer that there should be no control whatsoever. Clearly a new plan would have to be devised. The Committee was still meeting daily and Charles was fully occupied. A chance arose to strengthen the foreign currency reserves when, in early October, J. P. Morgan & Co. informed the Bank that there was a large demand for sterling in New York at $3.95. Since the Bank's policy was to buy above $3.75, this was a good opportunity to redress the balance of the past weeks.

Though this plan looked useful it proved totally inadequate, since reserves were still far too meagre to face the strain, which mounted towards the end of the year when, once again, sterling's value fell. The Governor wrote in his diary that Hambro was sitting next door, keeping him informed of all events. Charles was working very closely with Norman, acting almost as his personal assistant. Professor Sayers, the highly acclaimed historian of the Bank of England, recognized that the relationship between these two men was one of the most interesting in the City at the time. Both were of independent character, yet they worked together extraordinarily well.

The Court of directors of the Bank of England, 1932. Charles Hambro, sitting at the far end of the table on the left, had been a director since 1928. In October 1932 he became an executive director and was intimately involved with the question of sterling and the exchange equalization account. In 1937 he was offered the position as Governor but for personal reasons he refused. Montagu Norman, at the near end of the table, remained Governor from 1920 to 1944. Reproduced with kind permission of the Bank of England.

Fortunately, exchange rates stabilized between Christmas 1931 and February 1932, and the bank rate was dropped to 5 per cent. On 25 February Charles noted that, with the influx of foreign money and half the August credits paid off, the Bank ought to intervene when sterling reached $3.65 and then reduce the bank rate again. During March the Bank's net reserve position improved considerably, and at last the time approached for the Bank to intervene formally in the market.

On 1 July 1932 the Exchange Equalization Account was formed with a special fund of £167,000,000 which would be used to check undue fluctuations in the exchange rate. It was to be administered on the Treasury's behalf by the Bank of England. Pressure on sterling increased in August and September, and so the Governor decided to appoint the first full time executive director of the Bank to be in charge of the administration of the Account. His choice was Charles Hambro. He began at a difficult time, when sterling was already under severe pressure, and at the end of November he was forced to abandon the idea of checking the decline in case the whole of the reserves were used up.

The purpose of the Account was only to maintain an orderly market and not to reverse the direction of a major movement.

By the end of September 1933 he had guided the Account through its difficult teething period and ensured a high degree of daily independence from the Treasury. Its role was of the utmost importance and it was regarded as one of the major innovations in the City in the 1930s. Even today it remains one of the Bank's most significant functions. Despite his comparative youth – Charles was still only thirty-four – he had become one of the leading members of the Court, and his distinguished service over the past two years meant that he was first choice as a permanent executive director at the Bank. Family commitments meant that he was unable to accept, but although he returned to Hambros Bank Limited he still retained his membership of the court and over the next four years continued to make a valuable contribution to the Bank of England's affairs, and retained his close relationship with Norman.

Indeed, when the Governor proposed that he intended to retire in 1937 both he and other members of the Court were unanimous in wanting Charles to be his successor. They thought that he had the right combination of a specialist and a traditional merchant banking family background. This was an exceptional honour and underlines the high esteem in which he was held. At first Charles wanted to accept, although he insisted that he should not be considered a 'lifer' like Norman, but that his position would be reviewed after five years. In the last analysis, however, overriding personal reasons forced him to refuse. Years later he wrote that he often 'looked back with great regret that Fate intervened in this way'. Other important roles, however, were yet in store for him.

Like the rest of Sir Everard's sons, Olaf was a tall, large man, dark-haired with a black moustache. Even in middle age he had a stern, imposing and often forbidding countenance, a gruff voice and an autocratic manner. He was a stickler for punctuality. From the depths of the chairman's office, at the north-east end of the 'partners' room' on the first floor of 41 Bishopsgate, at 1.15 pm each day he would command his colleagues 'Time for lunch', and with one accord the four or five other directors present would leave their desks, gather in the board room for a glass of sherry, and at 1.30 pm precisely proceed to the dining-room, where the butler would be waiting.

Olaf's pipe was his most trusted and devoted companion. Its permanent position – clenched firmly between his teeth – accounted for the inaudible mutterings which managed to escape the restricted exit. He always smoked a special blend from Robert Lewis' in St James's, and

Olaf Hambro, the youngest of Sir Everard's sons, was born in 1885 and became the third chairman of Hambros Bank in 1932. He governed with enormous skill and integrity until his death in 1961. He adored gardens and in the 1950s kept beautiful grounds at his country home, Linton Park in Kent, and also at Logan in Scotland, famous for its sub-tropical climate. Portrait by Edward Halliday, c. 1955. Hambro Family Archives.

390

Olaf's characteristic half-pound tins of tobacco were left strategically in all the first-floor rooms of 41 Bishopsgate.

Olaf became the undisputed chief of the bank. He made the decisions, leaving others to work out the details. His despotic rule, however, belied a warm-hearted nature; beneath the hard exterior there was a mischievous, finely-tuned sense of humour blended with an infinite compassion for others who needed his help. His own tragedy of August 1932 had taught him much about personal suffering, and so he developed a sensitive regard for fellow men in distress. Even in small ways he showed a deep consideration for others. Dunton, his chauffeur, recalls that if they had been up to Scotland and he had returned home by himself, leaving Olaf to catch the train a few days later, Olaf would always take the trouble to telephone Mrs Dunton to say that her husband was on his way back. In Dunton's words, 'He had a heart of gold.'

Olaf was a man of style. His lovely country estates and his flat over the West End branch of the bank in Pall Mall were obvious examples of his good taste. One of his great hobbies was to restore fine houses. His son Jocelyn once said, 'He adored pulling them to pieces and then putting them together again.' His first major attempt was at Kidbrooke Park which still stands on the edge of Ashdown Forest in Sussex. The main block of the house had been built in 1734, but in the nineteenth century a new wing and porch had been added. Olaf bought it in 1921 and radically altered the interior design. The entrance hall became a dignified library and the whole of the west front was transformed into a long drawing-room which he had decorated in Adam style, completed by a chimneypiece painted in the manner of Angelica Kauffmann. Vast lawns stretched out before the house and in the park beyond he created a water garden. Like his father he entertained royal guests and on 5 June 1934, Queen Mary arrived for tea.

In 1938 he sold Kidbrooke and bought Linton Park, an extensive house looking over the Weald of Kent. The centre portion had been built for Robert Mann in the eighteenth century, and then enlarged by the 5th Earl of Cornwallis in about 1825. Olaf demolished the sprawling additions, so that the original house with its fine proportions and interior design was left standing alone and intact. He created a swimming pool in the orangery where rhododendrons, azaleas, eucalyptus and other plants provided colourful and fragrant surroundings. Olaf adored flowers and over the years the sheltered grounds surrounding the house became a gardener's paradise.

Just after World War II, his quest for a sub-tropical garden in the Western Isles of Scotland brought him to Logan House, situated on the

Rhinns of Galloway – a long peninsula south of Stranraer stretching out into the warm waters of the Atlantic drift. He could not resist the challenge which the new property offered, and within a few years he had transformed the rambling Victorian mansion to its former elegance, discovering within its outer walls a fine Georgian house. Christopher Hussey wrote in *Country Life* in 1954 that the recovery was 'an architectural miracle, admirably performed and restoring, as far as may be, the most distinguished building of its date in this remote and delectable corner of Scotland'.

Its remoteness was part of its attraction to Olaf, who quite unlike his eldest brother or his nephew Charles was an introverted and lonely man. The London to Stranraer boat-train made the house quite accessible, and despite the distance Olaf frequently visited it for extended weekends or for much longer periods at the height of the flowering season. Gradually he managed to tame the garden, which had been neglected and allowed to run wild during the war years; in time it became one of the wonders of Scotland. There was always plenty of work to do and Olaf was often seen, shirt sleeves rolled up, dodging around the bushes, chopping and clearing rampant growth, and so recovering many rare species. Chopping trees and lighting bonfires were his passion.

In the warm, humid climate, sheltered by a tall belt of trees which filtered the westerly winds and the high stone walls of the former medieval castle which reflected the heat, a large variety of sub-tropical plants flourished, both aquatic and terrestrial. In particular, exotic water lilies, bird of paradise flowers, arum lilies, giant cabbage palms, tree ferns, eucalyptus, hydrangeas, azaleas and magnolias grew in abundance. But Olaf's speciality was rhododendrons, which thrived in the sub-tropical climate of Logan. He exhibited regularly at the Royal Horticultural Society Show in London, and won many awards for the large-leaved Chinese and Himalayan varieties which were his pride. Not surprisingly, Logan became famous among gardening enthusiasts from all over the world, and by the end of the 1950s some two thousand people visited it annually. One special guest in August 1955 was the Queen Mother, who shared Olaf's fervour for plants and wanted to try several Logan varieties at Windsor. As a result, when Dunton drove south the next week the boot of Olaf's black Silver Wraith Rolls Royce was packed with seedlings and cuttings.

Besides the gardens there were 250 acres of parkland and through the woods to the west was a lovely walk down to the sea where primulas grew waist-high, a multitude of pink, mauve, purple and red flowers with umbrella leaves. The grounds of Logan had the natural enchant-

Kidbrooke Park was the home of Olaf Hambro, who bought it in 1921 and sold it in 1938 after greatly altering the interior design. Reproduced by gracious permission of Her Majesty Queen Elizabeth II.

ment of a wild garden, informal in plan, exotic and lush in flavour. They formed a rich oasis in which Olaf could instantly forget the bank and other cares of the City.

Such was the man who, in 1932, suddenly became chairman of the bank. That year he was faced with a mountain of problems. In his personal affairs he was deeply shattered by the tragic death of Winifred. Meanwhile the whole family seemed to be in turmoil. Sir Eric's unexpected retirement had been quickly followed by the death of Charles' wife, Pamela. Disappointed by his father, and grieving for his wife, Charles had to wrestle with the problems over sterling at the Bank of England. He had little time to help Olaf in Bishopsgate who was trying to keep the bank intact while the country and the City faced one of its worst crises. Nearly 3,000,000 people were registered as unemployed – 23 per cent of the workforce. World trade was at a desperately low ebb as demand and prices slumped, and protectionist tariffs rose up like walls around the domestic economies. By 1933 the bank's balance sheet had slumped to £21,000,000, a third lower than at the end of the 1920s. Acceptances had fallen by the same proportion and in 1933 they barely reached £8,000,000.

393

Painting of Harold Hambro CBE
(1876–1952) by Thomas Dugdale RA.
Harold lived at Coldham Hall in Suf-
folk and farmed 1,000 acres of land
where he kept Percheron horses, Large
Black pigs and Red Poll cattle. He was
a scratch golfer and played cricket for
Bury and West Suffolk. He had a good
eye for pheasants and grouse, and was an
avid horseman – he was master of the
Suffolk foxhounds for 16 seasons.
Hambro Family Archives.

The courage and resilience with which Olaf faced these difficult times were of paramount importance to the eventual recovery of the bank. His drive and foresight were remarkable, as can be seen by his attitude towards foreign loans. Owing to pressure on sterling, the Bank of England had restricted new issues severely. Indeed, between 1932 and 1936, only £3,000,000 of new capital issues was raised in London for countries outside the Empire. But although the market was dampened, Olaf was still keen to look out for additional business opportunities and in 1933, under special circumstances, Hambros Bank undertook the issue of a £1,000,000 loan for Denmark, the proceeds of which would be used to construct a combined railway and road bridge between Zeeland and Falster. Two miles in length, it was to be the longest bridge of its kind in Europe, helping to link Copenhagen to the main railway network on the European continent. A condition of the loan was that all the constructional equipment for the project would be bought from the United Kingdom, and any remaining balance of funds would be used to buy other British goods. The terms were looked upon favourably by the Bank of England, since they would directly increase domestic employment.

This type of loan was exceedingly rare and throughout the rest of the decade the main source of 'new issue' business lay within the United

Kingdom and not abroad. In 1930 the bank had participated in the Bankers' Industrial Development Company, which had been established under Montagu Norman 'to examine, assist and finance the amalgamation, reconstruction, and reorganization' of important British industrial companies. Previous connections between British industry and the London issuing houses had never been close, but from this time onwards Hambros Bank adopted a more positive attitude. Thus in the mid-1930s, when opportunities to raise foreign loans were rare, the domestic industrial loan market was a welcome replacement. In May 1935 the bank issued a £2,000,000 4½ per cent 1st Mortgage Debenture Stock for John Brown & Co. Ltd, owners of the Clydebank Shipyard, who were at the time building the *Queen Mary*. A year later the bank was responsible for reorganizing the capital structure of the Consett Iron Company of Co. Durham.

The bank retained its reputation as one of the most aggressive of all the London issuing houses, and by the end of the decade it was the paying agent for eighty-six loans. Jack, a director since 1931, took the greatest interest in the issuing business and was particularly keen on the industrial sector which, though it was still small, was to become an important growth area in the future. Black-moustachioed, with horn-rimmed spectacles, he was regarded as 'a supreme technician', and like his father, Harry, paid meticulous attention to detail. He was, however, a warmer character, with a lively sense of humour and a wonderful charm – all essential ingredients of the best bankers.

Nigel, only son of Harold Hambro, was born in 1915. He went to Eton, and entered Hambros Bank in September 1930. Shortly before the war he joined the Royal Artillery and served in France, Holland, Belgium and Germany. Hambro Family Archives.

Another member of the family who had become a director in 1931 was Colonel Harold Hambro, Olaf's brother, who had been an officer in the army during the Boer War and World War I. One gentleman today remembers him from the 1930s as a 'great horsy sort of man with a tremendous laugh and a huge deep voice'. As a non-executive director he went to the bank only once a month for board meetings. His real interests lay elsewhere, and he was much more the country squire than the City financier. He lived at a beautiful Elizabethan mansion, Coldham Hall in Suffolk, surrounded by 1,000 acres of land which he managed himself. He kept a herd of Large Black pigs, a stud of Percheron horses and a herd of Red Poll cattle. Throughout his life horses were his great love and he enjoyed nothing better than a day's hunting. For sixteen years he was master of the Suffolk foxhounds.

As the decade progressed Olaf found that he had increasing support from the family. Harold's son Nigel, born in 1915, joined as soon as he left Eton, followed shortly afterwards by Evy, born in 1916, son of Major-General Sir Percy Hambro. In the autumn of 1933 Charles returned from his important work at the Bank of England and was able to add his valuable experience of foreign exchange matters to the general pool of ability provided by the other directors. By the late 1930s a large and flourishing foreign exchange department had been established in Hambros Bank. Meanwhile, Jack continued to concentrate on the issuing side of the business and over the course of the decade matured into a most able banker. Although other managing directors such as Gerard d'Abo and A. John Hugh Smith, and non-executive directors including Sir Joseph Priestley, Sir Karl Knudsen, Lord Glenconner, Lord Astor and Knut Wallenberg all added their own particular expertise and contacts, in reality Olaf, Charles and Jack were indisputably the key figures in the bank.

After the years of crisis in 1932 and 1933 the bank's position revived and profits almost regained the level of the late 1920s. The economic upsurge culminated in 1937 when acceptances reached a new peak of nearly £14,000,000 representing 42 per cent of the balance sheet total which then approached £33,000,000. The boom was short-lived, however, and before long the world plunged headlong into another war which brought an even more devastating effect on the international economy than had been the case in the years 1914–18. Olaf now faced his second economic crisis.

20   The Bank in World War II

The onset of war and the consequent danger of bombing in the City had caused Olaf considerable worry. His own house at Linton Park in Kent would not provide a viable alternative to the bank's premises in Bishopsgate, since it lay in the direct path of German bomber aircraft. Jack's home at The Hyde in Bedfordshire, some thirty miles north of London, was a much safer option and so, several weeks before the declaration of war, various members of the male staff left the City to prepare for the evacuation. Temporary dormitories were built in the grounds, and loads of office furniture were delivered and installed in the main building. Soon the new bank quarters were fully occupied, as many of the unmarried female staff and those of the male staff not yet called for active service left their homes around London and took up permanent residence in the country.

The men slept on canvas beds in the austere wooden huts which had been hastily constructed just a few weeks before, while the women slept in the attics and the wings of the main house. Conditions were cramped but the adaptation was made smoothly, and the work of the coupons, correspondence, new issues and ledger departments continued undisrupted. The strict blackout imposed by the government meant that on winter afternoons and evenings all work had to be conducted behind firmly closed shutters. Thus the staff worked and lived in their strange but lovely surroundings. Table tennis, billiards and film shows were available for indoor recreation, while a swimming pool and tennis court provided outdoor sport, and the local pub, the Leather Bottle, offered alternative entertainment.

Each weekend many of the staff went home by train. Few people ran cars, because of petrol rationing. One of the male clerks, Rex Gardner, remembers that cars were available very cheaply and he was able to buy a handsome Riley Saloon in 1940 for only fifty shillings and then paid seventy shillings to insure it! He recalls that in the summer of that year an invasion was thought to be imminent, and the people of The Hyde formed a detachment of the Home Guard. Each man was 'issued with baggy uniforms and eventually, after the "pitchfork" era, P14 rifles from the 1914–18 war'.

For the first six months Jack was responsible for the administration

The Hyde, near Luton in Bedfordshire, painted by Cecily Williams Ellis. She was the daughter of Harry Hambro, who bought the Hyde estate in 1925. It was inherited by his son Jack and became the home of the bank during World War II. In 1952–3 the main house was altered, one wing and the attic were removed completely. Hambro Family Archives.

of the bank's operations at The Hyde but soon he had more pressing wartime duties to perform in connection with the United Kingdom Commercial Corporation. Mr Arthur Purton, who was one of the bank's managers, then took over Jack's role and made certain that everything ran smoothly. He liaised with Olaf daily both by telephone and via the two bank messengers, one from The Hyde and one from Bishopsgate, who met each afternoon in the Underground station at Cockfosters where they exchanged despatch cases. With all the wartime dangers, they never once failed to keep their rendezvous.

Though the main offices in Bishopsgate escaped the air raids, in 1945 the West End branch at 67 Pall Mall was damaged when a large bomb obliterated the offices opposite. Fortunately the bank building was not affected too seriously, and the next day business was able to continue almost as usual. The main problem was the constant enquiries about the safety of certain valuables kept in the bank vault! The war had had other effects on the branch, and from the outset Olaf had been forced to adapt its operations. While on the one hand he had to close its once flourishing foreign exchange business, on the other he was able to open hundreds of accounts for Norwegian servicemen stationed in and around London. Like most of the bank's activities during the war, however, the overall volume of business was sharply reduced.

About sixty of the staff remained in Bishopsgate to look after the bank's credit, cash and collection departments. The war brought British trade with Europe nearly to a standstill, and Olaf found that many of his most valued customers in Norway, Finland, Denmark, Italy and eventually Greece were in enemy-occupied territory. On 31 March 1941 less than £750,000 worth of acceptances were registered on Hambros Bank's ledgers. Severe exchange restrictions, curtailment of foreign deposits, a total embargo on investments abroad and no new capital issues meant that the bank's balance sheet total fell below £12,000,000 while profits that year were reduced by a third to only £100,000.

Of course domestic trade still continued, though on a restricted basis, and the ever adaptable Olaf shifted the emphasis of the bank's acceptance operations to the finance of the inland movement of goods. His policy was a departure from traditional merchant banking but it proved to be a timely move. By 31 March 1943 only £28,000 was

The photograph shows 'the management' of the bank at its wartime home, The Hyde, with Jack Hambro sitting second from the left. Before long he had to leave his banking duties in order to run the UKCC *in London.* Hambro Family Archives.

connected directly with international trade finance, while inland acceptances approached nearly £2,000,000. This was a tiny figure compared with previous standards, but it was better than nothing and represented 13 per cent of the diminished balance sheet.

Fortunately, a profitable banking opportunity arose elsewhere. One of the by-products of the war was the dislocation of the traditional diamond markets in Antwerp and Amsterdam. Following the German occupation and vendetta against the Jews many of the traders abandoned their homes and businesses. With their wives and children they fled the country, clutching their precious bundles of uncut diamonds. They arrived in London and settled in and around the jewellery area of Hatton Garden. With his keen eye for new business Olaf recognized that these refugees had excellent collateral and expertise but no established means of credit. Overdrafts and revolving acceptance credits were offered up to 70–80 per cent of the value of rough or polished diamonds, which were then deposited with Hambros Bank.

Individual parcels worth between £10,000 and £100,000 were stacked in the safe at 41 Bishopsgate. Gutchen & Partners, A. Monnickendam and J. K. Smit were some of the first names to appear on the bank's diamond credit lists, but by the summer of 1943 the numbers had grown considerably and the total indebtedness of the diamond trade had reached £700,000, involving dealers and polishers in London, cutters in Birmingham and diamond tool companies in Wolverhampton. As the bank's experience with diamonds increased Olaf decided to become more directly involved, and so a subsidiary of the bank, called the Bishopsgate Trading and Export Co. Ltd., began to deal in rough diamonds. Hambro interests in the diamond business grew dramatically and proved to be a successful new venture, filling part of the void left by the lack of normal peacetime business. Olaf's shrewd assessment had paid off handsomely.

During most of the war period, Olaf remained the only family member permanently working in the bank. Young Nigel and Evy Hambro had both joined the Territorial Army before the war. Charles was appointed to the Ministry of Supply on the day that war was declared, and in 1940 Jack became wholly immersed in the pre-emptive purchases of goods considered valuable to Germany.

Altogether, four members of the family went off to fight. Nigel, the only son of Harold Hambro, followed in his father's footsteps and in March 1939 left the bank and joined the Territorial Army. Later he was given a commission in the Royal Artillery and was called up in August 1939, promoted to captain in 1941 and to major in 1943. He served in France,

Holland, Belgium and Germany, and was present at the D-Day land-ings in Normandy.

On one occasion in Holland he and a colonel in the 54th Division, plus two other soldiers, went out in a jeep behind the enemy lines to gather information about German troop movements. They drove for thirty miles without seeing anything of interest to report, and since it was seven o'clock in the evening they decided to stop outside a small village hotel for some refreshment. Nigel recalls the event vividly as he and the colonel went inside, only to be met by a worried hotel manager who flatly refused to serve them. But his colonel did not take 'No' for an answer and demanded food, whereupon he and Nigel walked straight into the dining-room. They were confronted by the sight of about forty German officers having dinner at a long table. Surprised beyond measure, they summoned their wits and with the words *'Heil Hitler!'* beat a hasty retreat through the doors. Fortunately they managed to escape, and when they reached camp they were able to report their discovery.

On 8 May 1945, the day of Germany's unconditional surrender, Nigel was driving down the main street of Wageningen, a small town near Arnhem in Holland, when suddenly a German official attracted his attention and surrendered himself. The man was none other than Dr Arthur Seyss-Inquart, the Nazi Gauleiter (governor) of Holland. Nigel took him into custody and delivered him to divisional headquar-ters.

By the end of May 1945 Nigel was in Germany and, as acting colonel, became the first British Military Governor of Dortmund. In this capa-city he was seconded as ADC to Sir Neville Laski, who was the British judge at the military trial of those responsible for the Belsen concentra-tion camp. Nigel attended the hearings for several gruelling weeks during the autumn of 1945. The same year he was awarded the TD, and he remained in the Army until April 1946. He never returned to the City, and with his wife Marjorie whom he married in 1938, along with their two children, Carl and Olga, he settled in the country. His main interest became farming and he established herds of pedigree Hereford cattle and Shetland ponies, which he exported all over the world. The cattle have been sold to China and Russia, and the ponies have been sent to America, Holland, Sweden, Malta and France. He is a council member of both breed societies. Like his father, he has always been a keen horseman and has been appointed master of three different packs of hounds.

Evy Hambro, named after his great uncle Sir Everard, had entered the Bank straight from Eton but, being a wild young man, his City career was subordinated to his social life and Olaf was not amused. Evy left the bank in 1937 and joined his father's old regiment, the 15th/19th Hussars, and was commissioned in the supplementary reserve of officers. His service with the colours lasted a year, during which time he was posted to Yorkshire where he trained in armoured warfare. There he met Mary Lyon, whom he married six years later. After he completed his service he returned to the City, not to the bank but to Robert Bradford & Co. Ltd, insurance brokers. Before long, however, war had been declared and his main army career began.

He landed in France on 19 May 1940 but soon afterwards was posted to Egypt where he served as staff captain to Brigadier John Currie and remained in the thick of battle throughout the war, whether in the Western Desert campaign, Sicily, Italy or north-west Europe. In 1942 he was appointed as DAA & QMG to the 4th Armoured Brigade – his main role was to ensure an adequate supply of army materials, petrol, ammunition, blankets, food and water. This was not an easy task, particularly in the desert, but his determination and initiative ensured that the brigade never lacked for anything. As one friend recalls, he would always be 'at the right cross-roads in the middle of the night', ready to galvanize 'a sleepy convoy, about to bed down for the night, into driving relentlessly on – Evy guiding them on, or more likely, chivvying from behind'. He was a tall, well-built man, and such an effervescent character that he was usually able to acquire whatever he needed.

He was mentioned in despatches while in Sicily in March 1944 and later that year he was awarded the MBE for service in Italy. The citation stated:

The administrative problems in supplying the Bde were considerable and were not made easier by the fact that the Bde was administered by two different Corps and two different Divisions in under two months. The Bde never went short of anything and by his zeal and foresight Major Hambro gave entire satisfaction not only to all units of the Bde but also to all senior 'Q' officers by whom the Bde was administered. No problem was too difficult for him to solve and no Commander ever had less anxiety as to his 'Q' situation throughout this campaign.

After the war, Evy returned to Robert Bradford where he built up the

---

Evy Bingham Hambro (1916–71), his wife Mary and their two sons, Tony in the boat and Peter on the right. For a short while before the war Evy worked in Hambros Bank but he later joined Samuel Montagu & Co. Ltd, where he became a director in 1954. Peter, the elder son, is a managing director of Smith St Aubyn (Holdings) Ltd and Tony works for Grindlay's Bank Ltd. Hambro Family Archives.

Jocelyn Hambro, aged twenty-three, married Silvia Muir on 28 March 1942 at St Mark's, North Audley Street, London. Like his father, he joined the Coldstream Guards and in 1944 was awarded the Military Cross for his notable contribution at the Battle of Caumont Hill in Normandy. Hambro Family Archives.

company's life insurance and pension fund business. Then, in 1953, David Keswick, a personal friend and director of Samuel Montagu, merchant bankers in Old Broad Street, asked Evy to join his bank and develop its insurance-related activities. He entered Samuel Montagu on 1 January 1954 and in March that year was appointed a director. Apart from his insurance work, one of his most valuable contributions to the company was his efforts to promote operations in the Middle East in the late 1950s and early 1960s, long before the oil scramble of the 1970s. As a result, Samuel Montagu became one of the first merchant banks to realize the implications of wealth in the Persian Gulf. Evy died in 1971, having lived life to the full. He left a wife, Mary, and two sons, Peter and Tony, who true to the family tradition have both followed successful financial careers. Peter has been appointed a managing director of Smith St Aubyn & Co. (Holdings) Ltd, one of the eleven discount houses in the City, and Tony works for Grindlays Bank Ltd.

Olaf's son Jocelyn had his first encounter with German hostility in 1936 when, having left Eton that summer, he was studying languages at Heidelberg University. Suddenly he received a summons from the Gestapo and two men in long black coats came to take him away. He thought he would be gone for good. They confronted him with the words, 'You are insulting the Third Reich', and Jocelyn saw before him a pile of rancid butter which he discovered had been sent weekly by his father's butler who had heard Goering's famous announcement that Germans should have guns rather than butter. He was eventually freed and without delay wired home to prevent the arrival of any more food parcels!

After Heidelberg, Jocelyn went up to Trinity College, Cambridge, to read history. Racing and golf were his delights, but following his father's advice he joined the supplementary reserve of the Coldstream Guards and during each of his summer vacations underwent a period of training at Wellington Barracks and Pirbright. He never completed his final year at Cambridge, as on 3 September 1939 he was recalled to join the Army. During the next four years he held various military appointments in England, and in May 1944 was promoted to the rank of major. Soon afterwards he took part in the European offensive and landed in Normandy where he commanded a tank unit, No. 1 Squadron, 4th (Tank) Battalion, Coldstream Guards.

On 1 July he was positioned near a strategic high point called Caumont Hill, map reference 309, which General Montgomery considered vitally important for the British Army to capture if it was ever to succeed in its advance on Paris. Normal army tactics dictated that tanks should never move forward without infantry support, but in this particular instance, where speed was all-important and there was no immediate hope of the infantry's arrival, Jocelyn's squadron was ordered to advance alone. The hill was strongly held by the Germans; however, under his leadership the tanks rushed forward, defeated the enemy and succeeded in reaching the top of the hill. For the moment his squadron was in command, but its position was extremely vulnerable as without the infantry it lacked essential support. Nevertheless it was able to control the hill until the infantry appeared.

Captain Christopher Bridge, Jocelyn's second-in-command, remembers the occasion clearly, and particularly recalls the dash, courage and inspiration which Major Hambro had shown. General Montgomery was extremely pleased with the victory and wanted to know who had been responsible for it. As a result, Jocelyn was awarded the Military Cross. At twenty-five this had been his first experience of battle.

Six weeks later, while still in Normandy, Jocelyn attended a conference with his superior officers to decide upon the tactics of the next assault. He provided the tank expertise. The meeting was held in an open field, and while the brigadier was talking a shell landed directly on

Alec, son of Angus Hambro, died in 1943 at Tripoli in north Africa from shellfire wounds received in the desert. Hambro Family Archives.

the group. The spot became a bloodbath. Several men were killed outright and Jocelyn was wounded severely. This marked the end of his military career and he was flown back to Britain where, in a Birmingham hospital, one of his legs was amputated. But with his characteristic courage and tenacity he was not to be defeated, and before too long was able to play a good game of tennis and enjoy grouse-shooting once more. Typical of his personality, his comment today is lighthearted: 'What a day to be shot, the 12th of August.'

Unlike his cousins, Alec, born in 1910 and by this time the only surviving son of Angus Hambro, had no army training before the war. On leaving Eton he had become an estate agent in Bournemouth and in 1934 had married Barbara, the sister of the famous photographer, Cecil Beaton. Immediately war broke out he joined his father's regiment and became a gunnery officer in the Queen's Own Dorset Yeomanry. He was posted to North Africa where he was badly wounded by shellfire in the desert. After treatment he appeared to have recovered, but unfortunately not all the shell fragments had been removed, and after he had returned to active service at Tripoli the wound festered. Several months later, on 9 August 1943, he died. Barbara was left with two small children, Alexandra, then aged eight, and Rosamund, aged three.

Although Jack was initially responsible for the bank's operations at

The Hyde, he soon became deeply involved with economic warfare and, like his father, acted on behalf of the British government in buying various raw materials. Jack's role, however, was of a more clandestine nature and in April 1940 he joined the newly established United Kingdom Commercial Corporation (UKCC) as one of the two managing directors under the chairmanship of Viscount Swinton. At the beginning the company had a capital of £500,000, but a year later this was increased to £1,500,000, the Treasury being the sole shareholder. This money was to be used by Jack and his colleagues to buy commodities considered useful to the enemy. Their aim was to carry out a programme of pre-emptive purchases so that steadily Germany would become starved, or at least seriously short, of certain types of foodstuffs, fibres and minerals. With the help of strategic information from the government they were to trade, as far as possible, on a commercial basis, being equally responsible for the risk of profit or loss.

Within two months of its creation, representatives had been established in many countries such as Egypt, Iran, Iraq, Turkey, Greece, the Balkan countries, Spain and Iceland, but after March 1941 the territorial scope widened even further to South America, the Far East, the Middle East and the Pacific. The company's success rested on the persuasive powers of the management and its representatives, since in many of these countries the UKCC had to break down established trade agreements with Germany and often heavy bribes were the only answer. Thus in return for chrome from Greece, supplies of wheat were offered from Australia. As a result, large cargoes of German-bound goods were diverted to the Allies, exchanged with commodities from neutrals, offered as bribes, or simply dumped. The whole operation took on a cloak-and-dagger style. Few knew about the connection between the UKCC and the government, even fewer realized the extent of its operations.

Jack admitted that he enjoyed his life as a buccaneer, outwitting the enemy, capturing cargoes, cornering commodities, and in many ways reverting to his family's original role as a merchant. He liked it best in the early years, when he thought the most effective business was accomplished. Later, towards the end of the war, the organization grew much larger, more regulated and remote, a situation he found personally to be much less rewarding. In spite of its disadvantages, the operation was regarded as a great success and Jack was able to return the capital with profit. In 1944 he was made a CMG in recognition of his services.

Undoubtedly the family's greatest contribution to the British war

Jack Hambro CMG *(1904–65) was one of the two managing directors of the* UKCC, *a cloak-and-dagger-style organization established in 1940 to carry out a programme of pre-emptive purchases against the enemy.* Hambros Bank Archives.

effort, however, was made by Charles Hambro who, in 1938, had been critically ill with cancer of the tongue. For months he was absent from work, incapable of speech and confined to bed under the devoted attention of Sir Ernest Rock-Carling, one of the most eminent surgeons in London. Charles underwent a major operation followed by a long course of radium treatment and this, together with his strong will to survive and the unfailing support of his second wife, Dorothy, pulled him through. Although his sense of taste was impaired, his speech returned to normal. Only a scarred throat indicated to the outside world that there had once been a desperate struggle for survival.

Charles had no sooner recovered from his illness than the rumblings of war were to be heard and Lord Halifax, the Foreign Secretary, asked him to join the Ministry of Economic Warfare (MEW). Charles was ideal material. His military experience as a guardsman in World War 1, his wide knowledge of world monetary matters gained from his intimate connection with the Bank of England and, in particular, his expertise on Scandinavian affairs which he had acquired through his work at the bank all helped to provide him with the necessary background for his new assignment. Moreover he was a character who immediately commanded respect and was able to obtain the best results from those in his charge. In short, he was a great leader and just the sort of man the Ministry needed.

On the day war was declared, Charles left his family in Dorset and boarded the first train to London in order to take charge of the Scandinavian section of the ministry. Just as his father, Sir Eric, had been concerned with this region in World War I, now Charles' turn had arrived. Harry Sporborg, another of Lord Halifax's special recruits from the City, was Charles' subordinate responsible for Sweden. After Cambridge, Harry Sporborg had become a solicitor with Slaughter and May where, at the age of thirty, he was made their youngest-ever partner. His experience of City firms and City affairs in general were valuable assets for his new role. Banker and lawyer worked closely together and quickly became great and lasting friends. Indeed, after the war, Harry Sporborg joined Hambros Bank as a director, a position which he held until 1970.

Through MEW Charles became intimately involved in the details of the war-trade agreements which Britain negotiated with the Scandinavian governments. These were drawn up to ensure that supplies of essential materials imported into the Scandinavian countries through the British blockade were used domestically in those countries and were not allowed to be re-exported to Germany. The neutral Scandinavian governments were not totally in sympathy with the British requests, and just as the Swedish negotiations had proved long and difficult for Eric in the summer of 1915, so Charles found the Scandinavians

Charles Hambro and his second wife, Dorothy, former wife of Marcus Wallenberg, at their farm near Milton Abbas in Dorset. They were married in 1936 and had one daughter, Sally. Hambro Family Archives.

tough bargainers at the beginning of World War II. A particularly tricky question arose over Norway's exports of iron and copper, which Britain was afraid would find their way into the German war industry. Already Lord Glenconner, a non-executive director of Hambros Bank, who was in charge of the Norwegian section of the ministry, had tried to win a concession on this point. He had failed, and so Charles flew to Oslo on 11 February 1940 to add more weight to the British argument.

The conclusion of the Norwegian war-trade agreement had been delayed long enough. Until it was signed Norway refused to implement the important shipping agreement whereby the Allies would have the use of the Norwegian mercantile fleet, which was the fourth largest in the world and considered to be the equivalent in value of one million fighting men. Although Charles failed to enforce all the British demands over iron and copper he did extract various other concessions, and on 11 March 1940 the war-trade agreement was signed. Of course, Hitler's invasion of Norway the following month rendered much of the document worthless, but at least the shipping agreement had been satisfactorily concluded and the Allies continued to benefit from it during the remaining years of war. Meanwhile Hambros Bank, which had established close links with several of the Norwegian shipping companies in the 1920s, became bankers to Nortraship, the organization formed to administer the fleet.

With the whole of Denmark, Norway, Belgium, Holland and Luxembourg overrun by German troops in April and May 1940, followed by France only a few weeks later, those within MEW realized that any British blockade was almost useless against the vast area of natural resources to which Hitler had now gained access. Policy had to be reformulated, and in July 1940 both Charles and Harry Sporborg were asked to join a new secret government organization called the Special Operations Executive (SOE). It was to be responsible to the Minister of Economic Warfare, but its existence was never to be revealed to those outside.

Winston Churchill, who was by then head of the newly-formed coalition government, called a meeting at 10 Downing Street and informed those present, including Charles, Harry Sporborg and Dr Hugh Dalton, chief of MEW, that SOE

. . . was to be an unavowable secret organization to carry out two tasks. First, it was to create and foster the spirit of resistance in Nazi-occupied countries. Secondly, once a suitable climate of opinion had been set up, SOE was to establish a nucleus of trained and equipped men who would be able to assist as a fifth column in the liberation of the country concerned whenever the British were able to invade it.

Europe was to be set ablaze. Industrial and military sabotage, propaganda, riots, terrorist acts against German leaders, strikes and other means of labour agitation were all weapons encouraged by those in command to be used under a cloak of complete secrecy.

Charles' original role in SOE was to be responsible for northern Europe. He performed his duties with distinction and in 1941 was made a KBE. When in May the following year the chief, Sir Frank Nelson, retired due to ill-heath, Sir Charles was promoted chief in his place, and befitting his new position was made an honorary air commodore. Under him, Harry Sporborg was responsible first for Scandinavia and later for western Europe.

Only a few months earlier their minister, Sir Hugh Dalton, was replaced by Lord Selborne who was quite different in character from Sir Charles. Indeed one acquaintance described them like chalk and cheese, and although they were friends socially they were incompatible over matters concerning work. Sir Charles tried to maintain the independence of SOE while constantly being obliged to inform Lord Selborne and thus the prime minister and the war cabinet of its affairs. Eventually, after sixteen months, Sir Charles resigned and Major-General Gubbins was appointed to his position. By 1944 the world strength of the organization had grown to approximately 15,000 men and women.

Following his resignation as chief of SOE in September 1943, Sir Charles was sent to Washington as the UK member of the Combined Raw Materials Board and as head of the British Raw Materials Mission. His experience with American businessmen and finances, and his expertise as a banker, eminently suited him for the job, which led him into one of the most delicate of all wartime areas.

Through this work he sought to obtain supplies of various commodities for the Allies, but within this field of activity uranium was his main concern. Nuclear research had advanced quickly since the discovery of fission in 1939; its potential use had already been recognized and work on the production of the atomic bomb had been started. Research by British and American scientists had led to particular areas of specialization but finally, in August 1943, after long and arduous negotiations, co-operation was formalized by the Quebec Agreement. This established that, in future, US and British scientists would collaborate to produce the atomic bomb. At the same time both sides accepted the implication that together they should seek out sources of the relevant new materials of which uranium was the chief.

General Groves, the US Army representative in charge of the American atomic energy project, was keen that world uranium production should be 'locked up', and believing a purely American approach might alienate certain other countries the British proposed that a Combined Development Trust (CDT) be established with representatives from the USA, Britain and Canada. At this delicate stage the unique qualities and experience of Sir Charles were brought in and, as head of the British Raw Materials Mission in Washington, he and Frank Lee from the Treasury represented Britain as Trustees of CDT under the chairmanship of the general. The aim of the CDT was to obtain control of existing uranium mines wherever possible, and through the organization of intensive geological surveys and the study of literature to carry out a detailed search and so discover new sources for the Allies.

Strategically, their immediate major concern was the rich uranium deposits in the Belgian Congo, where the mines had been flooded at the beginning of the war and therefore rendered unworkable. The Trust was anxious that they should be re-opened and that all the output should be sold to the Allies. General Groves and Sir Charles tried to bring pressure on Monsieur Sengier, who was the chief administrator of Union Minière, the company which owned the mines. Negotiations were complex, and further complicated by the need for them to be conducted through quiet commerical channels and without political fuss. Secrecy was vital. Sir Charles played a crucial role in the talks and General Groves admitted that it was only through his colleague's determination and efforts that agreement was ever reached. The contract was signed in September 1944.

The general was a tough, single-minded character who believed that the British only wanted co-operation so that they could profit from the peacetime uses of atomic energy after the war was over. Considering the difficult period of Anglo-American discussions prior to the Quebec Agreement, signed a year earlier, the joint accomplishments of these two men over the Belgian Congo contract were indeed noteworthy. Sir Charles' natural ability to get on well with people eventually overcame even the general's difficult disposition, a result which few other British colleagues ever achieved.

Sir Charles' aptitude to win the general's respect is clearly described by Margaret Gowing in her official history *Britain and Atomic Energy 1939–1945*. She wrote:

Hambro had sufficient standing to impress and win the confidence of Groves and so persuade him to give the British willingly something like a co-equal place in the raw material field. Groves came spontaneously and sincerely to accept the Trust as an effective and useful body, and in Lee's judgement this was due solely to his confidence in Hambro and Hambro's constant hard work

Sir Charles Hambro joined the Special Operations Executive in the summer of 1940 and was responsible for northern Europe. In May 1942 he was appointed chief of the entire underground movement and made honorary air commodore. Hambro Family Archives.

in connection with such matters as the Belgian contract. Hambro's presence as a trustee was considered so indispensable that when he left his main Washington post at the end of 1944 and returned to London he remained the senior British member of the Trust and visited Washington for this purpose.

When Sir Charles left Washington just before Christmas 1944 he insisted that a London group of the CDT should be formed so that the British work should continue and be co-ordinated with that of the Americans. Thus, in the following January, a London arm of the Trust was established with Sir Charles as chairman and Richard Sayers, Charles Davidson and Michael Perrin as the other three members. Between them they combined expertise on finance, economics, geology, technical and Intelligence matters. One of their most important decisions was the acquisition of the Portuguese uranium mines at Urgeirica. Already the controlling interest of the company lay in the hands of the United Kingdom Commerical Corporation (UKCC) of which Jack Hambro was one of the two managing directors. Sir Charles visited Portugal in order to inspect the mine and the hotel which belonged to it. Repeating his tactics over the Belgian Congo affair, he considered political action might be harmful, and that commercial means would be the most effective way of obtaining the supply that would give the Trust a strong foothold in a country where other minor sources were being discovered. In February 1945 he concluded the agreement whereby the Trust would purchase the UKCC's controlling interest.

Another area of prime importance was Germany itself. No one was certain how far developed was its atomic research, but conceivably the Germans might have progressed as far as the Allied efforts. This was doubted by British Intelligence though there was evidence that a project had been started. One clue was the disappearance of the large supply of uranium oxide from the Union Minière Company at Oolen in Belgium. This had been captured by the Germans in 1940, so they had had access to the raw materials for the last five years. Steadily more information had been gleaned, until eventually steps could be taken to destroy any future German wartime research or production.

General Groves established a mission called 'Alsos' which aimed first to capture this uranium oxide; secondly, to round up the German nuclear scientists; and thirdly, to seize their papers and equipment. Such a task was difficult enough, but it was made further complicated by the extreme delicacy of the whole affair. The Allied development of the atomic bomb had been kept a tight secret throughout the war. Only a comparatively small number of officials in either the USA or Britain knew anything about the project. Not even all the British War Cabinet ministers knew of its existence. Therefore, in the middle of April, when the mission travelled eastwards across Europe they had to avoid all contact with the liberating armies of France and later Russia, who were still completely oblivious of their task.

The mission which combined American and British scientific and technical expertise assembled at Rheims, and then split. One part including Sir Charles went to Stassfurt in Eastern Germany, which lay very close to the Russian line of advance and where the uranium oxide seized from the Oolen store was known to be stored. 1,100 tons were found in rotting barrels which had been hidden in a shed. Within three days, 20,000 new barrels were procured from a factory nearby and all the uranium was shipped safely to an airport hanger at Hildesheim, whence it was sent to Britain and eventually to the USA. Sir Charles then travelled to southern Germany, where the main American team with Perrin and Welsh had gone to find and interrogate the German scientists and collect their equipment. In a cave at Haigerloch the experimental atomic pile had been found, but the uranium and heavy water to be used in it had vanished. Intensive questioning revealed that the uranium blocks had been buried in a field close at hand, while the heavy water had been concealed in oil drums in a cellar at a disused country mill. The mission was a total success and as a result the German atomic project was brought to an abrupt end.

Successful attempts to acquire uranium were thought to be one of Britain's foremost contributions to the later stages of the wartime atomic project. In this respect, Sir Charles' role was of paramount importance. His forceful personality, his ability to win people's allegiance and to command respect, particularly from Americans, were all essential ingredients to his success as an administrator and co-ordinator. Meanwhile his skill in the financial aspects of the negotiations was crucial. Sir Michael Perrin, who as assistant director of the British 'Tube Alloys' project worked closely with Sir Charles, remembers him vividly and has warm praise for the man who won the friendship of the formidable General Groves: 'He was an ideal man to have been brought in at a very senior level.'

Outwardly Sir Charles revelled in the excitement of wartime escapades and the dangers with which he was confronted, but for all his experiences he remained a modest and secretive man and never once divulged information even to his wife about his role in the Alsos mission or his work in SOE. From the days in 1938 when he had been critically ill with cancer, he had risen with great courage to shoulder the enormous responsibilities with which he was confronted. He survived his wartime activities but they all took their toll and by the time peace came he appeared considerably older. His, indeed, was a notable contribution.

21 The Post-War Era

Critics of the City highlight the inertia that characterized the merchant banks during the early years of peace which followed the 1930s' depression and wartime retraction. Images have been drawn of stuffy old men retreating into their mahogany parlours with blinkered vision and faltering steps as their acceptance businesses floundered and their issue departments crumbled. To the merchant bankers a devalued, unstable and restricted currency, and a domestic credit squeeze coupled with enforced curtailment in foreign lending, were all loathsome reflections of the post-war period undermining the very basis of their normal business.

Fortunately for Hambros Bank, Olaf was more resilient than many of his counterparts in other merchant banks. It is true that he was shy, introverted and already sixty by the time the war was over but like his father, Sir Everard, he had the ability to adjust to the changing circumstances; his shrewd judgements enabled him to capitalize new opportunities and thus reshape the bank's former business. He was fortunate, moreover, that two other members of the family, Sir Charles and Jack, were both extremely able merchant bankers. In 1945 they both returned to the bank bringing with them the valuable fruits of commercial wartime experience.

The complementary trio of Olaf, Sir Charles and Jack represented an outstanding team. Many senior people in the City today hail Olaf as one of the soundest merchant bankers that they have ever known, but, typical of many of the older City personalities he hated publicity and loathed foreign travel; he preferred to stay quietly in his chairman's room at 41 Bishopsgate where he could control the policy decisions. By contrast, Sir Charles adored travelling, feeling just as much at home whether he was in New York or Cape Town, and is still considered one of the best known and most loved bankers of his era. During his wartime adventures he had become an international character with a huge circle of friends throughout the world. His charm and vivacity brought many new introductions to the bank, though not all of them could be described as good financial risks. They were sifted, however, by Olaf whose wise decisions were intuitive and, ultimately, his alone. Jack, the youngest of the three, was known in the bank as the 'human face' of the family. He always had a cheery grin and friendly glint in his eyes and the staff found him far more approachable than Olaf or Sir Charles. He was an active, working director involved in the bank's daily affairs, fulfilling the role of 'housekeeper' and keeping it on steady lines through a mastery of detail. He was the anchor man. Together the three men formed a striking balance, a range of ability and age, yet bound by the common strength of the Hambro name.

In the early post-war period the British economy was suffering from

Three chairmen of Hambros Bank. From left to right: Jack, Sir Charles and Olaf Hambro on their way to the wedding of Patsie Hambro, second daughter of Major-General Sir Percy Hambro, on 1 March 1938. Hambro Family Archives.

a severe imbalance of payments. Heavy wartime borrowing and a huge cut in British exports had created a desperate situation which needed an immediate remedy. The great loan which Keynes managed to arrange with the United States was a partial answer aimed to tide the country over the difficult period of peacetime adjustment but, in addition, the government and the Bank of England both emphasized the necessity of increased exports which would earn valuable dollars for Britain.

Olaf was keen to promote the export drive, recognizing it as a new opportunity for business. He chose his son Jocelyn, the youngest Hambro in Bishopsgate, to visit the American West and develop a market

Jocelyn Hambro, his wife Silvia and their three sons Rupert (standing), Richard (on the left) and James (on the right). The photograph was taken in the grounds of Coopersale House in 1961. Eleven years later Silvia died, aged only fifty-two. Hambro Family Archives.

for British goods. Jocelyn and his wife Silvia had just returned from New York where Jocelyn had been training with Brown Brothers Harriman & Co., the oldest private bank in the United States. The experience helped him become accustomed to American business and banking techniques but, in reality, it was a far cry from his export ventures in Chicago, Dallas and San Francisco which soon proved raw country compared with sophisticated New York.

First Jocelyn had to find suitable British goods to sell, and after searching the Midlands and north he decided upon motorcycles and pottery. Then, with an authorization of $10,000 from the Bank of England and export finance from Hambros Bank, he established a subsidiary in New Orleans, called the Hambro Trading Corporation of America Incorporated. It was thought that the unexploited Mid-west would provide a potentially greater market for British goods than the eastern seaboard where the names of British manufacturers were already well known. For a while, the sales of motorcycles were good, but when the American automobile industry returned to its usual peacetime working they quickly went out of favour.

Jocelyn decided to sell cars instead and, realizing that the idea of a sports car had never occurred to anyone in America, he put his faith in the small MG and began to introduce it to the cowboy towns of Texas. To gain publicity, he gave the Mayor of Dallas a grand tour through the streets in one of his cars, but afterwards the Mayor likened it to the first cousin of a malted milk machine! Initial bewilderment was only one of

Jocelyn Hambro purchased Coopersale House, Essex, in 1946. On the adjacent farm he established a very successful herd of pedigree Friesians and then a herd of pedigree Jerseys. He sold Coopersale in 1972 and moved to Redenham Park in Hampshire, adjoining the well-known Redenham Stud where he bred racehorses. Painting by Julian Barrow. Hambro Family Archives.

Jocelyn's problems – much more serious was the organization of the sales network. MGS would have been far easier to sell through a system which had been established already, but as the American car manufacturers would not allow their distributors to handle imported cars Jocelyn had to find his own team. In Dallas he chose the local jukebox salesman; in California his distributor was the Philco radio dealer. There were a few setbacks, but fortunately the new image of the sports car caught on quickly and from the early beginnings in 1948, when only six were sold, the numbers rapidly increased to an annual total of 33,000 by 1958. In the year ending 31 March 1959 the subsidiary earned $53,000,000 through its car sales alone. Dollars had certainly been earned for Britain as well as profits for the bank.

Jocelyn's adventures with kippers and honey were not so successful! In 1950 he established the Hambro House of Design on East 54th Street, New York, to sell traditional British and Scandinavian items such as glassware, linen, furniture and food. The goods were to be of luxury quality, aimed at wealthy customers. Scottish kippers were one of his special lines and he advertized them under the name 'Queen of Scots', denoting a large succulent fish fit only for the best table. Large crateloads arrived at the docks, but the 'Queen of Scots' turned out to be small and insignificant, and they proved impossible to sell to the class of customer which Jocelyn had envisaged. The smell of rotting fish was an uncomfortable reminder in the weeks that followed. Purchases of honey were another disaster. Hundreds of pots were kept in a refrigerated warehouse where unexpectedly the electricity supply was cut off. In high summer temperatures the honey fermented and the pots exploded, so that when the mess was discovered the ceiling and floor were found coated with the glutinous stuff. It had to be scraped off at great cost and the whole lot was dumped. Further trouble arose with several other types of goods and in 1956, after a significant loss, the bank decided to close its high-class shop. By then the car sales were booming and the directors were only too happy to concentrate their efforts on the British Motor Corporation franchise. The subsidiary trading company changed its name to the Hambro Automobile Corporation, which then employed a staff of 500 people.

Another unusual and successful diversification of the Bank's activities immediately after the war was the development of the diamond trade. Some banking experience had already been gained during the early 1940s but, from 1945 onwards, Olaf's attitude became one of aggressive expansion. In April that year, Hambros Bank purchased a 50 per cent share in I. Hennig & Co., a diamond broking operation run by George Prins who was regarded as one of the world's most knowledgeable people in the rough diamond business. Only a month later, in May 1945, the bank bought a substantial share in the Diamond Development Company Ltd which had been formed in 1934 to classify diamonds, on behalf of outside producers, before they were sold to the central selling organization which was run by De Beers. Then, in May 1946, the bank paid £1,000,000 for a 100 per cent holding in Diamond Realizations Limited and thus obtained a crucial entry to the annual sights held at the Diamond Trading Company (DTC) in Charterhouse Street where sales of the world's diamonds take place.

Within a year of peace, Olaf had ventured into the brokerage, classification and trading of diamonds on a large scale. Not only was he able to draw on the expertise of George Prins but also he gained Sir Ernest Oppenheimer, the Chairman of De Beers, as a non-executive director on the board of Hambros Bank. Sir Ernest, then aged sixty-five, was an experienced financier used to large-scale operations and, furthermore, had a brilliant grasp of the diamond market. Appointed in 1946, he remained a director until his death in 1958.

Meanwhile, Hambros Bank's diamond banking service, which had been established in the early 1940s, continued to prosper. The diamond department occupied two rooms on the third floor of 41 Bishopsgate. Ralph Sheffield, a former naval officer, now secretary of Hambros Bank, remembers being posted there when he returned to the bank after the war. Several times a month he and another clerk were sent to the DTC in Charterhouse Street, two miles from Bishopsgate, where they collected parcels of diamonds worth up to £50,000 which the bank's customers offered as collateral against the credit finance which they received. There were no armoured cars for protection, taxis were not allowed, and the risky return journey from the DTC to the bank was made by bus. Sheffield often used to carry the parcel of diamonds in his pocket, but if the package was especially large he would wrap it up in newspaper and hold it under his arm like a packet of fish and chips. A dirty raincoat and a hat pulled well down would complete the disguise! Fortunately, every journey was made without loss or mishap.

Besides being inconvenient and risky, the operation grew too big for the existing accommodation in Bishopsgate and in 1946 a branch of the bank was opened in Audrey House close to the DTC. Then in 1957, a new and more spacious Holborn branch was opened nearby at 1 Charterhouse Street. Two main services were given; firstly, large credits were offered to the DTC clients and, secondly, overdrafts or rollover facilities were offered to the small merchants either on a yearly basis or against a particular transaction. Total trustworthiness was an essential ingredient throughout the trade, and the small, clannish world of

From left to right: King George VI, HRH *Princess Elizabeth, Queen Mary,* HRH *Princess Margaret, the Queen, and the bridal couple: Jean Hambro (Angus' fourth daughter) and the Hon. Andrew Elphinstone (the Queen's nephew) on the occasion of their wedding, 29 May 1946. Early in 1945, Jean had been appointed as a lady-in-waiting to* HRH *Princess Elizabeth and in one of the lifts at Buckingham Palace Jean first met her future husband. As lady-in-waiting, she helped with correspondence and the organization of official functions; attended the wedding of Princess Elizabeth; accompanied her on a tour of Canada and attended her at the coronation.* Hambro Family Archives.

Hatton Garden appealed to Olaf's shy but shrewd character. Hambros Bank was unique among the London merchant banks in its diamond specialization and it soon became referred to as the Diamond Bank.

Although now an old man and much less concerned with banking details, Olaf continued to rule with an iron will, strongly supported by Sir Charles, Jack and Jocelyn, until his death in 1961. Two other family recruits also became managing directors. First, Jack Woodroffe was appointed in 1955, having replaced his father-in-law, Angus Hambro, as a non-executive director the previous year. Before joining the bank he had been a director with his family's trading company, Gordon Woodroffe Ltd, which had given him a valuable knowledge of Hong Kong, India and North Africa.

The second appointment came in 1957 through the retirement of

Gerard d'Abo, the former general manager of the British Bank of Northern Commerce, who had served Hambros Bank for thirty-five years. He was replaced by Charlie Hambro, the present chairman of the bank, who was then twenty-seven. As a boy, Charlie had been evacuated for most of the war years, first in Stockholm with the Wallenberg family and then for three years with the Morgans in New York. On his return to England in 1943 he went to Eton, where he quickly lost his American accent and was chosen for the cricket XI. After Eton he joined the Coldstream Guards. He entered Hambros Bank in 1952 and was promptly sent to banks in Stockholm and Oslo for several months. On his return he gained experience in various banking departments of Hambros Bank, and in 1955 went to New York to work for the Empire Trust Company, an American investment bank with which Hambros Bank at that time had close relations.

By the late 1950s the only non-family member among the six managing directors was Harry Sporborg, the successful City solicitor who had worked under Sir Charles in the MEW and SOE. He was appointed to the board in 1951, replacing A. John Hugh Smith who retired, aged seventy. The four new post-war recruits – Jocelyn, Jack Woodroffe, Charlie and Harry Sporborg – all injected a wider, more dynamic approach to merchant banking which laid the foundations for much faster growth during the course of the next decade.

Charlie Hambro is the present chairman of Hambros Bank. His mother died when he was a baby and he spent much of World War II in Sweden and the United States. He returned to England in 1943 and went to Eton, where he played for the school cricket eleven. Hambro Family Archives.

Meanwhile a notable change had taken place in the middle hierarchy. In 1953 Mr Percy Plucknett, who had been the general manager since the mid-1920s, retired. With no obvious successor, a team of five managers was appointed consisting of Mr Anton Martens, Mr Roy Clark, Mr Frank Stone, Mr Arthur Purton and Mr Fred Pennington. With Thomas Honniball, secretary to the bank for many years who had an exceptional knowledge of the law of banking, they represented a powerful and professional group of men jointly responsible for the daily affairs of the bank's various departments. Under their control was a rapidly expanding staff, increasing from approximately 350 in 1955, to 400 in 1961, to 500 in 1965. Their numbers grew as the pace of the bank's activities quickened.

One of the most quickly expanding areas of the bank was the foreign exchange department. During the war the market had been closed, but by 1953 it had re-opened for both forward and arbitrage dealings. Here was a chance for Sir Charles to re-establish the department which had flourished so well in the turbulent currency period of the 1930s. However, exchange rates were far more stable during the 1950s and most of the dealing profits came from commissions on customer business. Therefore the directors realized that they would have to tap new sources of foreign exchange business if they wanted to increase the income.

An opportune occasion arose in 1957, when the partners of one of London's four bullion-dealing firms, Messrs Mocatta & Goldsmid, decided that they would be more successful if they were closely attached to a bank. Jocelyn was a friend of Sir Henry d'Avigdor-Goldsmid, and so Hambros Bank was an obvious choice. But instead of the tenuous link which had been envisaged at first, the bank acquired the partnership and converted it into a limited liability company as a wholly owned subsidiary. The main benefit to the bank was the ability to deal in much larger amounts of foreign exchange business; hedging against movements in the prices of gold and silver and covering forward transactions. Edward ('Jock') Mocatta was appointed senior director of Mocatta & Goldsmid Limited and became a permanent figure in the bank. Of medium height and thick-set build, he had the specialized mind of a dealer, easily capable of dealing with a buyer on one telephone and a seller on another, taking only seconds to calculate the prices. He had the natural flair of a born trader and brought exceptional expertise to the bank's foreign exchange desk.

The bank's managing directors knew little about the bullion market and so Jock Mocatta was the bank representative at the ritual fixing of the gold price which took place at Rothschilds Bank in St Swithin's

Sir Charles Hambro, Chairman of the Anglo-Danish Society in London 1949–54, receiving the Duke and Duchess of Gloucester at the Dorchester Hotel on 21 April 1950, in commemoration of the Society's twenty-fifth anniversary. Sir Charles' son, Charlie, was vice-chairman from 1967 until 1971 when Rupert Hambro became his successor. Nordisk Pressfoto, Copenhagen.

Lane at 10.30 am each day. A similar ceremony occurred on the second floor of 41 Bishopsgate, where representatives from the bullion companies came to Hambros Bank to fix the silver price. Meanwhile all the gold and silver bars which the bank had acquired through its subsidiary remained in their familiar stacks in the vaults of the company's premises in Throgmorton Avenue. However on one exceptional occasion a considerable amount was secretly transferred to the safe at 41 Bishopsgate. Only a handful of people knew that a glittering pyramid of gold, silver and platinum bars was being built, three feet high and worth precisely one million pounds, as a special curiosity for Queen Elizabeth II to see when she came to the bank for lunch on 28 March 1961.

The New Issues Department was also growing, but its work revolved around domestic issues almost entirely as foreign ones were forbidden for many years after the war. Formerly the problems of the market had been resolved by the Accepting Houses Committee but Olaf was determined to establish a separate body and so, in 1945, fifty invitations were sent out to various London issuing houses to join the new Issuing Houses Association. Jack Hambro was the bank's representative, co-opted on to its committee since he was the main instigator of much of the bank's issue business, applying his meticulous brain to the tedious detail of the prospectuses. London Assurance, Norway Shipping, Taylor Woodrow and the *News of the World* were all examples of the bank's post-war clients, while one of the companies which the depart-ment had been involved with in the 1930s, the Consett Iron Co. Limited, now made a reappearance.

The Consett denationalization issue was a particularly notable one which might have taken a less organized team three months, but it took Jack three weeks. Just before Christmas 1955 the issue opened and 200,000 applications were received. They filled two rooms up to the ceiling. 'Compulsory volunteers' were drafted from other departments and then from outside the bank, so that on the first Thursday a total of 600 people were involved. Many worked through the night, then a new contingent took over, and so on throughout Friday and Saturday until on Sunday at 3.30 pm when finally the allotment letters were posted. The colossal exercise was executed smoothly under Jack's close scrutiny. He was a hard taskmaster, but he drove himself even harder and worked thirty-six hours non-stop during part of that weekend. The deadline was reached and on the Monday morning the new shares could be traded on the Stock Exchange.

The bank's liaison with industry had been conceived in the 1930s but, even after the war, the corporate finance side of industrial banking was still regarded as unknown territory by many of the more senior merchant bankers while it remained an unexplored area to the younger ones. From 1951 onwards the bank's subsidiary called Bentworth Trust Limited, which had offices further down Bishopsgate, became more involved in this area of banking, doing all those things which, at that stage, the blue-blooded bankers would not deign to touch.

Public flotations became its speciality, dealing in small industrial issues of less than £100,000 where profit margins were considered too small for the larger banks. Gradually the Trust built up a good reputa-tion and larger issues followed. Working with small companies, mean-while, had the advantage that there were always further developments

---

Jack Hambro became the fifth Chairman of Hambros Bank in 1963, and is here photo-graphed sitting at the chairman's desk in 41 Bishopsgate. He was appointed a part-time member of the National Coal Board in 1949, and at one time was a director of twenty-four companies, including five investment trusts, and treasurer of the Middlesex Hospital. He was a keen skier even in his fifties, and a notable rose grower at The Hyde in Bedfordshire. Hambros Bank Archives.

to follow with later mergers, takeovers or rights issues so that advising, arranging and negotiating terms became normal business. By the mid- to late-1950s the takeover and merger business was gathering momentum and, regardless of previous attitudes, the bankers in the main office at 41 Bishopsgate were now being forced on to the scene. It was, after all, just part of their continuing service to industrial clients.

Occasionally this field of banking became the scene of fierce battles reminiscent of Sir Everard's fight with Rothschilds over the huge Italian loan of the early 1880s. In the winter of 1958–9 the City held its breath while Hambros Bank and Lazard Bros & Co. pitted their strength against S. G. Warburg & Co., J. Henry Schroder and Helbert Wagg. The pawn in the conflict was the British Aluminium Company.

For many years Olaf Hambro had acted as merchant banker for the British Aluminium Co. In 1957, however, its managing director, Geoffrey Cunliffe, son of Lord Cunliffe who had been Governor of the Bank of England during World War I, decided to take his business to Lazard Bros & Co. where one of the directors was a personal friend. When Cunliffe told Olaf of his proposal the old merchant banker felt rebuked and shocked but as he was anxious not to lose the business altogether he suggested a compromise. He proposed that his bank would act jointly with Lazard Bros & Co.; a solution to which Cunliffe readily agreed.

Although a cheerful figure, Cunliffe could be very difficult and, on one particular occasion, he offended Siegmund Warburg who was Chairman of S. G. Warburg & Co., merchant bankers in Gresham Street. Warburg was a powerful newcomer to the City, envied by many of the old guard. Born in 1902, he originated from a Jewish banking family in Hamburg, and when in 1925 he visited London as a young man he trained with N. M. Rothschild & Sons. Escaping from Nazi Germany in the 1930s he settled in London, and in 1946 established his own bank. He was a scholarly man with a modern, aggressive approach to business, and he quickly built up a team of single-minded, professional banking experts. In the course of a single decade and without the benefit of personal wealth or social prestige he had established a small but active business and, in 1957, he merged successfully with Seligman Bros, one of the older merchant banks which had a good acceptance credit business. As a result he gained access to the Accepting Houses Committee which represented the inner group of sixteen merchant banks. From then onwards the growth of his company was remarkable.

Cunliffe's lack of tact proved ominous. Warburg's attention focused on British Aluminium, which he regarded as a sleepy industrial concern which ought to be under the ownership of a far more dynamic institution. His insight into its business was right as, indeed, it was ripe for a takeover. The company shares had been trading at only 45 shillings, much lower than previous levels, and while current earnings were relatively small, potential profits were considerable. It needed capital to expand and, with this idea in mind, Warburg managed to interest an American aluminium giant, Reynolds Metals Company of Virginia, which shortly afterwards entered into partnership arrangements with Tube Investments. This was a large British industrial company which had its own aluminium interests and was jointly represented by the merchant bankers, J. Henry Schroder and Helbert Wagg. Warburg had masterminded a formidable partnership which was capable of raising vast amounts of money. It was easily large enough to gobble up British Aluminium. Using nominees, he began secretly to buy shares on the Stock Exchange for the Reynolds-Tube Investments (R-TI) partnership and stealthily managed to build up a significant holding.

Cunliffe soon realized that someone was buying British Aluminium shares on the Stock Exchange and sought the aid of his merchant bankers, Hambros and Lazards. They advised that the authorized ordinary share capital of the company should be increased from £9,000,000 to £13,500,000, but they emphasized that the additional £4,500,000 should remain, at present, unissued. The shareholders sanctioned the increase in May 1958. It represented one third of the capital and so gave Cunliffe his required safety valve. As yet unissued, the shares could not be purchased on the open market, so no one could obtain control of them without the board's express consent. Moreover, the directors alone had the full right of disposal, since once the sanction had been obtained the shareholders had no further legal power.

By October 1958 the R-TI partnership had purchased 10 per cent of the British Aluminium shares. The smouldering conflict now came out in the open. On 3 November Sir Ivan Stedeford, Chairman of Tube Investments, approached British Aluminium and made it clear that his company wanted an association. But the idea was abhorrent to Cunliffe who wanted nothing to do with Warburg's clever scheme. He nonchalantly cast aside Sir Ivan's suggestion by saying that he was already negotiating with another group. It was a shrewd tactical move since, unknown to the R-TI partnership, the £4,500,000 unissued shares had been offered to the Aluminium Company of America (Alcoa) which was a great rival of the Reynolds' empire. Both Lord Portal, Chairman of British Aluminium, and Cunliffe had enjoyed a warm relationship with the directors of Alcoa for many years. Now the friendship was to be put on a more formal basis with three of their directors joining the

British Aluminium Board. Without delay Lord Portal flew to North
America to settle the terms of the proposed agreement.

Sir Ivan and Warburg, though rebuffed, were not beaten and were
determined to fight back. They began to formulate a specific offer and
on 24 November Sir Ivan disclosed his terms. The R-TI partnership
would give the equivalent of 78 shillings per share, cash, and one Tube
Investment share, worth 78 shillings, for every two of the 9,000,000
ordinary British Aluminium shares, providing that there was no
change in the existing capital structure. Four days later Cunliffe was
able to declare the offer completely unacceptable on the grounds that
the Alcoa agreement had already been signed, subject only to Treasury
consent. Since the agreement would automatically alter the capital
structure, any negotiations with the partnership would be fruitless.

Both Sir Ivan and Warburg must have been dumbfounded by the
outright rejection of their terms which they realized had never been put
formally before the British Aluminium shareholders. They were
determined that their generous offer should be made known and, on the
same day that they received Cunliffe's refusal, they called a press
conference at which the details were made public. It was an unusual
method of attack but it successfully struck at one of the weakest points
of the Alcoa agreement – that it had been arranged without any
reference to the shareholders. Legally the directors of British
Aluminium had been quite within their rights, but many took the view
that such a major decision affecting the structure of the company
should have been approved by those who had put their money at risk.
Sir Ivan was quick to point out, too, that they should also have had the
opportunity to consider the R-TI offer. That weekend, the last in
November, the City and its personalities loomed large in bold news-
print and for the first time Hambros and Lazards began to face public
scrutiny. Over the next six weeks news coverage intensified as public
opinion was swayed first one way and then the other, courted by both
sides of the conflict.

Even then, victory appeared to be within the grasp of Hambros,
Lazards and Cunliffe, but Treasury consent still had to be given. It was
widely acknowledged that British industry was short of investment
finance but there was a strong fear of American control. The Alcoa
agreement would give 33 per cent of the shares to an American company, whereas the R-TI offer would give 49 per cent. However, in the
case of the latter offer, the other 51 per cent would be fixed automatically in British hands, while the Alcoa deal would not necessarily be so
decisive and in the future its shareholding might be increased considerably. Press reports highlighted the argument and for a long while the

Treasury delayed its answer. Eventually, on 4 December, it announced its decision: the shareholders should decide for themselves.

Lord Portal and Cunliffe were trapped by the Treasury's proposal. A meeting of the shareholders would be suicidal, as the R-TI offer of 78 shillings per share or equivalent was sure to look more attractive to the shareholder, in the short term, compared to the Alcoa agreement by which only 60 shillings would be subscribed to their company for each of the unissued shares. They were left with no choice but to drop the deal and search for an alternative solution. Quickly they decided upon new tactics. Future backing would have to be British and the battle would have to be fought in the City where Hambros and Lazards had a joint record of business stretching over 200 years. Their appeal would go to the old guard to keep the 'British' in British Aluminium and thus resist American domination. Underlying the warcry was the attempt to squash the successful upstart Warburg. Before long the whole City was rent apart.

The peaceful spirit of Christmas went unnoticed in those dark wintry days as Sir Charles, Jack and Harry Sporborg walked the City streets drumming up the support of their friends in other banks and finance houses. Together with Lazards, they drew around them a large group containing some of their oldest associates. Morgan Grenfell & Co. and Brown Shipley and Co. were both included, and so was Samuel Montagu, the merchant bank of which Evy Hambro had just been made a director. Another ally was Robert Fleming & Co., only established in 1909 but specializing in investment management. Fourteen banks and financial institutions were named; others offered their support but dared not reveal themselves openly. By 31 December they had formed a consortium and were ready to declare their hand.

They pledged £7,000,000, money which would be used privately to buy British Aluminium shares at 82 shillings each. Their price was 4 shillings above the R-TI offer, although it was only a partial bid. They would pay cash for half a shareholder's holding but the other half was to remain frozen until 31 March 1959. City opinion including banks, finance houses and the institutions seemed to favour them, not solely for financial reasons but out of a sense of loyalty as well. By the end of the year Hambros and Lazards were convinced that they had the silent backing of the holders of 2,000,000 shares, all of whom had promised that they would not sell to the R-TI partnership. The grand alliance had been formed and the situation retrieved. The new year would herald their victory.

The consortium had not reckoned with the open defiance which Warburg was about to show. On 1 January 1959 he took the battle on to the Stock Exchange and, with the £300,000,000 worth of assets which the R-TI partnership represented, he began to flaunt his funds and tempt the institutional shareholders to sell at a large profit. He knew that Hambros and Lazards could not match the same amount of money and he realized full well that the pension fund managers and the assurance company managers could not afford to miss the opportunity of selling all their shares at over £4 each. He would raise the market price above the consortium's offer and thereby erode their so-called backing.

On that Thursday morning the price of British Aluminium shares soon reached 84 shillings and 500,000 units were sold on the Stock Exchange. They were immediately taken up by the R-TI partnership; the consortium made no attempt to buy – its funds being strictly for private sales under the terms of its offer. The next day bidding opened at 85 shillings and it was clear, by now, that some of the institutional holders had sold. The headline of the leading article in the *Financial Times* read 'Huge Dealings in British Aluminium Stock'. It sounded the death knell of the consortium, and with each day that followed their mood grew more despondent until on 6 January it became almost certain that they had lost the battle. They had no more weapons to use. Wednesday 7 January proved to be the day of final surrender. Crushed and disappointed, Hambros and Lazards publicly admitted defeat.

For the last six weeks the story of the takeover battle had dominated the front page of the *Financial Times* and had appeared frequently in other newspapers too. Olaf had been incensed with their disapproving attitude and he made his bitterness apparent in a letter which was published in *The Times* on 12 January 1959. He pointed out that the consortium had enjoyed the support of nearly every finance house in the City: 'This being so it is very unclear why the majority of the City Editors of the Press seemed to be against City opinion and openly in favour of the takeover bid.' Even after defeat, Olaf had likened his own opinion, together with the consortium's, to that of the whole City and he was not allowed to forget his unfortunate mistake. The press did not take kindly to his seemingly arrogant assumption, and published several letters which openly attacked his attitude.

Olaf had lost the contest but he had learnt at least one important lesson. He took stock of the past few weeks' happenings and finally came to recognize the immense power of the press and the distinct advantage of having them on his own side. Without further delay he approved the appointment of a public relations firm which would offer professional advice to the bank in all its dealings with the city editors. Thus Hambros became one of the first merchant banks in London to adopt this modern attitude. The old ways of warfare had changed. In the future, new tactics and weapons were necessary.

The British Aluminium affair proved to be only a temporary setback for the bank's industrial finance group, and before long a team of technical experts had been built up and a separate department established called the Financial Advisory Department. Sir Charles was keen to promote the business and announced at the Annual General Meeting held on 14 June 1963:

> The scope of Merchant Banking is very wide and can, and should, cover all aspects of finance . . . flexibility . . . is the lifeblood of our business. We pride ourselves on being able to supply all kinds of money and are very keen that anyone in industry should feel he can come to us at any time with any problem relating to the development of financing of his business whether in sterling or dollars.

By the late 1960s Hambros Bank could pride itself that it was one of the most aggressive of all the London merchant banks in this sphere of its operations.

Sir Charles' reference to dollar finance provides an important clue to a dramatic new phenomenon which was beginning to change the pace of merchant banking during the early 1960s. The development was associated with the growth in the Eurodollar market which was centred on Europe, and particularly on the London banks. It attracted dollar deposits particularly from the state banks in eastern Europe, which preferred to keep their dollars in London and Paris rather than risk having them blocked in New York. It also drew deposits from foreign subsidiaries of giant American companies which found they could earn higher interest rates by lending to the European banks than to those in the United States. Soon Eurodollars came to refer to any dollar deposits held for the account of a non-resident of the United States.

Shortage of sterling in the 1957 crisis gave an added boost to the movement when the British banks substituted dollars for sterling in their efforts to finance world trade. The shipping department of Hambros Bank found that it was losing customers because of the restrictive limits on its sterling loans. Otto Norland, then a young Norwegian official in the department, remembers trying to persuade Olaf that Eurodollars were the answer to their problems. With the threat of lost business, Olaf reluctantly agreed and the first Eurodollar deposit, at fixed interest for five years, was taken on to the bank's books and immediately lent to the Norwegian shipping industry.

The older bankers were extremely suspicious of the Eurodollar deposits, which in many cases were not commercial deposits at all, simply borrowings from the market. A sudden change in the policy of

Jocelyn Hambro's main interest in racing dates from 1950 when he registered his colours and put his first horse, Courier, in training with F. Armstrong at Newmarket. In 1959 he became a member of the Jockey Club of which he became a steward in 1976. In 1971 he purchased Redenham Stud in Hampshire but five years later he moved his breeding interests to the Waverton Stud in Gloucestershire where he is now building a new country home. His second wife, Elizabeth, widow of the sixth Duke of Roxburgh, also shares his enthusiasm for horses as do his three sons, who each have their own racing interests. Photograph taken at Newmarket in 1968. Berlingske Tidende, Copenhagen.

central banks or a reversal in the US balance of payments deficit might make the pool dry up and then they would have no easy accessibility to dollars with which to repay their borrowings. Moreover, there would be no lender of last resort, which function, of course, had always been fulfilled by the Bank of England in respect of sterling. As a result, both Jack Hambro and Jack Woodroffe thought that they ought to strengthen their banking ties in America, and in 1961 Hambros Bank entered into a limited partnership with Laidlaw & Co., one of only two private banks in the United States which maintained membership of the New York Stock Exchange. This gave them a fully-fledged banking business on the other side of the Atlantic. Besides providing access to dollars within America, it opened up many new areas of activity, including a very successful foreign exchange operation in New York, for example.

By 1962 the size of the bank's Eurodollar deposits were much more substantial, and Sir Charles showed them separately on the published balance sheet. He was still convinced, however, that they were a temporary phenomenon. In March that year deposit accounts in foreign currencies reached the equivalent of £28,000,000, whilst the year before the figure had been only £9,000,000. By March 1963 they had grown to £37,000,000, representing 22 per cent of the balance sheet and as much as 47 per cent of the sterling deposits. Significantly, after 1964 the figures were no longer shown separately since they were then considered as a permanent feature of the accounts. Meanwhile, the ability to attract these huge deposits directly increased the bank's lending power and so enabled it to grant large foreign currency loans, then on a renewable short-term basis, to shipping companies and industrial customers.

While Jack Hambro and Sir Charles were still wary of these Euro-dollar deposits the younger bankers, especially Jocelyn and Charlie, were keen to explore the new avenues of business which now lay open. One area which attracted them more than the others was the international loan market. For many of the post-war years, sterling issues for foreign governments and companies had been virtually forbidden by the Bank of England, and so Hambros Bank had been forced to give up those specialist activities which it had executed with such enormous skill in the days of Carl Joachim and Sir Everard. In the early 1960s, however, the window opened for a very short period and Hambros Bank was asked to issue sterling loans for Iceland in 1962 and Denmark in 1964. Nevertheless, it was the Eurodollar market which provided the main opportunity for the bank to re-establish its reputation as an issuing house.

In January 1963, Hambros Bank and one other London bank joined a syndicate of European banks which undertook a private placement loan for the Norges Kommunalbank. This was the first foreign currency loan in which the Hambros had ever partaken, and marked the beginning of a frenzied period of activity. Between March 1964 and March 1965 issues totalling $190,000,000 were arranged by the bank, including a $30,000,000 issue for the Kingdom of Norway, one of the bank's traditional customers which had first approached Joseph Hambro in Copenhagen over 140 years previously. Old links had not been forgotten. Although the early Eurodollar loans in 1963 and 1964 had relied on European investors almost entirely, the emphasis began to change, and by 1965 the bank was trying to place a greater percentage of the bonds with British institutions. This meant that it would not have to rely so much on foreign banks as co-managers, and moreover it would gain a greater control of the issue. Between 1963 and 1966 only three British banks pioneered and monopolized this new market. Besides Hambros Bank there was the old rival N. M. Rothschild & Sons and the new rival, S. G. Warburg & Co.

However active the bank had become in all these other areas, the acceptance business remained undeniably its primary function. In 1955 its total acceptances outstanding stood at £21,000,000; by 1960 the figure had reached £27,000,000 and by 1965 it had risen to £45,000,000. In the late 1950s curtailment of trade and restrictions on foreign credit led to a downturn in the volume of London acceptances, but the bank was left unscathed by the general trend and actively went out into the market to create new business. It began its Scandinavian Service which explained to medium-sized and small firms, particularly in the Midlands and north, that traded with Scandinavian companies how to make fuller use of trade finance. The exercise was a great success and introduced a large amount of new business to the bank. Whilst other accepting houses found their acceptance figures falling, Hambros Bank increased its total volume and commanded a growing proportion of the London market. By 1960 it was at the top of the accepting houses league, a position which it still retains today.

In 1965 Hambros Bank was in an extremely powerful position. In its traditional field of banking, the acceptance business, it was the strongest. In the new Eurodollar market it had already built up a very good reputation and had once again established its name as one of the leading merchant banks in the issue of foreign loans; it had a monopoly in the diamond trade and was called the Diamond Bank; it controlled one of the four London bullion firms; its American banking business, property, leasing and investment trust operations were all beginning to

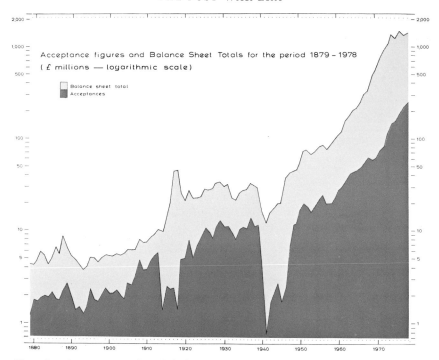

2,000
1,000
500

Acceptance figures and Balance Sheet Totals for the period 1879 – 1978
(£ millions — logarithmic scale)

☐ Balance sheet total
■ Acceptances

100
50

10
5

1

1880   1890   1900   1910   1920   1930   1940   1950   1960   1970

Financing the movement of goods in international trade was the primary business of the bank and, apart from the duration of the two World Wars, the acceptance figures always accounted for a considerable proportion of the balance sheet. Hambros Bank Archives.

grow – its deposits were second only to one other London merchant bank and increasing much faster; its declared profits were higher than any other merchant bank and had been for the last four years. The results showed clearly on the balance sheet totals. Over the past ten years they had grown from £81,000,000 in 1955 to £215,000,000 by 1965. During the last half of the 1950s the annual growth rate had been 5 per cent. During the first half of the 1960s it was 20 per cent. Even so, the present directors of Hambros Bank consider the period from 1965 onwards as the time of real expansion.

22 The Bank Today

Although the early 1960s were a time of remarkable growth, it was also a period of tragedy for the family. Olaf's great era ended on 25 April 1961, when he died at the age of seventy-five. He had given over fifty years' service to the bank and been chairman for nearly thirty years. He had succeeded his brother during the crisis of the 1932 depression and had continued to steer the bank through the difficult war years, until by 1960 it was on the brink of unprecedented growth. He had governed with vision and integrity and, although a reclusive man, had won the affection of all his employees. Upon his death everyone recognized that the old era had passed, but there was no doubt about who would succeed him.

Naturally, Sir Charles, who commanded immense respect from the City, filled the gap. Within a year, however, he too was desperately ill. His cancer had returned and he died on 28 August 1963. A memorial service was held for him in St Paul's, and such was his renown that the great City cathedral was packed to capacity. Sir Charles had been a director of the Court of the Bank of England for thirty-five years, and befitting his notable contribution Lord Cromer, then the Governor of the Bank, was asked to read the lesson. Although the family and the bank had expected Sir Charles' death for some while, there was a distinct feeling of emptiness at 41 Bishopsgate for many months afterwards. People were aware that one of the bank's most remarkable personalities had been lost.

Two chairmen died within two years, yet the family could still produce another experienced and successful banker to replace Sir Charles. Thus Jack Hambro became the fifth chairman of the bank. At fifty-nine he seemed a much younger man than his predecessors, and his appointment signalled a period which would bring many years of continuous leadership. But fate cast its hand a third time, and on 4 December 1965 Jack died of a heart attack whilst pheasant shooting in Hertfordshire. The man who was so well loved by his employees for his modesty, understanding and humour was snatched away before he even had a chance to exert his full influence. The outstanding combination of Olaf, Sir Charles and Jack had come to an abrupt end, and the death of three chairmen in five years left the entire bank stunned.

438

Jocelyn Hambro was Chairman of Hambros Bank from 1965 until 1972 and has been Chairman of Hambros Ltd, the quoted parent company, since it was established in 1970. He was Chairman of Hambro Life from 1971 to 1978 when he became Chairman of Phoenix Assurance. He has given strong support to British cancer charities, his special involvement being with the Businessman of the Year Award. Photograph taken in 1970. Hambros Bank Archives.

One of the family's traditional strengths, however, has been its capacity to produce able bankers. Many other family concerns have fallen after two or three generations, but Sir Charles and Jack were both fifth generation bankers and still there was another cousin to take over. In December 1965 the chair reverted to Olaf's side of the family and at the age of forty-six Jocelyn Hambro became the sixth chairman of Hambros Bank, with Charlie, who was a sixth generation banker and a seventh generation Hambro, then aged thirty-five, as the deputy chairman. This heralded the beginning of a modern era when the emphasis was on youth, flair and flexibility. Aggressive and adventure-some in their approach, none of the seven managing directors had ever worked in the bank before the Second World War. Besides Jocelyn, Charlie, Harry Sporborg and Jack Woodroffe there were three new additions, including John Clay – son of Sir Henry Clay who had been an advisor to the Bank of England and a close associate of Sir Charles – who was appointed managing director in 1962. There were soon several other directors, all men in their early or mid-thirties. The team which emerged provided a startling contrast to the middle-aged management of the previous decade.

The recent tragedies had left the family representation in the bank severely depleted but, as always, young members continued to be welcomed, tried and tested so that they could also make their contribution to its strength. Andrew Gibson-Watt had joined in 1953 after his

Charlie Hambro became the seventh Chairman of Hambros Bank in 1972. He is also Chairman of the Royal National Pension Fund for Nurses which his great-grandfather, Sir Everard, helped to establish in the late 1880s; and deputy chairman of Guardian Royal Exchange Assurance. He enjoys many sports including shooting, flying and racing, and runs an arable farm in Gloucestershire. Photograph taken in 1975. Hambros Bank Archives.

marriage to Charlie's sister, Pamela Hambro. In 1960 he was appointed secretary to the bank and in 1968 he became a director. Peter Hill-Wood, grandson of Violet Hambro who was Olaf's only sister, joined the bank in 1961 and became a director in 1968. He was appointed executive director of the Investment Management Division in 1973. Simon Woodroffe, the son of Jack Woodroffe and the grandson of Angus Hambro, entered the bank in 1962, followed by Jocelyn's three sons, Rupert, Richard and James, who began their careers in 1964, 1966 and 1969 respectively.

Rupert Hambro was appointed a director in 1969, executive director of the International Division in 1974, and of the International Marketing Division in 1979. Within this Division are his two brothers: Richard, who has been executive director of Hambro America Inc. in New York since 1976 and a director of the bank from 1978; and James, who was appointed a director of the bank in 1979. Hamish Leslie Melville, meanwhile, the eldest of Sir Charles' grandsons, joined the bank in 1968 and was appointed a director in 1975. Four years later he became executive director of the International Banking and Issues Division. The most recent family recruit is Andrew Martin Smith, another grandson of Violet Hambro, who entered Hambros Bank in 1975 – the only relation to join in the 1970s. Sir Everard's outstanding ability has been passed through the successive generations so that there are now eleven members of the family in the bank who are all his direct descendants, including two grandchildren, seven great-grandchildren, and one great-great-grandchild.

Of these, no less than five bear the Hambro surname, headed by Jocelyn who retired as Chairman of Hambros Bank in 1972 but who retained his position as Chairman of Hambros Limited, the quoted parent company created in 1970. His sons are in their early and mid-thirties: Rupert, who married an American journalist, Robin Boyer, and has two children, Jonathan aged five and Flora aged three; Richard, who married Charlotte Soames (daughter of Lord Soames and grand-daughter of Sir Winston Churchill) and has one daughter, Clementine, aged three; and James, who is the youngest of Jocelyn's family. Of the same generation is the present Chairman of Hambros Bank, Charlie, who succeeded Jocelyn in 1972. Within the next few years his two sons, Charles and Alexander, may also join the business, but at present Charles is following in the footsteps of his father and grandfather by serving in the Coldstream Guards, while Alexander is still at Eton.

Ever since Carl Joachim established the London firm of C. J. Hambro & Son in 1839, its attention has always been focused overseas, particularly on Scandinavia, whence came its origins, much of its business, many of its staff and, after 1920, several of its significant shareholders. Its traditional functions first as an accepting house and secondly as an issuing house provided the basis of the bank's international business,

From left to right: Rupert, Richard and James Hambro, Jocelyn's three sons, who entered the bank in 1964, 1966 and 1969 respectively. After studying at foreign universities and then in accountancy, they each gained practical experience with banks and investment banks in Scandinavia, Switzerland and the United States. Hambros Bank Archives.

which by its very nature has been constantly subject to the influence of worldwide market conditions. The family's signal quality as bankers lies in its enduring ability to withstand the recurring storms in the international economy and the consequences of them, and so to be ready when the cycle turns to recoup their business and strike out in new areas of activity. Flexibility is crucial to their success. In the 1940s it was highlighted by Olaf's pioneering efforts in the diamond trade, and in the 1970s by Jocelyn's venture with Mark Weinberg and his highly successful Hambro Life Assurance team. Diversification into both these areas showed remarkable foresight which has been amply rewarded.

Even with the many Hambro subsidiaries and associate companies in Australia, Hong Kong, the Middle East, Europe and North America, present operations remain small compared with that of the large London clearing banks and the many competitors in the international banking market. The size of Hambros Bank, however, is part of its strength, since it always has been, and still is today, an exceedingly personal business where the style of approach is individual and the lines of communication are short and direct.

Clearly the family's role is essential and provides the key to the whole operation. Although there have always been other non-family partners and directors, there has never been a time when a Hambro has not been the senior partner or chairman. By no means all the Hambro family have proved themselves to be able bankers, but each generation has produced at least one of outstanding quality who has carefully guarded and nurtured the inheritance for future members.

The saga of Calmer and Thobe's descendants over the last 200 years has now come to a close. As can be seen from the genealogical trees at the front and back of the book, new lines in the eighth generation augur well for the future of the Hambro family. Obviously, however, the lives of contemporary members of the family, not only in England but in Norway too, cannot be described in their entirety yet.

Their story has still to be told.

Bibliography

Frederick Lewis Allen. *The Great Pierpont Morgan.* Harper & Row, New York 1965
William Ashworth. *A Short History of the International Economy 1850–1950.* Longmans, Greens & Co Ltd, London 1952
Philip S. Bagwell and G. E. Mingay. *Britain and America 1850–1939.* Routledge & Kegan Paul, London 1970
Geoffrey Bell. *The Euro-Dollar Market and the International Financial System.* The Macmillan Press Ltd, London 1973
Oscar Bendix. *Hambro Bank Ltd 1839–1939.* London 1939
Carl Bernhardt. *Erindringer.* København 1848
Nicolai Bøgh. *Jens Adolf Jerichau.* København 1884
Poul Borchsenius. *Historien om de danske Jøder.* København 1969
Elias Bredsdorff. *H. C. Andersen og England.* København 1954
Francis Bull. *Minner om Mennesker.* Oslo 1962
George Bull and Anthony Vice. *Bid for Power.* Elek Books Ltd, London 1958
Th. Bull. *Købmand i Bergen Edvard Isach Hambro og hans Efterslaegt. Burdett's Official Intelligence 1882–1897.* Privattryk, Oslo 1933
Vincent P. Carosso. *Investment Banking in America.* Harvard University Press, Cambridge, Mass. 1970
Hedley A. Chilvers. *The Story of De Beers.* Cassell and Company Ltd, London 1939
Sir John Clapham. *The Bank of England*, vol. II. Cambridge University Press 1944
Sir Henry Clay. *Lord Norman.* The Macmillan Press Ltd, London 1957
P. L. Cottrell. *British Overseas Investment in the Nineteenth Century.* The Macmillan Press Ltd, London 1975
Virginia Cowles. *The Rothschilds A Family of Fortune. Dansk Biografisk Leksikon.* Weidenfeld and Nicolson Ltd, London 1973
J. Davidsen. *Fra det gamle København 1–2.* København 1881
T. K. Derry. *A History of Modern Norway 1814–1972.* Clarendon Press, Oxford 1973
– *Det norske Storting gjennem 150 år 1814–1964.* Bind 3 1908–1964. Oslo 1964
Aytoun Ellis. *Heir of Adventure. The Story of Brown, Shipley & Co Merchant Bankers 1810.* Privately printed, 1960
Harald Faber. *Danske og norske i London.* København 1915
Paul Ferris. *The City.* Random House, New York 1961
Joseph Fischer. *Slaegten Levisohn fra Hamburg Mosaisk Trossamfund (maskinskrevet).* København 1957
M. R. D. Foot. *S O E in France.* Her Majesty's Stationery Office 1966
Carlo Maria Franzero. *Il Conte di Cavour e i Suoi Banchierei inglese.* Turin UA
Frederiksberg Bibliotek. *Breve fra Carl Joachim Hambro til Adolf Jerichau og Elisabeth Jerichau-Baumann.*
Trond Gabrielsen. *C. J. Hambro som jeg Kjendte ham.* Oslo 1967
Olle Gasslander. *History of Stockholms Enskilda Bank To 1914.* Privately printed, 1962
Karen Glaesel. *Simon Hambros Slaegt.* Duplikeret privattryk, København 1954
Margaret Gowing. *Britain and Atomic Energy 1939–1945.* The Macmillan Press Ltd, London 1964
– *Slaegten Gyberg Duplikerede slaegtsoplysninger.* København UA
Carl Joachim Hambro. *Far og Søn.* Oslo 1948
Christopher Hibbert. *Edvard VII. A Portrait.* J. B. Lippincott Company, New York 1976
David Irving. *The Virus House.* William Kimber Ltd, London 1967
Lennart Jörberg. *The Industrial Revolution in Scandinavia 1850–1914.* Fontana Books, London 1970
Harald Jørgensen. *C. N. David 1–2.* København 1950
Harald Jørgensen. *Statsradets Forhandlinger 1848–1863.* København 1958
Richard Kellett. *The Merchant Banking Arena.* The Macmillan Press Ltd, London 1967
Københavnske Meddelelser. *De hambroske Bade- og Vaskeanstalter.* København 1920
J. A. S. L. Leighton-Boyce. *Smiths the Bankers 1658–1958.* National Provincial Bank Ltd, London 1958

Erik Lindahl, Einar Dahlgren and Karin Kock. *National Income of Sweden 1861–1930*. P. S. King & Son Ltd, London 1937

Michael Lubbock. *Cecil Lubbock 1872–1956*. Privately printed, 1960

Peter Mathias. *The First Industrial Nation*. Methuen & Co Ltd, London 1969

W. N. Medlicott. *The Economic Blockade*, vols. I & II. Her Majesty's Stationery Office and Longmans' Green and Co, London 1952

Oscar Mendelsohn. *Jødernes historie i Norge*. Oslo 1969

A. Milward and S. B. Saul. *The Economic Development of Continental Europe 1780–1870*. George Allen & Unwin Ltd, London 1973

Frederic Morton. *The Rothschilds*. Secker & Warburg, London 1962

– *Nekrologiske samlinger 1849 Joseph Hambros nekrolog*. København 1849

Johannes Nordal and Valdimar Kristinsson (ed.). *Iceland 1966. Norsk Biografisk Leksikon*. Reykjavik 1967

Stewart Oakley. *The Story of Denmark*. Faber and Faber Ltd, London 1972

Boris T. Pash. *The Alsos Mission*. Award House, New York 1969

Raymond Phillips. *The Belsen Trial*. William Hodge & Co Ltd, London 1949

Sidney Pollard. *The Development of the British Economy 1914–1967*. Edward Arnold Ltd, London 1962

Mathilde Reinhardt. *Familieerindringer*. København 1887

C. F. Ricard. *Rejsebreve*. København 1954

Rigsarkivet i København. *Korrespondance mellen Joseph Hambro og Johan Møsting Nicolai von Holten og A. W. Moltke 1824–38*.

Marcus Rubin. *Frederik 6.s tid Bind 2 1814–39*. København 1895

Julius Salomon. *Bidrag till dank-jødisk Historie 1820–45*. København 1918

Julius Salomon og Joseph Fischer. *Mindeskrift i anledning af 100-arsdagen for anordningen af 29. marts 1814*. København 1914

R. S. Sayers. *The Bank of England 1891–1944*, vols. I and II. Cambridge University Press 1976

R. S. Sayers. *A History of Economic Change in England 1880–1939*. Oxford University Press 1967

C. S. Schilbred. *Slekten Bull fra Trøndelag*. Oslo 1976

Fritz Stern. *Gold and Iron. Stock Exchange Year-Book 1890–1914*. George Allen & Unwin Ltd, London 1977

Just Mathias Thiele. *Af mit livs årbøger 1–2*. København 1917

Thorvaldsens Museum. *Breve fra Joseph Hambro til Bertel Thorvaldsen 1830–35*.

Chr. A. R. Christensen (ed.). *Vårt Folks Historie* Bind 8 og 9. Oslo 1961

Joseph Wechsberg. *The Merchant Bankers*. Weidenfeld and Nicolson Ltd, London 1967

Joseph Wechsberg. *Profiles: an Accepting House. The New Yorker*, 5 February 1966

C. H. R. Whittlesey and J. S. G. Wilson (ed.). *Essays in Money and Banking in honour of R. S. Sayers*. Oxford University Press 1968

Anthony Wood. *Europe 1815 to 1945*. Longman Group Limited, London 1964

Index

Page numbers in *italic* refer to the illustrations and their captions

Accepting Houses Committee, 428
Adam, Robert, 301
Aftenposten, 118; *89*
Aichelin, Lore, 118
Alexander II, Tsar, 279
Alexandra, Queen, 275–6, 279; *230*
Alfred, Prince, Duke of Edinburgh, 272–4, 276
Aluminium Company of America (Alcoa), 429–31
Amalie, Queen of Greece, 279
Ancker, Andreas, 51, 53–5
Ancker, Carl, 53–6; *56*, *206–7*
Ancker, Henriette (*née* Hambro), 45, 49, 51, 53
Ancker Foundation, 56
Andersen, Hans Christian, 72–3, 228–32, 249–50, 259; *40*, *231*
Anglo-Danish Society, *425*
Anne, Queen of England, *274–5*
Appert, Françoise, 204
Army Golfing Society, 354
Arneberg, Arnstein, *130*, *134*
Asmussen, Des, *281*
Astor, Lord, 396
Aumont, Louis, *121*
Avebury, Lord, 354

Baerentzen, Emilius, 52–3; *55*, *195*
Balduino, Commander, 315
Bank of England, 300, 319–20, 332–6, 355, 376, 378, 385–9, 393–4, 396, 408, 417, 419, 428, 434, 435, 438; *305–7*, *333–5*, *388*
Bank of France, 320
Bank of Norway (Norges Bank), 64, 97
Bankers' Industrial Development Company, 395
Banque d'Escompte, 310–14
Barclay, Bevan, Tritton & Co., *306–7*
Barclay, Charles, 298

Bardenfleth, 246
Baring, E. C., *see* Revelstoke, Lord
Baring, Francis, 319
Baring Brothers, 212, 240, 242, 246, 264, 309, 310, 314–16, 318, 319–23, 324; *306–7*
Barrow, Julian, *419*
Baumann, Elizabeth Jerichau, 256–8, 259, 260, 261
Beaton, Barbara, *see* Hambro, Barbara
Beaton, Cecil, 406
Beaulieu, Elizabeth, *37*
Bedfordshire County Council, 384
Bendixson, H., *372*
Bentworth Trust Limited, 426–8
Berg, Paal, 97, 105, 110
Bergen Feminist Association, 77
Bernhardt, Carl, 184–8
Berntsen, Ingrid, *see* Bull, Ingrid
Berntsen, Klaus, 135
Bingham, Brigadier-General, 354
Bingham, Marjorie, *see* Hambro, Lady Marjorie
Bishopsgate Trading and Export Co., 400
Bismarck, Prince Otto von, 244, 262–3
Bissen, H. W., 196, 222–4; *224*, *235*
Bjørnson, Bjørnstjerne, 116, 123, 127, 134, 135–6; *126*, *135*
Bjørnson, Caroline, *135*
Blackburn, Mary Ann, *see* Hambro, Mary Ann
Blore, H. R., 352
Board of Trade, 365
Bødtker, Anne Kristine, *see* Hambro, Anne Kristine
Bødtker, Johannes Sejersted, 136, 140; *139*
Boer War, 297, 350–2
Bonsor, Edith, *see* Hambro, Edith
Bonsor, Henry Cosmo, 326–7, 335; *334–5*, *346–7*

445

Bonsor, Mrs, *346–7*

Bontoux, M., 312

Borop, Eline, 42

Borup, Hans, 42

Borup, Johan, 42, 73; *41*

Borup, Julius Theodor, 39–42, 65, 73; *40*

Borup, Lars, *38*

Borup, Marie, 41–2; *40, 41*

Borup, Niels, 11, 38–9, 64; *37, 38*

Borup, Zipora (Hanne Sophie; *née* Hambro), 11, 12, 21, 25, 32, 33, 34–42, 46, 48, 64, 172; *35, 36*

Botcherby, 284, 287–8

Boyer, Robin, *see* Hambro, Robin

Bradford (Robert) & Co., 402–4

Bramsen, Luis, 208

Brandes, Edvard, 72

Brandt, (William) Sons & Co., *306–7*

Brauer, Curt, 97, 102–3, 104

Bridge, Captain Christopher, 405

British Aluminium Company, 428–33

British Bank of Northern Commerce (BBNC), 367–8, 370–2, 377, 423; *371*

British Expeditionary Force, 355

British Intelligence, 414

British Motor Corporation, 420

British Raw Materials Mission, 411–12

British South Africa Company, 354–5

Brock, J. P., 72, 74, 78

Brown, Capability, 253–4; *251*

Brown, (John) & Co., 395

Brown Brothers Harriman & Co., 418

Brown, Shipley & Co., 317, 431

Brun, Constantin, 142, 163

Brun, Frederikke, 163

Buenos Aires Water Supply and Drainage Company, 319

Bull (Norwegian minister), 105

Bull, Angelique, *see* Hambro, Angelique

Bull, Barbara, 135

Bull, Edvard (son of Edvard Isach Hambro Bull), 129–34; *128, 130, 133*

Bull, Edvard Jr, 129; *134*

Bull, Edvard Isach Hambro, 120–2, 124–9; *124, 126, 127, 135*

Bull, Francis, 129, 134–8; *128, 135, 137, 139*

Bull, Georg Jacob, 68; *120*

Bull, Gina, 124–5

Bull, Ida Marie, 125, 129; *128*

Bull, Ingrid, 135, 138

Bull, Johan Peter, *128*

Bull, Johan Randulff, 120–2; *120*

Bull, Karen, 129

Bull, Lucie, 129, 133–4

Bull, Marie Louise, *128*

Bull, Niels, *134*

Bull, Theodor, 124–5

Bull, Theodora (*née* Hambro), 67, 120–3; *121*

Burdett, Sir Henry, 303

Burns, Walter, 328

Bute, 2nd Marquess of, 300

Carl XIII, King of Sweden, *223*

Carl XIV Johan, King of Sweden, 221–2; *223*

Carl XVI Adolf, King of Sweden, *223*

Carl Albert, King of Sardinia, 266

Caroline, Crown Princess of Denmark, 50

Caroline Mathilde, Queen of Denmark, 154–6

Cavour, Camillo, 249, 250, 262–72; *263, 265, 268, 269, 271*

Chamberlain, Neville, 90

Chambers, Sir William, 252–3; *252–3*

Channel Tunnel Company, 330

Chapman, Ella, 284–7

Chapman, Mr, 284–5

Charlton, Vanda St John, *see* Hambro, Vanda

Christensen, C. A., 88, 90

Christensen, Gyda, *see* Hambro, Gyda

Christian IV, King of Denmark, 201

Christian V, King of Denmark, 59; *161*

Christian VII, King of Denmark, 17, 28, 146, 154–6

Christian VIII, King of Denmark, 61, 196; *58, 62–3*

Christian IX, King of Denmark, 275, 279

Christian X, King of Denmark, *371*

Christian Michelsen Institute, Bergen, 118

Church of England Children's Society, 303

Churchill, Sir Winston, 108, 410, 441

Clark, Roy, 424

Clay, Sir Henry, 439

Clay, John, 439
Cleminson, Hugh, 361
Clover, Dr, 296
Clover, J. P., 298
Cobbold, Pamela, *see* Hambro, Pamela (wife of Sir Charles Jocelyn Hambro)
Cohen, Alfred, *318*
Cohen, G., 315
Cohen, (Louis) & Co., 315
Cohen, (Nathaniel) & Co., *306–7*
Cohn, Isaak, 28
Coldstream Guards, 358, 360, 405, 423, 441
Combined Development Trust (CDT), 412–14
Combined Raw Materials Board, 411
Comptoir d'Escompte, 320
Connelly, Marc, 81
Consett Iron Company, 395, 426
Copenhagen, battle of (1801), 142; *144–5*
Copenhagen, battle of (1807), 156; *155*
Copenhagen University, 57, 72, 164
Cornwallis, 5th Earl of, 391
Country Life, 346, 392
Credit Mobilier, 310, 315
Cromer, Lord, 438
Cunliffe, Geoffrey, 428–31
Cunliffe, Lord, 428
Currie, Brigadier John, 402

d'Abo, Gerard, 372, 377, 380, 396, 423; *376*
Dagbladet, 89
Dahl, J. D., *69*
Dahl, Siegwald, *124, 233*
Dalhousie, Earl of, 324, 385; *325*
Dalton, Dr Hugh, 410–11
Danchell, Hanne Frederikke (*née* Hambro), 45, 49–51, 52
Danchell, Henrich Leonhard, 51, 52–3; *54, 55*
Danish Industrial Association, 52–3
Danish Navy, 45; *46–7*
David, Adelaide, *see* Gerson, Adelaide
David, C. N., 188
David, Nathan, 188
Davidson, Charles, 413
d'Avigdor-Goldsmid, Sir Henry, 424
De Beers, 421

De Coninck, 142
Deuntzfeldt, 142
Devonshire, HMS, 106–7
Diamond Development Company, 421
Diamond Realizations, 421
Diamond Trading Company (DTC), 421
Dighton, Richard, *193*
Donner, Conrad Hinrich, 185–8, 194; *184*
Dreier, J. F. L., *58*
Drexel Morgan & Co., 301, 307, 317
Drossopoulos, 379
Drucker, 340
Dugdale, Thomas, *394*
Dunton (chauffeur), 391, 392

Eastern Extension Australia and China Telegraph Co., 384
Eastern Telegraph Co., 384
Eckersberg, C. W., *175*
Economic Warfare, Ministry of, 408–10
Eddelien, Heinrich, *44, 45, 54, 55*
Edward VII, King of England, 272, 275, 279, 298, 323, 346–7; *230, 322, 346–7*
Elizabeth, Queen Mother, 392; *422*
Elizabeth II, Queen of England, 425; *422*
Elphinstone, Andrew, *422*
Elphinstone, Jean (*née* Hambro), *422*
Elphinstone, Lord, *379*
Elverum Authority, 100–2; *101*
Emmet, *37*
Empire Trust Company, 423
Erichsen, Erich, 142, 147, 158, 182–3, 185, 188; *146, 147*
Eton, 385, 423, 441; *384*
Evans, William, *384*
Exchange Equalization Account, 388–9

Falkenberg, Johan, *83*
Falsen, Gina, *see* Bull, Gina
Federal Reserve Bank (USA), 380
Federation of Swedish Mine-Owners, 221
Fehlis, Heinrich, 112
Ferdinand VII, King of Spain, 216, 222
Financial Times, 432
Find, Ludvig, *41*
Fischietto, *265, 268, 269*
Fleicher, Professor, 73
Fleming, (Robert) & Co., 431

447

Folk High School, 42
Fosters & Co., 317
Franz Josef, Emperor, *271*
Freckland, Jens Hansen, 48–9
Frederik VI, King of Denmark, 12, 28, 30–1, 46–7, 49, 52, 62, 146, 147, 148, 156, 167, 170, 174, 178, 183, 185–6, 192, 202, 214, 219, 221–2, 224; *32*, *156–8, 163, 175, 176*
Frederik VII, King of Denmark, 246, 277; *243*
Fritz, J. F., *184*
Fürst, Haller & Co., 26, 150, 157

Gamborg, Knud, *168, 169*
Gardner, Rex, 397
Garibaldi, Giuseppe, *273*
George, Prince of Denmark, *274–5*
George I, King of Greece (Prince Vilhelm of Denmark), 276–80; *277*
George II, King of Greece, 108
George III, King of England, 154–6
George VI, King of England, 107; *422*
Gerard, Françoise, *223*
Gerhardsen, Einar, 110
Gerson, Adelaide, 188–9
Gerson, Georg, 157–8, 173–4, 183, 188–9, 196; *158, 189*
Gertner, J. V., *156, 217, 243, 244*
Gibbs, (Antony) & Sons, *306–7*
Gibbs, Henry Hucks, 303, 334–5
Gibbs, Joseph, 298
Gibson-Watt, Andrew, 439–40
Gibson-Watt, Pamela (*née* Hambro), 382, 440
Giersing, Peder, 30
Glenconner, Lord, 396, 410
Gloucester, Duchess of, *425*
Gloucester, Duke of, *425*
Glyn, Mills, Currie & Co., 320; *306–7*
Goering, Hermann, 405
Goldschmidt, Adolf, 190–2; *193*
Goldschmidt, (Adolf) & Co., 162, 172–3, 182–3, 192
Goldschmidt, Otto, *230*
Görbitz, Johan, *64, 65*
Gordon Woodroffe Ltd, 422
Gornsen, E. M., *435*
Goschen, Viscount, 319–20

Gostenhofer, Caroline, *see* Hambro, Caroline
Gostenhofer, Mrs, 259
Gostenhofer, Theofilius, 212–13
Gowing, Margaret, 412–13
Granville, Lord Gerald, *346–7*
Great Northern Telegraph Co. (Denmark), 307
Greene, Benjamin, 335
Grieg, Cato, 86
Grieg, Edvard, 123, 127; *126*
Grieg, Gudrun, *see* Hambro, Gudrun
Grieg, Harald, 136, 138; *139*
Grieg, Johan, 86
Grillo, 314
Grindlays Bank, 404
Gröger, C. F., *186*
Gröger, F. G., *147*
Grønlund, Johannes, 276
Groves, General, 411–12, 414, 415
Grundtvig, N. F. S., 42
Grut, Emma, *see* Hansen, Emma
Grut, Thomas, 190
Guaranty Trust Company of New York, 385
Gubbins, Major-General, 411
Guest, Montagu, 290–1, 292; *285, 293*
Guldbrandsen, O., *126*
Günther, 105
Gustmeyer, Frederik, 30
Gutchen & Partners, 400
Gutfeld, Frederik Carl, 37
Gyberg, Carl Hambro, 52
Gyberg, Hektor, 52
Gyberg, Ida (*Née* Hambro), 45, 49, 52
Gyldendal, 136, 138

Haakon VII, King of Norway, 84, 97, 99, 100, 103–4, 106–8, 109–10, 116, 132; *95, 105*
Hagelin, Albert, 111; *93*
Haldemann & Sons, 172–3, 182–3
Hale, (S.B.) & Co., 319
Halifax, Lord, 408–9
Halle, Mirjam von, *see* Hambro, Marianne
Halle, Priwche von, 154
Halle, Wulf Levin von, 154
Haller, Martin Joseph, 150; *151*

Halliday, Edward, *390*

Hambro, Agneta, 290, 292

Hambro, Alec, 357, 406; *406*

Hambro, Alexander, 441

Hambro, Alexandra, 406

Hambro, Angelique, 68–9, 71, 120; *68*

Hambro, Angus, 302, 357–8, 406, 422, 440; *301, 327, 346–7, 356, 358, 379*

Hambro, Anne Kristine (Stine), 138, 140; *141*

Hambro, Arabella, 296–7, 337, 351

Hambro, Augusta, 55–6

Hambro, Barbara, 406

Hambro, Bernt Anker, 140–1; *140*

Hambro, Bertram, 297, 359; *359*

Hambro, Calmer Joachim, 11–13, 15–17, 20–32, 34, 43; *13, 22, 32, 33, 206–7*

Hambro, Carl (son of Carl Joachim Hambro), 94, 118, 120; *85, 119*

Hambro, Carl (son of Nigel Hambro), 401

Hambro, Carl Joachim (son of Isach Hambro), 67–71; *68–70*

Hambro, Carl Joachim, Baron Hambro (son of Joseph Hambro), 11–12, 20, 40, 68, 154, 162–5, 174, 176–7, 190, 194, 196, 198–200, 202, 208–14, 218, 222, 224–36, 237–61, 262–83, 284–90, 295–6, 301, 304; *31, 159, 199, 206–7, 212, 219, 225, 227, 245, 247–59, 259, 278, 280–2*

Hambro, Carl Joachim (son of Edvard Isach Hambro), 76, 78, 80–116, 132, 236; *75, 81, 83, 87, 89, 103, 109, 111, 113, 117*

Hambro, Carl Simon, 11, 12, 21, 25, 32, 34, 43–52, 64, 158, 172; *44–51, 206–7*

Hambro, Caroline, Baroness Hambro (wife of Carl Joachim Hambro), 212–14, 225–6, 228, 230, 250–1, 256, 259, 260, 284; *215, 225*

Hambro, Caroline (daughter of Colonel Charles Hambro), 290

Hambro, Caroline Frederikke, 11, 45, 49–51; *53*

Hambro, Caroline Marie, 214, 228

Hambro, Cathrine, *81*

Hambro, Cato, 94, 118; *85, 119*

Hambro, Cecilia, 234

Hambro, Cecily, *see* Williams Ellis, Cecily

Hambro, Colonel Charles (son of Carl Joachim Hambro), 214, 238, 251, 255, 260, 284–95, 298, 326, 337; *229, 285, 286, 292, 293, 325*

Hambro, Charles (son of Charlie Hambro), 441

Hambro, Sir Charles Jocelyn, 104, 303, 354, 359–60, 377, 382, 383, 385–9, 396, 400, 408–15, 416–17, 422, 424, 431, 433–5, 438–9; *327, 376, 378, 384, 388, 409, 413, 417, 425*

Hambro, Charlie (son of Sir Charles Jocelyn Hambro), 303, 382, 423, 435, 439, 441; *384, 423, 425, 440*

Hambro, Charlotte (wife of Richard Hambro), 441

Hambro, Christian, 67, 138–40

Hambro, Clementine, 441

Hambro, Cynthia, 382

Hambro, David, 344

Hambro, Diana (daughter of Bertram Hambro), 359

Hambro, Diana (daughter of Sir Charles Jocelyn Hambro), 382

Hambro, Dorothy (daughter of Percival Hambro), 297

Hambro, Lady Dorothy (wife of Sir Charles Jocelyn Hambro), 408; *409*

Hambro, Lady Ebba (wife of Sir Everard Hambro), 348; *374–5*

Hambro, Edith, 326–7, 341–2

Hambro, Edvard, 64, 67, 225, 232–4, 236, 237; *234*

Hambro, Edvard Isach (son of Carl J. Hambro), 65–7, 69, 71–9, 80, 84, 85; *72, 73, 75, 77*

Hambro, Edvard Isach (son of Christian Hambro), 140; *141*

Hambro, Edvard Isak (son of Carl Joachim Hambro), 94, 108, 109; *85, 115, 119*

Hambro, Eliza, Baroness Hambro, 260–1, 279, 283, 337–8; *261*

Hambro, Elizabeth (second wife of Jocelyn Hambro), *434*

Hambro, Sir Eric, 302, 326, 328–32, 338, 343, 346, 354, 355, 360, 361–9, 370, 372, 376, 378–80, 382, 385, 393, 409;

Hambro, Sir Eric – *contd.*
289, 325, 327, 329, 343, 346–7, 364, 366, 379

Hambro, Evelyn, 94, 104; *85*

Hambro, Sir Everard, 189, 228, 230, 251, 259, 262, 272, 283, 292, 296, 298–336, 339, 343–9, 354, 355, 370, 372, 374–6, 386, 416, 440; *258, 285, 289, 299, 311, 318, 321, 322, 325, 327, 339, 343, 346–7, 353, 364, 374–5*

Hambro, Everard Bingham (Evy), 354, 382, 396, 400, 401–4, 431; *353, 403*

Hambro, Faith, 359

Hambro, Flora, 441

Hambro, Grace (wife of Percival Hambro), 296, 326; *297*

Hambro, Grace (daughter of Percival Hambro), 296

Hambro, Gudrun, 85–6, 94, 97, 98, 104, 105, 108–9; *83*

Hambro, Gyda, 114–16; *114*

Hambro, Hanne Frederikke, *see* Danchell, Hanne Frederikke

Hambro, Colonel Harold, 302, 350, 354–5, 356–7, 396; *327, 355, 357, 394*

Hambro, Harry, 323, 326–8, 329, 337–44, 355, 368–9, 372, 380, 383–4; *292, 338*

Hambro, Henriette, *see* Ancker, Henriette

Hambro, Henry, 296, 297

Hambro, Hermione, 302, 374

Hambro, Ida, *see* Gyberg, Ida

Hambro, Isach, 12, 21–2, 24–6, 32–3, 34, 39, 42, 46, 48, 52, 57–69, 71, 72, 234–6; *58, 61, 64, 66*

Hambro, Jack, 384, 395, 396, 397–8, 400, 406–7, 413, 416–7, 422, 426, 431, 434–5, 438–9; *399, 408, 417, 427*

Hambro, James (son of Jocelyn Hambro), 440, 441; *418, 441*

Hambro, Jean, *see* Elphinstone, Jean

Hambro, Jeanette, 44, 48, 52, 53; *45, 50–1*

Hambro, Jocelyn, 383, 391, 404–6, 417–20, 422, 423, 424, 435, 439, 441, 442; *374–5, 404, 418, 419, 434, 439*

Hambro, Johan (son of Isach Hambro), 64, 67, 138, 232–4, 236; *233*

Hambro, Johan (son of Carl Joachim Hambro), 94, 108, 109, 118; *85, 119*

Hambro, Jonathan, 441

Hambro, Joseph, 11–12, 21–6, 28–30, 32–3, 34, 39, 44, 57, 64, 67, 142, 148, 150–65, 166, 172–7, 178–200, 201–33, 237–40, 264, 298, 436; *37, 53, 143, 159, 204–7, 210–13, 235, 239*

Hambro, Katherine, 354–5

Hambro, Marianne (Mirjam), 44, 152–4, 162, 174–6, 194, 196, 198, 222–4, 228, 237, 284; *159, 224*

Hambro, Marie, 61, 64, 120; *65*

Hambro, Lady Marjorie (wife of Sir Percy Hambro), 354, 382; *353*

Hambro, Marjorie (wife of Nigel Hambro), 401

Hambro, Marjory (wife of Bertram Hambro), 359

Hambro, Lady Mary (wife of Sir Everard Hambro), 296, 300–2, 323, 344–6, 358, 374; *300, 325, 327, 343*

Hambro, Mary (wife of Evy Hambro), 402, 404; *403*

Hambro, Mary Ann (wife of Edvard Hambro), *234*

Hambro, Maud, 357

Hambro, Maurice, 302, 374

Hambro, Michael, 357

Hambro, Nicoline, 74, 76–7, 79, 80; *75, 78*

Hambro, Nigel, 356, 396, 400–1; *395*

Hambro, Lt Norman, 297, 350–2; *351*

Hambro, Olaf, 302, 331–2, 358–9, 360, 369, 372, 377–8, 380, 382–3, 389–96, 397–400, 402, 416–17, 420–2, 425–6, 428, 432–3, 438, 442; *289, 301, 325, 327, 343, 346–7, 358, 381, 390, 393, 417*

Hambro, Olga, 401

Hambro, Pamela (wife of Sir Charles Jocelyn Hambro), 382, 385, 393; *383*

Hambro, Pamela (daughter of Sir Charles Jocelyn Hambro), *see* Gibson-Watt, Pamela

Hambro, Patricia (Patsie), *see* Tapley, Patsie

Hambro, Peggy, 357

Hambro, Percival, 214, 237, 251, 260, 284–8, 290, 295–7, 298, 304, 326; *229, 285, 297, 325*

Hambro, Major-General Sir Percy Otway,

288, 296, 297, 350, 352–4, 355–7, 358, 380–2; *352*
Hambro, Peter, 404; *403*
Hambro, Richard (son of Sir Eric Hambro), 354
Hambro, Richard (son of Jocelyn Hambro), 440, 441; *418, 441*
Hambro, Robin (wife of Rupert Hambro), 441
Hambro, Rosamund, 406
Hambro, Rupert (son of Jocelyn Hambro), 440, 441; *418, 425, 441*
Hambro, Sally, *409*
Hambro, Silvia (first wife of Jocelyn Hambro), 418; *404, 418*
Hambro, Susan (wife of Colonel Charles Hambro), 288–93, 295; *285, 293*
Hambro, Susan (daughter of Sir Percy Hambro), 354, 382; *353*
Hambro, Sybil (wife of Sir Eric Hambro), 328–9, 346, 348, 354, 360; *327, 343, 346–7, 364, 367*
Hambro, Theodora, *see* Bull, Theodora
Hambro, Thobe (Dorothea), 11, 13, 15–17, 20–4, 32–3, 34, 37; *23*
Hambro, Tony, 404; *403*
Hambro, Val, 359–60, 384; *360*
Hambro, Vanda, 358; *356*
Hambro, Violet, *see* Smith, Violet Martin
Hambro, Winifred, 358–9, 382–3, 393; *343, 374–5, 382*
Hambro, Zelia, 354
Hambro, Zipora, *see* Borup, Zipora
Hambro America Inc., 440
Hambro Automobile Corporation, 420
Hambro House of Design, 420
Hambro Life Assurance, 442
Hambro Orphanage for Girls, 302–3
Hambro Trading Corporation of America Incorporated, 419
Hambro Trust Limited, 380
Hambros Skole, Bergen, 74–9, 84, 85; *77*
Hamilton, Cecilia, *see* Hambro, Cecilia
Hamsun, Knut, 124
Hansen, (A.N.) & Co., 190
Hansen, Andreas, 173, 179, 189–90, 201, 204–5, 226, 237; *191, 210, 213*
Hansen, Emma, 190
Harbitz, Nicoline, *see* Hambro, Nicoline

Hardwicke, 4th Earl of, 288–9
Harraden, R. B., *289*
Haslewood, Edward, 269
Haslewood, Lewis, 269
Heidelbach & Ickelheimer, 307, 317
Heidelberg University, 404–5
Hein, Piet, *191*
Heine, Heinrich, 154
Heine, Salomon, 154, 178, 181, 221
Helbert Wagg, 428, 429
Hennig, (I.) & Co., 420–1
Henriques, Henrik, *152*
Henriques, Leif, *152*
Henriques, Moses Ruben, 28
Henriques, Ruben Jr, 147–8, 151–2, 154; *152, 153*
Henriques, Sally, *152, 153*
Herholdt, Counsellor, 222
Heriot, Robert, 304, 320–2, 326, 329, 331
Heriot, Walter, 326, 329
Hetsch, G. F., 198; *197*
Hicks, G. E., *336*
Hill-Wood, Peter, 440; *345*
Hitler, Adolf, 91–2, 102–3, 410; *93*
Hoffenberg, *122*
Holberg, Ludvig, 134
Holm, H. G. F., *31, 165, 225*
Holmboe, C. A., 72
Holten, Nicolai von, 54, 166, 181, 194, 208–9, 216, 222, 224; *183, 206–7*
Holter, Christine, 118
Home Guard, 397
Honniball, Thomas, 424
Hoppe, *192*
Hornemann, Christian, *158*
Hornsrud, Christopher, 132
Hoskier, Emile, 309
Hoskier, (Emile) & Co., 317–18, 326
Howard, Esmé, 363
Howitt, Mary, 228
Hugh Smith, A. John, 300, 396, 423
Hugh Smith, Colin, 300–1, 335, 344; *334–5*
Hugh Smith, Constance, 300–1, 344
Hugh Smith, Launcelot, 361, 365
Hunæus, A. H., *35*
Hungarian Land Mortgage Bank, 378
Hussars, 350, 402
Hussey, Christopher, 392

Ibsen, Henrik, 116, 123, 127, 129, 134, 135–6; *126*, *135*

Ibsen, Lillebil, 114

Ickelheimer, Mr, 322

Illustreret Tidende, *278*, *280*

Inconstant, HMS, 361

Indemnity Mutual Marine Assurance Co., 384

Indrebø, Adolf, 97

Induno, Gerolamo, *267*

Information, 102

International Court of Justice, 116, 118

Irvin, John, 365

Isabella II, Queen of Spain, 216

Issuing Houses Association, 426

Jacob, Raphael, 34

Jacobson, Daniel, 198

Jæger, Hans, 141; *140*

Jahren, G. A., 90

Jenisch, Martin Johan, 187–8; *186*, *187*

Jensen, C. A., *143*, *162*, *163*, *191*, *231*

Jensen, J., *56*

Jerichau, Adolf, 249–50, 255, 256, 260, 261; *257*

Jylland, 275–9

Katenakis, Dionysos, 274

Kauffmann, Angelica, 391

Keswick, David, 404

Keynes, John Maynard, 417

Kielland, Alexander, 123, 136

Kings Royal Rifle Corps, 350

Kitzerow, 151

Klæstrup, Peder, *28*, *171*, *173*, *176*

Kloumann, T., *89*

Knudsen, Sir Karl, 396

Knudsen, Peter, 59

Koht, Dr Halvdan, 92, 97, 99, 103

Kolstad, Peder, 91

Komintern, 131

Koren, Wencke, 118

Korsaren, 84

Krebs, Johanne, *40*

Kristiania Arts Association, 127

Kristiania University, 72, 73–4, 125–7, 129, 130, 135; *125*

Krogh, Per, *137*, *139*

Lahde, G. F., *29*, *49*, *155*

Laidlaw & Co., 434

Landsbanki Islands, 377

Lang, Captain, *346–7*

la Rue, Emile de, 263–4, 270

Laski, Sir Neville, 401

Lausanne, Treaty of (1923), 378–9

Lavery, Sir John, *321*

Lazard Brothers, 428–32; *306–7*

League of Nations, 88, 90, 92, 114

Lee, Frank, 412

Lehmann, Orla, 239

le Maire, Emile, 237, 262; *235*, *239*

Lerum, Gustav, *135*

Leven and Melville, Earl of, 335

Levi, Elkele (Dorothea), 21; *23*

Levi, Isach Joseph, 15–16, 17, 20–2; *23*

Levi, Thobe, *see* Hambro, Thobe

Levy, Isaak, 15

Levy, Jekev, 15

Levy, Jokev, 15

Levy, Mathias, 15, 22, 26, 33, 57, 150, 151

Levy, Nachman Joachim, 15–17, 20, 22, 23; *24*

Lib, *311*

Lidderdale, William, 319–20

Lie, Jonas (1833–1908), 123, 136

Lie, Jonas (d. 1945), 111

Lie, Trygve, 102

Lind, Jenny, 229, 232; *230*

Ljungberg, Birger, 96

Lloyd, Yarbrugh, 298

Lloyds, 161–2

London Assurance, 426

Lorentzen, C. A., *144–5*

Lowzov, A. G. von, 30

Lubbock family, 304, 354

Lubbock, Edgar, *334–5*

Lubbock, Marjory, *see* Hambro, Marjory

Lubbock, Sir Neville, 359

Ludwig, Elector of Hesse, 146

Lunde, Gulbrand, 111

Luton Bute Hospital, 384

Lyon, Mary, *see* Hambro, Mary (wife of Evy Hambro)

Madvig, J. N., 72

Maffei, Count, 309

Magliani, 309–10, 314

Malling, Ove, 30
Manchester Ship Canal, 330
Mann, Robert, 391
Mann, Thomas, 108
Mansell, Alfred, 190, 201–2, 205; *199*
Mansell, Louise, 190
Marconi's Wireless Telegraph Co., 384
Marcus, Moritz, 177
Margaret, Princess, *422*
Marietta and North Georgia Railroad, 309
Marstrand, M., *183*, *242*
Martens, Anton, 424
Märtha, Crown Princess of Norway, 104
Martin & Co., *306–7*
Martin family, 304
Mary, Queen, 391; *381*, *422*
Maud, Queen of Norway, 84
Maurice, Henry, 365
May, Frank, 332; *333*
Mayne, Grace, *see* Hambro, Grace
Mayne, Major Henry Otway, 296, 350
Medical Association (Norway), 125
Melville, Frederick Leslie, 298
Melville, Hamish Leslie, 440
Mercantile Industrial Association (Denmark), 53
Merton College, Oxford, 295
Meyer, David Amsel, 147, 170–1, 174; *156*, *157*
Meyer, Moses, 28
Meyer & Trier, 147, 166, 170; *156*, *157*, *171*
Middlesex Hospital, *427*
Milton, Lady Caroline, 283
Milton, John, 108
Milton, Lord, 252–4, 256, 283; *252–3*, *292*, *340–1*
Mocatta, Edward ('Jock'), 424–5
Mocatta & Goldsmid, 424–5
Møller, Emil, 54, 55
Moltke, Count A. W., 194, 214, 218–19, 239–40; *183*, *217*
Monnickendam, A., 400
Montagu, Samuel, 404; *318*
Montagu, (Samuel) & Co., 404, 431; *306–7*
Montgomery, General, 405
Morgan family, 423
Morgan, Harry, 385; *379*

Morgan, (J. P.) & Co., 329, 385, 387
Morgan, (J. S.) & Co., 301, 309, 317, 328; *306–7*
Morgan, John Pierpont, 301, 328–9, 330; *303*
Morgan, John Pierpont Jr, 328–9, 385; *379*, *386*
Morgan, Junius Spencer, 301, 303, 328; *302*
Morgan Grenfell & Co., 431
Morgenbladet, 84, 86–8
Morley, Samuel, *334–5*
Møsting, Johan Sigismund von, 30, 146–7, 166, 172, 179, 182–5, 192, 194; *163*, *183*
Mowinckel, J. L., 90, 91, 92, 132
Muir, Silvia, *see* Hambro, Silvia
Munch, Edvard, 124, 141; *123*, *140*
Mynster, J. P., 177

Napoleon I, Emperor of the French, 142, 147; *19*, *155*, *223*
Napoleon III, Emperor of the French, 279; *271*
Napoleonic Wars, 52, 57, 157, 264, 276
Nathan, Jeanette, *see* Hambro, Jeanette
Nathanson, Mendel Levin, 41, 147, 166–7, 171, 172, 185, 186; *40*, *156*
National Association for Mental Health (Norway), 118
National Bank of Greece, 379
National Bank of Italy, 310, 314
National Coal Board, *427*
National Debt Commission (Denmark), 166, 182–3, 185, 190, 194
National Mortgage Bank of Greece, 379
National Theatre (Norway), 127, 136
Nelson, Sir Frank, 411
Nelson, Lord, 142
News of the World, 426
Nexø, Martin Andersen, 42
Niven and Wigglesworth, 372
Norddeutsche Bank, 317
Norges Kommunalbank, 436
Norland, Otto, 434
Norman family, 304
Norman, Arabella, *see* Hambro, Arabella
Norman, Montagu, 385–9, 395; *388*
Norsk Gyldendal, 136

North, Mr Justice, 338
Northern Assurance Co., 384
Nortraship, 410
Norway Shipping, 426
Norwegian Biographical Encyclopaedia, 131, 136
Norwegian Commercial Institute, 118
Norwegian Farmers' Party, 91
Norwegian Translators' Association, 118
Nye Danske Brandforsikring, 208
Nygaardsvold, Johan, 81–2, 91, 92, 96, 99–100, 103, 108, 110, 132–3; *133*
Nyhus, Haakon, *140*

Oehlenschlager, Adam, 199
Olav V, King of Norway, 84, 104, 110, 112; *109, 111*
Olsen, Andrea Rockmann, *134*
Oppenheimer, Sir Ernest, 421
Ørsted family, 135
Ørsted, H. C., 68; *120*
Oslo Commercial College, 118
Otto I, King of Greece, 274, 279

Paasche, Professor, 136
Paget, Dr, 296
Paludan, Ida Marie, *see* Bull, Ida Marie
Parker, Admiral, 142
Paton, W., *379*
Pedersen, Viggo, *40*
Pedrinelli, *271*
PEN Club (Sweden), 105
Pennington, Fred, 424
Perez, Don Julian a, 222
Perkins, Mr, 375
Perrin, Sir Michael, 413, 414–15
Peter II, King of Yugoslavia, 108
Petersen, Wencke, 118
Petit, M., 204
Phelps, Stokes & Co., 307
Philip, Aaron, 28
Philip, Moses, 28
Philipson, P. G., *160–1*
Pignatelli-Ruffo, Prince Antonius, 188–9
Pitt family, 304
Pius VII, Pope, 194
Pløyen, 190–2
Plucknett, Percy, 424
Ponsonby, Sir Frederick, *346–7*

Portal, Lord, 429–31
Portalington, 6th Earl of, 251
Powell, David, 335
Priestley, Sir Joseph, 396
Prins, George, 420–1
Privatbanken, 317
Punch, 333
Purton, Arthur, 398, 424

Quebec Agreement (1943), 411, 412
Queen Mary, 395
Queen's Own Dorset Yeomanry, 291, 293, 357–8, 406
Quisling, Vidkund, 91–2, 99, 103, 104–5, 111; *93, 112*

Raphael, Jacob, 34
Raphael, Joseph, 34, 170
Raphael, Lazarus, 34–5, 170, 172
Raphael, Lazarus Jr, 35, 39
Raphael, Thea, 35, 39
Raphael Brothers, 34–5, 170; *168*
Raverat, Elisabeth, 118
Rawlings, Edward, 304, 326
Rediess, Wilhelm, 112
Ree, Heckscher & Co., 166–7
Reinhardt, Johannes, 163–5, 176–7, 198; *159, 165, 206–7*
Reinhardt, Mathilde, 164, 165, 212–13
Reinhardt, Nicoline, 163–5, 174, 176–7, 198
Revelstoke, Lord (E. C. Baring), 309, 319–23, 324; *308, 311*
Reventlow, Count Frederik, 244–6
Revold, Axel, *87*
Reynolds Metals Company, 429–32
Ricard, C. F., 279
Richard, Captain, *357*
Rieter, J. A., *204–5*
Riisnaes, Sverre, 111
Robarts, Lubbock & Co., *306–7*
Roberts, General, 350
Rock-Carling, Sir Ernest, 408
Roggen, Marie, *see* Hambro, Marie
Roosevelt, Theodore, *37*
Rosenberg, Friedrich, *149*
Rothschild family, 15, 146, 262
Rothschild, Baron Alphonse de, *313*

Rothschild, Amsel Salomon, 192–4, 216–19
Rothschild, Baron Carl, 264
Rothschild, Charlotte, 192
Rothschild, Baron James, 190–2, 216, 264, 266, 268–9
Rothschild, Baron Lionel, 246
Rothschild, (N. M.) & Sons, 428, 436; *306–7*
Rothschild, Nathan, 162, 192, 212, 216, 244–6, 264; *193*
Rothschild, Lord Nathan 'Natty', 303, 319, 323, 363; *311, 318*
Rothschild, Nathaniel, 298
Rothschild, Baron Salomon, 192, 264
Rothschilds Bank, 166, 182, 192–4, 214–18, 240, 242, 264, 266, 268–9, 272, 309–15, 318, 320, 375, 424–5
Rowe & Pitman, 361
Royal Air Force, 358
Royal Artillery, 350, 400
Royal College of Arms, 246, 247–8
Royal Commission on Wheat Supplies, 369
Royal Exchange Assurance Corporation, *305*
Royal Horse Artillery, 359
Royal Horticultural Society, 392
Royal National Pension Fund for Nurses, 303
Ruge, General, Otto, *103*
Russell, Lord John, 270, 279
Russian Revolution, 1917, 131
Ryberg, 142

Sacheri, Giuseppe, *317*
St Aubyn, Edward, 298
St Quintin, Miss, *285, 293*
Sassoon, (David) & Co., *306–7*
Savile, Lady, *346–7*
Savile, Lord, *346–7*
Sayers, Professor, 387
Sayers, Richard, 413
Scandinavian Youth, 129
Scandinaviska Kreditaktiebolaget, 317
Schanck, Ragnar, 111
Scheel, 92
Schimmelmann, Count Ernst, 142, 146, 147, 166, 198; *162, 163, 165*

Schousboe, Eline, *see* Borup, Eline
Schoutz, Augusta von, *see* Hambro, Augusta
Schroder, J. Henry, 428, 429
Scientific Association (Norway), 125
Scott, Sir Gilbert, 255, 283; *255, 282*
Scott, Katherine, *see* Hambro, Katherine
Secher, S., *435*
Selborne, Lord, 411
Seligman Bros., 428
Sengier, M., 412
Seyss-Inquart, Dr Arthur, 401
Sheffield, Ralph, 421
Sikorski, General Wladyslaw, 107–8
Simplicissimus, 126
Simpson, Professor, 238, 241
Slaughter and May, 409
Smidt, Wilhelm, 237, 262; *235, 239*
Smit, J. K., 400
Smith family, 309
Smith, Andrew Martin, 440; *345*
Smith, Audrey Martin, 329
Smith, Cecily Ridley, 358; *343*
Smith, Emily Ridley, 300, 358; *343*
Smith, Everard Martin, *343, 345*
Smith, Francis, 298; *285*
Smith, Martin Ridley, 298–300, 304, 328, 358; *343*
Smith, Martin Tucker, 298; *285*
Smith, Mary Martin, *345*
Smith, Sybil, *see* Hambro, Sybil
Smith, Violet Martin (*née* Hambro), 302, 348, 440; *301, 325, 327, 343, 345*
Smith, Winifred Ridley, *see* Hambro, Winifred
Smith, Payne and Smith, 298; *306–7*
Smith, St Aubyn & Co. (Holdings) Ltd, 404
Soames, Charlotte, *see* Hambro, Charlotte
Soames, Lord, 441
Sonne, Jørgen V., *240–1*
Sørensen, Øivind, *89, 113*
Sørensen, S. O., *435*
Sorø Akademi, 40–1
Southern Mahratta Railroad, 307
Special Operations Executive (SOE), 410–11, 415
Spiller, Captain Eberhard, 100

Sponneck, Count Wilhelm, 242–6, 250, 279; *244*
Sporborg, Harry, 409–11, 423, 431, 439
Stavropaulous, Constantin, *115*
Stedeford, Sir Ivan, 429–30
Steele, W., *379*
Stenberg, E., *362*
Stenstadsvold, Haakon, *117*
Stiernholm, General Frederik, 56
Stock Exchange Committee, 320
Stockholms Enskilda Bank, 361, 370
Stone, Frank, 424
Stonehaven, Lord, 358
Streatfield, Colonel, *346–7*
Strömer, Johan Henric, *220–1*
Stuart, Cecily, *see* Smith, Cecily Ridley
Stuart, Henry, 300
Stuart, Mary, *see* Hambro, Mary
Students' Association, Kristiania, 84, 140
Students' Choral Society, 40
Sturgis, H. P., 291
Supply, Ministry of, 400
Sutherland, Dr Alexander, 226
Svane, Claus, 59
Swinton, Viscount, 407
Symons, Sir Penn, 350–1

Tapley, Patsie (*née* Hambro), 349, 354, 382; *353, 417*
Taylor Woodrow, 426
Tenniel, John, *333*
Terboven, Josef, 111, 112
Territorial Army, 381–2, 400
Thant, U, *115*
Thaon de Revel, Count, 266
Thiele, Just Mathias, 181–2, 194
Thomsen, Vilhelm, 72
Thornwick, Miss, *346–7*
Thortsen, Bernhard, 26–31
Thorvaldsen, Bertel, 194–6; *195*
Thorvaldsen Museum, Copenhagen, 196
Tietgen, C. F., 309; *316*
The Times, 240, 241, 348, 432
Trans-Caucasian Railroad, 307
Trap, *122*
Treschow, Frederik, 241–2; *242*
Trier, Ernst, 41, 42
Trier, Marie, *see* Borup, Marie

Trinity College, Cambridge, 288, 298, 328, 331, 405; *289*
Trondheim University, 134
Tube Investments, 429–32
Turner, Eliza, *see* Hambro, Eliza

Union Générale, 312
Union Minière, 412, 414
Union of Norwegians, 86, 88, 91–2, 108, 118
United Kingdom Commercial Corporation (UKCC), 398, 407, 413–14
United Nations, 116; *115*

Vansittart, Robert, 361
Vernet, Horace, *195*
Victor Emanuel II, King of Italy, 266, 272; *267, 269, 273*
Victoria, Princess, *251*
Victoria, Queen of England, 212, 228, 272–4, 279
Vigeland, Gustav, 124
Vilhelm, Prince of Denmark, *see* George I, King of Greece
Vogt, Nils, 86
Voss, Lucie, *see* Bull, Lucie

Waifs and Strays, 303
Waight, *349*
Wallenberg family, 423
Wallenberg, A. O., *362*
Wallenberg, Knut A., 361–3, 370, 396; *362*
Warburg, (S. G.) & Co., 428, 436
Warburg, Siegmund, 428–32
Waterloo, battle of, 147, 160
Weinberg, Mark, 442
Wellington, Duke of, *155*
Werenskiold, Erik, *127*
Wergeland, Oscar, *62–3*
Westminster Bank, 384
Whyte, Ebba, *see* Hambro, Lady Ebba
Wilhelmina, Queen of the Netherlands, 107
Williams Ellis, Cecily, 398
Wilson, Thomas, *193*
Wilson, (Thomas) & Co., 192–4, 218
Women's National Council of Norway, 79

Woodroffe, Jack, 422, 423, 434, 439, 440
Woodroffe, Simon, 440
World War I, 86–7, 92, 297, 331, 355–60, 361–9
World War II, 91–112, 136–8, 397–415
Wortley, Captain, 350–1
Wulf, Caroline, 35
Wulf, Gustav, 36, 39; *37*
Wulf, Wulf Marcus, 35–6, 172

Wulf-Borup, Carl Wilhelm, 36, 39–40, 177; *37*
Wulf-Borup, Wulfine, 36, 37, 39, 41; *37*
Wynn, 185

Yorke, Henry, 288–9
Yorke, R., *285*
Yorke, Susan, *see* Hambro, Susan (wife of Colonel Charles Hambro)

(1)

Calmer Joachim Hambro
1747–1806.
Born in Rendsburg, grew up in Hamburg, arrived in
Copenhagen 1778,
granted work permit 1779
and created the firm C. J. Hambro & Son, in Copenhagen.
m. 1778 **Thobe Levi,**
1756–1820,
daughter of a Danish merchant who had obtained Danish
citizenship in 1751.

(2)

DANISH FEMALE LINE:	ENGLISH LINE:	NORWEGIAN LINE:
Zipora Hambro 1779–1852. See front "end page".	**Joseph Hambro** 1780–1848. See front "end page".	**Isach Hambro** 1782–1865. Baptised Edvard Isach in Denmark 1810. Merchant in Bergen 1810–65. m. 1812 **Johanne Marie Roggen** 1791–1841.

Besides two daughters.

(3)

Carl Joachim Hambro
1813–78.
Merchant and manufacturer in Bergen
m. 1838 **Angelique Bull**
1815–39.

Besides several daughters.

Johan Hambro
1816–80.
Banker in C.J. Hambro & Son
in Copenhagen and later
in London 1836–48.
Manufacturer in London
1849–79.
m. (1) 1844 **Christine Bødtker**
1822–44.
m. (2) 1856 **Cecilia Hamilton**
1836–99.

Theodora Hambro
1818–49.
m. 1844 **J. Randulf Bull**
1815–94, Military
Surgeon in Bergen.
Known as "Long Bull".

(4)

Edvard Isak Hambro
1847–1909.
Founder of Hambros School in Bergen.
m. 1880 **Nicoline Harbitz**
1861–1926.

All seven daughters were
nurses, only one married
in Portsmouth, 1887.

Edvard Isak Hambro Bull
1845–1925.
Surgeon.
m. (1) 1869 **Gine Falsen**
1849–79.
m. (2) 1880 **Ida Paludan**
1861–1957.

Besides three daughters

Besides two sons

(5)

Carl Joachim Hambro
1885–1964.
President of the Norwegian Storting.
m. (1) 1910 **Gudrun Grieg**
1881–1943.
m. (2) 1946 **Gyda Christensen**
1875–1965.
Actress and theatre manageress in Oslo.

Besides one daughter

(6)

Edvard Isaac Hambro
1911–77.
Norwegian Ambassador
m. 1940 **Elizabeth Raverat**
b. 1916.

Cato Hambro
b. 1911.
Psychologist, O.B.E.
m. 1946 **Wencke Petersen**
b. 1922.

Carl J. Hambro
b. 1914.
Lecturer at Oslo
University and author.
m. (1) 1939 **Wencke Koren**
b. 1916.
m. (2) 1951 **Christine Holter**
b. 1931.

Johan Hambro
b. 1915.
Secretary General of
Normandsforbundet.
m. 1945 **Lore Alchelin**
b. 1918.

(7)

Carl Joachim Hambro
b. 1944.
Lawyer.
m. 1965 **Lillian Fleischer**
b. 1945.

Christian Hambro
b. 1946.
Director
m. **Sissel Markhus**
b. 1945.

Nicholas Hambro
b. 1947.
Lawyer.
m. **Siri Steen**
b. 1945.

Edward Hambro
b. 1949.
T.V. producer

Lars Hambro
b. 1945.
Physicist, Phd.
m. **Vivi Myhre**
b. 1941.

John Michael Hambro
b. 1946.
Computer Specialist.

Peter Edward Hambro
b. 1948.
Lawyer.

(8)

Three children.

Two children.

One child.

Two children.